Memoirs of the protectoral-house of Cromwell; deduced from an early period, and continued down to the present time; collected chiefly from original papers and records Volume 2 of 2

Mark Noble

Memoirs of the protectoral-house of Cromwell; deduced from an early period, and continued down to the present time; ... collected chiefly from original papers and records, ... together with an appendix: ... Embellished with elegant engravings. By Mark Nob Volume 2 of 2

Noble, Mark
ESTCID: T135737
Reproduction from British Library
With an engraved dedication and a list of subscribers in vol.1.
London : printed for G. G. J. and J. Robinson. 1787.
2v.,plates : ports. ; 8°

Gale ECCO Print Editions

Relive history with *Eighteenth Century Collections Online*, now available in print for the independent historian and collector. This series includes the most significant English-language and foreign-language works printed in Great Britain during the eighteenth century, and is organized in seven different subject areas including literature and language; medicine, science, and technology; and religion and philosophy. The collection also includes thousands of important works from the Americas.

The eighteenth century has been called "The Age of Enlightenment." It was a period of rapid advance in print culture and publishing, in world exploration, and in the rapid growth of science and technology – all of which had a profound impact on the political and cultural landscape. At the end of the century the American Revolution, French Revolution and Industrial Revolution, perhaps three of the most significant events in modern history, set in motion developments that eventually dominated world political, economic, and social life.

In a groundbreaking effort, Gale initiated a revolution of its own: digitization of epic proportions to preserve these invaluable works in the largest online archive of its kind. Contributions from major world libraries constitute over 175,000 original printed works. Scanned images of the actual pages, rather than transcriptions, recreate the works *as they first appeared.*

Now for the first time, these high-quality digital scans of original works are available via print-on-demand, making them readily accessible to libraries, students, independent scholars, and readers of all ages.

For our initial release we have created seven robust collections to form one the world's most comprehensive catalogs of 18th century works.

Initial Gale ECCO Print Editions collections include:

History and Geography
Rich in titles on English life and social history, this collection spans the world as it was known to eighteenth-century historians and explorers. Titles include a wealth of travel accounts and diaries, histories of nations from throughout the world, and maps and charts of a world that was still being discovered. Students of the War of American Independence will find fascinating accounts from the British side of conflict.

Social Science

Delve into what it was like to live during the eighteenth century by reading the first-hand accounts of everyday people, including city dwellers and farmers, businessmen and bankers, artisans and merchants, artists and their patrons, politicians and their constituents. Original texts make the American, French, and Industrial revolutions vividly contemporary.

Medicine, Science and Technology

Medical theory and practice of the 1700s developed rapidly, as is evidenced by the extensive collection, which includes descriptions of diseases, their conditions, and treatments. Books on science and technology, agriculture, military technology, natural philosophy, even cookbooks, are all contained here.

Literature and Language

Western literary study flows out of eighteenth-century works by Alexander Pope, Daniel Defoe, Henry Fielding, Frances Burney, Denis Diderot, Johann Gottfried Herder, Johann Wolfgang von Goethe, and others. Experience the birth of the modern novel, or compare the development of language using dictionaries and grammar discourses.

Religion and Philosophy

The Age of Enlightenment profoundly enriched religious and philosophical understanding and continues to influence present-day thinking. Works collected here include masterpieces by David Hume, Immanuel Kant, and Jean-Jacques Rousseau, as well as religious sermons and moral debates on the issues of the day, such as the slave trade. The Age of Reason saw conflict between Protestantism and Catholicism transformed into one between faith and logic -- a debate that continues in the twenty-first century.

Law and Reference

This collection reveals the history of English common law and Empire law in a vastly changing world of British expansion. Dominating the legal field is the *Commentaries of the Law of England* by Sir William Blackstone, which first appeared in 1765. Reference works such as almanacs and catalogues continue to educate us by revealing the day-to-day workings of society.

Fine Arts

The eighteenth-century fascination with Greek and Roman antiquity followed the systematic excavation of the ruins at Pompeii and Herculaneum in southern Italy; and after 1750 a neoclassical style dominated all artistic fields. The titles here trace developments in mostly English-language works on painting, sculpture, architecture, music, theater, and other disciplines. Instructional works on musical instruments, catalogs of art objects, comic operas, and more are also included.

GUIDE TO FOLD-OUTS MAPS and OVERSIZED IMAGES

The book you are reading was digitized from microfilm captured over the past thirty to forty years. Years after the creation of the original microfilm, the book was converted to digital files and made available in an online database.

In an online database, page images do not need to conform to the size restrictions found in a printed book. When converting these images back into a printed bound book, the page sizes are standardized in ways that maintain the detail of the original. For large images, such as fold-out maps, the original page image is split into two or more pages

Guidelines used to determine how to split the page image follows:

• Some images are split vertically; large images require vertical and horizontal splits.
• For horizontal splits, the content is split left to right.
• For vertical splits, the content is split from top to bottom.
• For both vertical and horizontal splits, the image is processed from top left to bottom right.

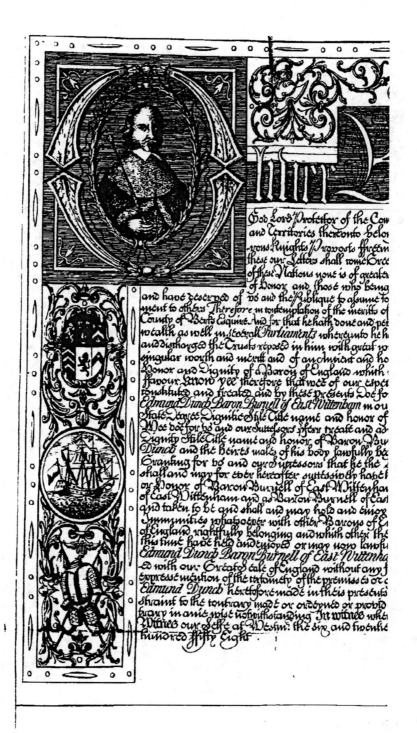

To the Right Hon.ble George Earl of Leicester;
This Plate engraved from the Original Patent & given by
...Is dedicated with the sincere...

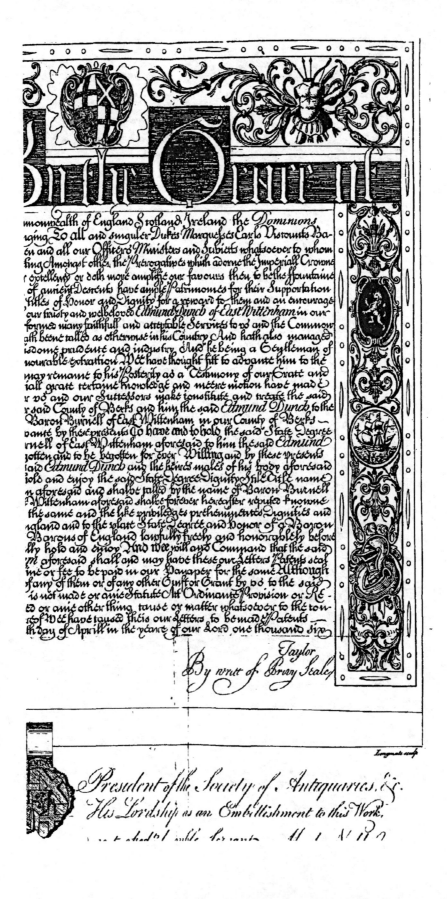

MEMOIRS

OF THE

PROTECTORAL-HOUSE

OF

CROMWELL;

DEDUCED

FROM AN EARLY PERIOD, AND CONTINUED DOWN TO THE PRESENT TIME,

AND, ALSO

THE FAMILIES ALLIED TO, OR DESCENDED FROM THEM:

COLLECTED CHIEFLY

FROM ORIGINAL PAPERS AND RECORDS,

Taken from Public Offices, &c or communicated by several
Persons, many of whom are of the highest Rank.

THE FIRST VOLUME CONTAINS

PROOFS AND ILLUSTRATIONS,

TOGETHER WITH

AN APPENDIX:

AS ALSO THE

LIVES OF SUCH PERSONS AS WERE DISTINGUISHED BY THE CROMWELLS, BY HONORS AND GREAT EMPLOYMENTS

EMBELLISHED WITH ELEGANT ENGRAVINGS.

By MARK NOBLE, F. A. S. of L. & E.

RECTOR OF BARMING IN KENT

THE THIRD EDITION, WITH IMPROVEMENTS

VOL II

LONDON

PRINTED FOR G G J AND J ROBINSON,
PATERNOSTER-ROW.

MDCCLXXXVII.

CONTENTS

OF

VOLUME II.

A 2 *bart.*

No.

No.

protector

No.

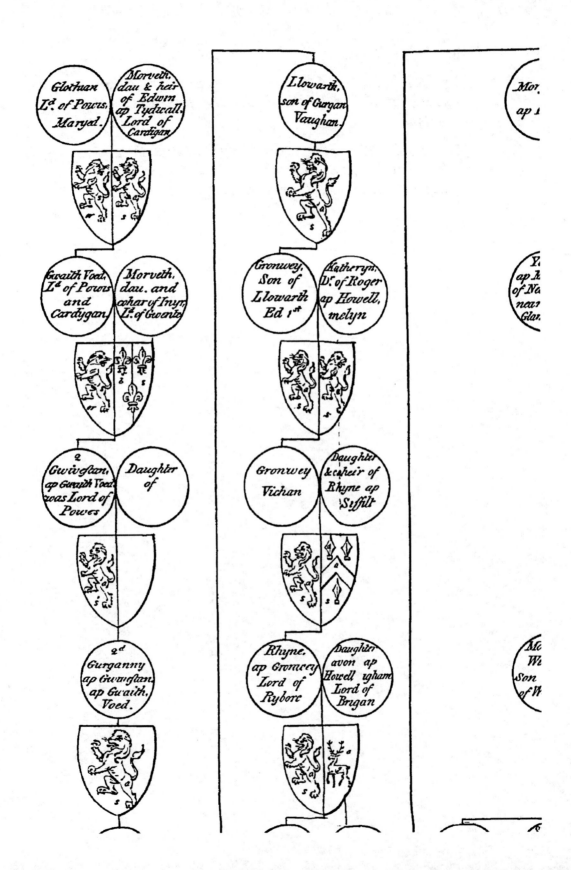

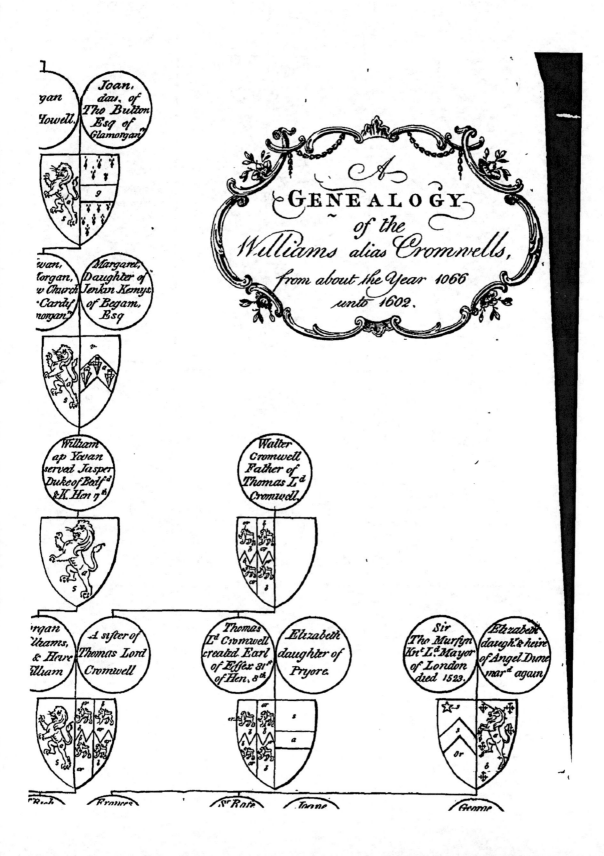

A
GENEALOGY
~
of the
Williams alias Cromwells,
from about the Year 1066
unto 1602.

Joan,
dau. of
Tho Button
Esq of
Glamorgan

Margaret,
Daughter of
Jenkin Kemys
of Begam,
Esq

…wan,
…organ,
…w Church
…Cardf
…morgan

William
ap Yavan
served Jasper
Duke of Bedf.d
& K. Hen 7th

Walter
Cromwell
Father of
Thomas Ld
Cromwell

…rgan
…lliams,
& Heire
…lliam

A sister of
Thomas Lord
Cromwell

Thomas
Ld Cromwell
created Earl
of Essex 31st
of Hen. 8th

Elizabeth
daughter of
Pryore.

Sir
Tho Murfyn
Knt Ld Mayor
of London
died 1523.

Elizabeth
daugh. & heire
of Angel Dune
mard again

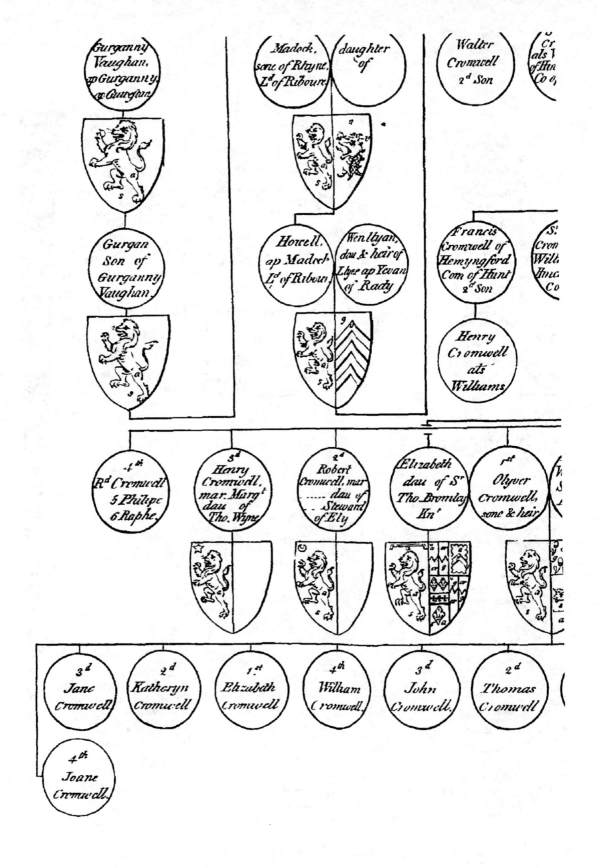

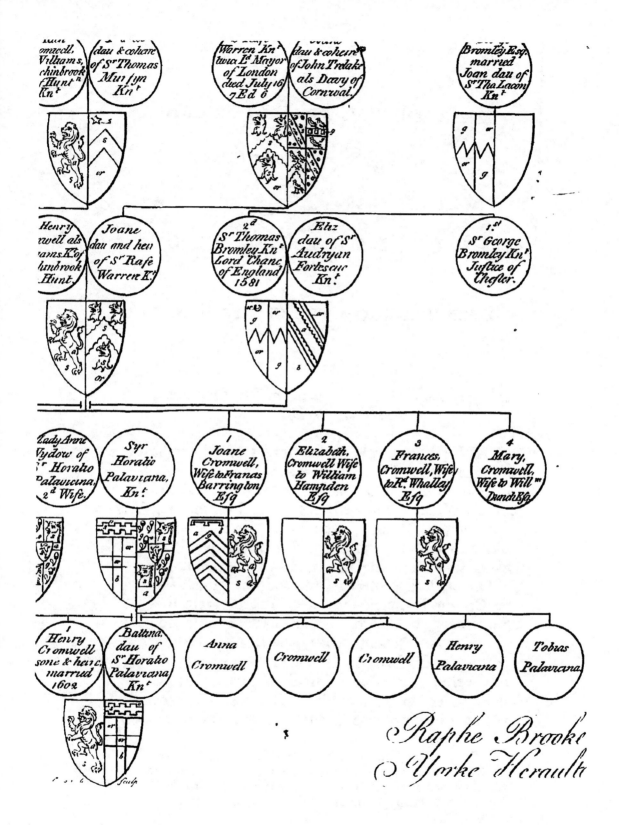

GENEALOGICAL AND HISTORICAL

MEMOIRS

OF THE

FAMILIES ALLIED TO,

OR,

DESCENDED FROM THE CROMWELLS.

No. I.

History of the earl of Essex, and the lord Cromwells, earls of Arglass.

FEW families rose to a more exalted height than that of the Cromwells*, and none from a less beginning. Thomas, its founder, was the son of Walter Cromwell, first a blacksmith, then a brewer, at Putney; who dying, left this son, and a daughter, who married mr. Morgan Williams, a welch gentleman, great-great-grandfather of Oliver, lord protector, the widow of this Walter Cromwell married, after his death, again to a Shearman, in London. Tho. had his education at a private school, where he learnt reading, writing, and a little latin; when he grew up he discovered great abilities, with as great unsteadiness, ever changing his situation: we know not how he employed himself at this time; but

NUM. I.
Cromwells.
Thomas, earl of Essex, and vicar-general.

*The name of Crumwell, or Cromwell, is taken from that of a village, but in what part of the kingdom is impossible to say, there being several so called: the ancient lord Cromwells had theirs, probably, from one in the county of Nottingham.

like all thoſe who puſh their fortunes, he underwent variety of viciſſitudes, ſometimes much reduced, at others, probably, as much elevated.

Not content with ſo ſmall a ſpace as his native
country, he obtained his deſire of travelling into
various kingdoms, but how he was enabled to do
this, is not now to be diſcovered. His induſtry
and reſtleſſneſs whilſt there, led him into many
ſtrange ſcenes, all which he improved to gain a
knowledge of men and manners; nor did he
omit attaining the languages of each country he
viſited. His knowledge and prudence joined with
his great good ſenſe and ready wit, made him
looked upon as a fit perſon to be employed in the
moſt arduous concerns · the engliſh factory at
Antwerp, then a very reſpectable community, retained him as their clerk or ſecretary, but this
did not ſuit his love of novelty, he reſigned it
in 1510, to go to Rome, at the perſuaſion of two
perſons, who were going from England to ſolicit
his holineſs to renew the charter of privileges and
indulgencies to a religious houſe in Boſton, in
Lincolnſhire, and finding themſelves incapable of
the embaſſy, ſolicited him; he went with them,
and by pleaſing the palate of pope Julius II.* by
making him ſome jellies after the engliſh manner, obtained his ſuit. He ſtaid ſome time after
this in Italy, and engaged in many adventures;
he ſerved under, and was with the duke of Bour-
bon, when he ſacked and took the city of Rome†;
he was involved in great diſtreſs upon the defeat
of that army which had pillaged the holy city,
but a generous italian of the name of Friſcobaldo‡,

* Pope Julius II. was elected pontiff in 1503, and died in
1513

† Rome was taken by ſtorm in 1527, and Clement VII. made
a priſoner.

‡ Cromwell's behaviour to Friſcobaldo was to the greateſt
degree noble. Some years after his return to England, when

lent him a confiderable fum in gold, with horfe and armour, fo that he was able afterwards to perform great fervice to his prince in contributing to the efcape of John Ruffell, efq. (afterwards earl of Bedford, and anceftor to the prefent duke of Bedford) who was near being fent to France, a prifoner from Bologne, becaufe employed in fome fecret fervice by king Henry VIII. againft the fee of Rome.

NUM I.
Cromwells.
Tho earl of
Effex, and vi-
car-gen.

Whilft in Italy, Cromwell learnt Erafmus's tranflation of the new teftament by rote. Upon his return to England, he was taken into the fervice of cardinal Wolfey, and was one of the very few that ftood by his mafter in his fad reverfe of fortune, his fidelity met its reward; Henry VIII. was pleafed with it, and on that account took him into his fervice. Like his late patron, his rife in power was rapid; the king, who affected to defpife the ancient nobility (perhaps from a dread of their power), was always raifing up from the commons a favorite that he placed above them: this gentleman was one of thefe favorites —— favorites of a tyrant, who knew no bounds to his love or hatred: it would fill very many pages to mention the places he beftowed upon him. In 1531, he was knighted, made a privy counfellor, and mafter of the Jewel-houfe, in the year following, clerk of the Hanaper, and chancellor of the Exchequer; in 1534, principal fecretary of ftate, and mafter of the Rolls; and upon his majefty's declaring himfelf head of the church, he conferred

---

in all his grandeur, he faw this humane italian, in a mean drefs, as he went in proceffion through London ftreets, immediately upon recollecting him, he left the proceffion, and difcovered himfelf to his benefactor, and finding that he had fallen into great misfortunes, he fo amply returned the former obligation with intereft, that Frifcobaldo left England with a renewal of his fortunes this was only one of the many of his requitals for former benefits.

upon

4

NUM I

Cromwell.
Tho earl of
Eſſex, and vi-
car-gen

upon Cromwell the new title of vicar-general of all ſpirituals and viceroy; in 1537, chief-juſtice itinerant of all foreſts beyond the Trent, and knight of the garter; in 1538, conſtable of Cariſ-brooke caſtle, and in 1539 (upon the death of Henry Bourchier, the premier earl in England, by a diſlocation of his neck, from a fall from an unruly horſe) earl of Eſſex, and ſoon after lord high chamberlain of England, a title ever before held by the earls of Oxford. His fortune, too, bore pace with his titles, Henry gave him a grant of the caſtle and lordſhip of Oakeham, with many others, to a prodigious amount. From this dangerous height he fell to riſe no more, being arreſted at the council-table, july 9, 1540, and condemned, unheard by the parlement, an horrid practice he himſelf had begun, and though he wrote a moſt pathetic letter to the king, it only moved him for a moment, ſo that he was beheaded on Tower-Hill the 28th following. At the ſcaffold he was perplexed in his ſpeech, and endeavoured to give as little offence as poſſible, on his ſon's account: from what he ſaid there on the ſubject of religion, both romaniſts and proteſtants have ſuppoſed he died in their faith. Biſhop Burnet has amply vindicated his character againſt the former, in his hiſtory of the reformation: his moderation, integrity, and very extenſive abilities, deſerved a better fate; a fate incurred only by obtaining a princeſs for his ſovereign, who was every way undeſerving of her*, and ſpiritedly reſenting an affront† put upon him by the duke

---

* Biſhop Burnet is ſingular in ſuppoſing the marriage not one of the great reaſons why poor Cromwell loſt his head

† K. Hen VIII. when he put forth the bloody ſix articles, was fearful it ſhould too much diſtreſs archbiſhop Cranmer, and amongſt other means to convince him that he did, and ever ſhould highly value that moſt upright man, ſent the dukes of Norfolk and Suffolk, with Cromwell, to dine with him,

and

of Norfolk, who reproached him with the meannefs of his birth. The earl married Eliz. or Jane
daughter and co-heirefs of fir John Pryore, knt.
and widow of Tho. Williams, efq. of an ancient
family in Wales*, by whom he had Gregory lord
Cromwell, and Jane who married Will. Hough,
of Leighton in Worrall, in Chefhire, efq.

Gregory, only child of the earl of Effex, was baron Gregory 1ft
lord Crom-
well
of Wimbleton, three miles fouth of Putney, in Sur-
ry, by defcent, as his father's fecond title, and
which was not legally loft by his attainder, and alfo
created baron Cromwell, of Okeham, in the county
of Rutland, by fummons and patent, dec. 18,
1540, about five months after his father's death †.
he was a fervant in the court of k. Henry VIII.
and created by him in 1546, knight of the bath,
but diftinguifhed by no place. It will appear a little extraordinary that lord Cromwell was dean of
Wells, but during the reign of k. Edw. VI.
many of the nobility had appointments to church
preferments where there was no cure of fouls,
a proceeding neither proper, nor juft. His lord-

---

and to acquaint him of his entire regard for him. In the courfe
of converfation, Cromwell drew a parallel between the cardinal
and the archbifhop, how much the one leffened his friends by
his haughtinefs, whilft the other procured the favor even of his
enemies, by his condefcenfion and gentlenefs, the duke of Norfolk faid ‘ he muft be a good judge, as he was his man,’ which
nettled Cromwell, who anfwered, ‘ he would not have been
‘ the cardinal's admiral, had he become pope,’ Norfolk replied,
with a great oath, he lied; with much more bad language.
Cranmer, in vain, attempted a pacification.

* The pedigree drawn out by one of the Cromwell family,
does not give the countefs of Effex's father as knighted, which
Lilly the herald does, but he varies in her chriftian name,
giving it Jane

† Milles, Brooke, York, Vincent, &c. take notice only of
lord Gregory's title of baron of Okeham, but Gwillim ftates
it as above, except falfely dating his patent and fummons 18
july, 18 Hen. VIII. 1536, but this Rymer's Foed. corrects.

fhip

ſhip was buried at Launde-abbey, in Leiceſterſhire: he married Eliz. daughter of ſir John Seymour, of Wolfehall, in the county of Wilts, knt.
and ſiſter to the firſt and great duke of Somerſet,
who was lord protector during the minority of
k. Edw. VI. to which ſovereign her ladyſhip was
aunt, ſhe was the widow of ſir Anth. Oughtred,
knt. His lordſhip with his lady had a grant of
the manor of Laddington, in the county of Rutland, from k. Edw. VI. during their lives and the
royal pleaſure. Lord Gregory left three ſons and
two daughters; 1. Hen. who ſucceeded to the
title. 2. Edw. 3. Tho. 4. Frances, who was married to Edw. Stroude, of Devonſhire, eſq. and
had iſſue Will. Stroude, eſq. and Cath. who
became the wife of John Stroude, of Parnham, in
Dorſet, eſq.

    Henry lord Cromwell, eldeſt ſon and heir of
lord Gregory, probably was a minor at his father's death, for he was not ſummoned to parlement until the 5th of q. Eliz. He died in 1593,
and was buried at Launde-abbey. By Mary,
daughter of John Paulet, marquiſs of Wincheſter,
he left three children: 1. Edw. the third lord
Cromwell. 2. Sir Gregory Cromwell, lord of the
manor of Langham, a chapelry belonging to
Okeham, in Rutlandſhire. He was knighted at
Bever-caſtle, by k. Ja. I. april 23, 1603. He
married Fra. eldeſt daughter of ſir Edw. Griffin,
of Dingley, in Northamptonſhire; created a knt.
of the Bath at the ſame ſovereign's coronation,
and anceſtor of the preſent Sir John-Griffin Griffin,
bart created, or rather confirmed, lord Howard
of Waldon, by his preſent majeſty. Upon ſir
Gregory's marriage Langham was ſeparated from
Okeham, and ſettled upon them, but they obtained of q Eliz. leave to alienate the manor to
ſir Andr. Noel, knt. 3. Cath. married to ſir

Lionel

Lionel Tollemache, of Helmington, in Suffolk, created a bart. by k. Ja. I. may 22, 1611, anceftor to the earls of Dyfert.

NUM I.
Cromwells

Edw 3d lord
Cromwell.

Edward lord Cromwell, was of the age of 33 when he fucceeded to the title, he was fummoned to parlement, feb. 19, 1593-4, and admitted the 27th following. and 1598, he ferved with Rob. earl of Effex, in the fea expedition againft Spain. His lordfhip received the honor of knighthood from the hands of that nobleman in Ireland, and from his partiality to him was near being involved in his ruin, but obtained (probably with difficulty) an efpecial pardon, dated july 9, 1601. This lord Cromwell difpofed of all his patrimony in England, with his barony of Okeham, and in 1606 purchafed a large eftate in the barony of Lecale, in the county of Downe, in Ireland, from Mountjoy earl of Devonfhire. He died in 1607, and was buried in the cathedral of Downe. His lordfhip married firft a daughter of ———— Umpton, efq. and fecondly, Fra. daughter of Will. Rugge, in the county of Norfolk, efq. who furviving his lordfhip, re-married to Rich. Wingfield, marefchal of Ireland, and created lord vifc. Powerfcourt, by that nobleman fhe had no iffue, and in him the title of Powerfcourt became extinct, but was afterwards revived. Of this lady Cromwell, the Wingfield family have this anecdote: When Oliver Cromwell in 1644, was marching northwards, the town of Stamford fhut their gates againft him, at which he was fo much enraged, that he determined to level the town. Her ladyfhip at that time lived in the parifh of St. Martin's, in a houfe now occupied by the mifs Mohams, whom the inhabitants requefted to mediate between them and the general: lady Cromwell accordingly wrote to Oliver, claiming relationfhip, and telling him that much of her

fon's

son's property confisted of houses in that town, and hoping for her fake he would draw off his artillery. He granted her petition, and the gates were opened to him*. Mrs. Wingfield is in poffeffion of an original portrait, which reprefents this countefs extremely fat and very low, with hard mafculine features, fhe had feveral original letters that paffed between her ladyfhip and Oliver, with many others, but they were all lately loft by an unlucky accident†. Tho lord Cromwell had only one child by his firft lady, and 3 by his fecond; 1. Eliz. who was married firft to fir John Shelton, of Shelton, in Norfolk, knt. and fecondly, Tho. Fitzhughes, of Oxfordfhire, efq. 2. Tho. his fucceffor. 3. Fra. married to fir John Wingfield, of Tickencote, in the county of Rutland, knt. and 4. Ann, the wife of fir Will. Wingfield, knt. eldeft fon and heir of lord vifcount Powerfcourt, in Ireland, and anceftor of the prefent nobleman of that title.

Tho. lord Cromwell was fummoned to parlement 18 k. Ja. I. he was created, in 1625, vifcount Lecale, was a ftrenuous advocate for k. Cha. I was one of the lords that accompanied that monarch to Oxford, and became a part of

---

* An anecdote fimilar to the above is alfo related of Oliver by the Wingfield family, who, when he came to Burleigh, the feat of the earl of Exeter, then a minor. who had oppofed his party, he retreated from thence, through the intreaty of the countefs dowager. who had received him with much hofpitality, in return for which, at his departure, he prefented her ladyfhip with a half-length portrait of himfelf, by Walker, which ftill remains in one of the dreffing-rooms in that houfe and it is alfo obfervable, that the earl of Exeter had a miniature of the elder protector.

† Sir Will Dugdale, in his baronage, mentions only one lady of Edw. lord Cromwell. but the books in the heraldsoffice agree in the above pedigree in giving two, but reverfe them, however the collections made by one of the family deferve more credit than either of the others.

what

what his majefty called his mongrel parlement:
in 1641, he commanded a regiment of horfe in
Ireland, and for his good fervices he was created,
in 1644, earl of Arglafs in that kingdom, but
feeing the ruin of his mafter inevitable, he made
his peace with the parlement, after paying 460l.
for his delinquency. His lordfhip died in 1653,
at the age of 59, and was buried at Tikencote.
His countefs was Eliz. daughter, and fole heirefs
of Rob. Maverell, of Throwley, Staffordfhire, efq.
by Eliz. daughter of fir Tho. Fleming, knt. lord-
chief-juftice of the King's-Bench *. She died
1653, and was buried by her lord at Tikencote.
The iffue of the earl and countefs of Lecale were
fix children: 1. Wingfield, who fucceeded to his
father's titles, 2. Vere-Effex, who, upon the death
of his nephew, earl Tho. fucceeded to his honors;
3 Oliver died unmarried, 4. Frances; 5. Jane;
both died infants, and, 6. Mary, who was married
to Will. Fitzherbert of Tiffington, in Derbyfhire,
efq by whom fhe had 5 fons and 5 daughters, all
of whom died unmarried, except two daughters,
one married to ——— Port, of Ilam, in Staffordfhire,
efq. who only left one daughter, Cath. who died
unmarried in 1724; the other married to Mr.
Fitzherbert of Somers-Hall, in Derbyfhire, but
died without iffue.

Wingfield, lord Cromwell, vifc. Lecale, and
earl of Arglafs, was born fept. 12, 1622. His lordfhip was an advocate for the royal caufe, for which
he was brought a prifoner to Chefter, in april 1649.
This earl died Oct. 3. and was buried in the church
of Ilam in Staffordfhire. He married a daughter of
fir Will. Ruffell of Shenfham in Worcefterfhire,

NUM I.

Cromwells.
Tho 4th lord
Cromwell,
created vifc.
Lecale, and
earl of Arglafs.

Wingfield, 2d
earl of Arglafs.

---

* Rob. Maverell, efq. died feb. 5, 1626-7; his widow, aug.
5, 1628, they are both buried in the church of Blore in Staffordfhire.

bart.

bart. alſo a loyaliſt, by whom he had two children,
1. Tho. who ſucceeded him, and 2. Mary, who
died unmarried in 1683.

Tho. third earl of Arglaſs, was born nov. 29,
1653; he married Honora, ſecond daughter of dr.
Tho. Michael Boyle, archbiſhop of Armagh, lord
chancellor, and primate of Ireland. He died april
11, 1682, and was buried in the church of Ilam,
and leaving no iſſue, his titles devolved to his
uncle.

Vere-Eſſex, who accordingly became lord
Cromwell, viſc. Lecale, and earl of Arglaſs; his
lordſhip was born in 1623, and died nov. 26, 1687,
and lies buried in the old cathedral of Downe. By
his counteſs Cath. daughter of Ja. Hamilton of
Newcaſtle, in the county of Downe, eſq and widow of Rich. Price, eſq. whom he married in
1672, he had an only child, a daughter,

Eliz ſole
hereſs of
Vere-Eſſex,
earl of Ar-
glaſs, mar to
Edw South-
well, eſq.

Elizabeth, born dec. 3, 1674, who ſucceeded to
none of the titles of her anceſtors, they being male
fiefs, though ſhe herſelf ſuppoſed that one of the
baronies of Cromwell deſcended to her, and as ſuch
walked in the proceſſion of q. Mary's funeral, but
it was afterwards found to be want of attention in the
officer whoſe duty it was to ſettle ſuch claims. She
married Oct. 29, 1704, Edw. Southwell, eſq whoſe
anceſtors were long ſettled in Norfolk, and ſince
then in Ireland, but more lately in Glouceſterſhire. Mr. Southwell having received a good
ſchool education, was ſent to Merton college in
Oxford, where he commenced gentleman-com-
moner, and applied ſo cloſe to his ſtudies, that he
gained ſuch a general knowledge of moſt branches
of polite literature, as to be thoroughly qualified
for the high offices which he afterwards ſo deſervedly enjoyed, being appointed principal ſecretary
of ſtate and a privy councellor of Ireland, returned
for Kinſale in the parlement of that kingdom, and
laſtly,

laftly, firft clerk of the privy council of this. Mrs. Southwell died in childbed, march 31, 1709, and was buried in the church of Henbury, in Gloucefterfhire: fhe was a truly amiable perfon. Mr. Southwell re-married Ann, daughter of Will. Blathwayt, efq. fhe died july 1, 1717, aged 27, having been a wife but little more than one year; and he himfelf in Spring-gardens, London, dec. 4, 1730, aged 63, and was buried near the remains of his firft wife. The iffue of the heirefs of the lord Cromwells was 3 fons and a daughter: 1. Edw. of whom below, 2. Rob. 3. Tho. and 4. Eliz. The three laft died in their infancy.

NUM. I.
Southwells.

Edward, the eldeft fon of the hon. Edw. Southwell by Eliz. daughter and heirefs of the earl of Aiglafs, was born june 1, 1705, he was one of the members in the irifh parlement for Downe-Patrick, and alfo in the britifh as one of the reprefentatives for the city of Briftol in 1739, and the two following parlements. He died march 16, 1755, having obtained the love of all by the rectitude of his conduct, both in his public and private character. By Cath. daughter of Edw. Watfon, lord Sondes (fon of Lewis, earl of Rockingham by lady Cath. Tufton, eldeft daughter and co-heirefs of Tho. earl of Thanet), whom he married aug. 21, 1729, he left 2 fons, 1. Edw. whom I fhall particularly notice; 2 ——— Southwell, efq. married to Arabella, daughter of Hen. Pye of Farringdon, Berks, efq. and 3. Cath. born dec. 11, 1740, who died march 17, 1748.

Edw Southwell, efq.

Edward, born june 6, 1738, the fole heir both to the Cromwell and Southwell eftates, was knight for the county of Gloucefter, when, by the death of the baronefs Clifford, and countefs dowager of Leinfter, he became intitled to the baronies of Clifford, Weftmoreland, and Vefcie, and the claim being allowed in 1776, he receive this fummons

Edw 1ft lord Clifford of the Southwell family

to

NUM I.

Southwells

Edw 1ᵈ lord
Clifford of the
Southwell fa-
mily

Edw the 2d
and present
lord Clifford
of this family

to the house of peers as baron Clifford. His lordship died nov. 1, 1777, and was buried at Henbury, in Gloucestershire, having married Sophia,
third daughter of Sam. Campbell, of Mount-
Campbell, in the county of Leitrim in Ireland,
the issue of which alliance was four sons and five
daughters; 1. Edw. the present lord Clifford, born
june 20. 1768; 2. Rob. born april 20, 1770, who
died at King's-Weston in aug. 1777, 3. Henry, born
march 30, 1773, 4. John, born oct. 19, 1774, and
died april 5, 1778; 5. Mary, born sept. 15, 1766;
6. Cath. born sept. 19. 1768, 7. Sophia, born
june 10, 1771; 8. Eliz. born june 11, 1776; 9.
Henrietta, born may 19, 1777.

I have been more particular in giving what relation I could collect of these lord Cromwells, because they were allied to, and left they should be
mistaken for any of the protectorate house of
Cromwell, the descendants of the earl of Essex,
the vicar-general, having resided latterly in Ireland, is the reason why their history is so little
known in England.

I am informed by a friend that was at King's-
Weston, near Bristol, the seat of lord Clifford, that
there are many portraits of the Cromwells, Southwells, and other persons allied to them*.

* For a more particular account of Tho. earl of Essex, see
Fox's book of martyrs, Stow's chronicle, Drayton's poems,
Burnet's hist of the reformation, Biographia Britannica, &c.
The genealogy of the lord Cromwells is taken from a M S.
pedigree, collected by one of the name, probably a Tho. Cromwell, esq who, the Biographia Britannica says, wrote some
notes for an history of his ancestors, and another pedigree of the
Wingfield family, drawn up and finely emblazoned by an herald; both of them are possessed by mrs. Wingfield of Stamford,
who was pleased to permit dr Hodson, then of that place, to
copy out the former, and such parts of the latter as related to
the history and genealogy of this family, who, in the most handsome and friendly manner, communicated them to the author.

Harleian

No. II.

The Family of St. John, in-cluding others.

The life of Oliver St. John, lord-chief-justice of the Common-Pleas, a cousin by marriage to Oliver lord protector.

THE family who now bear the firname of St. John, are paternally defcended from Hugh de Port, who poffeffed 55 lordfhips in the county of Hants in the time of Will. the conqueror; whofe vaft eftates may be feen in domefday book, under the article of terra Hugonis de Port, which is the more fingular, as he was evidently a native englifhman, from his enjoying at leaft two manors, Cerdeford and Efchetune, in Hants, from his anceftors before the norman invafion. This Hugh de Port left Henry, who was the father of John, whofe fon, Adam de Port, was a great baron, and feated at Bafing in Hants. He married Mabel, the daughter and fole heirefs of Reginald de Aurevel; by Muriel, the fole daughter and heirefs of Roger St. John (by Cicily, daughter and fole heirefs of Rob. de Haya, lord of the manor of Halnac, in Suffex, which he received from his relation k. Hen. I) William, the eldeft fon of this Adam de

NUM II.
St John's origin.

Harleian M.S S. in the Britifh mufeum, M.S. pedigrees of Lilly and others, in the poffeffion of mr. Longmate, Dugdale's fummonfes, and his baron ge, Camden's life of q Eliz Spelman's hiftory of facrilege, Le Neve's monumenta anglicana, fir John Temple's hift. of the irifh rebellion, Rudder's hift of Gloucefterfhire, extinct peerage, laft edition of Collin's peerage, with mr Longmate's fupplement, together with fome additions and corrections from that gentleman, and fome other friends, M S. cathaloge of batchelor knights, made by our fovereigne lorde k. James, &c,

Port,

Port, by Mabel, the reprefentative of fo many
great families, and one of them allied to the norman kings, affumed the firname of his grandmother by the mother's fide, viz. St. John, writing
himfelf Willielmus de Sancto Johanne, filius et
hæres Adæ de Port.   The St. Johns were inferior
to no family in defcent or power.   Will. de St.
John accompanied k. Will. when he came to
feize the crown of Harold, and then enjoyed the
very honorable place of grand mafter of the cavalry, for which reafon he took for his cognizance
the horfehames, or collar, his name is in the roll
of Battle-Abbey, with others that attended their
fovereign at the battle of Haftings, which decided
the fate of the kingdom, and placed the crown of
the englifh king upon the head of the norman
duke.   The Ports, or St. Johns, kept up their
fituation, continuing to increafe their riches and
greatnefs by the nobleft alliances, and became relations to the royal houfe of Tudor*, as their pro-
genitors had been to the norman princes, and for
the eminent fervices they have rendered the ftate,
feveral of them have been ennobled.

Alexander, the third fon of fir John St. John,
knt. (the anceftor of various peers of this family)
was feated at Thorley in Herts, he was the father of Henry, whofe fon, Oliver St. John of Cay-

---

* Both the houfe of St. John and Tudor defcended from
Margaret, fifter and fole heirefs of John de Beauchamp of Blet-
fhoe, in Northamptonfhire, knt. a junior line of thofe of Po-
wick, branched from the old earls of Warwick, as appears by
the following fketch.

fir O v St. Jonn, krt = Marg Beauchamp =		John Beaufort duke of
from hom defcended the		Somerfet, grandfon of
eal , ns and baronets		John of Gaunt, d of
of his family.		Lancafter, fon of k Edw
		III
Margaret = Edm Tudor, earl of Richmond		
K Hen VII.		

ſhoe, in Bedfordſhire, knt. was returned a member for his county in the parlements held in the 12th and 21ſt years of the reign of k. Ja. I. and for the two held in the firſt year of k. Cha. I.; this Oliver had two ſons, Oliver, whoſe life I am going to give, and John, who left no child, and a daughter, named Elizabeth.

Oliver St. John, the eldeſt ſon of the gentle-man of both his names, received his education in Trinity college, Oxford, where he received his bachelor of arts degree, July 8, 1630, from Ox-ford he was removed to Lincoln's Inn, his ad-miſſion is thus regiſtered,—Oliverius St. John Fi-lius & Hæres apparens Oliveri, St. John de Cay-ſhoe Com. Bedford Admiſſus eſt in ſocietatem iſtius Hoſpitij—22 die Aprilis Anno Reg. Regis Jacobi 17°.—Mancaptores Richd. Taylor, Sami. Brown *, to the latter gentleman (afterwards a judge) his father moſt affectionately recommend-ed him, requeſting him to take care of him, and give him good counſel : whilſt here he made

Oliver St. John, lord-chief-juſtice of the Com-mon Pleas.

* M.S. ſuppoſed to be written by Oliv. St. John's ſon, to re-fute the aſſertion of lord Clarendon, which he has repeated in his hiſtory of the rebellion, that he was a natural ſon of the houſe of Bolingbroke Wood, in his faſti, has alſo miſcalled him the ſon of ſir John St. John of Lydiard-Tregoſe in Wilts, knt. I have relied upon the pedigree of the St. Johns in M.S of lord Liſburne, and others, in the poſſeſſions of mrs. Warren, the wife of the lord biſhop of Bangor, and of col. Neale of Alleſley, in Warwickſhire, both of which confirm the admiſſion of St. John entered in Lincoln's Inn.—We muſt ſuppoſe that ſir Oliver was knighted late in life the baronetage ſays, that ſir Oliver's lady was Sarah, daughter of Edw Buckley of Odell, in Bed-fordſhire, eſq, mrs. Warren and mr. Neale's pedigrees, that ſhe was Judith, eldeſt of three daughters of ———— Neale, of Woolaſton, in Northamptonſhire, eſq and that her two ſiſters were Mary, married to———— Franklin, of Bolnhurſh, in Bed-fordſhire, eſq. and Alice, married to ——— Fitz-Jefferies, of Creakers, in the ſame county, eſq.

a great

NUM. II

S: Johns
Oliver St
John, lord-
chief-juftice
of the Com.
Pleas.

a great proficiency in the law, became eminent as
a pleader, and as he was attached to the caufe of
liberty, he foon raifed himfelf to confequence.——
The court heightened his averfion, and made him
ftill more popular, by imprifoning him upon fome
groundlefs jealoufies *; but after fuffering an examination in the Star-chamber, he was honorably
releafed from his confinement. Ever after this he
was an open oppofer of all the king's arbitrary
proceedings. He pleaded mr. Hampden's caufe
refpecting fhip-money, in which he obtained great
reputation: he was alfo one of the council againft
the earl of Strafford, for taking the militia from
the crown, and abolifhing epifcopacy, the king
vainly endeavouring to foothe him, by appointing
him folicitor-general. He reprefented the county
of Bedford in the 3d parlement called by k. Cha.
I. and Totnefs in the 15th and 16th years of the
fame reign; he took the proteftation in 1642, and
the covenant in 1643, was nominated one of the
affembly of divines, one of the commiffioners of
the parlement great-feal, and was alfo appointed
their attorney-general, and a commiffioner to treat
with the king. Upon the death of lord-chief-
juftice Banks he was conftituted lord-chief-juftice
of the Common-Pleas, and though averfe to the
violent death of his fovereign, and for that reafon
excluded the parlement in 1648, yet he was one
of thofe who accepted their places under the commonwealth, and which he held through all the re-

---

* Mr St John, with the earl of Bedford and fir Rob Cotton, were taken into cuftody, as being the fuppofed difperfers
of a libel, intitled, ' a propofition for his majefty's fervice, to
' bridle the impertinency of parliaments', which was found to
have been the production of the much-injured fir Rob Dudley,
fon of the earl of Leicefter, the favorite of q Eliz. then in the
court of the grand duke of Tufcany, where he was known by
the title of duke of Northumberland.

volutions,

]

PART I

N⸱° 1

N⸱° 2

N⸱° 3

N⸱° 4

N⸱° 5

N⸱° 6

PART III

Arch 1

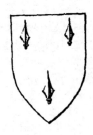

2

3

PART II

ANNO DOMINI 1602

Nº 1

Nº 2

Nº 3

SVDORE NON SOPORE

The Seal of Sr Richd William
alias Crumwell 32 Hen 8

5

6

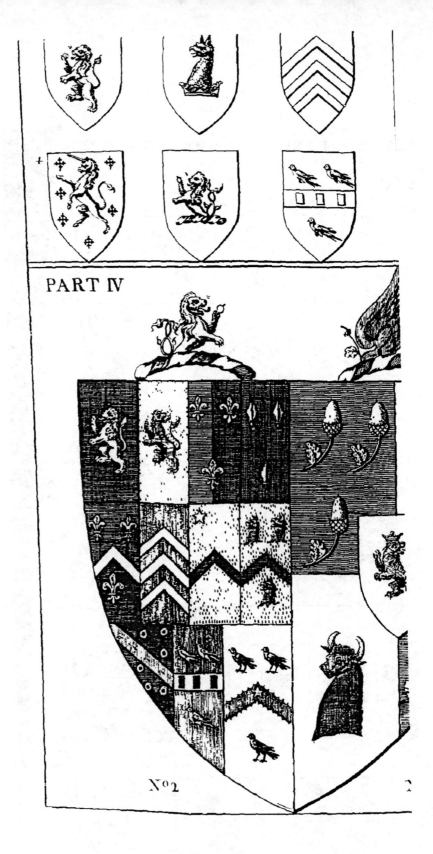

PART IV

Nº 2

Nº 1.

volutions, until the reftoration: he was alfo elected
one of the council of ftate in the years 1649, and
1650.

NUM II.

St. Johns.
Oliver St
John, lord-
chief-juftice
of the Com-
Pleas.

He was fixed upon, with mr. Walter Strickland
(afterwards one of Oliver the prot.'s lords), to go
into Holland, as ambaffador from the commonwealth to the ftates; which, though difagreeable
to himfelf, as well from the danger of the employment, as from lofing the perquifites of his office
as a judge, and although he petitioned the parlement to excufe him, yet he was obliged to fubmit, however, to prevent the ambaffadors experiencing the fate of Doriflaus, the former ambaffador (whom fome loyalifts had affaffinated), they
were allowed 10,000l. to defray their expences,
and forty attendants for their protection; but this
did not prevent his receiving perfonal affronts;
particularly from prince Edward, fon to the q. of
Bohemia, who, meeting St. John by accident, at a
turn-ftile at Verhout, where the prince, with his
fifter Henrietta leaning upon his arm, had walked
out for the air, and expected St. John, who came
at that inftant, to wait until he and his fifter had
paffed, but St. John, regarding his quality as ambaffador, and to put a flight upon a prince of the
blood, endeavoured to force his way firft, upon
which the prince pulled off his har, calling him
many opprobrious names, as dog and traitor; and
faying, ' learn, traitor, to refpect the relation of the
' king thy lord.' St. John, with as little refpect,
replied, ' I regard neither thee, nor the perfon
' thou fpeakeft of, but as a race fugitive,' and it
was with difficulty that they were prevented fighting. The populace in Holland were enraged at
St. John, and affembled before the houfe, where he
and Strickland lodged, with a refolution to ftorm
it, nor was it fafe for them, or any of their attendants, to go out, and feveral advices were given

NUM II

St. Johns.
Oliver St
John, lord-
chief-justice
of the Com.-
Pleas.

them of defigns againſt their perſons. Their high mightineſſes, upon application of the ambaſſadors, and fear of enraging the new commonwealth, were obliged, to ſave appearances, after the moſt tedious delay, to ſummon the prince to the Hague, but he refuſed compliance, ſaying, he was a prince of the empire, and therefore not ſubject to their juriſdiction, and retired from their dominions. To ſatisfy them, however, they were allowed a file of ſoldiers as a guard, and the ſtates ſent a meſſage to the princeſs of Orange, forbidding either her, the duke of York, or the q. of Bohemia, giving them any further diſturbance; and they alſo pub-liſhed a proclamation, prohibiting all injuries or violence to them; but this had not the deſired effect; and mr. St. John returned home (after re-maining there from the latter end of march, 1650, until towards the end of may, 1651), diſguſted with the Dutch, who did not liſten to the terms he offered, for which they were brought to repentance; but he was happy to be recalled from an employ-ment attended with ſo little pleaſure, and ſo much danger, and, as he himſelf declares, without any emolument; for the plate, furniture, beds, and other things, claimed formerly by ambaſſadors, were returned by them to the wardrobe; and the ſtates, at their departure, as a gratuity, promiſed to ſend to each of them, when in England, 1,000l. in gold, which was refuſed; and he proteſted, that all the favor which he received in reward for this embaſſy, was, that he obtained the cathedral of Peterborough, which was propounded to be ſold and demoliſhed, to be granted to the citizens of that place. In 1651, he was appointed one of the ſeven commiſſioners of union of Scotland with England, and the ſame year he was choſen chan-cellor of the univerſity of Cambridge, upon the earl of Mancheſter's being ſuperſeded, for not

taking

taking the engagement, but which he loft to that
nobleman again at the reftoration, and he was pa-
pointed one of the vifitors of that univerfity in 1654.

NUM. II.

St Johns.
Oliver St
John, lord-
chief-juftice
of the Com.-
Pleas

Notwithftanding he was allied to the protectors,
it was with difficulty he was kept from giving fuch
open umbrage, as not to be permitted to hold any
place of truft under their governments; though
they feduloufly endeavoured to keep him their
friend, and he refufed to fit in the parlement called
in 1653, or in the other houfe, though always fummoned, which is the more remarkable, as he continued to fit in the long-parlement from his return
from Holland in 1651, when he was reftored to
his feat, until the members were forcibly expelled
by Cromwell. Not content with abfenting himfelf
from the convention parlement in 1653, he acted
quite contrary to the acts paffed in it, in his judicial capacity, for which complaints were made
againft him both to the elder protector and to his
counfellors, and he had the boldnefs to difcharge
any that came before him that had been committed by the major-generals; nor could he be prevailed upon to act as one of Oliver's council, or as
a commiffioner of his treafury, nor did he receive
any falary on either of thofe accounts. It was very
feldom that he attended the courts of the protectors, except in the beginning, and at the end of the
terms; however, he chofe to retain his place as
judge under every form of government; the reafon of this was his avarice, which got the better of
his political fentiments, thofe in power knew his
love for wealth, and gratified him accordingly. He
had the granting of all pardons to the delinquent
loyalifts, which amounted to the enormous fum of
40,000l. nor did he fcruple accepting bribes for
places under the protectorate of Oliver; and when
the republicans had again got hold of the helm,

and

NUM II

St. Johns
Oliver St.
John, lord-
chief-justice
of the Com-
las

and the patriotic part of them wifhed to make fuch as had enriched themfelves at the expence of the public, refund their ill-gotten money, he obtained an exprefs claufe to indemnify himfelf, for fuch offices as he had difpofed of during Oliver's adminiftration, Ludlow, by oppofing it, made him his enemy ever after: indeed, his whole mind feemed occupied in acquiring wealth. When the parlement wifhed to fet afide all the long expenfive proceffes of the law, he, with Whitlock, promifed the leading members in the houfe, that the lawyers fhould, jointly with the clergy (to excufe the abolition of tythes) pay 100,000l. as a compofition, which effectually ftopped all further proceedings in the matter.

He was appointed, in 1660, one of the council of ftate, but he refufed to fit becaufe of the oaths, and oppofed the abjuration oath in the houfe of parlement, coming to London purpofely, if he is to be believed, to do it, and made the motion, march 11, for the calling a new parlement, which was carried; this, however, probably proceeded from the certainty that fuch an event muft take place, preparatory to what every one forefaw, the reftoration of the monarchy under the houfe of Stuart; when it at length happened, he found that his compliance with that government would not be accepted; and it is moft reafonable to fuppofe, that he faved his life, or at leaft perpetual imprifonment, by the expanfion of the ftrings of that purfe which he had taken fuch pains to fill and keep clofed. K. Cha. II. was difappointed and hurt by his efcaping, even with life, for when it was told his majefty, he faid, ' I wifh he had been ' excepted without any ftipulation.' There can be no doubt but he remembered the infult to the royal family when St. John was in Holland, and

his

his propofal, in 1660, not to recal his majefty
without fubfcribing to fome terms *, was not forgotten. His large fortune might likewife be a
temptation not eafily overcome by fo expenfive
and profligate a monarch, or by needy courtiers,
efpecially as his fon, in a paper he drew up to vindicate his father's character, fays, that the lord-
chief-juftice having lately built a houfe in the country, which, from the manner and ftyle of its architecture, little ufed in England before, rather than
from its fize, made more talk than it really deferved, and was magnified by fome, either on purpofe to create him envy, or through their own ignorance, beyond the truth: this reaching court, it
was too high a prize not to be defired. Lord Clarendon (as St. John himfelf mentioned, when his
fon was prefent) fent for him foon after the reftoration, requefting to fpeak with him, when he told
him he had fome intentions of building an houfe,
and ' that having heard much talk of one mr. St.
' John had lately built, he would be glad if he
' would give him a defcription of it.' The late
lord-chief-juftice was as fagacious as the then lord-
chancellor, for pretending ignorance of his meaning, he replied, that ' he had not the vanity to
' think his houfe, of five or fix rooms on a floor, a
' fit pattern for his lordfhip,' which put a total
ftop to the conference, and perfect filence enfued.
But his riches were too great for his enemies to
give up their expectation of fharing them with
him, they therefore accufed him of various things
he never had committed, efpecially of promoting
the death of k. Cha. I. and juftifying it when done,
fetting up a commonwealth, of wifhing to raife up

NUM. II.

St Johns.
Oliver St.
John, lord-
chief-juftice
of the Com.-
Pleas

* An Author fays, St. John made the above propofal in the
council of ftate, but he himfelf fays, he never fat in that
of 1660.

a govern-

NUM II.

St. Jonns.
Oliver St.
John, lord-
chief-justice
of the Com.-
Pleas.

a government by the long fword, and of affifting in
advancing Oliver and Rich to the protectorate, as
alfo in endeavouring to reftore the latter when depofed, from all which he well defended himfelf,
in a printed anfwer addreffed to the houfe of commons; this, with lord Clarendon's avaricioufnefs,
which he was fearful of having difcovered, prevented the act to pafs, fpecifying what pains and
penalties he was to fuffer. As a further confirmation of what I have juft advanced, refpecting lord
Clarendon's conduct towards him, I will tranfcribe
a paffage from his fon's vindication of him: ' I had
' this' (fays he) ' alfo from a perfon concerned in
' it, a near relation of Oliver St. John, who being
' in the lobby of the houfe of commons, foon after
' paffing the vote for a bill of pains and penalties,
' was accofted very abruptly by a gentleman, a
' great intimate of lord Clarendon's, with this
' queftion—Sir, what brings you hither? to which
' the other replied, with fome warmth, that he
' came to complain of his (the other's) great man:
' whereupon that gentleman faid, no, don't, don't,
' there fhall not need, or to that effect, and ufed
' arguments to perfuade him to be quiet.' Secretary Thurloe alfo rendered him the greateft affiftance at this time, by generoufly affuring fir Har-
bottle Grimfton, fpeaker of the houfe of commons,
that ' he was neither inftrumental in the king's
' death, nor in Oliver's, or Rich.'s exaltation, and
' was fo far from being even a confidant to Oliver,
' that fome who loved and valued him, had fome-
' thing to do to preferve him under that govern-
' ment, nor did he, he thinks, ever wifh the re-
' ftoration of Richard.' Thefe allegations he certainly cleared himfelf of, for he was the open and
avowed enemy of the Cromwell family, yet I cannot believe him, that he was attached to the government by king, lords, and commons, and that
he

he wifhed the reftoration of k. Cha. II. he was too

NUM II.
St Johns.
Oliver St
John, lord-
chief-juftice
of the Com-
Pleas.

great a politician for that, for he could not think
that the royal family would forgive him the enmity
he had fhewn to k. Cha. I. nor the affront he had
put upon prince Edw. and his reflection upon the
royal family when at the Hague, nor can I fuppofe him free from avarice, one of the greateft
faults a judge can have, though his fon defends
him in this refpect, by faying, that what *he left* to
his family was not the fourth part fo much as had
been procured by fome others of that profeffion,
in lefs time, and in offices not fo beneficial, but
the reafon why he did not leave fo much was, becaufe his enemies obliged him to part with large
fums of it to procure his own perfonal fafety,
which he did with great difficulty: moft probably
what he retained was but a very fmall part of the
vaft wealth he once poffeffed · Cha. II.'s minifters at the reftoration, were as poor as they were
mercenary.

He regained the royal favor in fome meafure,
efpecially if his fon has ftated this anecdote of
him right, 'that a fon of lord Sandwich (who
' brought over the king) told him that he had
'' heard his father fay, that the king, after his re-
' ftoration, did offer the continuance to mr. Oliver
' St. John in his place of chief-juftice of the
' Common-Pleas, which mr. St. John refufed on
' account of the violent heats many people were
' running into.' For various reafons, yet under
pretence of health, he retired to the continent,
he was firft at Utrecht, from thence he went to
France, where he made fome ftay: He was at
Augfburg in 1669, and died upon the continent
dec. 31, 1673, aged about 75 years. Dr. Echard
wifhed much to have known his laft fentiments.
He was proud, retired, and morofe; he has been
called the dark-lanthorn-man, but certainly he

was

NUM II

St. Jorn..
O.. er St.
Jorn, lord-
ch er-juftice
o the Com-
plee.

was not fo to the protector Oliver, to whom he
was very ungrateful, for as he chofe to act under
his government, he ought to have fupported it,
and not have returned fo ill all the obligations
that celebrated man was conftantly laying upon
him, as his relation and friend; but lord Clarendon
feems to have done him injuftice in faying he was
revengeful. He certainly is deferving of the greateft
praife for projecting the act of navigation, the
bulwark of the future grandeur of Britain : indeed
his abilities were fuperior to moft, and have never
been queftioned. There is a fine whole length portrait of him at Longthorpe, by Vandyke. He had
three wives, his firft was the daughter and fole
heir of fir Ja. Altham, of Layton, in Effex, knt.
maternally defcended from the Cromwells, by
whom he had four children; his 2d. was Eliz.
eldeft daughter of Hen. Cromwell, of Upwood,
efq. uncle to the prot. Oliver, by whom he had two
children, and his 3d was the widow of one Cock-
craft, merchant and citizen of London, whom he
married probably for her rich dowry: by her he
had no child.

C--- -- of
Oliver S
Jone, c o-
ch c - f ce
o s firt
wife

Fra. S Jo n
e , c ct
for o the
lo d-cm..-
Juftce

*The iffue of Oliver St John, lord-chief-juftice, by his
firft wife.*

1. Fra. St. John of Longthorpe, efq. who was
educated at Emanuel college, in Cambridge, and
ftudied the law at Lincoln's-Inn, he was returned
a member for the city of Peterborough, in Oliver
and Rich.'s parlements, held in 1656, and 1658-9,
and alfo in feveral future ones, but with the other
parts of his family abfented himfelf when the petition and advice was voted to give the protector.
Oliver the crown, that he might not give his confent, nor difpleafe by refufing it. He died in 1705,
having twice married, firft, Mary, heirefs of Dio-
nyfius Wakeringe, of Kelvedon, in Effex, efq. and
after her death, Mary, eldeft daughter of Daniel
Foorth,

Foorth, alderman of London, by the firft he had
only Oliver, who died unmarried in France, upon
his travels The iffue of the fecond marriage
was 5 fons and 3 daughters: 1. Dannett, who
died before his father, when young. 2. fir Francis
St. John, of Longthorpe, who was high fheriff of
Northamptonfhire in 1714, and created a baronet
in the following year. He married Mary, eldeft
daughter of fir Nath. Gould, knt. by whom he
had two daughters, Fra. and Mary, the youngeft
of whom was married to fir John Bernard, bart.
3. Will. who died young. 4. Oliver, who died
unmarried. 5. Walter, a merchant in London.
6. Joanna, who died an infant. 7. Mary, married
to Sam. Browne, of Arlefey, in the county of
Bedford, efq. who left an only daughter: and 8.
Elizabeth.

NUM II.

St Johns.

Children of
Oliver lord-
chief-juftice,
by his firft
wife.

2. Will. St. John, efq. fecond fon of the lord-
chief-juftice, he died a bachelor. This gentleman, for fome reafon now unknown, left his
father: who, that he might regain him, requefted
mr fecretary Thurloe to iffue out warrants for
apprehending him.

3. Joanna, the eldeft daughter of the lord-chief-
juftice St. John, married to fir Walter St. John,
of Lydiard-Tregoze, in Wilts, bart. fon of the
loyal fir John St. John bait*. This fir Wal-

Joanna, eldeft
daughter of
the lord-chief-
juftice, mar.
to fir Walter
St John,
bart.

* Sir John St. John, the firft bart was nephew to Oliver St.
John, baron Tregoze, in England, and vifc. Grandifon, in
Ireland, privy counfellor of both kingdoms, and lord-lieut.
of the latter. fir John had feven fons, Oliver, who was father
of fir John St. John, who died before he was of age, and unmarried; Will. Edw. John, and Nich all of whom died without iffue, the three former fell in the civil war, fighting for
k. Cha. I Henry, of whom in a future page, and a daughter,
married firft to fir Hen Fra. Lee, bait (father by her to the
firft earl of Litchfield of the name of Lee, who married a natural daughter of k. Cha. II.) and to her 2d hufband, Henry
lord Wilmot, afterwards earl of Rochefter, general of the
horfe

NUM II.

Sᵗ John

Joanna, eldeſt
daughter of
the lord-
en an-juſtice

ter St. John ſucceeded to the title of bart.
upon the death of his nephew of both his names,
and to the eſtates of Lydiard-Tregoze, Batterſea,
and Wandſworth, he was returned a member for
the county of Wilts, for Oliver's parlement in
1656, in which he followed the example of his
brother-in-law, mr. Fra. St. John, in abſenting
himſelf whilſt the petition and advice was debat-
ing, as did all the other relations of the family:
He was alſo in the parlement called by the prot.
Rich. and in two held in the reign of k. Ch. II.
In 1679-80, he preſented a petition to that monarch, to requeſt that the parlement might continue ſitting, as it was ſuppoſed the nation was
in danger from popiſh plots; to whom his majeſty returned for anſwer, ' Have you had direc-
' tions from the grand jury? ' No.' ' Why ſay
' you then that you come from the county? You
' come from the company of looſe, diſaffected peo-
' ple. What do you take me to be? And what
' do you take yourſelves to be? I admire that
' gentlemen of your eſtate ſhould animate people
' to mutiny and rebellion; you would not take
' it well I ſhould meddle with your affairs, and
' I deſire you would not meddle with mine, eſ-
' pecially with a matter that is ſo eſſentially a
' part of my government.' In the ſecond year
of the reign of k. Will. and q. Mary, he was alſo
returned for the county of Wilts. He died at
Batterſea, his uſual reſidence, july 3, 1708, in
his 87th year, and was buried in the church there.
Dr. Patrick, afterwards biſhop of Ely, was do-
meſtic chaplain to ſir Walter, to whom he
dedicated his menſa myſtica in 1659, and
profeſſes himſelf much obliged to this baronet

horſe to k Cha. I father by her of John earl of Rocheſter,
equally celebrated for his wit, poetry, and penitence.

and

and his lady for many civilities. Sir Walter was
famed for his piety and all moral virtues. By Joanna, he was the father of Henry, who was a member of parlement for 21 years, and for his great worth created by k. Geo. I. baron St. John of Batterfea, and vifc. St. John, whofe eldeft fon, the favorite of q. Ann, and friend to Pope, was alfo created, 1712, baron St. John, of Lydiard-Tregoze, and vifc. Bolingbroke, which title, by the limitation in the patent (as his lordfhip died without iffue) reverted to the heirs of his father, and is now enjoyed by the prefent lord vifc. Bolingbroke and St. John.

Sir Walter St. John, Bart ∞ Joanna, daughter of Oliver St. John, lord-chief-justice.

Mary, 2nd daughter and co-heir... to Rob. Rich earl of Warwick.

Henry St John, m p for Wilts 21 years, created baron St. John of Battersea, and visc St John, july 2, 2 Geo I died in april 1742, in his 90th year.

∞ Angelica Magdalena, daughter of Geo Pelletry, treasurer gen of the marine, and superintendant of all the ship and galleys of France, temp Lewis XIV in France, she died in 1736

Barbara ∞ sir John Topp, bart.

Ann ∞ Tho Cholmondeley, of Vale Royal, in Cheshire, esq.

Fra daughter & coheress of sir J. Winchcomb k t

Henry, created baron St. John and visc Bolingbroke, he was the favourite of Q Ann, and friend of Pope, he died dec 15, 1751 S P

Maria Clara des Champ de Marcilly, niece to the celebrated Madam de Maintenon and relict of the marq de Vilette

Geo St John, secretary to the english plenipo at Turnelle, Utrecht, died unmarried at Venice, july 11, 1747

Ann, dr of sir Rob ... bart she died 1716

John St John, died in 1748-9

Hester eldest wife St John, dr of Ja Clark, of Watton, Herts, esq. she died march 8, 1752 S P

Hollis St John exchequer-... to q Ann, died unmar 1738

Henrietta, died in 1756 S P

Rob earl of Catherlough in Ireland

Frederick St John, visc Bolingbroke, and St John, ... baron St John of Lydiard-Tregoze, and baron St John, of Battersea

Diana, daughter of Chs duke of Marlborough, from whom he is divorced

Henry St John, M P groom of the bedchamber, and aid de camp to his Majesty

Eldest dr of Tho Bladen, and sister to the countess of Essex.

John bred to the law, late his majesty's surveyor gen of the crown lands, and M P for Eye.

Ann, Louisa, died infants.

Louisa ∞ Sir Will Bagot, bart created in 1780, baron Bagot, of Bagot's-Bromley, Staffordshire

---

George-Rich, M P for Cricklade Wilts ∞ Charlotte daugh of the rev ---Collins, of Winchester.

Frederick.

4. Cath. the 4th child, but 2nd daughter of the lord-chief-justice St. John, married to Henry St. John, youngest brother of sir Walter St. John, bart. her sister's husband. her father, in a letter dated from Forty, jan. 7, 1650-1, to Oliver Cromwell, then lord-governor of Ireland, says, ' what con-' cerns the publique you have from the well-head, ' by sir Roger and your brother Herne,' (probably the husband of a sister of Oliver Cromwell's wife) ' those which now come from Forty, concern ' only the œconomiques, in that I have lately ' married my two daughters to two brothers of ' my own name, sons to sir John St. John, of ' Wiltshire; the youngest is concerned in Ireland; ' they are both such as fear God, and such as my-' self and their wives, I hope, shall find a blessing ' in'. He was a member of parlement for Wotton-Basset, in Rich. the prot.'s parlement. By Cath. he left Ann, an only child, who married to Anth. Bowyer, of Camberwell, in the county of Surry, esq.

Children of Oliver St. John, lord-chief-justice, by his second wife, Eliz. daughter of Henry Cromwell of Upwood, esq. uncle to the prot. Oliver.

5. Oliver St. John, the 5th child, but 3d son of the lord-chief-justice; married Eliz. daughter of ——— Hammond, of Kent, esq. by whom he had a son named Oliver; the lady was, no doubt, a relation to col. Hammond, who married Mary, daughter of the patriot Hampden.

6. Eliz. the 3d. daughter, but the 6th child of the lord-chief-justice; she became the first wife of sir John Bernard, bart. he died in june, 1679*

marginal notes:
NUM II.
St Johns.
Children of Oliver St. John, lord-chief-justice, by his 1st wife.
Cath. 2d. daughter of Ol lord-chief-justice, mar. to Hen St. John, esq.

Children of Oliver St John, lord-chief-justice, by his 2d wife.

Oliver St. John, esq. only son of Oliver lord-chief-justice, by his 2d wife.

Eliz only da. of Ol lord-chief-justice, by his 2d wife - she mar to sir John Bernard, bart

* Sir John Bernard, bart. was son of sir Rob. serjeant-at-law, the first of that title, so created in 1662 he was named a justice of peace for Huntingdon with O. Cromwell, esq. (afterwards prot.)

leaving by his lady 6 children. 1. Sir Rich. Bernard, bart. of whom below. 2 Eliz. 3. Ann. 4.
Lucy, all of whom died young, or unmarried.
5. Mary, married to Tho. Brown, of Arlesey, in
Bedfordshire, by whom she had seven children;
dr. Brown, of Arlesey, was the heir. 6. Grace. 7.
Fra. married to John Pedley, esq. 8. Joanna, who
married to the very learned dr Rich. Bentley,
archdeacon and prebendary of Ely, Regius profes-
sor and master of Trinity college, Cambridge; he
died in 1742, leaving three children, a son and two
daughters, Rich. Bentley, Eliz. wife of Humphrey Ridge, of Portsmouth, esq. by whom she had
no issue, and Joanna, who was the Phœbe upon
whom the late dr. Byram wrote his elegant pastoral,
given in no. 603, in the Spectator, beginning, 'My
time, O ye Muses, was happily spent,' &c. when
he wrote this he was a student, or fellow of Trinity
college, Cambridge· miss Bentley, however, was
not won by this plaintive sonnet, she surrendered her charms to dr. Denison Cumberland,
bishop of Clonfert and Killaloe, in Ireland, and
grandson of dr. Rich. Cumberland, bishop of
Peterborough; by his lordship she had three
children, 1. Rich. Cumberland, of Portland-
Place, esq. well known in the republic of letters, by his dramatic, and other writings: he
was employed a few years ago, as negociator by
his majesty to Spain, and was accompanied by
his lady, who injured her health by the heat of
the climate: his eldest daughter was married,
dec. 23, 1782, to the right hon. lord Edw. Ben-

pror j which borough he represented in the long parlement, in
1640, he married, first Eliz daughter of sir John Tallakerne,
knt and 2dly, Eliz. relict of Rob. lord Digby, by the former
he had many children, by the latter none he died in 1666,
aged 65, and was buried in the north ayle of Abingdon church.
Sir John Bernard, bart. re-married to Grace, daughter of sir
Rich Shuckburgh, of Shuckburgh, in Warwickshire, knt. by
her he had no issue

tinck,

tinck, brother to the duke of Portland. 2. Joanna, died single. and 3. Eliz. married to dean Allcock in Ireland.

NUM II

Bernards.

Sir Rich. Bernard, bart. member for the county of Huntingdon, in 1688, married Ann, daughter of Rob. Weldon, of London, esq. who re-married to Tho. first lord Trevor, by sir Rich. Bernard she had only sir John, who succeeded to the title of baronet, and 5 daughters, Ann, Mary, and Eliz. who died before their father, and Ann and Mary, who died unmarried. *Sir Richard Bernard, bt.*

Sir John Bernard, bart. died dec. 16, 1766, he married in jan. 1736-7, Mary the youngest daughter of sir Fra. St. John of Longthorpe, bart. by whom he had 5 sons and 4 daughters, 1. Sir Rob. the present bart. of whom below. 2. John. 3. Rich. 4. Rich. all of whom died infants. 5. Fra. who died at the age of 12 years, in 1750, or 1751, at Bishop-Stortford, where he was at school. 6. Will. who died at Thorpe, in the 15th year of his age, feb. 8, 1766. 7. Mary, married to Rob. Sparrow, of Worlingham, near Beccles, in Suffolk, esq. by whom she has Rob. Bernard Sparrow, and Mary, and Fra. who died a child. 8. Ann, who died an infant. 9. Eliz. who died at the age of 7 years; and 10. Fran. who died unmarried, in the 19th year of her age.

Sir. Rob. Bernard, bart. the only surviving son of sir John, was a member of parlement for the county of Huntingdon, and for the city of Westminster, in two successive parlements*. *Sir Robert Bernard.*

---

* The life of the lord-chief-justice St John is taken from
' the case of Oliv St. John, esq. concerning his actions during
' the late troubles, presented to the House of Commons in the
' 1st parlement after the restoration of k Cha. II. ann. 1660,
' and then printed,' and a M S written by his son tending to
further prove his innocence, both most obligingly lent me by
lady Bernard; from several contemporary authors, as Whitlock,

No. III.

The hiftory of the family of Neale, defcended from Anna, youngeft daughter and coheirefs of Henry Cromwell, efq. of Upwood, uncle to Oliver lord protector.

NUM. III
Neales
Antiquity

THE family of Neale is originally of Stafford-shire; Rich. Neale of that county, efq. had two fons, the elder of whom fettled at Woolafton in Northamptonfhire*; Tho. the younger, feated

lock, Clarendon, Ludlow, Heath, Wood, &c. and feveral general hiftories of England, and the hiftory of his family, and his defcendants, is chiefly taken from the baronetages, and the London Mag. for 1774, from pedigrees moft politely lent me by the earl of Lifburne, and col. Neale, with various additions and corrections by the earls of Sandwich and Lif-burne, L. Brown, efq and mr. Longmate.

* As a further explanation of what I have written of the St. John family, I will fubjoin fome of the defcendants of Mr. Neale of Woolafton

Rich Neale of Staffordshire, efq

— Neal of Woolafton, efq = Goodrith, dr of Rich Throg-morton, efq younger fon of i r Rob Throgmorton of Coving-ton, in Warwickfhire, by —— dr of Beaufov of Emfcote, alfo in the co of Warwick, efq

| John Neale o Woolaf ton, efq who left de-fcendants | Jane=Oliv St. John of Cayfhoe, Bedfordfhire, efq | Mary=— Franklin of Bolm-hurft, in Bedford-fh efq | Alice = — Fitzjef-feries of Creakers, Bedf fh. efq |

Oliv St John, lord-chief-juftice

The Neales of Woolafton continued long there, and were confiderable in their county; they were loyalifts, Edm Neale of that place, efq was fined for his attachment to k Cha I. 5821.

hun-

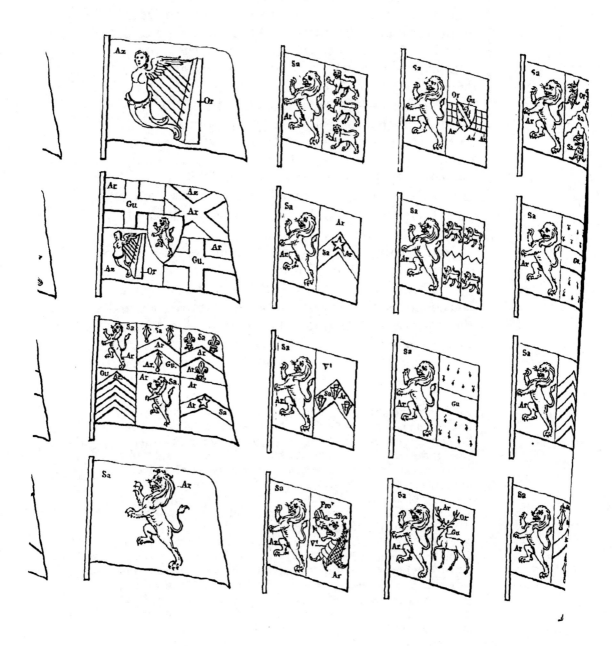

himfelf at Ellefborough, in the county of Bucks, and was the father of Rich. who removed to Dean in Bedfordfhire, he married Alice, daughter and coheir of Tho. Moore, of Buckton, in the county of Bucks, efq. by whom he had two fons, and three daughters, Tho. the eldeft fon, married Ann, daughter of —— Daurell, of Lamport, Bucks, efq. the iffue of this marriage was 3 fons and a daughter *; John, the eldeft, married Bridget, daughter of ——— Moore, of Wing, in Bucks, efq. by whom he had the numerous family of 10 fons and 2 daughters; the eldeft fon is he of whom I intend particularly to fpeak, and whofe defcendants are here given †.

John Neale, of Deane, in the county of Bedford, efq. the eldeft fon of John, was born dec. 20, 1612, he married Anna, the youngeft daughter and coheirefs of Henry Cromwell, of Upwood, in the county of Huntingdon, efq. third fon of fir Hen. Cromwell, knt. fhe was firft coufin to O. Cromwell, efq (afterwards lord protector) who was one of the truftees mentioned in the marriage

John Neale; efq.

---

* Peter, the 2nd fon of Tho. was the father of Noah, whofe fon, alfo named Noah, by Eliz. daughter of Hen. Warren, of St. Martin's in Stamford, efq had 3 fons and 7 daughters; Eliz the 2nd, married John Wilbore, of Peterborough, efq. Fra a daughter of theirs, married Hen Southwell, of Wifbech, in Cambridgefhire, efq Eliz. his eldeft furviving daughter, is the wife of dr John Warren, the lord bifhop of Bangor, to which lady I am indebted for the ufe of the curious M.S. pedigree from which the above is taken

† Jof. Neale, of Gray's-inn, London, efq another fon of John, gave lands at Little-Catworth, in the parifh of Long-Stow, in Huntingdonfhire, to the value of between 20 l. and 25 l. per ann for founding a charity-fchool at Nether-Dean, where 20 poor boys, 10 of them of Dean, 5 of Shelton, and 5 of Swinefhead, were to be taught gratis this endowment was made aug. 27, 1702; and he died at London, april 23, 1710 · mr. Neale alfo gave feveral books for the ufe of the minifter of the parifh of Dean.

settlement, part of which is still remaining in the possession of the present representative of the family. Mr. Neale was a parlementarian, and it was scarce possible to be otherwise with one who was the brother-in-law to Oliver St. John, the lord-chief-justice, and the near relation of the celebrated O. Cromwell, and Hampden the patriot. He was appointed one of the committee to put in force the parlement ordinances in Bedfordshire, for levying money upon the estates of the loyalists, to pay their army, and he was one of the representatives for that county in 1654. There is no doubt but that he was much respected by the prot. Oliver, for col. Neale has a good portrait of that great man, taken late in life, and which, we may be pretty certain, was a present from his highness himself to the Neales*. He died oct. 28, 1680, and was buried in the church of Dean: in the south ayle is a handsome monument of marble erected to perpetuate his memory, upon the inscription of which he has this character: 'He ' was a good and religious man.' His wife died sept. 23, 1651, and is buried in the same church. Near the monument of her husband is one of stone for her, a part of which is worthy transcribing: ' She was one of the most faithful servants of Jesus ' Christ, wholly devoted to the holy scriptures, and ' to the exercises of religion, both public and pri- ' vate; a most sincere observer of truth, a me- ' morable pattern of perfect humility; and a most

---

* The portrait of Oliv. the prot in the possession of col. Neale, is a very fine piece of painting, in the late mr. Neale's time it was greatly neglected, owing to the hatred he had to the character of his famous relation The picture gives Oliver in armour, the whiskers and hair below the under lip are very grey. It is a great likeness of Cromwell's best portraits, and is no doubt an original, but by whom is uncertain, perhaps sir Peter Lely.

‘ shining example of every virtue.’ There still remains in the church an hatchment with the Neales arms impaling those with the Cromwells. The issue of this marriage was two sons and three daughters, 1. John Neale, of Dean, esq. who married Hester, daughter of John Stephens of Lippiat, in the county of Gloucester (a family very many times allied by intermarriages to the Neales); by her he had Tho. who died young, Ann, married to Tho Stephens, of Lippiat, esq. father by her of another Tho. and Hester married to Rynard de-la-Bere, of Southam, in Gloucestershire, esq. of a venerable family, who came into England with Will. I.*. As there was no issue of this marriage, mr. de-la-Bere left the manor of Southam to Will. Bagot, of Besbury, esq. (son of his sister Ann) who, in conformity to the will of his uncle, took the name of de-la-Bere; and by Hester, daughter of Tho. Stephens, of Lippiat, esq. left Tho. Bagot de-la-Bere, the present possessor of Southam   2 Henry, who continued the name, of whom hereafter   3. Ann, married to Tho. Stephens, of Little-Sadbury, in Gloucestershire, esq by whom she had a son named Edw. who by Sarah, daughter of D. Burthy, left no issue. 4 Bridget, who died unmarried, and 5. Eliz. who was born in 1650-1, and buried may 11, 1664.

---

* The de-la-Bere’s, says Guilhm, bear for their arms, az. a bend arg cotoised, or betw. 6 martlets of the last, but Edmondson, az. a bend oz. cotoised, arg betw. 6 martlets of the 2nd, and in consideration of sir Rich. one of this family’s, rescuing Edw the black prince, at the battle of Cressy, k Edw. III gave them for a crest, out of a ducal coronet, or, a plume of ostrich feathers, party per pale, arg and az. Their seat at Southam is a magnificent pile, built in the reign of k. Hen IV. several of the apartments are laid with painted bricks that once belonged to Hales-Abbey.

Henry

NUM II'

Neale

Her Neale, efq

Henry Neale, efq fecond fon of John Neale, efq. by mifs Cromwell, was born in 1651; he was fheriff of Bucks in 1696, he afterwards fettled in Warwickfhire, at the pleafant village of Allefley, two miles from Coventry, where he had a noble feat, and a very confiderable eftate, the manor and patronage of the church being his · the former he purchafed of the widow of Tho. Flint, ferjeant-at-law. He married Anna-Maria, fole daughter and heirefs of John Hanbury, of Feckenham, in Worcefterfhire, efq. with whom he lived more than 40 years, and furvived her only 2 months and 25 days. She died feb. 11, 1729-30, aged 60 years, and he, may 6, 1730, aged 79. There is an elegant marble monument, recording their many virtues, in the chancel of Allefley church *; by which it appears, that they left fix fons and a daughter; 1. John Neale of Allefley, and of Cherington, in Gloucefterfhire, efq. He was returned a member for the county of Warwick in the 8th year of k. Geo. I. and again the 1ft of k. Geo. II. was a member for Coventry in 1734, 1736, and 1739, as there was a ftrong conteft in fome of thefe elections, though he was fuccefsful, yet it much injured his fortune; and he was obliged to part with the advowfon of the church. The court gave him the place of comptroller of the houfehold to the young princeffes · he died dec. 19, 1746. By Fra. daughter of Roger Pope, of Ofweftry, efq. which Fra. was dreffer to q Caroline, he had iffue 3 daughters,—Caroline, who died young and unmarried, Ann, who married, in april 1742, to Ja. Stonehoufe, M.D. who refided firft in Coventry,

---

* Upwood, the feat of Henry Cromwell, efq. uncle to the prot Oliver, and father of the mifs Cromwell who married mr Neale, is, by miftake, upon the monument, faid to be in the county of Effex, but it is in Huntingdonfhire, as is elfewhere mentioned.

and afterwards in Northampton, and was the friend
of the gloomy mr. Harvey, who mentioned him in
his meditations, and has there given her monument.
He has been some years in the church, and now resides in Bristol universally beloved. He has had 3
or 4 children by miss Neale, one of whom is married to mr. Vansittart. And Frances married to
sir John Turner, of Warham, in Norfolk, bart. so
created april 27, 1727. He was returned a member of parlement for King's-Lynn, and was constituted a commissioner for executing the office of
treasurer of the Exchequer. Lady Fra. died dec. 25,
1761, the title is extinct, sir John having only two
daughters, one of whom married sir Martin
Folkes, bart. president of the Royal-Society, by
whom he had, it is thought, one son, sir Martin,
the present baronet, and 3 daughters. the other
daughter of sir John Turner married to a gentleman of Lynn. 2. Joseph Neale, esq. 2nd son of
Henry, was a captain in the horse-guards, he was
buried in the chancel of Allesley church, where
there is a neat monument erected to his memory,
with this concise inscription :

Ah! poor Joe Neale,
ob. the 29th sept. 1730.
Aged 42.

3 Henry Neale, esq also died a bachelor, and
was buried at Allesley. 4. Tho. Neale, esq. of
whom I shall speak, as the continuator of this
line. 5. Hanbury Neale, esq. who died unmarried, feb 29, 1756, aged 56 years. 6. Will.
Neale, esq. who married a daughter of —— Hanbury, of Herefordshire, esq by whom he had no
issue. 7. Eliz who married to John Nott, of
Braidon, Wilts, esq she left 3 sons,—capt. John-
Neale-Bledell Nott· he was killed on board a
man of war, of which he was commander : by miss
Andrews he was father of 2 sons and as many

D 3 daughters,

daughters, Jof. Nott, and Roger Nott; the former of thefe died a bachelor in the Eaft Indies, and Roger, if alive, is now in Jamaica. 8 Anna-Maria, and 9 Mary, both of whom died children; the former fept. 3, the latter dec. 19, both in 1693.

Tho. Neale, 4th fon of Hen. Neale, was feated at Allefley. He married Ann, daughter of Mich. Macpherfon of Scotland, by whom he had 8 children, only two of them arrived at the age of manhood.

1. Jofeph-Macpherfon Neale, of Allefley, efq. who died a bachelor, and was fucceeded in that eftate by his only brother.

2. John Neale, efq. who is a colonel in the britifh army, but now refides at his feat of Allefley-Park. This gentleman was high-fheriff of Warwickfhire in the year 1783. He married Mary, daughter of —— Hill, of Dinmock, in the county of Gloucefter, efq by whom he has no iffue *.

* The hiftory of the family of Neale is taken from a pedigree, and fome MSS fent me in the moft obliging manner by mrs Warren, the lady of the lord bifhop of Bangor; and another in the poffeffion of col. Neale, who alfo kindly permitted me to take extracts from it, from the monuments in the church of Allefley, &c Col. Neale, befides the portrait of Cromwell, and part of the marriage-fettlement upon Anna Cromwell, has fome other curious writings relating to the prot. Oliver, as well as fome family portraits of the Neales.

No. IV.

No. IV.

The history of the baronet family of Barrington, descended by a female from the protectoral-house of Cromwell.

SIR Francis Barrington, bart. uncle by marriage to Oliver lord prot was descended from
the Barringtons, or Barentones, of Barrington-
Hall, in Herts, who trace their pedigree up to
the norman conquest, and from saxon descent.
They were much enriched in the reign of k. Stephen, by the estate of the lords Montfitchet, and
their blood ennobled by sir Tho. Barrington, knt.
marrying Winifred, widow of sir Tho. Hastings,
knt. second and youngest daughter, and coheiress
of Hen. Pole, lord Montagu *, son of sir Rich.
Pole, knight of the garter, by Marg^t. Plantagenet,
countess of Salisbury, sister and sole heir of Edw.
earl of Warwick, and daughter to Geo duke of
Clarence, brother to k. Edw. IV. and k Rich. III.
The issue of this illustrious marriage was sir Fra.
Barrington, who was created a baronet, Hen.
Barrington, a gentleman pensioner, who died
without issue, and Cath who married Will. son
and heir of sir Ralph Bourchier, of Benningborough, in Yorkshire, knt †.

* Catherine, the eldest daughter and coheiress of Hen. lord
Montagu, married Fra. earl of Huntindgon, eldest brother to
sir Tho Hastings.

† The grandson of the above marriage was Barrington Bourchier, esq of Benningborough, in Yorkshire, who was to have
been a knight of the royal oak, and whose estate was 1000l. per
ann. The Bourchiers of Benningborough are descended from

NUM IV

Barringons

Sir Francis
Barringto,
...u-
ce... o
the... t
Oliver

Sir Fra. Barrington was seated at Barrington-Hall, he was returned a member for the county of Essex, in the parlement assembled 43d of q. Eliz. in which reign he distinguished himself by signing a petition to parlement in behalf of the puritan ministers of Essex. Upon the accession of k. Ja. VI. of Scotland, to the english throne, he was knighted at Theobald's, may 7, 1603, and created a baronet upon the institution of that order in 1611. Sir Fra. was one of the representatives of Essex in all the parlements during the reign of k. Ja. I and in the 3 first of k. Cha. I. He was justly alarmed at the encroachments of the crown, and with a boldness to be commended, refused to contribute to the loan in 1627, for which he suffered an imprisonment: happy for himself, he died july 3, 1628, before his country was deluged in a civil war. By Joan, daughter of sir Hen. Cromwell, knt. aunt to the prot Oliver, he left 4 sons and 5 daughters 1. Sir Tho Barrington, bart. of whom below. 2 Rob. Barrington, esq. He was one of the representatives for the borough of Newton, in the parlement called in the 3d year of

---

Ja Bourchier. eldest natural son of John Bourchier, lord Berners Sir John Bourchier, of Hanging-Grimston, in Yorkshire, knt and son of sir Ralph Bourchier, of Benningborough, knt was a rigid independent, and one of the king's judges happy for himself, he died just before his trial would have taken place, he was then old and infirm, and had surrendered himself within the time limited by the proclamation he died at the house of one of his daughters, where he obtained permission to remain instead of going to the Tower his relations pressing him much to express his sorrow for the part he had acted respecting the king's death, he rose up from his chair, which he had not done for some days before without assistance, and exerting himself, said, It was a just act, God, and all good men will own it Having said which, he calmly sat down again and soon after expired He was no relation to the prot. Oliver as it is, as appears by his seal in the warrant for k Cha. I's execution.

k. Cha.

k. Cha. I's. reign. He was much careffed and trufted by the long-parlement (who made him one of their committee for Effex) and by his coufin, the prot. Oliver. he fettled at Hatfield-Broad Oak, in Effex, and married Dorothy, daughter of fir John Eden, of Sudbury, in Suffolk, knt. and widow of ———— Barret, by whom he had feveral children *· his male defcendants were long feated at Lacelly's, in Staple-Bumfted, in Effex: the laft of the name was Juan Barrington, married to mr. Gyles, of the Six-cleiks office. 3. Fra. Barrington, efq who firft fettled at London; but in the civil war took up arms, and was a field officer in Jamaica, after it was taken by the prot. Oliver; he fettled there, and took vaft pains to cultivate the plantations he was fo much beloved, that col. d'Oyley, the governor, recommended him, in 1657, to fucceed him in that employment, as he wifhed to decline it, becaufe, fays he to the protector, ' he is allied to your highnefs, is a man ' of known integrity, competent abilities, and fuf- ' ficient experience in the place ' He married the daughter of Rich. Dowfet, by whom he had a fon of both his names. 4. John Barrington, efq. one of the gentlemen of the prot. Oliver's bedchamber, member of parlement for Dunwich, in 1658, 1659, and 1660 at the reftoration he left Britain, and retired to Germany, where he ferved in

* During the government of the prot Oliver, the names of Geo Henry, and Abia Barrington, all of Effex, occur as perfons trufted by him, Henry was member for Effex, in 1653; as alfo one of the parlement committee for Effex, and the town of Colchefter. Query, Were not they fons of the above Rob. ? Winified, one of his daughters, was married to John Ellifon, a clothier he died in dec. 1665, leaving John, Peter, and Oliver Ellifon, the latter was a phyfician —Another Winified, daughter of fir John Barrington, of Broad-Oak, married Rob. Wifeman, of Torrell's-Hall he was a volunteer, and killed at the fiege of Buda. She died may 7, 1684, leaving no child.

the

the army. One of thefe fons of fir John Barrington, bart. I apprehend, was major Barrington, who
was difplaced from his commiffion by col. fir Cha.
Coote, for murmuring at fir Cha. making his
3 brothers, and his coufin fir Geo. Coote, colonels · fir Cha. at any other time would have been
inexcufable, but the times demanded fuch only
to be trufted, who could be entirely depended
upon. however, it was the greater hardfhip, as
major Barrington was alfo anxious to have his
royal mafter reftored, and he was treated by fir Cha.
with great feverity, by the freenefs of his repri-
mands, as well as by depriving him of his poft:
and it is moft probable, that another of thefe fons was
the mr. Barrington who was clerk of the green cloth
in the protectorate of Oliver. 5. Eliz. Barrington. She was twice married, firft to fir Ja. Altham, of Markefhall, in Effex, knt. who died
july 15, 1610, by whom fhe had an only daughter, Joanna, married to Oliver St. John, lord-
chief-juftice of the Common-Pleas. Her defcendants have been already given After fir Ja.
Altham's death, his widow married to fir Will.
Mafham, bart *. 6. Mary Barrington, who
married to fir Gilbert Gerard, of Harrow-on-the-
Hill, Middlefex, created a baronet in 1620. He
was a member for Middlefex in the 18th and 21ft
years of the reign of k Ja. I. and the 1ft, 15th, and
16th years of the reign of k Cha I. in the laft, which
is called the long-parlement, he fhewed himfelf an
enemy to the earl of Strafford, and afterwards to
the king, joining with the parlement againft royalty
itfelf, he was one of their committee for Middlefex and Bucks, and the liberty of Weftminfter †,

---

* Vide hiftory of the Mafhams. no. 5.

† Alderman fir Jacob Gerard, knt. one of the parlement
committee for London, and Gilbert Gerard, efq for Middlefex, and the liberty of Weftminfter, were probably near relations to fir Gilbert.

for the fervices he rendered them, he rofe to many confiderable places, he was made paym*fter of the parlement army, had three-pence in the pound allowance, worth 60,000*l* and alfo was appointed chancellor of the duchy of Lancafter: the plot. Oliver made him a lord of his upper houfe. His alliance to, and friendfhip for the Cromwells, occafioned the long parlement, after Richard's refignation, to refufe him admiffion into their houfe; but he had the courage to bring an action againft col. Alured, who had perfonally ftopped him as he was entering the houfe, but the parlement ordered the action to be dropped, as it was done by their order. the army foon after obtaining the fuperiority, he was nominated one of the new council of ftate, he was one of the officers who met at general Monk's quarters, feb 17, 1659-60, to confult with the members what fteps fhould be taken for fettling the nation. The title of baronet is now become extinct in this family: fuch of his defcendants as I have found are given in a note*;

---

* Sir Cha. Gerard, bart defcended from fir Gilbert, reprefented Middlefex in parlement, and died in 1701 By lady Honora, daughter of Cha. lord Seymour, of Trowbridge, and fifter of Cha duke of Somerfet, he left an only daughter, who married to Warwick Lake, of Canons, Middlefex, efq by whom fhe had Launcelot-Cha Lake, of Harrow-on-the-Hill, efq who married Letitia, daughter of John Gumley, efq commiffary-general Upon mr. Warwick Lake's death, his widow married to fir Philip Stapleton, of the Leward Iflands, but. by whom fhe had three children, Miles, Ann, and Frances, fhe was a vaft fortune to her firft hufband, great part of the family eftate centering in her, though the title came to fir Fra Gerard, brother to her father, who was then in Spain he enjoyed his dignity but two years, dying in aug. 1704, leaving only two daughters, the eldeft of them married to —— Lethieullier, efq and Ifabella, the other, in 1725, to fir John Fryer, bart lord-mayor of London, in 1720, fhe re-married, after his death, to lord vifc Palmerftone the title defcended to fir Fra's younger brother, fir Check Gerard, bart. who died at Harrow-on-the-Hill,

NUM IV
Barrington s
Younger chil-
dren of Sr Fra
Barrington, bart.

observing, first, that John, a younger son of sir Gilbert, was fellow of King's-college, Cambridge, and died in 1690, aged 53. 7. Winifred Barrington, married to sir Will Mewes, or Meaux, of Kingston, in the isle of Wight, created a baronet dec. 11, 1641; which title became extinct in sir Will. Meaux, bart. who died unmarried in 1705, aged about 21 years. He left sisters. 8. Ruth Barrington, wife of sir George Lamplugh, of Cumberland, knt. Of this family was dr. Lamplugh, archbishop of York, who died in 1691, aged 76. 9. Joan Barrington, married to sir Rich, Everard, bart.

Sir Thomas Barrington 2d bart
&c cousin to the
pret O!.

Sir Tho. Barrington was knighted in the lifetime of his father, and upon his death succeeded him in the title of baronet. He was one of the representatives for Newtown, in the parlements called in the 12th, 18th, and 21st years of the reign of k. Ja. I. and for both those called in the first years of the following reign, and was returned for the county of Essex in the 3d and 15th years of that king, but for Colchester, in the following year. He followed his father's example in oppos-

---

Hill, in feb 1715-16, in whom the title became extinct. The Gerards are branched out into many noble families, the Fitz-Geralds, earls of Kildare, as also the earls of Plymouth and Macclesfield, and the barons of Gerards-Bromley, are of this family, besides several of less note. Lord Gerard was one of k Ch I.'s generals, and an exile with k Cha. II. his lordship engaged in a plot to assassinate Oliver the prot for which his relations, sir Gilbert Gerard, afterwards a lieutenant in k Cha. II.'s guards, col. John Gerard, and mr Cha. Gerard, brothers, were taken up; Cha. by confessing, saved his life, John was beheaded It is singular, the brother of the Portugueze ambassador died the same day for killing a gentleman, whom he mistook for this colonel, sir Gilbert, the eldest, was set down for a knight of the royal oak, was much favored by k Cha. II. but forsook the court towards the latter part of that reign.

* Vide history of the Everards, no 6.

ing

ing the royal tyranny, having given such offence to the court, by the freedom of his speeches in parlement, in 1629, that he was brought before the privy-council, and in 1640, he presented a petition to the long-parlement, from his county, stating the grievances complained of. He was a committee-man in that county, took the protestation in 1641, and the covenant in 1643, and was one of the lay assessors in the assembly of divines: he died in 1644. He married twice; first, Fra. daughter and coheir of John Gobert, of Coventry, esq. and secondly, Judith, daughter of sir Rowland Lytton, of Knebworth, Herts, knt. (member of parlement for Hertfordshire in 1656 and 1658-9) and widow of sir Geo. Smith of Annables, in that county, knt. She died in 1657, aged 65, without issue. By the first lady sir Tho. had four children: 1. sir John Barrington, bart. whose history will be given. 2 Oliver Barrington. 3. sir Gobert Barrington, of Tofts, in Little-Baddow, in Essex.

He was a parlementarian, but carried himself so well at the restoration, that he received the honor of knighthood: he died about 1695. Sir Gobert married twice; first, Lucy, daughter of sir Richard Wiseman, of Torrells-Hall, Essex, knt. and secondly, Eliz. relict of Hugh Lawton, or Lorten, esq. who died in 1703: by the former he had six sons, Tho. born in 1648; Fra. Rich. Rob. John, and Theophilus, the four last died young, and also six daughters. Tho. Barrington was a col. in the army; and having greatly injured his fortune, requested his brother, Fra. Barrington, who was a very rich merchant of Tunis, to purchase it. Fra. dying first, and without issue, by the daughter of Sam. Shute, esq alderman of London, in 1681, left the estate to his brother Tho. but with limitation to John Shute, esq. his wife's brother, if Tho. died with-

I

out issue; which happening, mr. Shute became heir, both to his large fortune and his ancient name Few persons have been more fortunate than this mr. Shute Barrington, for John Wildman, esq. though very remotely allied to him, adopted him heir to his great estates. He married the sole heiress of sir Will Daines, of Bristol, a very wealthy knight. He was by k. Geo. I. created visc Barrington, in Ireland · he was deserving of all these riches and honors, which are descended to his son, the present Will. Wildman visc. Barrington · another of his sons is the hon. Daines Barrington, esq. so well known for his valuable publications. 3 Lucy Barrington, married first to sir Will Chency, of Chesham-Boys, Bucks, knt. who died member for Amersham, in the long-parlement: after his death she re-married to sir Toby Tyrrell, of Thornton, Bucks, bart. · The Tyrrels are a most noble and ancient family : it is supposed that k. Will. sirnamed Rufus, was by accident shot with an arrow by one of them, there certainly, in his reign, was a knight of that name, who was a relation to the king. It must also be observed, that sir Toby Tyrrell was the second son of sir Edw Tyrrell, bart. who, out of displeasure to his eldest son Rob. surrendered up his patent, and took out a new one, limiting the title to his son Toby, but with precedency from the original grant to him of that title, viz oct. 1. 3 Cha. I†. Whether Lucy, daughter of sir Thomas Barrington, had any

---

    - Sir Toby had a former wife, who was Edith, daughter of sir Fra. Windebank, knt secretary of state to k. Cha I by whom he had Fra. married first to sir John Hewet, bart. and secondly to Philip Cotton, esq. third son of sir Tho. Cotton, bart.

    † It was generally looked upon that the king could not legally deprive Rob sir Toby's elder brother, of his succession: he died unmarried.

children

children by fir Will. Cheney, is uncertain; but by fir Toby fhe had fir Tho. his fucceffor; fir Timothy Tyrrell, knt. who died oct. 24, 1701, leaving no child; and Francis. alfo Lucy, married to —— Shipton, of London; Hefter to Fra. Gosfright, of London, merchant; and Mary. Sir Toby died in 1671, and was buried at Thornton. Sir Thomas Tyrrell, bart. fucceffor to fir Toby, married Fra. only daughter of fir Hen. Blount, of Tittenhanger, Herts, knt. by whom he had a numerous iffue. Sir Henry Tyrrell, bart. his eldeft fon, married Hefter, eldeft daughter, and in the end heir to Cha Blount, of Blount-Hall, in Staffordfhire, efq fecond fon of the above fir Henry Blount. Sir Henry died nov. 6, 1708, leaving 3 fons and 2 daughters, 1. fir Tho. Tyrrell, bart. who died unmarried, in 1719. 2. fir Harry Tyrrell, bart who alfo died unmarried, nov. 9, 1720. 3. fir Cha. Tyrrell, bart. married at Geneva, when upon his travels, in 1726, Jane-Eliz only daughter of monfieur Sellon, of that city, by whom he had James, born at Geneva, 1727, and died there, 1729, and Harry-Cha. Gafpard, born alfo at Geneva, 1728, and died at Paris, 1729, and a daughter, named Hefter-Maria. Upon fir Charles's death, this title became extinct, as is the title of baronet in the Tyrrells of Hanflape and Caftle-Thorpe*.

r It is a matter of doubt, whether the Tyrrells were moft loyal or otherwife, in the time of the greateft trial, feveral of them proved themfelves much attached to the perfon and office of the king others (though many of their anceftors bore places of great truft and honor near our kings) diftinguifhed themfelves by their zeal for the parlement, of the former was fir Timothy Tyrrell, of Oakley, Bucks, and Shotover, in Oxfordfhire, knt one of the privy chamber, to k Cha I a col. in his fervice, governor of Cardiff, and general under lord Gerard, afterwards earl of Macclesfield, and was fined 750l. as a compofition for his eftates, as a delinquent. He married Eliz the daughter of the celebrated and venerable archbifhop Ufher. On the other fide, fir. Tho Tyrrell, of Hanflape and

Caftle-

N∪ᴹ IV
∿∿∿
Barringtons
Youneer chil-
dren of Sr Tho
Barrington, bart

Sir John Barrington, bart. was alſo knighted in his father's life-time, and was likewiſe a friend to civil liberty, he was a member of parlement in 1640, for the borough of Newtown; he was one of the parlement committee for Eſſex and the iſle of Wight, but when he ſaw what lengths his party went, he virtuouſly, as well as prudently, declined following them, though probably they expected he would go to the extremeſt length, for he was one of thoſe nominated to ſit in the pretended high-court of juſtice, to try k. Cha I. but he never could be prevailed upon either to attend any of the meetings, or to ſign the warrant for the execution of that moſt unfortunate of ſovereigns, probably this did not oblige the republicans, but would endear him to Oliver, when he became poſſeſſed of the ſupreme power, who appointed him ſheriff of Eſſex, in 1655, after the reſtoration, he lived privately until his death, which happened march 24, 1682. By Dorothy, daughter of ſir Will. Lytton, of Knebworth, knt. who died oct 27, 1703, he had 5 ſons, and 9 daughters. 1. Tho. Barrington, eſq. who died in his father's life-time, ſee below. 2. Francis Barrington, who died young. 3. John Barrington, of Dunmore-Park, eſq he married Eliz. daughter of Edw. Hawkins, of Biſhop's-Stortford, gent. by whom he had Mary, Ann, Rich. and Mary, who died young, or unmarried, and ſir John Barrington, bart. father of the preſent baronet. 4. Fra. Barrington, eſq. who died a

Caſtle-Thorpe, elder brother of the firſt baronet of thoſe places, was a col. in the parlement army, judge of the Common-Pleas, and one of the commiſſioners of the great ſeal to Oliver lord prot. Will. Tyrrell, ſecond ſon of another ſir Timothy, of Oakley, Bucks, and maſter of the buck-hounds to Hen. pr. of Wales, and k. Ch. I. was killed in the civil wars, at Cheſter, in 1644.

bachelor

bachelor. 5. Will. Barrington, who married NUM IV.
Sarah, daughter and heirefs of Rich. Young, of
London, merchant, by whom he had no child. Barringtons.
Only two of the nine daughters of fir John are
mentioned in the pedigrees of this family, viz.
6 Winifred Barrington, married to fir Rich.
Wifeman, of Torells-Hall, in Effex, knt. and 7.
Lucy Barrington, who became the wife of John
Walter, of Chepftow, in Monmouthfhire, efq.

Tho. Barrington, efq. eldeft fon of fir John Tho Barrington, efq
eldeft fon of
fir Jn Bar-
rington, the 3d
bart. Barrington, bart born aug. 29, 1643, and died in
the life-time of his father, jan. 31, 1681-2, aged 38
years. He married the lady Ann, eldeft daughter
of Rob. and coheir of Cha. Rich, earls of Warwick,
with whom he had very large eftates. Lady Ann
re-married to fir Rich. Franklyn, bart. by her
he had 3 fons and 2 daughters. 1. Sir John
Barrington, bart. 2. Sir Cha. Barrington, alfo
baronet, their lives are given below. 3. Rich.
Barrington, efq. died a bachelor. 4. Mary Barrington, who died unmarried, in oct. 1727, and
5. Ann Barrington, who became the wife of mr.
Cha. Shales, goldfmith for 45 years to q. Ann,
k. Geo. I. and k. Geo. II. he died oct. 5, 1734;
fhe, nov. 17, 1729. They had two fons, 1. Rich.
who died before his father; and 2. John Shales,
who took the name of Barrington, and refided at
Hatfield-Broad-Oak.

Sir John Barrington fucceeded to the title of Sir Jn Barrington, 4th
bart baronet upon his grandfather's death. He was
born oct. 16, 1670; was educated at Trinity-
college, in Cambridge: upon his returning from
the continent, oct. 20, 1691 (whither he had been
for his improvement) he was prematurely cut off,
nov 26th following, by the fmall-pox: as he was
unmarried, the title and eftate devolved upon his
fecond brother.

NUM IV.

Barringtons.
Sir Charles
Barrington,
the 5th bart.

Sir Cha. Barrington, bart. who twice married; first, Bridget, only daughter of fir John Monfon, of Broxborn, bart. (by Judith, daughter of fir Tho. Pelham, bart. grandfather to Tho. late duke of Newcaftle), and after her death, Anna-Maria, daughter of Will. lord Fitz-William, fhe died in july, 1717. Sir Cha. was feven times returned a member of parlement for Effex, againft a very powerful oppofition · He was appointed deputy-lieutenant and vice-admiral of that county by q. Ann. He died, generally lamented, jan. 29, 1714-15, and was buried in St. Catherine's chapel, at Hatfield-Broad-Oak, with his anceftors. Sir Cha. dying without iffue, the title of baronet became extinct in the elder branch: the eftates he poffeffed in the ifle of Wight he permitted to go to his next heir male, fir John Barrington, bart. his nephew, that in Effex he gave to his fifter Ann, wife of mr. Shales, for life, and to her furviving children, with orders to bear the name of Barrington, in addition to that of Shales.

Sir John Barrington, the 6th bart.

The title of baronet came to fir John Barrington, fon and heir of John Barrington, efq. third fon of the baronet of thofe names, and grandfather of the laft fir Cha. Barrington, bart. This fir John Barrington, bart. died in auguft, 1717. He married Sufan, daughter of Geo. Draper, of Hitchin, in Herts, gent. by whom he had 3 fons and 2 daughters. 1. Sir John Barrington, bart. his life is given hereafter. 2. Cha. Barrington, efq. who died without iffue, april 3, 1764. 3. Sir Fitz-William Barrington, bart. who fucceeded fir John his brother, of whom below. 4. Sufan Barrington, married to Barrington Flacke, of Linton, in Cambridgefhire, efq and 5. Sarah Barrington.

Sir John Barrington, 7th bart.

Sir John Barrington, bart fon and heir of the laft baronet of the fame names, was elected a mem-

ber for Newton, in the isle of Wight, in the 7th
and several succeeding parlements of Great-Britain.
He married Mary, daughter of Patricius Roberts,
esq who died june 17, 1752. Sir John himself
died in april, 1752, leaving no child. His title
descended to his third brother.

Sir Fitz-William Barrington, bart who was
sheriff of Hertfordshire in the year 1754. He
has married twice; first, the daughter and sole
heir of capt. Tho Mead, and after her death,
miss Jane Hall, by the latter he has, 1. John
Barrington, of Swaintone, in the isle of Wight, esq
member in the present parlement for Newton, in
Hants. 2. Fitz-William Barrington, esq. 3. Ann,
4. Winifred, and 5. Jane*.

* The history of the Barringtons is chiefly taken from the
baronetage, several hist of Engl especially relating to the reign
of k. Ch. I. and during the commonwealth and government
of Oliver lord prot Morant's hist of Essex, Willis's notitia
parliamentaria, observations communicated by mr Longman,
&c &c

No.

No. V.

The history of the noble family of Masham, descended from the Cromwells, through the Barringtons.

NUM V
Mashams
Sir Wm
Masham, 1st
bart.

SIR William Masham was created a baronet by k. James I. in the 19th year of his reign. He was sprung from an ancient and opulent family, seated at Oates, in Yorkshire, so early as the reign of k. Henry VI. Sir William was grandson of Will. Masham, alderman of London, and one of the sheriffs in 1583, and son of another William. Sir. Will. was a member for Malden, in the county of Essex, in the parlement called by k. Ja. I. in 1623, and was returned twice for the same place, in 1625, and for Colchester in 1640, and afterwards for Essex. In this parlement, called the long, from the length of its duration, he much distinguished himself by his warmth against the arbitrary proceedings of the court. He signed the protestation and took the covenant; was one of the parlement committee for Essex, and when the irish roman-catholics rose in arms against, and murdered the protestants, he subscribed 600l. to raise an army to reduce them. K. Cha. I. and his parlement having appealed to the sword to decide their quarrel, he ventured his person and estate in support of the latter, and was so highly prized by both parties, that when he had the misfortune to become a prisoner to the gallant lord Goring, he was exchanged for sir John Ashburnham, the king's favorite. He continued firm to the parlement interest to the last, and by them was appointed one of the commissioners of the high court of justice to try his sovereign, but that
being

being much againſt his judgment, he never attended, though he willingly ſubmitted to a republican
form of government, when it was erected, and
acted in the council of ſtate, in the years 1649,
1650, and 1651, yet cloſed with his relation the
protector's government, and in his parlement
called in 1654, he repreſented the county of Eſſex. By Eliz or Winifred*, daughter of ſir. Fra.
Barrington, bart. and widow of ſir Ja. Altham, of
Markſhall, in Eſſex, knt. he had ſeveral children :
his heir was,

NUM V.

Maſhams.

William Maſham, eſq appointed by the parlement one of the committee for Eſſex, and by his
relation, Oliver lord prot. one of the four commiſſioners of the treaſury, becauſe it was ſuppoſed
that he had ſeveral relations of conſiderable intereſt of the clergy party. He himſelf was by no
means pleaſed with the employment, not liking
Oliver's government, but having a numerous family, and but a ſlender income, as his father was
then living, he was (though with ſome difficulty)
prevailed upon to accept it. He died before his
father. By Eliz. daughter of ſir John Trevor,
knt. and ſiſter of ſir John Trevor, knt ſecretary
of ſtate to k. Cha. II. he had iſſue 4 ſons and 6
daughters. 1. Sir. Will. Maſham, bart. who died
unmarried 2. Sir Fra. Maſham, alſo bart. of
whom below. 3. John Maſham, eſq. who died a
bachelor. 4. Trevor Maſham, eſq. ſecretary to
Lockhart, ambaſſador from the prot. Oliver to the
k of France, whom he attended at the treaty of the
Pyrenees, as he alſo did lord Rocheſter, the ambaſſador to Poland, and was likewiſe ſecretary to
the earl of Eſſex, when his lordſhip went viceroy
to Ireland. He died unmarried. 5. Joan, mar-

Wm Maſham,
eſq eldeſt ſon
of ſir Wm the
firſt bart.

* Lady Maſham is called in the baronetage Eliz. but in the
peerage Winifred.

ried

ried to Mark Hildesley, of Lincoln's-Inn, esq.
6. Ann. never married. 7. Eliz. married to mr.
Knight, of Berks. 8. Mary, married first to mr.
Brownsword, and afterwards to mr Hay, of Suffex.
9. Margaret, married to the rev. dr. Walker; and,
10. Jane, who died unmarried.

Sir Francis Masham, bart. was member of parlement for Effex, 2nd, 7th, and 13th k. Will.
III. and 1ft and 7th of q. Ann, and was one of
the commissioners of the victualling-office. He
died at his feat at Oates, in Effex, march 2,
1702-3, in the 77th year of his age; having had
the misfortune to bury seven of his sons, and both
his wives, his first was Mary, daughter of Sir Will.
Scott, bart. feated at Rouen, in Normandy, and
marquifs de la Mezanfene, in France, by whom he
had 8 sons and one daughter, this lady dying, he
married Damaris, daughter of Ralph Cudworth,
D D. author of the ' intellectual fystem.' She
was born jan. 18, 1658-9, and died april 20,
1708, and has an infcription much to her honor,
upon her monument in the cathedral church of
Bath. The iffue of this fecond marriage was an
only fon, named Francis-Cudworth. 1. William
Masham, efq. eldeft fon of fir Fra. Masham,
bart. died unmarried, he was a lieutenant in
the earl of Oxford's royal regiment of horfe
guards 2. Henry Masham, efq. died a bachelor in Ireland. 3 John Masham, efq. who died
in Flanders, alfo unmarried. 4. Fra. Masham,
efq. he married Ifabella Burnet, a near relation of
the celebrated bifhop of that name, by whom he

had an only fon, named Francis, who fucceeded
his grandfather in the title of baronet, but dying
without iffue, the title and eftate devolved upon
lord Masham. 5 Winwood Masham, efq who
died 1709, leaving no child. 6. Rich. Masham,
efq who died abroad with fir Cha. Wheeler, and
left

left no family. 7. Cha. Masham, esq. who died
likewise issueless. 8. Sir Sam. Masham, who succeeded his nephew sir Fra. in the title of baronet,
and was created by q. Ann, baron Masham, in
1711, of whom below. 9. Hester, a most accom-
plished lady, she died unmarried. 10. Fra.-Cud-
worth Masham, esq. who was a master of the high
court of Chancery, accomptant-general of the said
court, and also foreign opposer in the court of
Chancery.

Samuel, first lord Masham, and baronet, was
page of honour to q. Ann, whilst princess of Denmark, and to his royal highness Geo. pr. of Denmark, to whom he was also one of the equerries,
afterwards gentleman of the bedchamber, and preferred by that prince to the command of a regiment of horse, and advanced to the rank of a brigadier-general of her majesty's armies, appointed
cofferer of the household, and jan. 1, 1711-12,
created lord Masham, of Oates, in Essex. And
having obtained a grant, in reversion, of the office
of remembrancer of the court of Exchequer, he
succeeded to it, oct. 23, 1716, upon the death of
Simon lord Fanshaw. His lordship married Abigail, daughter of Fra. Hill, an eminent Turkey
merchant, and sister of general John Hill, of En-
ville-Green, near Egham, in Surry: this nobleman and his lady had the peculiar happiness of
being favorites of their royal mistress q. Ann, and
of being beloved by that great philosopher John
Locke, esq. who spent ten years of his life with
them, and dying at Oates, was buried, according to
his own desire, in that church-yard. Lord Masham
died oct. 16, 1733, her ladyship dec. 6, 1734,
and were both buried at Oates. They had issue 3
sons and 2 daughters. 1. Geo. Masham, esq. who
died unmarried, and before his father 2. Sam. who
succeeded to his father's honors, his life is given

NUM V
Mashams

hereafter. 3. Fra. Masham, esq. who died a bachelor. 4. Ann, married to Hen. Hoare, of Stourton-castle, Wilts, esq brother of sir Rich, Hoare, knt. lord mayor of London, in 1745, she died march 4, 1727: and 5. Eliz who died in the 4th year of her age, oct. 25, 1724.

Sam 2nd
10th Masham,
and 5th bt

Samuel, second lord Masham, and baronet, was appointed groom of the bedchamber to his royal highness the prince of Wales, oct. 16, 1736. His lordship married Harriot, daughter of Salway Winnington, of Stamford court, in Worcestershire, esq. and sister of Tho. Winnington, commissioner of the admiralty, and treasurer and paymaster of the forces; with this lady he had a fortune of 20,000. She died july 1, 1761; and his lordship, may 2, 1762, re-married Charlotte, daughter of John Dive, of Westminster, esq. and one of the maids of honour to the princess dowager of Wales, her ladyship died may 21, 1773, aged 61. This nobleman dying in june 1776, without issue, his titles became extinct *.

* The hist. of the Mashams is taken from the peerage, general hist. of England, mr. Morant's hist. of Essex, &c.

No.

No. VI.

The history of the Everards descended from Joan Barrington, daughter of sir Tho. Barrington, bart. and grandaughter of Joan, the eldest daughter of sir Hen. Cromwell, knt. grandfather to the prot. Oliver.

THE Everards are of a very ancient descent, tracing their pedigree so high as the reign of k Hen. III, and have allied themselves to many of the best families; in their shield of arms they bear those of the Barnardistons, Maynards, Barringtons, Cornishes, &c. from having married heiresses of those names. Sir Richard Everard was created a baronet by k. Cha. I. jan 29, 1628-9; this did not prevent his joining in the great family combination, under Hampden the patriot, against his majesty. He married twice, first, Joan, the daughter of sir Tho. Barrington, bart and, secondly, Fra. daughter of sir Rob. Lee, of Billesly, in the county of Warwick, relict of sir Gervase Elwes, of Woodford, in Essex, knt. and mother of sir Gervase Elwes, of Stoke, in Suffolk, by the former he had 4 sons and 3 daughters. 1. Sir Rich Everard, bart. whose life is given hereafter. 2. Barrington Everard, esq. who died a bachelor. 3. Robert Everard, esq. who never married. 4 Hugh Everard, a clergyman, fellow of Emanuel-college, Cambridge. 5, and 6. Unknown. 7. Winifred, married to sir Will Luckyn, bart. by whom she left Ann, an only daughter, and sole heir.

Sir

Sir Richard Everard, bart. inherited the eſtate at Great-Waltham, in Eſſex, he was a conſiderable perſon in the reign of k. Cha. I. and was one of thoſe whom the parlement appointed a committee-man for his county, for which he was ſheriff, in 1644 · in the prot. Oliver's parlement held in 1654, and 1656, he was one of the repreſentatives for Eſſex; he lived during all the commotions that ſhook the kingdom, from the breaking out of the civil war to the revolution, and died aug. 29, 1694, in the 70th year of his age. He married twice, firſt, Eliz. daughter of ſir Harry Gibbs, of Falkland in Scotland, knt. groom of the bedchamber to k. Ja. I. and after her death, Jane, daughter of ſir John Finnet, maſter of the ceremonies to k. Ja I. and k. Cha. I *. She lived till oct 8, 1729, being then about 90 years of age: by this laſt lady he had no child, by the former, three. 1. Jane, who died young. 2. Sir Rich. Everard, who reſided at Borham, in Eſſex, and was knighted by k. Cha. II. he died before his father, and unmarried, which occaſioned the title of baronet to deſcend to his only brother.

3. Sir Hugh Everard, baronet, who, as a younger brother, was brought up to arms, and ſignalized himſelf in Flanders. He was a receiver-general of the land-tax, and juſtice of the peace for the county of Eſſex, and dying in jan. 1706-7, aged 51, was buried at Waltham. His lady was Mary, daughter of John Brown, M.D. of Saliſbury, by whom he had five children. 1. Sir Rich. Everard, who ſucceeded his father in the title of baronet. 2. Hugh Everard, eſq. lieute-

* Ja. Howell printed a manuſcript diary of ſir John Finnet, in 1658, and dedicated it to the right hon. Philip lord vile. Liſle, it is curious, and now become ſcarce.

nant of the ſhip Reſtoration; he was unhappily loſt NUM VI.
in the memorable ſtorm, in 1703. 3. Morton Everards.
Everard, eſq. who died in the ſervice of his country on board the Hampſhire, commanded by lord
Maynard. 4. Eliz. who was married to the rev.
John Oſborne, M. A. vicar of Great-Waltham,
rector of Hemmingfield, and alſo vicar of Thax-
ted, all in Eſſex. And 5. Frances, who died unmarried.

Sir Richard Everard, baronet, was obliged to Sir Richard
ſell the family eſtate of Langley, with the re-Everard,
mains of a ſcattered fortune he purchaſed Brom-4th bart.
field. He was governor of North-Carolina, under the lords proprietors, but being diſplaced
when the crown purchaſed that province, he returned to his native country, and died in Red-
Lion-Street, Holborn, feb. 17, 1733. Sir Rich.
married Suſannah, one of the daughters and co-
heirs of dr. Rich. Kidder, lord biſhop of Bath and
Wells (who, with his lady, was killed in bed by the
falling of a ſtack of chimnies, blown down in the
ſtorm 1703). By this lady, who died ſept. 12,
1739, he had two ſons and two daughters. 1. Suſannah, who married mr. David Mead, an eminent
planter and merchant in Virginia. 2. Ann, married to Geo. Lathbury, gent.

3. Sir Richard Everard, who ſucceeded to the Sir Richard
title of baronet, but never chuſing to marry, left Everard,
by his death, in march 1742, the title to devolve 5th bart.
upon the preſent baronet.

4. Sir Hugh Everard, bart. who went to Caro-Sir Hugh
lina, in North-America, but is now, I believe, in Everard, 6th
this kingdom. He is greatly to be pitied, as he is bart
left with a title, and ſcarce any fortune to ſupport
it.

* Hiſtory of the Everards is taken from the baronetage,
hiſt. of Eſſex, and ſome others.

No.

No. VII.

*The hiftory of the family of Hampden, defcended from
the Cromwells by the marriage of Eliz. daughter
of fir Henry Cromwell, knt grandfather of the
prot. Oliver, to Will. Hampden, efq.*

NO. VII.
Hampdens
Antiquity
of the
Hampdens

THE Hampdens are defcended from the moft
honorable family in Buckinghamfhire, and,
like moft other ancient houfes, take their name
from their habitation, which has been, for a long
feries of centuries, at Great-Hampden, in the
above county*.

* An old manufcript, dated 1579, reports, 'that the firft
' mention which is found to be made of any of the Hamp-
' dens, is to be feen in an ancient antiquitie, written in parch-
' ment' (and at that time undoubtedly) 'remaining at Hamp-
' den, whereof there be fundry copies in fundry parts of the
' fame fhire, and whereof it appeareth, that before the con-
' queft there was a commiffion directed to the lord of Hamp-
' den then being, that he fhould be affiftant with his aid to-
' wards the expulfion of the Danes out of this land, which by
' reafonable conjecture fhould be at the general avoidance of
' that nation, by Edw the confeffor, k. of England, in the
' year of our lord 1043, and before the conqueft 23 years.'
And by the pedigree of the Hampdens it appears, 'that the
' firft of the lords of Hampden, who is remembered by name,
' in any author, is one Baldwyn, of Hampden, of whom it
' appeareth by the book called doomfday-book (which re-
' maineth in the Exchequer, contuning a furvey of all Eng-
' land in the time of the conqueror, and is the moft ancient
' record at this day extant; that the faid Baldwyn was the lord
' and owner of Hampden, whereof, whether ever he was dif-
' poffeffed a the conqueft, or whether he deceafed before or
' after the fame, is unknown, only this is certain, that Ofbert
' his fon was returned into quiet poffeffion thereof, by the 20th
' year of the conqueror's reign, which was in the year of our
' Lord 1086.' The above is extracted from papers, and a very
accurate and full genealogy of the Hampdens, new drawn up,
and

The genealogy which commences in this Bald-wyn, informs us, that his son Osbert was suc-ceeded by a second Baldwyn, and he by Rob. de Hampden, the father of Simon de Hampden, whose son, sir Rob. Hampden, married Lora Giffard, the daughter of Walter Giffard, the conqueror's great friend, to whom he granted large possessions, and created him earl of Buck-ingham. This may probably account for the Hampdens being one of the very few ancient english families that were permitted to retain their great possessions under our norman kings: Bartholomew, his son, married one of the daugh-ters of Will. Fiennes, or Fyenes, ancestor of the lords Say and Sele, and the lord Dacre of the south, which two marriages greatly enriched and advanced this family, Sir Reginald, the next lord of Great-Hampden, married Agnes, daughter of sir Ingram Burton: to sir Reginald succeeded sir Alexander Hampden *, who married Marian, daughter of sir Brian Hardeby, knt. the issue of which marriage was Alex. who died unmarried;

and finely illuminated by the order of Griffith, the grandfather of the patriot, and continued down since that time. Both are now possessed by the right hon. lord visc. Hampden.

* Sir Alex Hampden was sheriff of the counties of Berks and Bedford, in the time of the barons wars, which was in 'the 49th year of the reign of Hen. III k. of England, and 'in the year 1264, and, as appeareth by record in the Tower, 'he died the same year, during the same troubles, after whose 'death, Alex. his eldest son (who died unmarried) made ac-'count to the king of his *sherriffe*, and inherited his lands, but 'shortly after the said Alex. deceased without issue· the whole 'inheritance fell to sir Reginald, 2d son of the said Alex. the 'father'—pedigree of the Hampdens Sir Alex. was sheriff of the counties of Bedford and Bucks for three years, com-mencing 34th k. Hen. III. for four years from the 43d; and from 47th of the same reign, until his death. Fuller's worthies, and Willis's survey of the town hundred, &c. of Buckingham.

sir

NVM VII.
Hampdens.
fir Reginald, his fucceffor, and three daughters. The pedigree from this time is very full, and carried into many collateral branches. Sir Reginald, the fon, and in the end heir of fir Alex. changed

Their arms.
the armorial bearings of his family, which were a raven proper upon a field argent, in the attitude and act of croaking, to argent a faltier gules between four eagles, difplayed azure, keeping the more ancient arms only for ' a badge and con-
' noifance, and purtenance for a fupporter,' and by the marriage of heireffes they have quartered the arms of Sidney, Cavendifh, Savage, Cave, Symeon, and feveral others.

From this Reginald defcended a long fucceffion of Hampdens, feated at the place fo named in Buckinghamfhire; to which county they have given fheriffs and members in almoft a regular fucceffion, until they became extinct, nor have they lefs diftinguifhed themfelves by arms. In

Their riches.
the fourteenth century, few families were fo opulent as this, but one of them having the prefumption to ftrike Edward, pr. of Wales, fon of k. Edward III. he was obliged to part with three of his beft manors, to fave his hand, which he was adjudged to lofe for that offence, this has given rife to a rude couplet, ftill remembered in that part of the kingdom:

> Tring, Wing, and Ivengo, did go,
> For ftriking the black prince a blow.

This, though a vaft lofs, did not prevent the Hampdens being one of the richeft families in their county, in which, and in feveral others, they enjoyed great eftates, particularly in Effex, notwithftanding feveral heireffes took confiderable

Younger branches.
fortunes into other families; and even the younger branches of the Hampdens, were amongft the greater gentry, fuch were thofe of Kembell, Wy-comb,

comb, Brails, Hartwell, Preſtwood, all in Bucks;
Emington, in Oxford, Abingdon, in Berks,
with many others *, beſides ſeveral ſettled in
London. Of the female Hampdens, none ren
dered themſelves ſo memorable as Sibel, daughter of John Hampden, eſq. (and aunt to Griffith)
who married to —— Penn, eſq. of Penn-houſe.
She was appointed nurſe to the Pr. of Wales,
afterwards k. Edw. VI. a truſt made ſtill more
important, by the ſituation of the prince, who, in
a few days after his birth, loſt the queen, his
mother. Mrs. Penn's merit, ſhewed itſelf by the
favois that were conſtantly beſtowed upon her,
by our ſovereigns, k. Hen. VIII. k. Edw. VI.
q. Mary I. and q. Eliz. At Penn-houſe, and
upon her monument in the chancel of Hampton
church, Middleſex, are honorable memorials of
her †.

* All the branches of the Hampdens have been long ſince
extinct, except thoſe of Abingdon, the pieſent repreſentative
of them has lately ſold his eſtates there, and removed into
Staffordſhire, where he has purchaſed others. There was a
perſon of the name of Hampden, who died at Great-Hampden,
in 1783, who was ſupported by the late and preſent lord
Hampden.

† At Penn-houſe, now the ſeat of mr Curzon, in the dining-
room, are the arms of k. Edw. VI. when pr. of Wales, viz.
England and France, quarterly, with a label of three points
and an ancient crown, or coronet, over it. it was formerly in
the nurſery, but removed to its preſent ſituation when great
part of the old edifice was taken down, and the remainder repaired The monument of mrs Penn repreſents her effigies in
a praying poſture, in the dreſs of the times, laid upon a tomb
under a canopy, ſupported by four fluted pillars, with richly
engraved pedeſtals, at the head, are the arms of the Penns;
at the feet, thoſe of the Hampdens, with many quarterings,
upon the back ground, above the effigy, is this inſcription.

Penn here is brot to Home, the Place of long abode,
Whoſe Vertu guided hath her Shippe, into ye quyet Rode
A Myrror of Her Tyme, for Virtues of ye mynde
A Matrone ſuch as in her Dayes, the like was herd to finde

No

Having premised thus much of this ancient and
venerable family, which produced one of the most
extraordinary characters this nation ever had, it
will now be proper to observe, that the Hampdens
early distinguished themselves 'as the friends of
civil liberty. Sir Alex. Hampden, of Hartwell,
knt. for refusing to contribute to an arbitrary loan,
illegally demanded by k. Cha. I. was imprisoned,
but by moving for an *habeas corpus* to the King's
Bench, released jan. 29th following. The great
Selden was sent to the Tower for espousing his
cause †.

Griffith

No Plant of servile Stock, a Hampden by descent
Unto whose Race 300 Years, hath friendly fortune lent
To Cowrte She called was, to foster up a king
Whose helpinge Hand long lingeringe Sutes, to speedie End did
    bring
Twoo Quenes yt Sceptre bore, gave Credyt to ye Dame
Full manye Yeres in Cowrte She dwelte, wthout Disgrace or
    Blame
No Howse ne worldly wealth, on Earth she did regarde
Before eche Joye, yea & Her Life, Her Prince's Health prefar'd,
Whose long & loyal Love, with skillful care to serve
Was such as did, thro' heavenlye Help, Her Prince's Thanks
    deserve
Woolde God ye Grounde were grafte wth Trees of such delighte
That idell Braines, ot fruitfull Plantes mt find just Cause to
    write
As I have plyed my Pen, to praise ys Penn withall
Who lyes entombed in ys Grave, untill ye Trompe her call
This restinge Place behold, no Subject place to fall
To wen perforce ye lookers on, your fleetinge Bodies shall.
Nov. 6th Day 1562*.

* A drawing of this monument, which makes no inelegant picture, hangs
up in mr Curzon's library, in Penn-house, and by an inscription upon it, we
are informed that it was taken from the monument itself in Hampton chancel,
b order of one of her descendants, Tho Penn, esq son of the hon Will Penn,
esq first proprietor of Pennsylvania, in 1768

† Sir Alex. Hampden, of Hartwell, knt. was sheriff of Bucks
33rd, and member for that county 43rd q. Eliz. was knighted
by

Griffith Hampden, of Great-Hampden, efq. grand-father of the patriot, was fheriff of Bucks, 18 q Eliz. and one of the reprefentatives for the fame county the 27th year of that reign: he is buried in the chancel of Great-Hampden church, and has this infcription upon his grave-ftone:

NUM. VII.

Hampdens.
Griffith
Hampden,
efq grand-
father of the
patriot

HERE LIETH THE BODY OF GRIF-FITH HAMPDEN ESQVIRE LORD OF GREATE-HAMPDEN & OF ANN HIS SECOND WIFE DAUGHTER AND HEIRE OF ANTHONY CAVE OF CHICHLEY ESQVIRE W^{ch} GRIFFITH DEPARTED THIS LIFE Y^e 27th OF OCTOB^r. 1591. & ANN DECEASED Y^e LAST DAY OF DEC^r. 1594.

By Ann, Griffith had 3 fons and 6 daughters. 1. Will. Hampden, efq. his heir; who married the aunt of Oliver lord prot. 2. Sir Edm. Hampden, of Preftwood, knt. who left defcendants; but this branch is now become extinct. 3. John, who died in 1578. 4. Eliz. married to fir Jerome Horfy, knt a member in feveral parlements in the reigns of q Eliz and k. James I. 5. Dorothy, married to Rob. Hatley, efq. member for the

by k. Ja. I in 1603, when his majefty honored him with a vifit. His fon and heir was Edm. whofe two daughters and co-heir efles, were Margaret, married to Tho lord vifc Wenman, a moderate parlementirian, and Mary, to the loyal fir Alex. Denton, knt. This branch of the Hampdens defcended from one of Great-Hampden, Rich Hampden in the eighth afcent before Alex. married Eliz. the heirefs of Tho. Shingleton, of Hartwell, Bucks, who obtained that manor by Agnes the heirefs of Tho Stokes, which Stokes poffeffed it as marrying Eleanor, heirefs of Sir Rob Luton, knt whofe grandfather married Alice, the daughter and heirefs of Will Hartwell, of Hartwell, efq. Alex. Hampden, efq. was imprifoned during life, for engaging in his coufin Waller's plot, and upon whofe evidence only, he was convicted, he had brought his majefty's laft meffage to the parlement. Query. Was not he the fon of fir Alex Hampden, knt?

town of Bedford 13 Eliz. 6. Ruth, married to
fir Philip Scudamore. 7. Mary, to mr. Ruffel.
8. Ann, to Rob. Waller, of Agmondefham, efq.
father of the poet. Thefe children are mentioned
becaufe of the families that they intermarried
with, fome of whom were great friends to the
patriot's defigns of curtailing the over-grown
prerogative; of thefe the Wallers were particularly confpicuous, at the head of whom, was the
celebrated poet, whofe father, by a virtuous œco-
nomy, acquired a fortune of 35,000l. per ann.
moft of which was loft by his fon's engaging in a
plot to difarm the contending powers, the king
and the parlement, and reftore the bleeding kingdoms to their priftine tranquility, and domeftic
harmony. There was alfo another reafon for
mentioning the children of Griffith, the grandfather of the patriot, which was to correct many
falfe relations in the hiftory of the Waller family,
given in the poet's works, that he was related
to the protector, which is an abfolute miftake*.

* The Wallers are originally of Spendhurft, in Kent. Rich.
Waller, of that place, efq took Cha. duke of Orleans. prifoner
at the battle of Agincourt, which prince remained at Spendhurft for 24 years. in reward for this, the gallant k. Hen. V.
gave, in addition to his coat of arms, a creft, viz. the arms of
Orleans hanging by a label upon an oak, or walnut tree, with
this motto, ' hæc fructus virtutis.' Their eftates at this time
were 7000l. per ann. Rob the poet's father, was defcended
from the above Richard, he married the fifter of the patriot
Hampden, by whom he had feveral fons and daughters; of
the fons, Edm. the poet, was the eldeft, three of whofe
brothers fettled in Ireland; two of them fell victims to the
bloody vindictive irifh, in the maffacre of the proteftants, in
1641. Rob a third brother, was employed in that kingdom by
the protectors, Oliver and Rich. and was anceftor of the Wallers, baronets of Ireland. Tho. another brother, was a colonel
in the parlement army, but was called to the degree of a ferjeant-at-law at the reftoration. Of the daughters, one married to Adrian Scroope, of Buckinghamfhire, efq. defcended

from

William Hampden, of Great Hampden, efq.
fon and heir of Griffith; he married the protector's aunt: no more of his life is known than
that he was member of parlement for Eaftlow, in
Cornwall, in the 35th of q. Eliz. and that he had

NUM VII.

Hampdens.
Will Hamp-
den, efq fa-
ther of the pa-
triot, and
uncle by mar.
to Oliver ld
protector

from the ancient lords of that name: it was he who interceded
with the parlement to permit his brother-in-law, Waller's return to England, but he found no friend to fave his own life
at the reftoration, at which time he was hanged for condemn-
ing k Cha I. to death, and figning the warrant for his execution.   Another of the fifters of the poet, was married to the
equally unfortunate mr Tompkins, clerk of the council to q.
Henrietta-Maria, who died for being in his brother-in-law
Waller's plot   A third fifter married to mr. Price, a great
parlementarian, it was this fifter who betrayed the poet to the
parlement.   A 4th fifter, Eliz. married to Maximilian Pettie,
of Thame and Tedfworth, efq alfo a friend to the parlement.
—What has given rife to the idea that the poet Waller was a
relation of the prot. Oliver, was their always calling coufin, a
ufual cuftom at that time, where any family connexions were,
though the parties were not actually allied, mrs Waller, the
poet's mother, was a loyalift, and would often tell Oliver, that
things would revert to their old channel, and leave him and his
friends in ruin, upon which he would take up a towel, as his
cuftom was, and throw it at her, faying, Well, well, aunt (as
he ufed to call her) I will not difpute the matter with you:
but when his highnefs found that ' fhe was more in earneft than
' he in jeft,' and that fhe held correfpondence with the royalifts, he put her under the cuftody of her daughter Price. but
although the prot. Oliver, called mrs. Waller aunt, and her
fon, the poet, coufin, yet there was no real relationfhip between them; the patriot, Hampden, indeed was firft coufin to
each, as this fketch will fhew

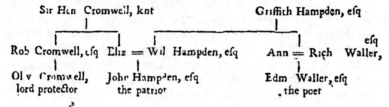

Sir Hen Cromwell, knt   Griffith Hampden, efq

Rob Cromwell, efq Eliz = Wil Hampden, efq   Ann = Rich Waller, efq

Olv Cromwell,   John Hampden, efq   Edm Waller, efq
lord protector   the patriot   the poet

The family of Waller, defcended from the poet, ftill refides at Beaconsfield, in the greateft affluence.—Edm. Waller,
efq. is mafter of St. Catherine's, his brother, Rich. Waller,
efq. is member in the prefent parlement for Agmondefham. At
their feat, at Beaconsfield, is one of the moft elegant beft pro-

NUM VIII.

Hampdens

the honor to entertain k. Ja. I. in july, 1603,
when his majesty conferred knighthood upon
sir Henry Baker; mr. Hampden was buried
in the chancel of Great-Hampden church: over
his grave is a blue marble stone, upon which
are two brass plates; one of them has a shield
of arms, of the Hampdens, with five others, viz.
2. Cavendish, 3. Savage, 4. Sidney, 5. Cave, 6.
ermines, 3 whales heads upon a bend, unknown,
impaling the arms of the Cromwells; with 5
other quarterings of the latter family: upon the
other plate, below this of the arms, is the following concise epitaph:

HERE LYETH THE BODY OF WIL-
LIAM HAMPDEN, ESQVIER, LORD OF
GRATE-HAMPDEN, SON AND HEIRE
OF GRIFFITH HAMPDEN & ANN HIS
WIFE, WHICH WILLIAM DEPARTED

portioned rooms in the kingdom; and, perhaps, the most
poetical in the world, built in honor of their ancestor, the poet,
who, as such, is more beloved by them, than disliked as the
diminisher of the very superb fortune his father bequeathed
him   Mrs Waller was so obliging as to shew me a miniature
of the poet, in the middle age of life, one of his mother, and
one of the beloved Sacharissa, with pearls of vast value appendant
to it, but scarce any when compared with the painting itself·
she is exquisitely handsome, and the execution is very fine·
the e is a portrait of her which is extremely beautiful, but it
hangs in a bad light, there are two portraits also of the poet,
one when he was at the age of twenty-three, the other late in
life, the former is intirely unlike the young face given for
him in the best edition of his works; the print is not near so
handsome, and the features are entirely different, the other,
which exhibits him late in life, in the same work, much re-
sembles the painting of him taken at that period.—It is remarkable, that one of mr Waller's sons is very like the poet;
the fine black eye runs through the family. Hardress Waller,
esq. one of k. Cha. I's judges, and sir Will Waller, knt a
parlement general, were near relations to the poet.—As the
above particulars are little known of this celebrated family,
no apology, it is hoped, is necessary for the length of this note

THIS

THIS LIFE THE SECOND DAY OF
APRIL, ANNO DOMINI, 1597*.

He married Eliz. fecond daughter of fir Henry
Cromwell, knt. grandfather of Oliver lord protector.—She continued a widow until her death,
which was 67 years after her hufband's, and was
buried in Great-Hampden church, feb. 21, 1664-5,
having lived to the very advanced age of 90 years.
What fingular revolutions did this lady fee! fhe
lived under the government of fix fovereigns;
fhe faw the Tudors expire in the perfon of q.
Eliz. and the british fceptre unite in that of k. Ja.
I. but wrefted from the hands of the impolitic k.
Cha. I. by his fubjects, who eftablifhed themfelves
into a republic, which was broken to pieces by
her nephew Oliver Cromwell, who feated himfelf
upon the throne, with the title of protector, and
peaceably bequeathed that dignity to his fon
Richard, her great nephew, who was foon driven
again to private life, by the men his father had
depofed; and thefe felf-reftored republicans again
difpoffeffed of their ufurpation, by the revival of
monarchy, in k. Ch. II. It muft have been an
unhappinefs to her, to fee fuch a great variety of
religious and political fentiments amongft her
neareft relations. Her father and eldeft brother,
fir Hen and fir Ol. Cromwell, knts. were orthodox and loyal, the family fhe allied herfelf to,
her defcendants, and feveral of the younger
branches of her own family, the Cromwells, dif-
liked the eftablifhed faith of their country, and
ftrove againft, and in the end overturned, even
monarchy itfelf The iffue of Will. Hampden,
efq. by Eliz. aunt to Oliver, lord piot. was only
two fons. 1 John Hampden, efq finamed the

Eliz wife of Will Hampden, efq mother of the patriot, and aunt to Oliver ld. protector

---

* Had I not feen this infcription I fhould have fuppofed that
the above Will. Hampden had been the fame who was knighted
at Whitehall, nov. 6, 1604.

patriot,

patriot, whofe life is given below, and, 2. Rich. Hampden, of Emington, in Oxfordfhire, efq. He was much trufted by the common-wealth, and the prot. Oliver, and recommended to the prot. Richard, by general Monk, as a proper perfon to be taken into his highnefs's council: perhaps he was raifed to that honor: he died without iffue in 1659, and was buried at Great-Hampden.

John Hampden, efq firnamed the patriot, firft coufin to Oliver lord prot

John Hampden, efq firnamed the patriot, fon and heir of William, reprefented the borough of Grampound, in the 18th year of k Ja I 's reign; Wendover in the two parlements called in the 1ft and 3d, and the county of Buckingham in the 15th and 16th of the reign of k. Cha I. After fpending feveral years in fafhionable diffipation, he bent his ftudy folely to ftop the progrefs of the wild chimera of his fovereign, to rule by his own arbitrary maxims only: he was the firft perfon who had courage to ftand forth the champion of liberty*: this procured him the honorable appellation of the patriot. In the height of his popularity, and when he was confeffedly the firft perfon of his party, both in the fenate and the camp, as well from the antiquity of his family, their honorable and numerous alliances, the greatnefs of their fortune, as from his own wrongs, his courage in feeking redrefs, the fteadinefs and confiftency of his conduct in oppofing the court; to thefe may be added, his fine parts, highly improved by his converfe with great men and good authors, his penetration, fkill, and affiduity in bufinefs, he received a mortal wound in a trifling fkirmifh, at Chalgrove-field, june 8, 1643, died the 18th, and was buried the 25th following, in the chancel of Great-Hampden church Echard, in his hiftory of England, fays, that he was in-

* Mr. Hampden tried the right of his fovereign to levy fhip money.

formed

formed from the beft authority, that the patriot
Hampden's death was occafioned by the burfting
of a piftol, which belonged to a cafe that fir
Rob. Pye, his fon-in-law, had prefented him with;
and when fir Rob. went to pay him a vifit in his
laft illnefs, he faid, ' Ah Robin, your unhappy
' prefent has been my ruin!' This relation of
the patriot's death feems confirmed, for when two
of the Harleys, and one of the Foley family were
at Farringdon houfe, in their way into Hertfordfhire, fir Rob. Pye, at whofe feat it was, gave this
relation of the patriot's death: That mr. Hampden, at the fkirmifh at Chalgrove-field, firing one
of the piftols, which his fon-in-law had purchafed
in Paris of an eminent artift, it burft, and fhattered his arm in fo terrible a manner, that he
could fcarce retire from the field of battle; as he
was fenfible that his death was near, he fent for fir
Rob. his fon-in-law, and acquainted him of the
accident · he replied, he was extremely hurt for
the misfortune, but that it was occafioned by no
fault of his, for he himfelf had proved them;
and upon examining the other piftol, it was difcovered, that it was loaded unto the top of the
barrel with fupernumerary charges, owing to
the ignorance of a country fervant whom mr.
Hampden had entrufted with the care of loading
them every morning, the late mr. Pye, inquiring
about the authenticity of this relation, could receive
no other fatisfaction, than that it was found written
upon a paper placed in a book which he had purchafed of the Harley family: this did not remove
mr. Pye's doubts, as he thought, had it been true,
fir Rob. who lived to be fo old, would have mentioned it to his family, which it was not remembered he ever had, however there appears to
me to be many reafons that it was really fo. The
houfe of Commons thought mr. Hampden had

ren-

rendered the nation vaft fervices; and to fhew their gratitude, voted, in 1647, that 5000l. fhould be paid to his executors out of the Excife.

From his profound diffimulation, it is impoffible to judge whether to clafs him amongft the true patriots or incendiaries, time only could have unfolded the myftery. It is certain, he refufed every folicitation for a reconciliation with offended majefty, which it has been (though with little reafon) fuppofed he would not have done, had he been declared governor to the pr. of Wales, and favored with fome other gratifications, but his conftantly ftudying d'Avila's hiftory of the civil wars in France*, fhewed that he well knew, that the conteft between the king and parlement could only be fettled by hoftile conqueft, as both were too much irritated againft the other, and had too much to gain or lofe, to fubmit to cool difpaffionate reafon, add to thefe weighty confiderations, the refentment he bore to the perfon of the king, for the unjuftifiable injuries both he himfelf, his neareft friends, and deareft interefts had experienced, and which called for, he thought, their whole force to fo circumfcribe the royal prerogative, that neither his prefent, or any future fovereign, fhould have it in their power, with impunity, to violate the rights of the people, but he knew that haughty monarch would never confent to the leaft diminution of abfolute fway, unlefs compelled to it by being reduced to the moft abject fituation that royalty could experience If he meant to go further, to dethrone the mafter whom he looked upon as a tyrant, who had violated the moft facred depofit that can be placed in the hands of

---

* From the patriot's always carrying d'Avila's hift. of the civil wars of France with him, wherever he went, it was called col. Hampden's prayer-book.

man,

man, and even to annihilate the regal power itfelf, his thoughts probably were thefe, that the
king himfelf would never be reconciled, as he had
been the firft to conteft his fovereign's will; and
this efpecially, as his majefty, from a very ftrong
attachment to arbitrary principles, conftrued every
oppofition to it rebellion; add to this, he knew
Charles's infincerity, and that his judgment was
fo foon biafed by thofe whom he loved and trufted, that no reliance could be placed in the moft
folemn affurances, and therefore it would be impoffible for himfelf to remain in fafety, whilft the
king continued upon the throne, however lowered
it might be; as when once the patriotic phalanx
was difarmed, favorable opportunities might offer
to punifh them at pleafure, and a fucceffor to the
crown would have the fame fentiments, becaufe
he would think he had fuffered the fame loffes:
it is not improbable, therefore, that the penetrating
fteady Hampden, when he drew the fword, for
ever threw away the fcabbard, and determined
that the king, and even monarchy with him,
fhould for ever ceafe: it may alfo be, that the
abufe of the monarchial power had made him diflike it, as much as it might occafion his rever-
encing a republican form of government. Different perfons and parties have had different fentiments of him: Thomfon has immortalized him
as the pureft patriot: earl Temple has placed him
at Stowe, amongft the Britifh worthies: Baxter has
gone higher, he has beatified him: he was the
oracle of his coufin O. Cromwell, afterwards protector, ' who followed his advice whilft living, and
' revered his memory when dead.' On the contrary, the friends of k Cha. I. have given him
the moft interefted and vindictive motives, and it
muft be obferved, that fir Geo. Crooke, when he
declared his judgment to be for him (in oppofition

tion to the other judges) with refpect to fhip-money, yet faid, ' he was a dangerous perfon, and ' that men ought to take heed of him.'

It is fingular, that there are feveral engravings of the celebrated Hampden, though, it is thought, there is not a portrait of him in being; the late mr. Hollis, in vain, endeavoured to obtain one, if there is an original portrait of him, it is that of mrs Baldwin in Grofvenor-fquare *, at Hampden-Houfe (now the feat of the right hon. lord vifc. Hampden, heir to his name and eftates) there is a fmall bufto of him, in ivory, well executed, and fuppofed to have been done in his life-time; it exhibits a thin long-vifaged man, with whifkers, there is the print of the patriot given in Peck, in another apartment, which I carefully examined with this, but there was no refemblance; the buft is thinner, and of a more melancholy caft of features; the nofe is aquiline and bending, almoft to the upper lip; the engraved portrait of Houbracken is undoubtedly his eldeft furviving fon, and very like him †.

Eliz. firft wife
of the patriot
Hampden.

The patriot married twice; firft, Eliz. fole daughter and heir of Edm. Symeon. of Pyrton, in Oxfordfhire, efq. She is buried in the chancel of Great-Hampden church, againft the fouth wall is a long plain black ftone, at the top of which are the arms of Hampden impaling Symeon ‡, and the

* The earl of Ludlow informed the author, that he had procured and prefented an original portrait of Hampden to the earl of Buckingham, but it is found that it is not genuine.

† See the life of the patriot Hampden in the Biographia Britannica, under that article, alfo examine the contemporary authors, Whitlock, Clarendon, Warwick, Ludlow, &c. I have omitted to write the patriot's life, as little new could be given, and for reafons mentioned in the preface to vol. I.

‡ The arms of the Symeons are party per feffe, fable and argent, a pale, counter-changed, on every piece of the firft a trefoil flipped of the fecond.

following

following infcription beneath, that fhews both the
time of her death, and gives an eftimate of her
worth, and the value the patriot had for her: it is

TO THE ETERNAL MEMORY
OF THE TRUELY
VERTVOVS AND PIUS
ELIZABETH HAMPDEN, WIFE OF JOHN
HAMPDEN, OF GREAT HAMPDEN, ESQVIER,
SOLE DAUGHTER & HEIRE OF EDMVND
SYMEON, OF PYRTON, IN THE COVNTY
OF OXON, ESQ. THE TENDER MOTHER
OF AN HAPPY OFFSPRING IN 9
HOPEFUL CHILDREN,
In her Pilgrimage
The ftaie and comfort of her neighbours,
The love and glory of a well-ordeied family,
The delight and happinefs of tender Parents,
But a Crowne of bleffings to a hufband.
In a wife, to all an eternal paterne of goodneffe,
and caufe of joye whilft fhee was.
In her Diffolvtion
A loffe vnvalluable to each yet herfelfe
bles't and they recumpenc'd in her
Tranflation from a tabernacle of claye
and Fellowfhipp wᵗʰ mortals to a Celeftiall
Manfion and Communion wᵗʰ Deity the
20th day of Auguft, 1634.
JOHN HAMPDEN, HER SORROWFVLL
HVSBAND, IN PERPETVALL TESTIMONY
OF HIS CONJVGALL LOVE HATH
DEDICATED THIS
MONUMENT*.

The fecond wife of the patriot was the lady
Letitia Vachell, who long furvived him. She died
in 1666, and was brought from Cooley, near Reading, and buried at Great-Hampden, march 29.
She had no child by mr. Hampden.   The iffue by

* It was almoft indifpenfably neceffary to give this infcription, to clear up fome miftakes in the Biographia Britannica.

the former wife was, 1. John Hampden, efq. who
died fome little time before his father, probably
either in 1641, or 1642. 2. Rich. Hampden,
efq. the heir of whom below. 3. Will. Hampden, efq. No fooner was this gentleman of age,
than he was much trufted and beloved by the protectors Oliver and Richard. he went with a commiffion into Ireland, and was difpatched by the lord-
lieut. Hen. Cromwell, to the prot. Rich. with the proclamation that had been iffued upon his highnefs's
acceffion to his fovereign dignity. He was returned a member for the borough of Wendover, in the
parlement called in 1658-9 by Richard. He died
a bachelor, and was buried with his anceftors, in
the chancel of Great-Hampden church, jan. 27,
1675-6. A writer, it is not recollected who, fays,
that of the patriot's fons, ' one was a cripple, the
' other fomething like a lunatic,' but with what
truth is not known. 4. Eliz. married to fir Rich.
Knightley, of Faufley, in Northamptonfhire, knt.
of the Bath *. She was the favourite daughter of
her father, and whom he had the unhappinefs to
bury. 5. Ann, married to fir Rob. Pye, of Farringdon, Berks, kt †. 6. Mary, who died a child,
buried march 18, 1626-7, at Great-Hampden.
7. Ruth, who married to fir John Trevor, of
Trevallyn, in Wales, knt. anceftor of the prefent
lord vifc. Hampden ‡. 8. Mary, firft married to
col. Rob. Hammond; after his death fhe re-
married to fir John Hobart, bart. anceftor of the
prefent earl of Buckinghamfhire §. 9. Judith,
died unmarried.

The right
hon Rich.
Hampden,
efq a lord of
the other
houfe, &c.

Richard Hampden, efq. fon and heir of the patriot, was highly valued by his relation Oliver,

---

* Vide hift. of the Knightleys, No VIII
† Vide hift. of the Pyes, No IX
‡ Vide hift of the Trevors, No X
§ Vide hift. of the Hammonds and Hobarts, No XI.

lord

loid protector, for his father's sake, and beloved for his own. He was returned one of the five knights for Buckingham, in Oliver's parlement, held in 1656; and, in the following year, he was called up to that protector's house of lords. He served in all the parlements of k. Cha. II. as one of the members for his own county of Bucks. He was ever a strenuous advocate for the bill to exclude the duke of York (afterwards k. Ja. II.) from the throne, very properly supposing it highly wrong that the imperial crowns of these realms should descend to a roman-catholic. This open opposing the person of James, did not prevent his being elected to sit in the parlements called by that misguided king in his first and second years for the above county. Finding that devoted sovereign was endeavouring (as he had apprehended he would) the subversion of the constitution, he was very forward in effecting the revolution, and engaged many persons of great worth and interest in it, he himself was trusted with most of the secrets attending that very important transaction. In requital for these services, april 8, 1689, he was appointed one of the lords commissioners of the treasury, he was also a member for Wendover, in the first parlement called by k. Will. and q. Mary, as he was for the county of Bucks, in that assembly in the following year: nov. 19, 1690, he had the chancellorship of the Exchequer given him in the room of Henry lord de-la-Mere, and about the same time he was sworn one of his majesty's most honorable privy-council. Though it is probable that, at the time of the restoration, he conformed to the establishment, yet he was always the patron of the ejected ministers, to whom he was ever a kind friend. He was buried in the chancel of Great-Hampden church, jan. 2, 1695-6. He married Letitia, second of the seven daughters of Will.

lord

lord Paget, by whom he had three children. 1, John Hampden, efq. who fucceeded to the family eftate, and whofe life appears in the following pages. 2. Rich. Hampden, who died young. 3. Ifabella, who married to fir Will. Ellys, of Wyham and Nocton, both in Lincolnfhire, bait *. The iffue of this marriage was 5 fons and 5 daughters; all of the fons, though they became men, died unmarried, except his fucceffor Will. He had a very large additional fortune from his uncle fir Will. Ellys, knt. one of the judges of the Common-Pleas. Sir Rich. Ellys, bart. eldeft fon of fir Will. the bart. was returned a member for Grantham in two parlements, and for Bofton, in Lincolnfhire, in three †, he married firft the daughter of fir Will. Huffey, bart. and after her death, Sarah, daughter and co-heirefs of Tho. Gould, of Ivor, Bucks, efq but having no iffue from either of his wives, he bequeathed his eftates, amounting to 4000l. per ann. and his fine feat of Nocton, built by his father (after the death of his furviving lady) to his relation the right hon. lord Hobart, afterwards earl of Buckinghamfhire. Sir Rich died feb. 14, 1742-3. The daughters of fir Will. were, 1. Ann, married to Edw Cheeke, of Pirgo, in Effex, efq. who died in 1717, having

---

* Sir Tho. Ellys, father of fir Will was created a baronet, junc 30, 1660, for his loyalty, though himfelf and family had been engaged againft k. Charles I. and much attached to the prot. Oliver. Sir Tno. was fprung from an ancient family, long feated in Lincolnfhire He married Ann, daughter of fir John Stanhope, of Elveftin brother to the firft earl of Chefterfield, by whom he had fir Will his fucceffor, John Ellys, efq who died at the age of 22, and was buried in the Temple church, and Jane, who was married to ———Strode, of Barrington, in Somerfetfhire, efq. by whom fhe had Will Strode, &c.

† See more of fir Will. Ellys, knt. at the end of the firft volume, amongft the protector's great lawyers

buried

buried all his children *. 2. Isabella, who married to Rich. Hampden, her first cousin. 3. Sarah, who died unmarried, feb. 10, 1735-6, and
two others, who did not live to become women.

John Hampden, esq. son and heir of the right
hon. Rich. Hampden, esq. had the greatest care
taken of his education; and to complete it, his
father sent him twice into various parts upon
the continent, particularly France, under the care
of Fra. Tallents, M. A. an eminent non-con-
formist, some time minister at Shrewsbury, under
whom he improved so much, that he was perhaps
the completest gentleman of his time; but most
unhappily he adopted the principles of father Simon, a most profligate man, which led him into
many and very great excesses: this did not prevent his attending to politics, for he took a
most active part against the house of Stuart: he
had not the coolness and deliberation of either
his father or grandfather, the want of it involved
him in misfortunes, which they, by their prudence,
escaped: he was amongst the foremost in the opposition in both the parlements held in the 31st of
k Cha. II's reign, and that in the following year:
in the two former he was returned a member for
the county of Bucks, and in the latter for the borough of Wendover. In 1683, he was concerned
in those practices against the licentious court of k.
Cha. II. that ruined the amiable lord Russell, for
which he was apprehended, but desiring not to be
pressed with questions, he was sent to the Tower;

John Hampden,
esq eldest son
of the right
hon Rich
Hampden, esq.

* The Cheekes are a very ancient and hon. family sir John
Cheeke, ancestor of the above Edw. Cheeke, esq was preceptor to k. Edw. VI. Edward's father was col Tho Cheeke,
lieut of the Tower to k Cha. II and k Ja. II and nephew
to the earl of Oxford, and son of ht Tho Cheeke, knt. a
member of the long-parlement, who took the protestation in
1641, and the covenant in 1643.

and

and feb. 6, 1683-4, he was tried in the King's-Bench, before that difgrace to humanity, judge Jefferies. The court's being able to produce but a fingle witnefs againft him, availed him nothing, though his crime was treafon, if any thing, but as that cannot be proved without two witneffes, the indictment was laid only for a mifdemeanor; and to enforce the neceffity of the jury finding the prifoner guilty, Jefferies *judiciously* obferved, that it was neceffary ' for them to bring ' him in guilty, or they would difcredit all they ' had done before.' This was, perhaps, more than enough to fatisfy their tender confciences; fo that upon the fingle evidence of lord Howard, he was convicted, and the court condemned him to a fine of 40,000 l. and to give fecurity for his good behaviour for life. Notwithftanding the enormity of the fum, he procured his liberty, but it was only to plunge himfelf into new difficulties. No fooner had the infatuated weak duke of Monmouth landed in England, in 1685, to attempt to dethrone his uncle k. Ja. II. than he joined that adventurer; for this he was tried at the feffions of the Old-Bailey, dec. 30, 1685, at which time he was told, that unlefs he pleaded guilty, he muft expect no mercy, and knowing that there was no want of legal evidence againft him, he confeffed the fact, and begged his life with much meannefs, for which he never forgave himfelf.

To a perfon of mr. Hampden's principles, and his fufferings under the royal brothers, k. Cha II. and k. Ja. II. we may fuppofe how defirable the revolution muft be. It is obfervable, that he was the perfon who carried up the refolutions of the commons to the lords, that the throne was become vacant. His conduct, after that event, was moft extraordinary, for when k William fent archbifhop Tillotfon, to affure him how

well

well he efteemed him; and that if he wifhed he
fhould be created either a baron or an earl, or if
he preferred a penfion, it was at his fervice, to
which he anfwered, ' that he would die a country
' gentleman, of an ancient family, as he was,
' which was honor enough for him, and that he
' would not take the king's money, and the king's
' fervants want bread, that he had always fpoken
' againft giving penfions to others, and, at fuch
' a time as this, it was oppreffion,' adding, that
' whilft he had a roll, or a cann of beer, he would not
' accept a fixpence of the money of the nation:'
yet this gentleman, who feemed fo little to court
titles, or value money, was ambitious of honorable
employments, and becaufe his majefty would not
give him the poft of fecretary of ftate, he was difgufted (though he was offered the embaffy to
Spain, which he declined, as unworthy of his fervices), and was ever after a conftant oppofer of the
miniftry with fir Edw. Seymour, but he always
diffented from that gentleman when the proteftant
intereft was concerned. Mr. Hampden was returned for Wendover 1ft of k. Will. and q. Mary,
and he had the honor of firft propofing the duchefs
of Hanover's being declared heirefs to the britifh
throne, after the deceafe of q. Ann, then princefs
of Denmark, but the parlement did not efpoufe
his propofition at that time, though they afterwards adopted that order of fucceffion, and he
carried up the feptennial bill to the lords after
paffing through the houfe of commons. His
fpirits were conftantly depreffed by his reflecting
upon what unmanly terms he received his life
from k. Ja. II. and ftill more from the remorfe
he felt for having gone fuch unjuftifiable lengths
in endeavouring to weaken the intereft of religion; the horror for which, and being deprived
of the confolation it would otherwife have afford-

ed him, occasioned his laying violent hands upon himself*. He was buried in the church of Great-Hampden with his ancestors, dec. 16, 1696. Bishop Burnet gives this character of him: ‘ he was a young man of great parts, one ‘ of the learnedest gentlemen I ever knew, for ‘ he was a critic both in latin, greek, and hebrew, ‘ he was a man of great wit and vivacity, but too ‘ unequal in his temper, he had once great prin- ‘ ciples of religion, but he was corrupted by F. ‘ Simon’s conversation at Paris.’ It would be unpardonable was I to omit giving an extract from a letter of mr. Hampden, written to the rev. mr. Dickenson, rector of West-Winch, in Nor- folk, and sent by mr. Tallents, his tutor, as it shews that he was influenced chiefly by vanity to profess his disbelief of religion, and that he was sincerely sorry for his conduct, and I am the more induced to publish it, as it perhaps may have some weight with such unhappy persons as, in youth and dissipation, abandon those re- ligious sentiments that have frequently been with such care instilled into them, but who, when in age, or overwhelmed with misfortunes, sink into the deepest distress, if not despair.— ‘ Having been in a most eminent manner under ‘ God’s afflicting hand, I think myself obliged to ‘ examine my conscience, concerning the cause ‘ for which it hath pleased the divine wisdome to ‘ inflict so many judgements upon me for some ‘ years past; and I freely confess, that among ‘ many other heinous sins whereof I am guilty, ‘ there is one especially, which causes me great ‘ trouble, and to which I was principally drawn by

* It has been asserted, that he applied to the clergy to know the lawfulness of putting an end to his life; and though they all gave their proper sentiments, yet it was not powerful enough to prevent his applying a knife to his throat.

‘ that

' that vanity and defire of vain glory, which are fo
' natural to the corrupted hearts of men. The
' particular is this, that notwithftanding my edu-
' cation, which was very pious and religious, and
' the knowledge which I had of the certainty of
' the truths of the chriftian religion, yet, to obtain
' the reputation of wit and learning (which is fo
' much efteemed in the world), I was fo unhappy
' as to engage myfelf in the fentiments and prin-
' ciples of the author of the critical hiftory of the
' old teftament, which yet, I plainly perceived,
' did directly tend to overthrow all belief which
' chriftians have of the truth and authority of the
' holy fcriptures, under the pretence of giving great
' authority to traditions, which afterwards is eafily
' turned and accommodated, as beft fuits the in-
' terefts of thofe who take upon them to cry
' it up I do likewife acknowledge, that though
' I had but weak arguments to fupport my liber-
' tine opinions, and fuch as I believed I eafily could
' have anfwered, and fuch as could not make any
' impreffion but upon thofe who were willing to
' caft off the yoke of their duty, and the obligations
' we are under to live in the fear of God, yet I
' was fo rafh and foolifh as to pretend I thought
' there was great ftrength in them, and I infi-
' nuated, rather than oppofed them to fome of my
' familiar friends, and I am afraid I have con-
' tributed thereby to caft fome into opinions, and
' perhaps practices, contrary both to the truth,
' and commandment of the chriftian religion. I
' do alfo acknowledge, that having difcourfed
' freely with the author of the critical hiftory, and
' having heard from his own mouth that he al-
' lowed yet lefs to the authority of the books of
' the new teftament than thofe of the old, which
' fhould have obliged me to avoid all communi-

G 2   ' cation

' cation with him, yet I furnished him with mo-
' ney to execute a design which he had formed
' of a critical Polyglott bible, which, after the
' declaration he had made to me, I think I ought
' to have considered as a design which tended to
' destroy the certainty of the books of the new
' testament, as well as the old. I believe this
' project of a Polyglott bible was innocent enough
' in itself, and might have been likewise consi-
' derably usefull in the manner it was agreed upon
' between father Simon and a friend of mine, and
' myself· but however that may be, I cannot for-
' give myself (after what I knew of that father's
' opinion concerning the authority of the scrip-
' tures) for embarking myself with a man who
' had so plainly declared his thoughts to me in
' that matter. and so much the rather, because,
' upon my consideration, I saw well enough how
' the execution of this design would have increased
' in me those loose principles, which I had al-
' ready received from the reading his critical
' history.   This confession I make with all possible
' sincerity, and with much grief, for having offend-
' ed God by so great a sin, for which I heartily beg
' pardon of him, and earnestly beseech all those
' who in any degree have been seduced either by
' discourses or example, that they would seriously
' reflect upon the danger they are in, and that they
' may be delivered from it in time, and from such
' judgements of God as he has been pleased to lay
' upon me. This confession I have written and
' signed with my hand, to the end that if I should
' dye before I can speak with those whom I have
' perverted by my example, they may return to
' themselves and to God, as I do by this solemn
' protestation which I make to them. The opi-
' nions which I have taught them, were nothing
                                                    ' but

' but the effects of my pride and vanity, which I
' unfeignedly condemn, defiring to live and dye
' in thefe which are contained in this paper.

J. HAMPDEN.'

Mr. Hampden muft be reckoned amongft the
writers of the laft century*. He married firft,
Sarah, and daughter of Tho. Foley, of Whit-
ley Court, Worcefterfhire, efq. and widow of Effex
Knightley, of Faufley, efq. She died in 1687,
and was buried at Great-Hampden. By her, he
had two children, Rich. mentioned below, and
Letitia. After this lady's death, he re-married
Ann Cornwallis, who died in an advanced age, in
july 1737, by whom he had John, whofe life is
given in a future page, and Ann. There are portraits of this John and his laft wife at Hampden-
Houfe, by which it appears they were both remarkably handfome. Letitia, the eldeft daughter, married to John Birch, ferjeant-at-law, by
whom fhe had no child. Ann, the half-fifter of
Letitia, married to Tho. Kempthorne, of Bexley,
in Kent, efq. In the chancel of Great-Hampden

---

* Mr Hampden publifhed ' fome confiderations about the
' moft proper way of raifing money in the prefent conjuncture,
' printed about the year 1692, fome fhort confiderations
' concerning the ftate of the nation, printed about nov.
' in the fame year He affifted major Wildman, and others,
' in writing, An enquiry, or difcourfe, between a yeoman of
' Kent and a knight of the fhire, upon the prorogation of the
' parlement to the 2d of may, 1693, and the king's refufing to
' fign the triennial bill, &c His moft generally known book
is, obfervations upon mr Sam. Johnfon's abrogation of k.
Ja II for the ufe of the duchefs of Mazarine, in which he endeavours to eftablifh k William's title under thefe heads, conqueft, providence, pofleffion, and vacancy of the throne by k.
James's abdication, which is fufficient to know that he had
no proper idea of liberty, is the greateft tyrant might have
ufed the fame claim to any, or all thefe ways, had he defended
it as the voice of the nation, with the confent of parlement, he
had fpoken much more rationally.

church,

church, againſt the north wall, is an elegant monument of various coloured marbles, at the top is an urn, with a wreath of flowers, under it the arms of the Kempthornes (viz. argent, three trees vert) impaling thoſe of the Hampdens, beneath are medallions facing each other, inſcribed THOMAS KEMPTHORNE, ANNA KEMPTHORNE, under which is this inſcription :

Here lie the Remains of THOMAS KEMPTHORNE, Eſq.
Who ſo loving the Example of his Anceſtors, ſerved
his King and Country in the Royal Navy,
And died Commiſſioner of Chatham-Yard, in July 1736.
Alſo, thoſe of ANNE his Wife,
Daughter of JOHN HAMPDEN, of Great-Hampden, Eſq.
By ANNE CORNWALLIS, his ſecond Wife.
She died in Sept 1723.
CHARLOTTE KEMPTHORNE, their only now
ſurviving Child,
Erects & dedicates this Monument, with all Duty and
Affection, to the Memory of her Parents.
MDCCLIX

Charlotte Kempthorne, the eldeſt daughter of this marriage, and in the end ſole heireſs (as Ann, her other ſiſter, died in France, unmarried) gave her hand to a perſon of the name of Wakefield, though then in the humble ſtation of a poſtillion, and at her death, without iſſue, in 1773, ſhe bequeathed him the whole of her fortune, amounting to near 50,000l He is ſtill living. his virtue deſerved the greateſt gifts of fortune, though his education and ſituation ſeemed to have precluded him from partaking of them ſo liberally at her hands

Richard Hampden, eſq eldeſt ſon and heir of John, was elected member of parlement in the beginning of the reign of q. Ann, both for the county of Bucks, and borough of Wendover, but made his election for the former, he was alſo returned for the ſame county in 1710, and for

Wen-

Wendover, the 8th of the following reign. As
the Hampdens had conſtantly ſhewed themſelves
the friends of liberty, and in ſo particular a manner in favor of the houſe of Brunſwick, his majeſty k. Geo. I. upon his acceſſion to the britiſh
throne, diſtinguiſhed him upon many occaſions;
he was appointed, june 22, 1716, one of the Tel-
lers of the Exchequer, which, march 18, 1718,
he exchanged for the treaſurerſhip of the navy,
and the 31ſt of the ſame month, he was ſworn
of his majeſty's moſt honorable privy-council;
but theſe were misfortunes, not ſervices to him;
for his poſt of paymaſter giving him the command of the public's money, he imprudently
truſted it in the ſouth-ſea ſcheme, and was one
of the moſt conſiderable ſufferers, loſing no leſs
a ſum than 95,000l. which ſwallowed up the whole
of his great eſtate, except 1,100l. a year, that
was fortunately ſettled upon mis. Hampden, his
wife · however, to ſave the principal family eſtate
of Great-Hampden, the creditors permitted him
to exchange the ſettlement from Dunton, to Great-
Hampden, mrs. Hampden giving up the former
to be ſold. This was a dreadful blow, and robbed
this ancient family of many eſtates in the vicinity
to that of Great-Hampden; he died july 27,
1728, at which time he was one of the knights
for the county of Bucks. Richard married his
firſt couſin, Iſabella, daughter of ſir John Ellys,
bart. by whom he had no iſſue; ſhe re-married
to Peter Bradbury, a preſbyterian miniſter, brother of the famous Tho. Bradbury, once at the
head of the diſſenting intereſt.

John Hampden, eſq. the youngeſt ſon of a
father of both his names, and half-brother of
Richard, ſucceeded him, but not at Great-Hampden till the death of his brother's widow. He
was in public employments in ſeveral reigns, was

John Hampden,
eſq half brother
and heir of the
right hon Ric.
Hampden, eſq.
and laſt of the
male line.

returned a member of parlement for the county of Buckingham, 14 of k. Will. III. in the latter end of whose reign, or in the beginning of the next, he was deputy to mr. Wyndham, clerk of the *habeas corpus* office, q. Ann appointed him one of her pages of honor, in the first and fourth years of that sovereigns reign, he reprefented Wendover, and the county of Buckingham the feventh, and afterwards was returned a member both for Wendover and Berwick-upon-Tweed, but made his election for the latter. Upon the acceffion of k. Geo. I. he was returned one of the county members for Buckingham, in the late reign, in the years 1734, 1740, and 1747, he was again member for Wendover, and in may, in the following year, he was appointed commif-fary-general of the ftores for the garrifon of Gibraltar. It is fingular, that though he con-ftantly voted with the minifter, he was fo well beloved, that he was never oppofed wherever he put up for. He died a bachelor, feb. 4, 1754, and by his will he bequeathed his eftates and name to the hon. Rob. Trevor, efq. afterwards lord Trevor, and created vifc. Hampden, and, for want of heirs male, to go to the earl of Buck-inghamfhire, or his reprefentative.

The late lord vifc. Hampden, in gratitude to him, and to perpetuate the memory of the patriot, and his defcendants, erected a moft fuperb monu-ment of various coloured marbles, it confifts of a farcophagus, upon the ends of which fit two mournful boys, one with the cap of liberty point-ing to his breaft, the other holding *magna charta*: above is a very large medallion, upon which is given the death of the patriot, or rather his re-ceiving his mortal wound in Chalgrove-field, the village and the church are vifible: he is re-prefented as being caught falling from his horfe,

which

which is under a large tree ; upon the butt of it, is a fhield of arms of Hampden, impaling Symeon, and in a fcroll underneath, *Veftigia nulla retrorfum.* The tree has five branches : upon the firft, is a fingle fhield of arms of the Knightleys, impaling Hampden. the fecond branch has feven fhields, 1. Hampden impaling Paget, 2. Hampden impaling on the dexter, Foley, and on the finifter, Cornwallis, 3 Ellys impaling Hampden, 4. Hampden and Ellys, 5. Kempthorne and Hampden, 6. Burch and Hampden, 7. Hampden alone, for John, in whom the male line became extinct Thefe two branches appear withered and dead: the third branch has only one fhield, Pye impaling Hampden, and is given as alive, but cut off, to fhew that there are ftill defcendants from this branch   The fifth arm of the tree has four fhields, 1. Trevor impaling Hampden, 2. Trevor and Searle, with a baron's coronet over it, 3. Hampden and Trevor, quarterly, for the late vifcount Hampden, before he was a nobleman, and 4. Kruyningin, for the lady of his late lordfhip*. Upon the farcophagus is this infcription:

JOHN HAMPDEN,
XXIIIIth hereditary lord of GREAT-HAMPDEN,
and Burgefs for Wendover in three Parlements,
dyed unmarried Febry 4th MDCCLIV aged 58.
Having bequeathed his Eftates and Name
To his Kinfman *THE* HON^BLE ROB^T TREVOR,
(now HAMPDEN)

* It would be needlefs to particularize to whom each fhield of arms belonged, as by referring to the preceding pages, the reader cannot but fatisfy himfelf. It is fomething remarkable, that no notice is taken of the Hobart family, now earls of Buckinghamfhire, though they are defcended from a daughter of the patriot Hampden, and may, by the limitation in the will of the laft John Hampden, efq fucceed to the eftate if that fhould be the cafe, perhaps, if they can find room, they may add a fixth branch.

Son

NUM VII

Hampdens

Son of *THE Rt HON*ble THO: *LORD* TREVOR,
Son of *THE Rt HON*ble SIR JOHN TREVOR,
by RUTH, daughter of JOHN HAMPDEN,
Slain in CHALGROVE-FIELD,
MDCXLIII
ROBT HAMPDEN
Dedicates this Monument,
With all due veneration,
To his GREAT-GRANDFATHER's
and to his BENEFACTOR's
Memories. *

* The history of the Hampdens is taken from original papers
communicated in the most obliging manner by the right hon
lord visc. Hampden, and dr Moss, the register and funeral
monuments at Great-Hampden, Willis's survey of the town,
&c. of Buckingham, Willis's not. parl Prynne's brevia parl.
rediviva; Fuller's worthies, a variety of histories during the
interregnum, secret history of Europe, several lives of Oliv.
lord prot. Annual Register, some visitations, &c.

No. VIII.

A sketch of the family of Knightley, allied to the protectorate house of Cromwell, by the marriage of sir Rich. Knightley, knt. of the Bath, to Eliz. daughter of the patriot Hampden.

THE Knightleys are originally from Staffordshire, taking their name from a manor so called, in that county, which they have possessed ever since the norman conquest; at that time Rinaldus, one of the followers of k. Will I. had a grant of it, but they removed to Fausley, in Northamptonshire, in 1415, when sir Ric. Knightley, knt purchased that manor. The Knightleys bear for their arms quarterly ermine, and paly of six, or, and gules, and quarter many others There is no private family in the kingdom has given more knights, none which has been more numerous in its branches, some of them have almost rivalled the eldest in consequence, and that settled in France surpassed them, having many centuries ago been declared noble, the alliances they have contracted have been equal to themselves, and the many high offices held by them in the state, have been exceeded only by the very large posessions they have constantly had. This family very early took exceptions to the church government, and distinguished themselves in the most striking manner in their endeavours to check the power of the royal house of Stuart, who threatened to extinguish the few liberties the haughty Tudors left, and even dared to shake those chains the former so openly were riveting.

margin notes: NUM VIII. Knightleys. Their origin.

Their religious and political sentiments.

I Sir

NUM VIII.

Knightleys
Sr Rich.
Knightley,
knt of the
Bath.

Sir Richard Knightley, knight of the Bath, lord of the manor of Fausley, eldest son and heir of sir Val Knightley, of Fausley, knt. by Ann, daughter of Edw. Ferrers, of Baddesley-Clinton, in Warwickshire, esq was one of the richest private subjects of his time, having landed property to the amount of 13,000l. per ann. He had an extreme aversion to the hierarchy, and to the decent ceremonies of the church of England, and would have wished to have gone after his relation, sir Tho Knightley, knt. serjeant-at-law (one of k. Hen VIII's head commissioners for inspecting religious houses), in depriving all dignified ecclesiastics of their honors and emoluments, and have levelled all to the genevan plainness, it is the more to be wondered at, as he spent his youth in gaiety and dissipation, his attachment to calvinism, however, gradually grew, until his zeal, or rather enthusiasm, at length gained the ascendancy of him so far, as to make him exceed his prudence, for, upon a nice scrutiny from whence so many dangerous libels against the church issued, they were, with much difficulty, discovered to have been printed in a room at the top of a small turret at Fausley, that was approachable only by a winding cork-screw staircase; for this offence his sovereign q. Eliz. summoned him before the Star-chamber, where he was deeply fined, but here he met with a friend, where he could only have expected an enemy, and this was archbishop Whitgift, for though it was chiefly against his grace that these pamphlets were written, yet he sued for, and obtained his pardon. This did not win him over to love his mother-church, for he still kept with her implacable foe, the puritans. He, with sir Edw. Montagu, and sir Fra. Hastings, with 60 or 80 other gentlemen, in 1605, presented a petition to

k. Ja.

k. Ja. I. in behalf of the puritan clergy of Northamptonshire, both himself and fir Edw. Montagu were most feverely reprimanded for their boldnefs, not only at the council table, but in the Star-chamber; at the former place they were told, ' What danger they had put themfelves in, ' by their affociations ; and that thus combining ' themfelves in a caufe againft which the king ' had fhewed his miflike, both by public acts and ' proclamations, was little lefs than treafon, that ' the fubfcribing with fo many names were Ar- ' matæ preces, and tended to fedition, as had been ' manifeftly feen, both in Scotland, France, and ' Flanders, in the beginning of thofe troubles;' and at the fame time their lieutenancy and commiffion of peace were taken from them, as alfo from fir Fra. Haftings, for drawing the petition, and acknowledging it, but the other gentlemen, making their fubmiffions, were pardoned: having failed in his aim, he with fir Fra. Haftings petitioned the parlement for a toleration of popery, for the fame reafon that k. Ja. II. wifhed to give liberty of confcience to the prefbyterians, and on the fame account it was refufed. So far did his diflike to the eftablifhed church carry him, that he left the patronage of his livings to truftees for ever, who fhould, upon every vacancy to an advowfon, appoint four perfons, out of which his heirs fhould name one. This was laying a burden upon his pofterity, which he himfelf could not bear. However, the reftoration effectually obliged thefe truftees to name none but thofe who would fubfcribe to the articles, fo that, fince that time, though the truftees ftill continue, yet their power is entirely nominal. Sir Rich. fat in feveral parlements in the reign of q. Eliz. and in the firft of that of k. Ja. I His death happened in 1615. He married, firft, Mary, daughter of

Will.

NUM VIII.
Kightleys

Will. Fermor, of Eafton-Nefton, efq. by whom he had two fons and one daughter, and after her death he re-married the lady Eliz 6th daughter of the great duke of Somerfet, protector to his nephew k. Edw. VI. She died in 1602, and is buried with fir Rich at Nocton   The iffue of this marriage was fir Seymour Kightley, and fix other fons; yet the male line became extinct in this branch, in 1695   this is the more to be wondered at, as moft of the fons of the fecond marriage had male iffue. but it is extraordinary that the eftate of Faufley came to another branch of the family long before there was a failure of defcendants from fir Rich. Knightley, knt. For Faufley was poffeffed by Richard Knightley, efq. eldeft fon and heir of Tho. Knightley, of Burgh-Hall †, in Staffordfhire, efq by Eliz daughter of John Shuckburgh, of Naveley, in Northamptonfhire, efq. which Tho was 3rd fon of fir Val. Knightley, and brother of fir Rich. Knightley, knt. of the Bath   He was probably the Rich. Knightley, efq. who was member of parlement for Northamptonfhire 21ft of k. Ja. I. and fheriff for the fame fhire the firft of k. Cha. I. and one of the reprefentatives for it in the parlement called in the third year of the fame reign, he was alfo, with his fon, of the committee for his own county with that of Radnor, in Wales, where perhaps he had eftates, he was one of the moft zealous of all the patriots againft the prerogative, wifhing nearly to annihilate it: it was at his houfe that the

---

Rich
Knightley
efq.

* There are two portraits of fir Rich. Knightley, knt and the lady Liz. Seymour, at Faufley, under his are fome lines explanive of his charactes, and the feverity of his fentiments in his old age

† Burgh-Hall, in Gnofall, in Staffordfhire, came to the Knightleys many centuries before, by the marriage of a Knightley with an heirefs of the De Burghs.

                                                                    plan

plan of retrenching that dreaded monster's power was formed, which was to be effected by taking away from the crown the right of making peace or war, vesting the militia in the parlement, which great body was to have the disposal of all places of trust and profit, and the royal revenues were to be placed in the hands of four several councils, appointed by, and accountable to, the parlement, which were to meet every year without writs or summons from the sovereign. He was no better pleased with the hierarchy and church worship than he was with the regal power; Ball was patronized by him to write ' his friendly ' grounds, tending to a separation, in a plain ' and modest dispute touching the unlawfulness ' of a stinted liturgy, and set form of common ' prayer; communion in mixed assemblies, and ' the primitive subject and first receptacle of the ' power of the keys, &c. printed at Cambridge ' in 1640.' It is much more to his credit, that he presented the worthy and learned dr. Dod *, and the still more celebrated mr. (afterwards dr.) Wilkins, the brother-in-law of the prot. Oliver, to his living of Fausley. Mr. Knightley died in 1650, aged 70. Jane, his widow, the daughter of sir Edw. Lyttelton, of Pillaton-Hall, in Staffordshire, bart. died in 1657, also aged 70 by her he had 9 sons and 4 daughters; his eldest son and heir was,

Sir Rich. Knightley, knt. of the Bath, he was returned a member for the town of Northampton,

Sir Rich Knightley, knt of the - Bath, who mar Eliz the eldest dr of the patriot Hampden, and cousin to Ol lord prot

---

* Dr Dod was presented to Fausley the latter end of the reign of k Ja I ' where his hospitality and charity were so ' great, that there was not a poor body left in his neighbour- ' hood, he having put them all in a way to live He was the ' puritan-cavalier, for though he never much liked the epis- ' copal government when it prospered, yet he was faithful to ' it when it suffered, declaring against the scandalous rebellion ' of the puritans ' Bishop Wilkins's life appears in this vol. he was presented, june 2, 1637.

in the parlements called in the 15th and 16th years of the reign of k Cha. I. and was as strenuous against the encroachments of that misguided prince, as his father, took the covenant, and was one of the committee of the parlement navy, yet he revolted at the idea of the violent death of his sovereign, for which he was secluded, with many others, from sitting in the house of commons; but when he saw monarchy, though by another name, restored in the Cromwells, he became an obedient (probably a satisfied) subject: he was appointed by that protector one of the assessors of the monthly taxes to be raised in his own county of Northampton, which he represented in the parlement called by the prot. Rich. in 1658-9. Upon the ruin of that short-governing prince, he shewed his attachment to the exiled king, for he was one of the council of state in 1660, which greatly promoted that event: at the restoration he was received with much grace by his majesty, who, just preceding his coronation, created him one of the knights of the Bath. he did not long survive this honor, dying june 29, 1661, and was buried near his father, and many of his ancestors, in Faußley church †.   A similarity in sentiments,

* In 1660 mr Jeremiah Stephens published sir Henry Spelman's hist of Sacrilege, dedicated to the right worshipful, and my much honored friends, John Crew, and Rich Knightley, esq. worthy patriots of our county of Northampton

† Besides the Knightleys of Faußley, and some branches in Northamptonshire, there were in the middle of the last century very opulent families (all descended from those of Staffordshire) in the counties of Hertford, Essex, Warwick, and Middlesex, the two former were great friends to the parlement cause, those of Offchurch, in Warwickshire, were created baronets in 1660, and sir Ed Knightley, of Lo. and Middlesex, knt was set down as one, who was to have been created a knight of the royal oak.

GENEALOGY of the FAMILY of KNIGHTLEY.

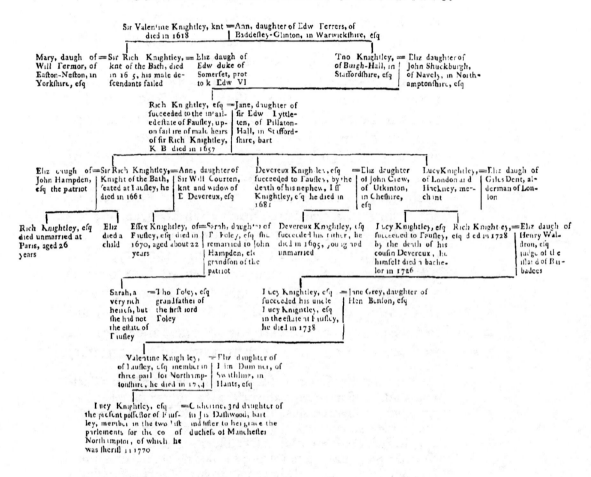

Sir Valentine Knightley, knt = Ann, daughter of Edw Ferrers, of
died in 1618 | Baddefley-Clinton, in Warwickfhire, efq

Mary, daugh of = Sir Rich Knightley, = Eliz daugh of   Tho Knightley, = Eliz daughter of
Will Fermor, of | knt of the Bath, died | Edw duke of   of Burgh-Hall, in | John Shuckburgh,
Eafton-Nefton, in | in 16 5, his male de- | Somerfet, prot   Staffordfhire, efq | of Navely, in North-
Yorkfhire, efq | fcendants failed | to k Edw VI | amptonfhire, efq

Rich Knightley, efq = Jane, daughter of
fucceeded to the intail- | fir Edw Lyttle-
edeftate of Faufley, up- | ten, of Pillaton-
on failure of male heirs | Hall, in Stafford-
of fir Rich Knightley, | fhire, bart
K B died in 1657

Eliz daugh of = Sir Rich Knightley, = Ann, daughter of   Devereux Knight ey, efq = Eliz daughter   LucyKnightley, = Eliz daugh of
John Hampden, | Knight of the Bath, | Sir Will Courten, | fucceeded to Faufley, by the | of John Crew, | of London and | Giles Dent, al-
efq the patriot | feated at Faufley, he | knt and widow of | death of his nephew, I ff | of Utkinton, | Hackney, mer- | derman of Lon-
| died in 1661 | E Devereux, efq | Knightley, efq he died in | in Chefhire, | chant | don
| | | 1681 | efq

Rich Knightley, efq   Eliz   Effex Knightley, of = Sarah, daughter of   Devereux Knightley, efq   Lucy Knightley, efq   Rich Knight ey, = Eliz daugh of
died unmarried at | died a | Faufley, efq died in | T Foley, efq fhe | fucceeded his father, he | fucceeded to Faufley, | efq d ed in 1728 | Henry Wal-
Paris, aged 26 | child | 1670, aged about 22 | remarried to John | died in 1695, young and | by the death of his | | dron, efq
years | | years | Hampden, efq | unmarried | cousin Devereux, he | | judge of the
| | | grandfon of the | | himfelf died a bache- | | ifland of Bar-
| | | patriot | | lor in 1726 | | badoes

Sarah, a = Tho Foley, efq   Lucy Knightley, efq = Jane Grey, daughter of
very rich | grandfather of   fucceeded his uncle | Hen Benfon, efq
heirefs, but | the firft lord   Lucy Knightley, efq
fhe had not | Foley   in the eftate at Faufley,
the eftate of   he died in 1738
Faufley

Valentine Knightley, = Eliz daughter of
of Faufley, efq member in | Tho Dummer, of
three parl for Northamp- | Swathling, in
tonfhire, he died in 1754 | Hants, efq

Lucy Knightley, efq = Catherine, 3rd daughter of
the prefent poffeffor of Fauf- | fir Jas Dafhwood, bart
ley, member in the two laft | and fifter to her grace the
parlements for the co of | duchefs of Manchefter
Northampton, of which he
was fheriff in 1770

and an equality in families, brought the Knight- NUM VIII.
Knightleys. leys acquainted with the Hampdens, and procured an alliance between them, as he married Eliz. the eldeſt daughter of John Hampden, of Great-Hampden, Bucks, eſq. ſirnamed the patriot, by which marriage he became allied to the protectoral houſe of Cromwell. This union gained a vaſt acceſſion of family intereſt againſt the royal power, and greatly contributed to make that already dreadful combination ſtill more forceably felt. After this lady's death he re-married Ann, one of the daughters of ſir Will. Courten, knt. and relict of Eſſex Devereux, eſq ſon and heir of ſir Walter Devereux, knt. ſhe died feb 5, 1702-3, at the advanced age of 88 . The annexed pedigree of the Knightleys will ſhew their deſcent, ſo far as relates to the ſucceſſion of the Fauſley eſtates, and the table following it gives their claim to the barony of Fitzwarine.

Fauſley is a grand ſeat, placed in a ſpacious and pleaſant park: there are three pieces of water near the houſe, one of them is very large, covering as much as 13 acres of land †. The ſtructure is partly ancient, partly modern the old hall is, perhaps, the largeſt in the kingdom, its windows are almoſt filled with ſhields of arms of the Knightleys, and their alliances, it is ſingular that one of them is exactly over the fire-place. The modern ſet of rooms is very commodious,

---

Sir Rich Knightley, knt of the Bath, beſides Eſſex, his ſon and heir by his firſt lady, had Luc married to ſir Edw Seabright, but inceaſor of the preſent ſir John Seabright bart. and by females to the preſent baronets, Boughton, and Hill of Hawkſton, and Jane, married to ſir Tho Dene, but

† Mr Pennant certainly overlooked the largeſt piece of water at Fauſley, is he acquaints us there are ſome inland ones, none of the three are very full, but one is a noble ſheet

NUM VIII.

Knightleys.

and the prefent poffeffor has ornamented them in a moft elegant manner. The family pictures are ill preferved, the other portraits, that are worthy attention, are thofe of Calvin, dr. Dod, and lord Grey, of Groby, with his page, the two laft are very fine paintings*.

* This fketch of the family of Knightley, is taken from records at Fauley, and particularly from an invaluable genealogy, commencing at the conqueft, and continued down until the year 166 it is the moft complete and the fulleft I ever faw This with whatever elfe was moft worthy attention, was fhewn, or has been fince fent to me, by Lucy Knightley, efq in a manner that will ever lay me under the greateft obligations Erdefwick's hift. of Staffordshire, various hift of England, Willis's not parl Dugdale's Warwickshire, Winwood's memorial, Mag Brit Neile's hift of the puritans B Mado reply to Neal, Vifitations of Northamptonfhire Peerage, Baronetage, &c,

No. IX.

The history of the family of Pye allied to the prot. Oliver, by the marriage of sir Rob. Pye, knt. with Ann daughter of John Hampden, esq sirnamed the patriot.

THE Pyes are a most ancient and honorable family, from whom two of the english kings descended, and they are now allied to many peers of the realm. The etymology of the name of Pye, is ap Hugh, the letter *u* having the same sound in welch, as *y*, the family conformed to the welch manner from residing near that principality; they bear for their arms, ermine, a bend lozengy, gules Will. Pye came over with the norman conqueror, and his family became champions to the first kings of that race. Hugh Pye, probably his son, was lord of Kilpec castle, in the Mynde Park, in Herefordshire, he had two sons, Tho. Pye de Kilpec, and John

Tho. the eldest, had an only daughter named Matilda, married to Stephen de la Bere, by whom she had also an only daughter, who was the lady of sir John Plonknet, or Plunket, from whom by females came, Joan, daughter of Rich. Fitz-Allan, 4th earl of Arundel and Surry, who became the wife of Humphrey Bohun, earl of Hereford, Essex, and Northampton, and constable of England, by whom she was mother of two daughters, Eleanor and Mary, the former married to Tho. Plantagenet, sirnamed of Woodstock, son of k. Edw. III. and uncle to k. Rich. II. Mary, the youngest co-heiress, married to Hen. Plantagenet, sirnamed Bolinbroke, who was saluted king of England by the name of

NUM IX
Pyes
Antiquity.

Will Pye, esq champion to the norman kings

Hugh Pye, lord of Kilpec castle, from whom descended k Hen V k Hen VI &c

Hen.

NUM IX.

Pyes.

Hen. IV. and from this marriage was born k. Hen. V. the father of k. Hen. VI. who was the parent of Edw. the unfortunate pr. of Wales.

John Pye, efq

John, the youngeſt ſon of Hugh, lord of Kilpec caſtle, is the progenitor of all of this name now in England. John Pye, or ap Hugh, held the ſixth part of a knight's fee, in Chenſton, in the valley of Dowre. In the reign of k. Hen. III. he was

Tho Pye, efq
Walter Pye, efq
Tho Pye, efq
Joan Pye, efq.

father of Tho. who was the father of Walter, and he the father of another Tho. whoſe ſon John, in the reign of k. Hen. VI. was retained to ſerve in the wars of France; he was ſeated at Sadlebow, in the county of ———, and married Eliz. the daughter of ſir John Scudamore, of Scudamore, knt.

John Pye, of the Mynde, efq.

from this marriage deſcended John Pye of the Mynde, in Herefordſhire, efq. who married Ann,

Joan Pye, efq.

daughter and coheir of Roger Andrews, of Hereford, gent. by whom he had John Pye, efq. ſeated at the ſame place, as were many of his deſcendants: he married Ann, daughter of ſir Rich. de-la-Bere, of Herefordſhire, knt. The eldeſt ſon and heir of

Walter Pye efq

this marriage was, Walter Pye, efq. who by Margaret, eldeſt daughter and coheireſs of Phil. Price,

Roge Pye, ef

of Orcop, in that county, efq. had Roger Pye, of the Mynde, efq. and poſſeſſor of the ancient caſtle of Kilpec, who married Bridget, daughter of Tho. Kyrle or Kirke, of Walford, in Herefordſhire, efq. he died march 31, 1591; his eldeſt ſon was Will.

W.. P.., ef.

Pye, efq. who died aug. 20, 1611[*]. He left iſſue 5 ſons. 1. Sir Walter Pye, of the Mynde, knt. 2. Sir Rob. Pye, of Faringdon, Berks, knt. the hiſtory of whoſe family I mean more particularly to treat of. 3. John. 4. Will. and 5. Tho. and 3 daughters. Before I proceed to take the deſcent of Rob. the ſecond ſon, I ſhall mention ſome particu-

---

[*] The above Will is omitted in the viſitations of Middleſex and Berks, in 1664, but is mentioned in Cole's Eſcheats, vol. page 116.

lars

lars of ſir Walter, the eldeſt, and his family. Sir
Walter was attorney-geneneral of the couit of
wards to k Cha. I. who knighted him for his ſervices at Whitehall, june the 20, 1640 : he was
member of the houſe of commons, and high ſteward
of Leominſter, in Herefordſhire, of which he was
deprived in 1640, for his *delinquency*, as was the
language of the oppoſite party, and his place given
by the houſe of commons to col. Birch, a member of that houſe, who requeſted it. Sir Walter
was fined for his loyalty 2649l. 6s. as was John
Pye, of the Mynde, gent. 200l probably a ſon of
this knight. Sir Walter married Joan, daughter
of Will. Rudſhall, of Rudſhall, in Herefordſhire,
eſq. by whom he had a daughter named Joyce,
married to Walter Calverly, by whom ſhe had ſir
Walter Calverly, created a bart. by q. Ann. Fra.
his fourth daughter, married to Hen. ſon and heir
of Roger Vaughan, eſq. which Roger died oct. 17,
1641.

The eldeſt ſon and heir of ſir Walter, was another ſir Walter Pye, of the Mynde, knt. he married
at Dinton, Bucks, in 1628, Eliz. daughter of John
Sanders, of Dinton, eſq*. by whom he had Walter
Pye, eſq. Rob. and Cath. This line of the family
being roman-catholics, retained their allegiance to
the royal houſe of Stuart, and diſpoſing of Kilpec
caſtle, retired to the continent, and were created by
James, ſon to k. Ja. II. (called abroad k. Ja. III.)
lord Kilpec. The caſtle of that name is now poſſeſſed by the bart. ſir Rich. Peers, who took the

NUM IX.

Pyes
Sir Walter
Pye, knt eldeſt
ſon of Will Pye,
eſq

Sir Walte Pye,
knt eldeſt ſon
of ſir Walter.

* John Sanders, eſq. was buried at Dinton, jan 21, 1623-4;
as was lady Pye, april 20, 1640. Sir Walter Pye had the patronage of this living, which he diſpoſed of to mr Rich Ser-
geant, of Aſton, in that pariſh, who conveyed it to Simon
Mayne, eſq. one of k. Cha I.'s judges, who loſt it upon his
attainder, but it was reſtored, with part or the whole of his
eſtates, to Simon Mayne, eſq. his ſon.

name

NUM IX

Pyes

Sir Rob Pye,
knt 2nd son
of sir Walter
Pye, ten knt

name of Symonds, whofe anceftors purchafed it of the Pye family : this eldeft branch of the family is fuppofed to be extinct.—Mifs Grace Pye, an heirefs to one of the eldeft branches, took a large eftate with the name of Walter into the baronet family of Blackett, of Northumberland.

Sir Rob. Pye, of Faringdon, Berks, knt. 2nd fon of the firft fir Walter Pye, of the Mynde, audi-tor of the receipt of the Exchequer to k. Ja. I. and k. Cha. I. the latter appointed him, in 1631, one of the commiffioners to inquire into the decay of St. Paul's cathedral. He was knighted at White-hall, apr. 21, 1641. Sir Rob. was deprived of his office of auditor, during the governments that fuc-ceeded the violent death of k. Cha. I. but he was reftored by k. Cha. II. He procured a very large fortune for his family; and purchafed the manor and feat of Faringdon, in Berks, of the Untons, which he refigned to his eldeft fon in his life time; and having a large fortune in Weftminfter, where he chiefly refided, he erected a chapel in St. John's parifh, Tothill-fields, which he liberally endowed: his defcendants were deprived of it by bifhop At-terbury, when dean of Weftminfter; the family now poffeffing no other right or privilege in it, except a family vault, and the liberty of appointing any perfon in holy orders to that finecure, which brings in 50l. per ann. and is now held by dr. Ben. Pye. As there is a copy of verfes addreffed to fir Rob. by Ben Jonfon, we may fuppofe him a lover of the mufes, and a friend to that poet. He died at his houfe in St Stephen's-court, in Weftminfter, may 19, 1662, and was buried in the vault he had provided as a refting place for himfelf and his fami-ly. He married Mary 2nd daughter and co-heirefs of John Croker, of Baltisford, in Gloucefterfhire, efq. Mr Croker died apr. 6, 1630. By this lady he had 1. fir Rob. Pye, of Faringdon, knt. of whom below,

below, 2. fir John Pye of Hone, in Derbyfhire, whom k. Cha. II. created a bart. by letters patent, dated jan. 13, 1664-5: this title is now extinct*.

Sir Rob. Pye, knt. eldeft fon of fir Rob. Pye, fen. was member for Woodftock in the long parlement. upon the breaking out of the civil wars, he went into the parlement army, and became colonel of horfe in general Fairfax's regiment. He gave 1000l. towards quelling the irifh rebellion in 1645. He was at the fiege of Briftol, and was one of thofe who figned the fummons to pr. Rupert, to furrender that city, and in the fame year he was one of the commiffioners at the treaty of Uxbridge. For fome caufe, now impoffible to be known, lady Pye, in 1647, petitioned for permiffion for her hufband fir Rob. to leave Britain, which was granted him at Thiftleworth, but upon his returning into the kingdom, he was met by fome forces of the army, and kept prifoner. However, upon application being made to the general, he was difcharged, and his horfes and goods reftored Notwithftanding he had been fteady to the parlement intereft, and performed feveral gallant actions in their fervice, particularly at the taking of Taunton; yet, becaufe he was known to wifh for a reconciliation between the king and parlement, he was, in 1648, fecluded from the houfe of commons. During the commonwealth he was neglected, but in the protectorfhip of his relation Oliver he was employed and trufted by him, and reprefented Berks in two of his parlements; yet he engaged in an attempt to reftore k. Cha. II. and was made one of the treafurers to apply fuch money as was fent for that purpofe. In 1654, he was arrefted at the fuit of mr. John

NUM IX.
Pyes

Sir Rob Pye, knt (eldeft fon of fir Rob. Pye, fen), he married the patriot Hampden's daughter.

* This was the fecond creation of the title of baronet granted to the Pyes, for k. Cha. I. apr. 27, created Edmund Pye of Leekhamfted, Bucks, efq. bart. but which title has been long extinct.

H 4 Spragne;

Spragne, but the parlement so highly resented it,
as a breach of privilege, that they ordered the
sheriff of Middlesex to oblige his under-sheriff to
repay the money his deputy had taken of sir Rob.
which not being performed, they ordered that both
the under-sheriff's deputy, and the plaintiff, should
be brought to them as delinquents.

Sir Rob with major Fincher, delivered, Jan. 25,
1659-60, an address to the parlement from Berks,
complaining loudly of insupportable grievances
and oppressions. The house having demanded whether they had signed it, they boldly acknowledged
that they had, and complained of the want of a settled government, and that the best expedient for it
would be the recalling the secluded members, by
free elections, to fill up all the vacancies, and that
the parlement might sit without oaths or engagements But this, just and wise as it was, was voted
seditious, a high breach of the privileges of parlement,
and tending to raise a new war, the consequence
of which was, they were sent to the Tower, but sir
Rob had the courage to move for an *habeas corpus*.
Newdigate, judge of the Upper-Bench, demanded
of the commonwealth's counsel, what objection they
had to the motion, and they replying, none, the
judge said, ' if you have not, I have, for as sir Rob.
was committed by an order of parlement, this
court, as an inferior one, cannot discharge him.'
But the commonwealth interest declining upon
Monk's coming to London, the secluded members
had leave given them, by that general, to return to
the house, when they immediately passed a vote to
relieve their champion from prison. He signed, with
several of the nobility and gentry, a declaration,
dated april 13, 1660, that they would bury all
animosities, and submit to the ensuing parlement
Sir. Rob thought it proper, though he had so
manifestly distinguished himself the friend of the
constitution.

constitution, and of the exiled monarch, to take
out a pardon under the great-feal it bears date in
1662. He obtained the confidence of his majesty,
which he certainly merited , he was appointed
equerry to that sovereign ; I apprehend he did not
long hold this place, but refigning all his public
employments, he fought happiness in retirement.
After a life spent in continual dangers and difficulties, he remained for near 40 years a quiet spectator of all the public fcenes that paffed before him.
Sir Rob. furvived his wife, Ann, eldeft daughter of
the patriot John Hampden, efq. only one week;
and when his fervant called him up the morning
following his lady's death, he faid he would never
rife again until the refurrection . they were both
buried in Faringdon church, where there is a monument with this infcription to their memories:

Here lies
Sir Robert Pye, Knt.
Lord of this Manor.
He was efteemed a fine Gentleman
By all who knew him.
Here alfo lies
Dame Ann, his wife,
A daughter of the famous Mr. Hampden ;
They lived together fixty years,
With great Reputation,
And both died A. D 1701.

By fir Robert's marriage with this lady, the Pyes
are allied to the vifc. Hampden and earls of Buckinghamfhire, who are alfo defcended from two fifters of lady Pye. The iffue of this marriage was, 3
fons and 2 daughters, 1. Hampden Pye, efq born
in 1647. he married very imprudently a fervant
of the family, for which reafon his father procured him an appointment, and fent him to fea,
where he was killed in an engagement upon the
coaft of Spanifh America, fome time before the
death

death of his father: there is fuppofed to have been no iffue of his marriage. 2. Edm. Pye, M. D. who, as continuator of the family, fee below. 3. Rich. who probably died young, or unmarried. 4. Eliz. born, march 21, 1657-8, buried at Faringdon, ap. 8, 1661; and 6. Letitia, born dec. 15, 1659.

Edmund Pye, M. D. 2nd fon of fir Rob. Pye, was born oct. 8, 1656, and upon the deaths of his elder brother, and his father, became poffeffed of the family eftates; he was bred to phyfic, which he practifed; he died at Knotting in Oxfordfhire, of the fmall-pox. Dr. Pye married a daughter of lord Crew of Stene, and widow of fir Harry Wright; fhe furvived her fecond hufband many years, and left all, except her jointure, which was the Dignam eftate in Effex, to a defcendant of fir Philip Carteret, who had married her niece Jemima, and was then poftmafter-general: by this lady the Pyes became allied to Hen. duke of Kent, the earls of Sandwich, and lord Grenville's family, both of the latter are by females defcended alfo from the lord Crews. The iffue of dr. Pye and lady Wright were, 2 fons and 3 daughters. 1. Henry Pye, efq. of whom below. 2. John Pye, efq. an officer in the army, and had two daughters, one married to mr. Wilkinfon, by whom fhe had no child, and Ann married to mr. Kelly. 3. Ifabella, married to ———— Nafh, of Wallerton, in Suffex, efq. they are both dead; their fon Rich. Nafh, efq. married his firft coufin, mifs Manwaring, by whom he has Rich. Nafh, late lieutenant in the 14th regiment of dragoons, but is now upon half pay, and Edw. Nafh, efq. a merchant in London. 4. Jemima married to Edw. Manwaring, of Witmore, in Staffordfhire, efq. by whom fhe had 4 fons and a daughter, Edw. Manwaring, efq. the prefent poffeffor of that feat, whofe

whofe fon and heir is Edw. Manwaring, of Iver,
Bucks, efq. he has alfo Will. Manwaring, who is
a merchant in London, and feveral daughters.
Tho. Manwaring, the 2d fon, married Fra. Pye,
by whom he left Hen. Manwaring, efq. a lieut.
in the army, now on half-pay. The rev. ——
Manwaring, the 3d fon, left 3 daughters; Ann,
married to Cha. Pye, of Wadley, efq. Sarah to
Tho. Wilkinfon, efq. and Urfula to John Ar-
buthnot, efq. Benj. Manwaring, efq. the 4th fon,
was an officer in the firft regiment of foot, he died
unmarried, and the daughter married to Rich.
Nafh, efq. 5. Eliz. married to —— Chace, efq.
by whom fhe had Stephen Chace, of Reading,
Berks, efq. and one of his majefty's juftices of the
peace for that county.

Hen. Pye, of Faringdon, efq. eldeft fon of dr. Hen Pyes
Edm. Pye, was born aug. 23, 1683, and died jan. efq
6, 1748-9, and was buried at Faringdon: he married thrice, firft, july 8, 1707, Jane, daughter of
fir Nath. Curzon, of Keddlefton, in Derbyfhire,
bart. anceftor to lord Scarfdale, and allied to
the noble and honorable families of Wentworth,
Milbank, Noel, &c. fhe died within the year:
2ndly, to Ann, only daughter of Benj. Bathurft,
knt cofferer of the houfhold to q. Ann, and fifter
to Allen, firft lord Bathurft, fhe died of the fmall-
pox, aug. 7, 1729: and 3dly, march 15, 1732-3,
mifs Ifabella Warren, of Wadley, Berks, fhe died
fept. 30, 1750, and is buried in Faringdon church.
By his firft marriage he had only one child, a fon,
by the fecond 8 fons, and 8 daughters, and by the
third no iffue. His children were, 1. Nath. the
child by Jane, was baptized mar. 16, 1705-6, and
buried at Faringdon, ap. 16, following. 2. Benj.
Pye, died an infant. 3. Hen. Pye, efq. of whom
hereafter. 4. Sir Tho. Pye, knt. admiral of
the white, and lieutenant of marines, born mar.

12, 1713, and died in 1785, leaving no child by his wife Mary Shank. 5. Rob Pye, L. L. D. prebendary of Rochester, born mar. 18, 1718; he married Ann daughter of sir Rowland Alston, of Oldhill, Bedford, bart. by whom he has an only daughter Ann, unmarried. 6. Cha. Pye, of Wadley, Bucks, esq born feb 9, 1721-2, he married Ann, eldest daughter of the rev. —— Manwaring. 7. Anth. Pye, esq solicitor in chancery, born june 27, 1722, he married Ann, daughter of John Blackstone, esq first cousin of sir Will. Blackstone, knt. he has Hen. Pye, of Merton coll. Oxford, and Charlotte, both unmarried. 8. The rev. Benj. Pye, L L. D. born nov. 10, 1723 Dr. Pye's poetic merit is too well known for any praise of mine to augment his fame, he married Eliz. daughter of John Sleigh, esq. and relict of —— Whitby, esq. by whom he has Bathurst Pye, a lieut. in the army, in the East-Indies, and Eliz. married to —— Watson, esq. 9. Will. Pye, esq born nov 20, 1726, he was an officer in the army, and was killed feb. 5, 1757, by a cannon ball at the battle of Plassy, in the East-Indies, where he acted as aid-du-camp to lord Clive. by Eliz. daughter of governor Saunders, he left Eliz married to dr Walker, a physician, also in the East-Indies; by her dr. Walker has one son, an infant. 10. —— a daughter, died an infant. 11. Ann, died of the small-pox, oct 6, 1729 12 Frances, born oct 11, 1710, and died in march 1781, she married Tho. Manwaring, of Whitmore, in Staffordshire, esq 13 Henrietta, born nov 10, 1711, she is married to the rev. John Baker, D D. vicar of Faringdon, where he was buried without any memorial, 1747, or 1748 · he had two daughters, Henrietta the eldest (since dead) married to Roger Drake, esq a governor in the East-Indies, by whom she had Geo. Drake, esq.

and

and Sarah, the youngeft, is unmarried.   14. Ann
Pye, born nov. 4, 1715: fhe has been married
twice, firft in nov. 1734, to Lionel Rich, efq the
iffue of which alliance was one fon and three
daughters. Hen. Pye Rich, a merchant at Am-
fterdam, who married a french lady, madamoifelle
Gieffeult, by whom he had one child, a fon, Ann
Rich, married to lieut. Goddard, who is dead,
leaving one daughter, and Phillippa Rich, married
to Tho. Randall, of Great-Shurdington, in Gloucefterfhire, efq. by whom fhe has two fons. Mifs
Ann Pye re-married after Mr. Rich's death to
Ja. Molloy, efq who is alfo dead, by him fhe had
capt Anth Pye Molloy, of the royal navy, who
has confiderably diftinguifhed himfelf, but particularly in the Weft-Indies, in the late war, for
which he received the thanks of Lord Rodney;
and Frances (fince dead) married to Will. Mat-
ford, of Gilbury, Hants, efq. a near relation of
the late duke of Northumberland, author of an
hiftory of Greece, and remarkable for his extenfive
and univerfal literature, the iffue of this marriage
is 4 fons, Will. Hen. John, and Bertram   15.
Eliz Pye, born mar. 1, 1716-17, fhe married to
fir Willoughby Afton, of Wadley, Berks, bart.
who died about 8 or 9 years ago in Wales, where
he is buried, lady Afton is living, their iffue is 1
fon and 2 daughters. Sir Willoughby Afton, bart.
married to lady Jane Henley, they have no child.
Eliz. married to capt. Cotton of the royal navy,
brother to fir Rob. Cotton, bart. they have one
child, a daughter, named Purefoy, married to the
hon.   Prefton, efq. brother to lord Gormaf-
ton, and Mary married to capt. Gordon of the
royal navy. 16. Finetta Pye, born fept. 1, 1719,
married to mr. Geo. Cruckfhank, an eminent merchant,

NUM IX
Pyes.

chant in Holland, who died in London, and it is supposed was buried in the vault belonging to the Pyes, in Weftminfter. after his death his widow married again to Mr. Mowbray, near Edinburgh, but now of Soho-fquare; he was near relation, and next heir, to the late mr. Cruckfhank; mrs. Mowbray has no iffue by either hufband. 17. Arabella Pye, born oct. 3, 1724, fhe married ———— Southwell, efq. uncle to lord Clifford, they are both living· the only iffue of this marriage is a daughter, born in 1760, married in 1782 to fir Cecil Bifhop, bart. Lady Bifhop has one fon.

Henry Pye,
efq fon of
Henry.

Henry Pye, of Faringdon, efq. eldeft fon, and heir to the laft-mentioned Henry, was born july 29, 1709. He reprefented Berks in four different parlements, and dying march 2, 1766, was buried in the church of Faringdon, by Mary daughter of the rev. David James, rector of Woofton, Bucks, the place of his refidence and death. Mrs. Pye is ftill living, their iffue was three fons and one daughter. 1. Henry James Pye, efq of him I fhall fpeak hereafter. 2. Rob. Hampden Pye, efq. a lieut-col. in the foot guards, but of which he has difpofed. He married at Faringdon, oct. 16, 1766, Joel Henrietta, relict of ———— Campbell, efq. fhe is now dead. By her he had only one child, Allen-Hampden Pye. 3. Walter Pye, efq. a barrifter at law, and unmarried. 4 Ann, who is a twin with Walter, fhe is alfo unmarried.

Hen James
Pye efq

Henry James Pye, efq. the prefent poffeffor of Faringdon, eldeft fon of the laft Hen. Pye, efq. was born feb. 10, 1744-5, and is now alfo one of the reprefentatives of Berks, he married, aug. 24, 1766, Mary, daughter of lieut-col. Will Hook, and

and firſt couſin to the counteſs Delewar: the children of this marriage are only two, Mary, born
in 1769, and Matilda Caroline, born nov. 18,
1775 *.

No. X.

*The hiſtory of the family of Trevor, now Hampden,
deſcended from Ruth, daughter of the celebrated
John Hampden, eſq. and couſin of Oliver lord
protector.*

THE family of Trevor is one of the moſt
ancient and noble in Wales, their pedigree is carried up higher than the time of k. Arthur, and it is ſaid that their anceſtor, Kariodock Urech Fras, was in that king's reign earl
of Hereford and Marcheogien. Tudor Trevor,
earl of Hereford, ſon of Rheingar, and grandſon
of Kariodock, married Ankaret, daughter of
Howell Dha ap Kadell, prince of North Wales.
The deſcendants of this marriage are branched
out into a prodigious number of families, which,
like moſt of thoſe in Wales, are more known by

---

* The hiſtory of the family of Pye, is taken from various
hiſt of England, Cole's Eſcheats, Viſitations of Hereford,
Middleſex, and Berks, extracts from the Regiſter of Faringdon, memorandums made in a bible in the poſſeſſion of H. J
Pye, eſq who with the utmoſt readineſs obligingly communicated that, and a variety of information reſpecting his family,
as did the late admiral ſir Tho. Pye, and through ſir Tho. the
rev. dr Pye.

their

their arms *, than their names, but even from the time of John, who firſt took the ſirname of Trevor, in the reign of k. Henry VII. many moſt reſpectable families in Wales, England, and Ireland, are known by the name of Trevor, and particularly the noble one of Trevor, viſcounts Dungannon, in Ireland. John Trevor, of Brynkynate, eſq who firſt aſſumed a ſirname, had five ſons, all of whom were founders of diſtinct branches. Rich. the third of them, by marrying an heireſs, became poſſeſſed of the manor of Allington, and was father of John Trevor, of Allington, eſq. whoſe eldeſt ſon was alſo John, ſeated at the ſame place; as was his eldeſt ſon, likewiſe named John, who became the father of four ſons, who all received the honor of knighthood †. Sir John Trevor, the ſecond of them, was ſeated at Trevallyn, in Flintſhire, he was knighted at Windſor, june 7, 1619, and by Margaret, daughter of Hugh Trevanion, in Cornwall, eſq. he had ſir John, his heir, who married the patriot's daughter, and ſeveral other children ‡.

---

* The arms of Trevor are, party per bend, ſiniſter, ermine and ermines, a lion rampant, or

† The four ſons of John Trevor, of Allington, eſq were ſir Rich. Trevor, of Allington, knt who left four daughters his co-heireſſes. Sir John, of whom in the following pages Sir Sackville, and ſir Tho. chief-baron of the Exchequer, he was impeached in 1641, but extricated himſelf with very great honor, and died in march 1656-7 Lloyd has written his life. His ſon and heir was ſir Tho. created a knight of the Bath at k. Cha I's coronation, and a baronet in 1641, which title, for want of male iſſue, became extinct at his death

‡ The other children of ſir John Trevor, knt. were, Cha. Will. and Rich. and three daughters, Ann, married to Rob. Weldon of London, eſq Jane, to ſir Fra Compton, knt. ſecond ſon of Spencer, earl of Northampton, and Eliz to Will. Matham, eſq eldeſt ſon of ſir Will. Matham, bart anceſtor of the lord Matham.

From

From this concife account of the Trevors, it may be expected, that an alliance was defirable by any family. The patriot Hampden particularly thought it fo, not only for their intereft in England, but for their command of fo large a part of Wales, their very numerous, and great family connexions, the political fentiments that were almoft common to all of them; and, what perhaps was ftill more interefting to the patriot, the vaft fway they bore in the houfe of Commons, having, befides feveral members allied to them by marriage, no lefs than five of their own name in parlement, of which, fir John, of Trevallyn, knt. was one, and his eldeft fon, of both his names, another. It is this fir John Trevor, junior, knt. (then only mr. Trevor), and his defcendants, that I fhall particularly treat of, as from the political reafons before enumerated, and the private amiable virtues of himfelf, and his family, the patriot fixed upon him for the hufband of Ruth, his 4th daughter, by which he greatly ftrengthened that union of families, which, firft under himfelf, and then the Cromwells at their head, endeavoured, and in the end overturned one of the moft ancient, and moft refpectable monarchies in the world; and in its place fubftituted a new form of government, which was at firft pretty evenly divided amongft this allied affociation, but in the end fell only to one family.

Mr. Trevor and his father were particularly trufted by the protectors, Oliver and Richard. He certainly was more inclined to a monarchy than a republic, and, therefore, it cannot be wondered at, that he fhould be better pleafed to fee a family, to whom he was known, allied to, and trufted by, upon the throne, than another, who he could not expect would have that partiality for him. But when his favorite intereft was entirely deftroyed, he wifhed for a reftoration of the royal line, rather than the establishment of a republic, though he was a particular loser by the king's return, as he had a grant of Richmond-park and ground, and the great park at Nonsuch, and a monopoly of 1500l. per ann. out of New-castle coals, all which advantages he was deprived of by that event; and he had the happiness either to satisfy his majesty, at the restoration, of his at-tachment to his person and government, so that he entirely forgot that ever he had been disloyal; or, which is more probable, Charles was willing to win over so powerful a family to his interest, for which reasons he conferred the honor of knighthood upon him, and, in 1668, sent him ambassador to the court of France. Upon his re-turn in the same year, he was sworn one of his majesty's most honorable privy council, and ap-pointed one of the principal secretaries of state. Whilst he held this office, he was attacked by a fever, which in the evening of the sixth day put a period to his life, may 28, 1672, in the 47th year of his age. His remains were deposited in St. Bartholomew's church in Smithfield. His fa-ther survived him about a year. By lady Ruth his wife, the daughter of the patriot Hampden, he had five sons. 1. John Trevor, esq who suc-ceeded, upon his grandfather's death, to the estate of Trevallyn. He married Eliz. daughter of ——— Clarke, esq. and widow of John Morley, or Glynd, in Sussex, esq She survived mr Trevor, and re-married lord visc. Cutts. The issue of her marriage with mr. Trevor was, John Morley Trevor, of Glynd-Stammerton, esq. who succeed-ed to the family estate in Wales, and represented Sussex, and the borough of Lewes, in several parlements. He died apr. 19, 1719, and by Lucy, eldest daughter of the hon Edw. Montagu, esq father of Geo the first earl of Halifax, he was father of another John Morley Trevor, esq. who

was

was also a member for Lewes, and was in the late reign a lord of the admiralty. He married Betty, daughter of sir Tho. Frankland, bart. and died in 1743. This last John Morley Trevor had 9 sisters, Lucy, the eldest, married to Edw. Rice, of Newton, in Carmarthenshire, esq. by whom she had col Geo. Rice, who married lady Cecil Talbot, created baroness Dinever; Lucy, who died unmarried, and Cath. who died an infant, Grace, living in 1784, Mary and Margaret, who are dead, Ann, wife of general Geo Boscawen, Ruth, wife of mr Roper, Gertrude, married to Cha. Tyler, esq. a capt. of dragoons, and one more. Tho. the youngest son of John Trevor, esq. died unmarried, Eliz. eldest daughter of John, married to David Polhill, of Otford, in Kent, esq. and Arabella, her sister, was twice a wife, first to Rob. Heath of Lewes, in Sussex, esq. and secondly to brigadier-general Edw. Montagu, only brother to Geo. 2nd earl of Halifax, she died at Egham, oct 11, 1734, leaving Edw. her son and heir. 2 Sir Tho. Trevor, knt. afterwards lord Trevor, of whom hereafter. 3. Rich. Trevor. 4. Hampden Trevor*. 5. Edw Trevor. The names of these three younger sons of sir John are only mentioned, so that whether they became men, or whether they lived single or married, cannot be ascertained. 6 Mary died unmarried, in a very advanced age, in apr 1738.

Tho. lord Trevor, the 2nd son of sir John Trevor, was himself also knighted by k Will. III. in oct 1692. He entered himself a student in the Inner Temple; and in the same year in which he was knighted, he was made solicitor-general, and in the following one attorney-general. It must

Tho ſt lord Trevor

---

* Hampden Trevor is not mentioned in lord Hampden's pedigree. Qu. If Mr. Trevor had such a son.

be

be obferved, that the Trevors, as friends to the freedom of the fubject, were greatly in favour at the revolution, for, befides the folicitor-general, fir John Trevor, knt. who had been fpeaker to the houfe of commons in 1685, was again chofen in 1690. He was twice appointed mafter of the Rolls, and twice commiffioner of the great feal*. Sir Tho. was called to be a ferjeant-at-law, June 29, 1701; and upon q. Ann's acceffion, june 5th following, appointed lord-chief-juftice of the Common-Pleas, fept 25, 1710, lord-chief-juftice of the Queen's-Bench; and jan. 1, 1711-12, her majefty called him up to the houfe of peers, by the title of lord Trevor, of Bromham, in Bedfordfhire. In the following reign, the royal favor ftill continued to him; for, march 6, 1725-6, he was appointed lord-privy-feal; and may 31, 1727, one of the lords juftices of Great Britain. His late majefty k. Geo. II. upon his acceffion, again conftituted him lord-privy-feal, and may 8, 1730, he was made prefident of the moft honorable privy council, in which elevated fituation he died, june 19 following, in the 72d year of his age, and was

---

* Sir John Trevor was the 2nd fon (Edw. the eldeft died leaving no child) of John Trevor, of Brynkynate, in Denbighfhire, efq. by Mary, daughter of John Jefferys, of Helon, in the fame county, efq Sir John was knighted at Whitehall, jan 29. 1670-1, he died at his houfe in Clement's-lane, may 20, 1717, and was buried in the Rolls chapel He married Jane, daughter of fir Roger Moftyn, of Moftyn, in the county of Flint, baro and relict of Roger Puliston, of Emeral, Flintfhire, efq fhe died in aug. 1704, and was buried in St Martin's, in Shropfhire, where fir John's eftates lie, by this lady he had 4 fons and one daughter 1 Edw Trevor, efq who had difpleafed his father, but, by fir John's dying inteftate, he fucceeded to a real eftate of 1500l per ann and a fhare of the perfonalty. 2. Arthur Trevor, efq ufher of the Rolls chapel. 3 John Trevor, efq mafter of the examiner's office in Chancery. 4 Tudor Trevor, a naval officer, and 5 Ann, who married fift ——— Hill, of Hillfborow, in Ireland, and fecondly, Alan lord Brodrick, lord-chancellor of that kingdom.

buried

buried at Bromham. It may be a difficult question to anfwer, whether he was moft unfortunate
in the commons' indignation who expelled him,
or happy in the love of fo many princes: the latter
certainly obliterates all traces of the criminality
fufpected by the former ; as he had the honor of
being employed by four fucceeding kings, in
whofe fervice he rofe higher in each reign, and
left his family both ennobled and enriched. His
lordfhip was fellow of the royal foc.ety, and governor of the Charter-houfe. He married firft
Eliz. daughter and coheir of John Searle, of Finch-
ley, Middlefex, efq. and after her death he re-
married Ann, daughter of col. Rob. Weldon, of
London, and widow of fir Rob. Bernard, bart. The
iffue of the firft marriage was, 2 fons and 3 daughters. 1. Tho. 2nd lord Trevor, of whom below.
2. John, 3d lord Trevor, alfo mentioned hereafter.
3. Ann, died unmarried. 4. Letitia, married to
Peter Cock, of Camberwell, in Surry, efq. fhe
died april 25, 1769, aged 71, and is buried in the
vault belonging to that family in Camberwell
church-yard, fhe left Matthew Cock, efq. and a
daughter married to ----- Crifpin, efq. 5 Eliz.
never married. 6. Rob Trevor, afterwards
Hampden, firft lord vifc. Hampden : his life is
given in a future page. 7. Rich. who was bifhop
of St. David's, and laftly of Durham. His lordfhip,
after a moft exemplary life, died with the greateft
refignation and compofure, june 9, 1771, in the
64th year of his age, and was privately buried (by
his own defire) in the church of Glynd, in Suffex,
which he had rebuilt His lordfhip never married *. 8. Edw. who died young.

There is an account of the exemplary death and character of bifhop Trevor, printed in the private prefs of my ingenious and worthy friend, Geo. Allen, of Darlington, efq. to
which is prefixed a good engraving of his lordfhip, by Collyer,
from a painting of Hutchinfon.

NUM X.

Trevors.

I 3

Tho.

Tho. 2nd lord Trevor, died march 22, 1733-4, and was buried at Bromham.   By his lady, daughter and sole heiress of Timothy Burrell, of Cuckfield, in Sussex, esq counsellor at law (which lady died aug 27, 1734) he had an only daughter, Eliz who, may 23, 1732, married to Cha. duke of Marlborough · the duke died oct. 20, 1758, her grace, oct. 7, 1761   their issue was Geo the present duke of Marlborough, who is a knt of the garter, born jan 26, 1738-9, and married, aug 23, 1762, the lady Caroline Russel, daughter of John duke of Bedford, by whom his grace has Geo Marq of Blandford, born march 3, 1766, lord Henry, born dec 20, 1770, lady Caroline, born oct 27, 1763; lady Eliz born dec. 20, 1764, lady Charlotte, born oct 18, 1769, and lady Ann, born nov. 5, 1773   2. Lord Cha. born march 31, 1740, member for Oxfordshire, a privy counsellor, and verdurer of Whichwood forest. By Mary, daughter of Vere Beauclerk, lord Vere of Hanworth, he has two sons, Geo. and Cha and had a daughter, Eliz. who died an infant. 3 Lord Rob. born may 8, 1747, member for the city of Oxford, a commissioner of trade and plantations, and L L D.   4 Lady Diana, born mar 24, 1734-5, first married, sept. 9, to Fred lord visc. Bolingbroke and St. John, since to the hon. Topham Beauclerk, esq only son of the late lord Sidney Beauclerk, 5th son of Cha 1st duke of St. Albans, and 5 Lady Eliz. born dec. 29, 1737, and married, mar. 13, 1756, to Hen. earl of Pembroke.

John, 3d lord Trevor, of Bromham, was bred to the law, and in the life time of his brother was a welch judge. His lordship married, may 31, 1731, Eliz. daughter of that celebrated wit, sir Rich. Steele, by whom he had an only daughter, Diana, who was born an idiot, lord Trevor died at Bath, sept. 27, 1764.

5   Rob.

NUM X

Trevors.

Rob 4th lor
Trevor,
created vifc
Hampden.

Rob. Trevor, born in 1718, who was the third, but eldeft fon of Tho. lord Trevor by his 2nd lady. He, in compliance with the will of his relation, John Hampden, of Great-Hampden, Bucks, efq. took the name and armorial bearings of that family, for which he inherited the eftate of that ancient houfe. In the year 1739, he was appointed envoy extraordinary and plenipotentiary at the Hague. In 1749, or 1750, he was conftituted a commiffioner of the cuftoms of Ireland; and in 1759, joint poftmafter-general. Upon the death of his half brother John, lord Trevor, without male iffue, he became 4th lord Trevor, baron of Bromham, and june 8, 1776, he was by his majefty raifed to the dignity of vifcount Hampden, of Great and Little Hampden, in Bucks. His Lordfhip was a fellow of both the royal and antiquarian focieties. He died at Bromham-houfe, aug. 22, 1783, of a dead palfy, which ftruck him upon wednefday in the preceding week, when he was in the intire enjoyment of all his faculties, and in perfect health, after fpending that day in his favorite diverfion, fifhing. This nobleman married in 1743, whilft in Holland, Conftantia, daughter of Peter Anthony de Huybert baron Van Kruningen, in Zealand, who died june 15, 1761*, of the fmall-pox. The iffue of this marriage was 4 children. 1. Tho 2nd vifc. Hampden, of whom below. 2. John, born in Albemarle-ftreet, London, feb. 21, 1748-9, and baptized march 26 following, he was minifter plenipotentiary to the

---

* The late lord vifc Hampden, with a modefty almoft peculiar, finding that he could not make any vault or grave in the chancel of Great-Hampden church, without difturbing his maternal anceftors, buried his lady in the cemetary at the weft end of the church, where his remains, by his particular defire, are alfo laid, over whom are two common brick tombs.

Elector-

Elector-Palatine, and minifter at the diet of Ra-
tifbon; and feb. 22, 1783, appointed his majefty's
envoy extraordinary and plenipotentiary at the
court of Turin.   He married aug. 9, 1773, Har-
riet, daughter and fole heir of the rev. dr. Dan.
Burton, late canon of Chrift-church, precentor of
Exeter, chancellor of Oxford diocefe, rector of
Slapton, Bucks, &c. by whom he left no child. 3.
Maria Conftantia, married may 25, 1764, to
Henry earl of Suffolk ; fhe died in child-bed, feb.
8, 1767, and was buried at Charleton, Wilts.   4.
Ann, who died unmarried, apr. 12, 1760.

Tho 2nd vifc.
Hampden

Tho. 2nd vifc. Hampden and 5th lord Trevor,
was born in Holland ; he was member for Lewes
in the laft parlement; and, upon the death of his
father, fucceeded him in the titles of vifc. Hampden and lord Trevor.   His lordfhip, june 13, 1768,
married Cath. only child of major-general David
Græme, of Braco-caftle, in North-Britain *.

* The hiftory of the Trevors is taken from Collyer, Jacob's,
and other peerages, feveral hiftories of England, Harl. MSS.
&c and corrected by the right hon lord vifc. Hampden The
hiftory of this family, is one of the moft defective in the peerages, though inferior to none in antiquity.

No.

No. XI.

The hiſtory of the families of Hammond and Hobart, allied to the Cromwells, by two gentlemen of thoſe names marrying Mary, daughter of the patriot Hampden.

THE Hammonds are a very ancient and knightly family; and in the laſt century were greatly divided in their religious and political opinions · ſome were as much attached to the national church and perſon of k. Cha I. as others were averſe to both. The moſt remarkable of the former was dr. Hen. Hammond, godſon of Hen. pr. of Wales, and the beloved chaplain of k. Cha I. His many great ſervices to that unfortunate ſovereign, brought upon him ejectments, fines, and impriſonments, he was one of the two epiſcopal clergy that dared to petition and remonſtrate to the army againſt putting the king to death. He was born at Cheitſey, in Surry, aug. 26, 1605, and died in retirement, in april, 1660, at the ſeat of ſir John Packington, in Worceſterſhire. He was an ornament to human nature, his writings upon divinity are numerous and valuable *. He was the brother of Rob. Hammond, eſq. who married the patriot's daughter, as was Tho. Hammond, eſq. one of k. Cha I.'s judges, and who ſentenced him to death, and ſigned the warrant for his execution †. The

NUM XI.

Hammonds Antiquity, religious and political ſentiments.

---

* Vide the life of di H. Hammond, in the biogr britann.

† Wood, in his Ath Oxonienſes, has written the life of Tho Hammond, eſq. one of the king's judges, he ſpelt his name Hamond, as ſeveral others of his family did, his ſeal of arms uponthe king's death warrant has three lions rampant, two and one, but in the additions at the end of vol. II. of Edmondſon, are the arms of Hamond, of Chertſey, in Surry, intirely different fiom thoſe nere mentioned There were other brotheis, who were likewiſe fiiends of the pailement, Tho. nephew of di Henry Hammond, was puiitanically educated, and was peiſuaded by his uncle Tho. to take up arms for the pailement,

NUM XI

Hammonds

Hammonds, at least some of them, early espoused the cause of the people against the unjust usurpations upon their liberties by the Stuarts, as sir Hen. Hammond experienced great severity from k. Cha I. for his freedom of speech in that monarch's third parlement [*].

Col Robert Hammond, who married Ruth, the patriot Hampden's daughter, and cousin of Oliver lord protector

Rob Hammond, esq. who married the patriot's daughter, was the son, and probably the eldest, of dr. John Hammond, physician to Hen pr. of Wales ; he was the intimate friend of the celebrated O. Cromwell, afterwards lord prot. by whom his relation, the patriot Hampden, was persuaded to give him Mary, his youngest daughter. Rob was always prejudiced against k. Cha. I. and his

parlement, and was captain-major under col Edw. Massey, he afterwards rose to be a col. of foot By the persuasion of his uncle, the divine, he repented joining the parlement, and expressed it to his majesty, when he was by that uncle on purpose introduced to the royal presence This col. Tho. in oct 1644, killed major Grey in a duel The sister of the rev dr Hammond married to sir John Temple, knt. master of the Rolls in Ireland, he wrote the hist of the irish massacre, and was father, by that lady, to the great and good sir Will. Temple, bart —Query Were sir Peter Temple, and James Temple, esq two of k Cha I's judges, and sir Purbeck Temple, knt. named a commissioner to try the king, but who refused to sit, any relation to the master of the Rolls r they bear the same arms. The Temples are a numerous family —A near relation to these Hammonds, was the loyal col Hammond, of Kent, a colchestrian cavalier, afterwards governor of the castle of Gowran, under the marquis of Ormond, who, by the mutiny of the garrison, was obliged to surrender up his trust, and was shamefully shot by the great Cromwell, then lord-governor of Ireland, though he had promised him his life John Hammond. of Edingham, in Norfolk, was fined 100l. by the parlement for his delinquency.

[*] Willis in his not parl does not give sir H. Hammond, knt. as a member of parlement, but we must suppose that he was returned upon the death or removal of some other member. in th t parlement Sir Tho Hammond, knt sat in the reign of k. Ja I more than in one parlement he bore arg on a chevron, engrailed between 3 martlets sable, as many cinque foils, or.

marriage

marriage entirely confirmed it; the parlement raifed him to the rank of a colonel, and appointed him governor of the ifle of Wight, where he was at the time that k. Cha I made his efcape from the army, and fled to this ifland Sir John Afhburnham, the royal fugitive's conductor, acquainted him where his majefty was, and befought protection for the wretched monarch, without previoufly obtaining his promife for his fafety, which his majefty no fooner knew, than he exclaimed, ' Oh Jack, thou haft undone me !' Sir John, offered to go down and put the governor to death, who was waiting below, but this the unhappy king, as knowing his enemies would have faid that he had been fent on purpofe to be deftroyed, would not permit, faying, he would fubmit to his deftiny. The colonel immediately difpatched a meffenger to the parlement, acquainting them where the king was, and that he waited their commands, to know how he fhould difpofe of his perfon, the parlement, who had been in the utmoft alarm when they heard of the royal captive's efcape, were fo well pleafed, that they voted him to have the charge of his majefty, and prefented him, for his fidelity to them, 1000l. in money, and 500l per ann. in land, and allowed him 20l. a week for fupplying his prifoner's table. The army grandees were not lefs ftudious to pleafe him, as they were fearful that he might be tempted by fome royal grants to at leaft connive at the king's flight O. Cromwell wrote him the moft obliging letters, as knowing how much now depended upon him, he put him in mind, by his excefs of tendernefs, of their long and uninterrupted friendfhip. Certainly his fituation was now moft important, and his declaring himfelf of the greateft confequence; for had he freed the king from captivity, had he tranfported him to France, which he might with eafe have done, no reward could

fcarce

scarce have been equal to the service, therefore honors and emoluments were no doubt at his command; and he might render the parlement or army the greatest kindness or injury, by declaring for either of them, in opposition to the other. But he seems to have aimed at what he thought the line of duty. The king had put himself into his hands, without any promise of protection; he was, therefore, he thought, not bound to give him liberty. The parlement had appointed him to the government of the island, and afterwards of the king's person, and had rewarded him for his zeal in their service, he therefore determined to continue faithful to their interest.

The peculiarity of his situation made his office disagreeable, and he gave but little satisfaction to any in it; the friends of the misguided prince thought he treated him with great severity, and have even pretended that he endeavoured to destroy him; on the contrary, the republicans reflected upon him as too much compassionating fallen majesty, the truth appears to be, that, until the king endeavoured to escape, he treated him with great tenderness, but ever afterwards with an excess of caution, sitting up often himself all night, doubling the guards, and sending away all that the king confided in, not permitting his own brother, the king's chaplain, to remain. Perhaps, had he known what would have been his prisoner's fate, he would have set him at liberty when he first came into his power, as he does not seem quite satisfied with the parlement's ordering him up to London, to be tried as a criminal, at the command of the soldiery, and the army were so fearful of his breach of trust, that they dispatched col. Eure, privately and disguised, to supersede him in his office, and he was obliged to go with Eure to London, to attend a secret charge against him. It appears by sir John Bowring's relation of
the

the laſt days of k. Cha. I. that col. Hammond adviſed the miſerable ſovereign to eſcape, telling him, that as by the treaty then on foot he had leave to be more at large, it would be no diſhonor to him, as the army had violated it, to get away, and promiſed not to oppoſe the deſign. But Charles, who always heſitated when action was requiſite, and betrayed his ſecrets to thoſe who were bribed by his enemies, loſt the opportunity of retiring, and he was ſent to Hurſt-caſtle, and ſoon after brought to London, to be tried, and then led to execution. After the king's decapitation, he had a penſion of 400l. per ann and accompanied his relation O. Cromwell, (afterwards prot.) to Ireland, by whom he was left at Dublin, with the title of one of the parlement commiſſioners; in which ſituation he remained until his death *, which happened oct. 24, 1654, occaſioned by a violent fever: his remains were depoſited with great funeral pomp in that city, nov. 2 following. In the ſame year the protector ſettled 200l. per ann. of lands in Ireland upon his widow and her children, for arrears due to him, as well as for other conſiderations. Mrs. Hammond re-married to ſir John Hobart, of Blickling, bart.

The Hobarts are of ancient deſcent in Norfolk. Sir James Hobart may be ſaid to have laid the foundation of their preſent greatneſs, he was bred to the law, and receiving his education at Lincoln's-Inn, he there ſo particularly diſtinguiſhed himſelf, that he was elected lent-reader of that ſociety, in the reign of k Edw. IV. and one of the governors he was appointed attorney-general to k Hen. VII. which office he retained to his death; he was made a knight of the ſword, at the creation

---

* A Rob Hammond, of Reading, eſq was returned for that borough, in the parlement called by the prot. Oliver, in 1654, who, it is reaſonable to ſuppoſe, was the patriot's ſon-in-law, though then in Ireland.—The patriotic family of Hammond, in Huntingdonſhire, are deſcended from thoſe of Surry.

of Hen. pr. of Wales, afterwards k Hen. VIII. he
died in 1507, and was buried in Norwich cathedral: he was deservedly esteemed by all good men,
his residence was at Halles-hall, in Norfolk. He
is ranked among the worthies of that county by
Fuller, who, amongst other acts of his piety and
munificence, mentions his building the church of
Loddon from the ground, and the bridge of St.
Olaves, called St. Tooley's, and making the cause-
way to it He married Marg. daughter of Peter
Naunton, esq. who died before him in 1494, and
is buried in Loddon church, by whom he had two
sons, 1. sir Walter, from whom, by his two wives,
Ann, the daughter of sir Hen Heydon, knt and
Ann, the daughter of John Ratcliffe, lord Fitz-
walter, and sister to Rob. earl of Suffex, are descended the families of Hobart of Halles-hall, and
Blyford, in Suffolk, and of Morley, in Norfolk.
2. Sir Miles, of whom below.

Sir Miles Hobart, 2nd son of sir Ja Hobart, kn.

Sir Miles, 2d son of sir James, was seated at
Plumsted, in Norfolk, by Eleanor, youngest
daughter of John Bleverhasset, of Frense, in that
county, esq. he had two sons, 1. Tho. of whom
below, and, 2 John, who married Ann, daughter
of sir Philip Tilney, knt. the founder of that
branch of the family that settled at Wavte, in
Norfolk, where he himself resided.

Tho Hobart, esq. eldest son of sir Miles Hobart, kt

Tho. the eldest son of sir Miles, inherited the
Plumsted estate, he married Audrey, daughter
and heir of Will Hare, of Beeston, in Norfolk,
esq. by whom he had two sons and two daughters,
1. Sir Miles Hobart, knt who inherited the estate
at Plumsted, but this branch failing, that estate
came to sir John, the 2d baronet of this family.
2. Sir Henry Hobart, created a baronet, of whom
hereafter. 3. Mary, and 4 Ellen.

Sir Henry Hobart

Sir Henry Hobart, seated at Intwood in Norfolk, was created a baronet by k Ja I in 1611,

he

he was the 9th in precedency, fir Hen. was chancellor to Hen. pr. of Wales, and after filling various other departments in the law, and in parlement, with fingular credit, died lord-chief-juftice of the common-pleas, dec. 26, 1625, and was buried in Chrift's church in Norwich. By Dorothy, daughter of fir Rob. Bell, of Beaupree-hall; Norfolk, knt. lord-chief-baron of the Exchequer, he had 16 children, moft of whom either died young or unmarried, two of them are particularly confpicuous, fir John and fir Miles.

Sir John, the eldeft furviving fon of fir Henry, was knighted with his father by k. Ja. I. in 1603, and fucceeded to the title of baronet upon his death, and to the eftate of Plumfted, upon failure of heirs of fir Miles, his uncle, but he refided chiefly at Blickling in Norfolk, where he built a magnificent feat, in that manor which his father by purchafe had added to the family poffeffions. He was returned a member of parlement for Corfecaftle, and alfo for Leftwithiel, in the reign of k. Ja I. and for Norfolk in the long-parlement called by k. Cha I. He greatly oppofed the arbitrary meafures of that foveieign, which endeared him to the parlement, who had commenced a war againft him, and appointed fir John of the committee for his county, to levy money to pay their army. He died in 1647, having married twice, firft, Philippa, daughter of Rob Sydney, earl of Leicefter, by whom he had only a daughter, named Dorothy; and fecondly, Fra eldeft daughter of John Egerton, firft earl of Bridgewater, by this lady he had 9 children, all of whom died infants, except a daughter, who was the fecond wife of her firft coufin John Hobart, fon of fir Miles Hobart, knt who by the failure of heirs male became fucceffor to the title of baronet, and, by this marriage, poffeffor of the feat of Blickling. But as the

hiftory

NUM. XI

Hobarts

Sir Miles Ho-
bart, knt 2nd
fon of fir Hen.}
Hobart, 1ft
bart.

hiftory of that knight is remarkable, I fhall particularly fpeak of him.

Sir Miles, the youngeft fon of fir Henry Hobart, the firft baronet, was born at Plumfted,
april 12, 1595, and knighted by k. Ja. I. at Salifbury, aug. 8, 1623, and created a knight of
the Bath in 1625: he was a member in that parlement which was called march 17, 1627-8, where
he diftinguifhed himfelf by oppofing the defigns of
the court; and, march 2, 1628-9, he, with feveral
other members, forcibly held the fpeaker of the
houfe of Commons in the chair, and locked the
doors, to prevent the parlement's being diffolved,
before they had publifhed a proteftation, declaring, that ' whoever fhould bring in innovation of
' religion, or by favor or countenance feek to
' extend or introduce popery and arminianifm, or
' difagreeing from the truth and orthodox church,
' fhall be reputed a capital enemy to this king-
' dom and commonwealth. 2. Whoever fhall
' counfel or advife the taking and levying of the
' fubfidies of tonnage and poundage, not granted
' by parlement, or fhall be an actor or inftrument
' therein, fhall be likewife reputed an innovator
' in the government, and capital enemy to the
' kingdom and commonwealth. 3. If any mer-
' chant, or perfon whatfoever, fhall voluntarily
' yield or pay the faid fubfidies of tonnage and
' pourdage, not being granted by parlement, he
' fhall likewife be reputed a betrayer of the liber-
' ties of England, and an enemy to the fame.'
For this he was imprifoned, and he did not regain
his liberty until 1631, and his death, which followed not long after, was occafioned by the blows
his keeper, Rich Plumley, efq. gave him, and
for which, it is faid, Plumley was made admiral
of the irifh feas. His memory was fo grateful to
the patriots, that in 1646, a vote paffed the houfe

of

of Commons, to pay his children 5000 l. as some recompence for the sufferings he had endured by this severity. Sir Miles, by Susan, the daughter of sir John Peyton, bart. had sir John Hobart, the 3d baronet, of whom hereafter, and Alice, married to sir John Jermy, of Bayfield, in Norfolk, knt.

Sir John Hobart, bart. who married the patriot's daughter, the widow of col. Hammond, was created a knight of the Bath; and by the death of his uncle of both his names, without male issue, became the 3d bart. Like his father and uncle, he was by no means pleased with arbitrary power, but he was equally averse to a republic; his aim was to see monarchy limited by law: these were the sentiments of the county of Norfolk, which returned him a member of parlement in 1654, when only 19 years of age. but interest and honor are powerful motives; they change our thoughts, however seemingly fixed: he, who had opposed as much as possible the cromwelian interest, no sooner allied himself to that family, than he forsook his former ideas, and became strenuous for, and attached to, the new sovereign*.

Sir John Hobart, 3d bart. cousin by marriage to Oliver ld. protector and one of his lords.

---

* Several of the Hobarts continued eminently loyal during the whole of the interregnum; amongst whom was Edm. Hobart, of Holt, in Norfolk, gent. descended from sir H. Hobart, lord-chief-justice of the Common-Pleas, who intended to have effected an insurrection in favor of the exiled king, in concert with some of the gentlemen of his county. but the plan not succeeding, he was obliged to secrete himself three days upon the top of a currier's house, in Holt, where the fuel was kept, and with difficulty escaped to London, where he hired himself to an honest loyal shoemaker, with whom he worked until the restoration. He once was near being discovered by the wife of one of Oliver's colonels, from the whiteness of his hands, she telling him ' those hands have not been used to shoemaker's ' wax, perhaps,' continued she, ' you may be some roguish ' cavalier;' to whom he pertinently replied, ' I must confess ' to your good ladyship, that I am an idle fellow; for which

' reason

NUM XI

H parts

This conduct, however, did not work any alteration in his relations, or in his conftituents, who had fhewed him peculiar regard; for they, difgufted with his alliance, openly reproached him with having married ' the *king's gaoler's widow*, who ' was not worth a groat,' which latter circumftance, had it been true, would have been the greateft proof of col Hammond's virtue. But the grant the parlement had made him, as well as the riches of the Hammonds, feems to forbid a belief to this poverty; the protector, however, amply made up for any deficiency of fortune, if any fuch there was; and though many, perhaps moft, of the freeholders in Norfolk were difpleafed with him, yet the fupport of the fovereign, aided by his own intereft, procured him again to be returned their member in the parlement affembled in 1656, the following year he was called up to the protector's houfe of lords, jan. 27, 1659-60, he, with lord Richardfon and fir Horatio Townfhend, bart. delivered a petition into the houfe of Commons in behalf of Norfolk, praying that the fecluded members might be reftored After the reftoration, he again defcended to the houfe of Commons; and in the three laft parlements in the reign of k. Cha. II. he was likewife one of the reprefentatives for that county which had formerly chofen him He had the honor to entertain his majefty king Cha II. at his feat of Blickling. but that fovereign fhewed evident marks of of his not deeming him his friend during the time of his dining there, as tradition fays; a circum-

' reafon my mafter employs me in carrying out work.' Upon k. Cha. II's return, he took his mafter from Turn-ftyle, Holborn, to his feat at Holt, and maintained him there as long as he lived. John Hobart, efq returned member for the city of Norwich in Oliver's parlements called in 1653 and 1656, and Richard's in 1658-9, was a fworn enemy ' to the ' protectorate and godly party.'

ftance by no means difadvantageous to the character of fir John. By Ruth, the patriot's daughter, he had four fons and two daughters. By
his laft lady, the daughter of fir John Hobart,
the preceding baronet, he had only one fon, who
died immediately after his mother: fhe fell a
martyr to the fmall pox, leaving the moft amiable of characters. The iffue of the firft marriage
was, 1. Sir Hen. the third baronet, of whom
below. 2. James, who died in 1670, when only
9 years of age, and was buried at Blickling. 3.
John, a brigadier-general in the army of his late
majefty, and captain and governor of Pendennis
caftle in Cornwall; he died nov. 7, 1734, and was
buried at Blickling. 4. Tho. of Lincoln's-Inn,
who died a bachelor. 5. Philippa, who became
the firft lady of fir Cha. Pye, bart. by whom fhe
had only two daughters; and 6. Mary, who never
married.

Sir Henry Hobart, the 4th baronet, was knighted by k. Cha. II. at the time his majefty honored
fir John with a vifit at Blickling. He was member of parlement, in the 23d year of that reign,
for Lynn-Regis, was one of the members for
Norfolk at the revolution, and was one of the
firft that concurred in that change. He attended
k. Will. as gentleman of the horfe, at the battle
of the Boyne, which determined the fate of Ireland · in the 7th year of this reign, he was returned again to reprefent his own county in parlement. Moft unhappily fir Henry prematurely
loft his life in a duel with Oliver Le Neve, efq.
occafioned by fome words which came from the
latter; this misfortune happened in 1697, for
which the victor was tried, and found guilty of
manflaughter: fir Henry's body was buried at
Thetford. The nation loft a true patriot, and
moft amiable character, by his death. He mar-

Sir Henry
Hobart, 4th
bart

ried

ried the eldeſt daughter and co-heireſs of Joſeph Maynard, eſq. ſon and heir of ſir John Maynard, knt. one of the commiſſioners of the great ſeal in the reign of k. Will III. Lady Hobart re-married to the hon. Hen. Howard, eſq. brother to Geo. earl of Suffolk : this lady died of a conſumption, aug. 22, 1701 ; by ſir Hen. ſhe had one ſon, and 3 daughters. 1. Sir John Hobart, 5th boronet, created earl of Buckinghamſhire ; whoſe life appears in the following pages. 2. Henrietta, who became counteſs to Charles 9th earl of Suffolk, his lordſhip died at Bath, ſept. 28, 1733 : ſhe, ſurviving him, re-married to the hon. Geo Berkley, eſq. 4th ſon of Cha. 2nd earl of Berkley. lady Suffolk died may 28, 1767, aged 86 ; their only child was Hen. earl of Suffolk, who married may 13, 1733, Sarah, ſole daughter and heir of Tho. Inwin, eſq. member of parlement for the borough of Southwark, his lordſhip died april 22, 1745, without iſſue. His counteſs re-married to lord viſc. Falkland. 3. Cath was married to Geo. Churchill, lieut. col. of the Coldſtream regiment of guards, died commander in chief in Scotland, ſon of the admiral of that name, and brother to the great duke of Marlborough. He died at Bath, ap. 27, 1745 ; and ſhe, june 22, 1725. 4. Dorothy, who never married.

John, earl of Buckinghamſhire, was born in the year 1692 ; ſucceeded by his father's death to the title of baronet, and after ſerving as member in two parlements, he was, may 28, 1728, created baron Hobart, of Blickling, in Norfolk, and ſept 5, 1746, earl of Buckinghamſhire : his lordſhip held many moſt honorable places and emploiments, he was a privy counſellor, and knt. of the Bath ; his lordſhip died ſept. 22, 1756, having married twice, firſt, Judith, daughter of Rob.

Rob. Britiffe, of Baconfthorpe, in Norfolk, efq. recorder of the city of Norwich, which he reprefented in parlement; by this lady he had 3 fons and 5 daughters: fhe died feb 7, 1726-7, in child-bed; upon which his lordfhip re-married, feb. 10, in the following year, Eliz. fifter of Rob. Briftow, efq. one of the clerks-comptrollers of his majefty's houfehold. this countefs died in 1762, leaving two fons. The iffue of the firft marriage was, 1. Hen. who died an infant. 2. John, the prefent earl of Buckinghamfhire. 3. Rob. who died may 8, 1733, in the 8th year of his age. 4. Dorothy, married to Cha. Hotham, efq. a captain of a company, but afterwards col of the firft regiment of foot guards, and aid-de-camp to gen. Ligonier, he was fon and heir of Beaumont Hotham, efq. one of the commiffioners of the cuftoms, he has fince taken the name of Thompfon, in purfuance of the will of a relation, he is now a major-general of his majefty's forces, and groom of the bedchamber to the king, and a knight of the Bath. The fifters of Dorothy died infants. The iffue of the earl of Buckinghamfhire, by his fecond countefs, was, 5. Geo. which name he received from his royal godfather, his late majefty; he poffeffes the Ellys eftate, and was a member for St. Ives in the parlement called in 1754, and for Beer-Alfton in the late parlements. when his brother was appointed ambaffador to Ruffia, he was named fecretary to that legation. He married in may, 1757, Albina, daughter of lord Vere Bertie, eldeft fon of Rob. firft duke of Ancafter, of the 2nd marriage, by whom he has 2 fons and 3 daughters, Rob. Geo.-Vere, Albinia, Harriet and Maria, twins. 6. Henry, who married july 22, 1761, Peggy, the eldeft daughter of John Briftow, of Quiddenham, in Norfolk, efq. member of parle-

ment

ment for Arundel, and fub-governor of the fouth-fea-company.

John, the 2nd and prefent earl of Buckingham-fhire, was born in 1722, and, during the late earl's life-time, was a member of the houfe of commons for the city of Norwich, and comptroller of his majefty's houfehold; and, fince his acceffion to the title, his lordfhip has been appointed one of the lords of his majefty's bed-chamber, and a privy-counfellor; in 1762, nominated ambaffador extra-ordinary and plenipotentiary to the court of Ruffia, where he remained near 3 years; and, in 1776, his lordfhip was appointed lord lieut. of Ireland, in which government he continued 4 years. His lordfhip married firft, july 14, 1761, Mary Ann, eldeft daughter and co-heirefs of the late fir Tho. Drury, bart. The iffue of this marriage was 4 daughters; 1. Henrietta, born april 4, 1762, and married march 25, 1780, to Armar-Lowry Corry, efq. knt. of the fhire for Tyrone, in Ireland, and, in 1780, created lord Belmore, of that king-dom. 2. Caroline Hans, born feb. 24, 1767. 3. Sophia, born apr. 5, 1768. And ——, born in dec. 1769, of whom her ladyfhip died in child-bed, and was buried at Blickling, and the infant herfelf alfo is dead. The earl, fept. 24, 1770, re-married, Caroline, daughter of Will. Co-nolly, of Stratton-hall, in Staffordfhire, efq. by lady Ann, daughter of Will. earl of Staf-ford, by this countefs his lordfhip has had, 1. John, born aug. 30, 1773, and died dec. 1, 1775. 2. Hen. Phil. born feb. 11, 1775, and died feb. 15, 1776. 3. Geo. born april 2, 1777, and died in oct. following. And 4. Amelia-Ann, born feb. 20, 1772, unmarried.

Upon the death of the prefent earl, if without male iffue, the titles of earl of Buckinghamfhire, and

and baionet, will defcend to his lordfhip's half-brother, the hon. Geo. Hobart, efq. or his defcend-ants in the male-line; and it is highly probable he may alfo enjoy the Hampden eftates, amount-ing to 3000 l. per ann. which were entailed by John Hampden, of Great-Hampden, efq. the laft male heir of that family, upon the Hobarts, in failure of heirs-male in the defcendants of the late loid vifc. Hampden *.

No. XII.

The hift. of the Whalley family, allied to the protec-toral houfe of Cromwell by the marriage of Fra. daughter of fir Hen. Cromwell, knt. to Rich. Whal-ley, efq. and particularly of col. Edw. Whalley, a defcendant of this marriage, who was one of k. Cha. I.'s judges, a major-general, and one of Oliver's lords.

THE Whalleys are of great antiquity; their arms aie arg. three whales heads erafed, fable, two and one, the creft a whale's head erafed, fable. There was a gentleman of the name of Whalley, who lived in the reign of k. Hen. VI †, two of whofe fons were ——— and Gilbert,

Whalleys.

—— Whalley, efq

* The hift. of the Hammonds and Hobarts are taken fiom papers communicated to me by verv high authority, various hift. of England, Collins' and Jacobs' pecrages; Thuiloe's ftate papers, Rudder's hift. of Glouceftefhire, lift of delin-quents, political and hiftorical effays, printed in or about 1726-7, &c &c

† John Whalley, who was fheriff of the counties of Derby and Nottingham, 24th k Edw III foi 5 years, as he was alfo on the 29th of the fame reign, was probably of the family whofe hiftory is here given.

the

the eldeſt left Rich. his ſon and heir, who, by Eliz. his wife, had an only daughter named Joan; for this reaſon, by his will, dated in the firſt year of the reign of k. Rich. III. he ordered his feoffees, ſir Gervas Clifton, ſir John Babington, knt. Tho. Leek, eſq. Rich. Whalley, prieſt, and Geo. Whalley, gent. to aſſign over his manor of Darlaſton, in Staffordſhire, to his widow for her life, and, after her death, to his daughter and heireſs, Joan; but he gave all his lands in Lancaſhire to the ſons of his uncle Gilbert, mentioned above; and the feoffees fulfilled the teſtator's will.

Rich Whalley, eſq.

Rich. Whalley, eſq. who appears to be the eldeſt ſon of Gilbert, a minor at the time of his couſin Rich.'s death, was, in the 9th year of k. Hen. VII.'s reign, paſſed over by ſir Henry Willoughby, his ward, to Tho. Leek, of Kirkſton; mr. Leek, with Jane his wife, covenanted, in 18th of k. Edw. IV.'s reign, to marry Elizabeth, their daughter and heir, to this Rich. Whalley, eſq who is called of Darlaſton: the eldeſt ſon and heir of this marriage was,

Tho Whalley, eſq.

Tho. Whalley, eſq. who ſeated himſelf at Kirkſton, in Nottinghamſhire, which came from the Leeks and Kirkſtons, whoſe ſeat it had been, and continued to be that of the Whalleys for ſeveral deſcents: he married Eliz. the daughter of John Shelly, of Woodborough, in that county *, by whom he had Thomaſine, married to Arnold Preresby, eſq. and,

Rich Whalley, eſq

Rich. Whalley, eſq. his ſon and heir, was alſo ſeated at Kirkſton, he was a gallant man, and much diſtinguiſhed himſelf at the tournaments held in

* The viſitation of Nottinghamſhire calls Tho. Whalley's wife, Filia Leeke, the Leekes were of great deſcent, and poſſeſſed vaſt eſtates in that county.

the

the reign of k. Hen. VIII. which probably greatly ingratiated him into that monarch's favor, in
the 32d year of whose reign he had licence
from his majefty to purchafe of Rob. Dighton,
Hardwick, Grange, and Wood, with all its ap-
purtenances, in Ofberton, Hardwick, and Work-
fop, and the fcite of the abbey of Welbeck, and
Henry alfo, in his 37th year, granted him Sibthorpe college, fubject to the life of dr. Magnus,
the manor and advowfon of Colfton, all in Nottinghamfhire. In the firft year of the reign of
k. Edw. VI. he reprefented Scarborough in parlement; and during the fplendor of the duke
of Somerfet, in the reign of k. Edw. VI. he
had great influence, as he was nearly related
to, and much trufted by, his grace: but the
fall and ruin that overtook that great fubject,
was fenfibly felt by mr. Whalley, who was his
fteward, but to whom he proved true; for when
he was examined refpecting his grace's intention
of getting himfelf declared protector in the en-
fuing parlement, he as ftedfaftly denied it as
the earl of Rutland affirmed it: but he confeffed his own mal-practices, as receiver of Yorkfhire, that he had lent out the public money,
paid one year's revenue with arrearages of the
preceding one, purchafed eftates with the royal
treafure, and made much profit by the fall of the
current coin. Surrendering this office, he fubmitted to fuch fine as his majefty k. Edw. VI.
and his council fhould affign him, but which he
did not pay until the reign of q. Mary, when he
was obliged to make ample fatisfaction: in the
firft year of that reign he was returned to ferve in
parlement for Eaft-Grinfted, and 1ft and 2nd and
2nd and 3d of k. Phil. and q. Mary, for Nottinghamfhire · his misfortunes and imprudences involved him in debt, to the amount of the enormous

mous fum of 48,866l. 13s. 4d. but which he difcharged in the firft year of the reign of q. Eliz. by felling his fair feat and noble manor of Welbeck: after having experienced the frowns of two fovereigns, he obtained the fmiles of Eliz. who, july 3, in her 3d year, granted him the demefnes and manors of Whatton, Hawkefworth, and Taunton, with the advowfon and rectory of Hawkefworth, late belonging to fir Maurice Denus, knt. He likewife obtained the lordfhip of Touton, by purchafe, from the Sacheverels, alfo the manors of Broxtow and Cotgave, with other lands in Nottinghamfhire: his riches at one time were fuperior to moft private fubjects in the kingdom; and notwithftanding the many loffes he fuftained, he left a prodigious fortune to his defcendants. He married thrice: his firft wife was Lora, daughter of Tho. Brookman; his fecond was Urfula, and his third Barbara, who furviving him, re-married to —— Burwell, whom fhe alfo outlived, and bui t two magnificent tombs for thefe her hufbands, mr. Whalley's at Stretton, and mr. Burwell's at Sibthorpe: the former is of alabafter, and very coftly, it exhibits his effigies recumbent, very long beard, hands raifed together, his head refting upon his creft, and his feet upon a whale, in three compartments, above his figure, are his firft wife, with 4 children; the fecond, his wife Urfula, with 11; and the third, as his laft wife, with 4; fo that he had 19 children by the three: round the verge of the altar ftone is, ' Here lyeth ' Ric. Whaley, efq. who lived all the age of 84 ' yeares, & ended this life the 23 of november, ' 1583:' at the weft end is T. W. fhield of arms and creft, and a coronet, in grateful memory of the patent defigned by k. Edw. VI. to create him earl of Nottingham, but which either his conduct, or that fovereign's death, prevented: and the effigies

gies of his eldeſt ſon, kneeling; round the top
are the initials of his wives names, L. W. V. W.
and B. W. with theſe lines beneath:

> Behold his wives were number three,
>   Two of them died in right good fame,
> The third this tomb erected ſhee,
>   For him that well deſerv'd the ſame,
> Both for his life and godly end,
> W^{ch} all that knew muſt needs commend,
> Since time brings all things to an end;
> And they y^t know not, yet may ſee,
> A worthy Whalley loe was he.

The children of the three marriages are not
given, except Tho. the eldeſt ſon by his firſt wife,
of whom below, Will. the heir of the ſecond, who
married Barbara, the ſiſter of his eldeſt brother
Tho.'s wife, by whom he had an only daughter, who
took one moiety of the lordſhip of Willoughby to
the family of Yarborough, and three of his daughters, one of whom became the lady of ſir John
Zouch, of Codnor, another married to a Belling-
ham; a third to John Nevil, of Grove, who was alſo
ſervant to the great duke of Somerſet, and on whoſe
account he himſelf ſuffered impriſonment in the
Tower, this Nevil had conſiderable grants of lands
belonging to the ſuppreſſed religious houſes. the
other children of mr. Whalley obtained moſt reſpectable alliances.

Tho Whalley, eſq. the eldeſt ſon and heir of
Rich. by his firſt wife, married Eliz. daughter
and co-heir of Henry Hatfield, of Willoughby,
in Nottinghamſhire, eſq. by Alice, one of the 8
ſiſters and co-heirs of ſir John Hercy, knt. but
which Alice re-marrying to —— Markham, eſq.
by whom having a ſon, none of Hercy's inheritance came to the Hatfields Mr. Whalley died
the year before his father, leaving, by Eliz his
wife, ſeveral ſons and daughters. 1. Rich. who
married the plot. Oliver's aunt. 2 Walter

Whalley,

Whalley, D. D. of Waterville, or Cherry-Or-
ton, he was educated at Pembroke-hall, in Cambridge, and married Eliz. daughter of Will
Howell, of Cambridge, by whom he had Walter,
John, and Eliz. 3 John, who died unmarried,
in june 1638. 4. Tho. educated in Trinity college, in Cambridge; he died a bachelor, in may,
1637; both of whom are buried at Screveton, in
the south ayle of which church is a grave-stone
to protect their remains. 5. Mary, wife of Arnold Reresby. 6. Ellen, who was married to
Tho. Draper, of Flintham, in Nottinghamshire,
by whom she had a son, Rich. Draper, who married the widow of Tho. Whalley, the eldest
grandson of this Tho. and several other daughters.

Richard
Whalley,
esq uncle
by mar to
Oliver lord
prot.

Rich. Whalley, esq. the uncle by marriage to
the prot. Oliver, succeeded his grandfather of his
names; he was a member in the parlement called
in the 43d year of q. Eliz.'s reign, for Boroughbridge, and was sheriff of Nottinghamshire, and
served that office with greater state than any of his
predecessors.   Unfortunately, he involved himself in many lawsuits, which, though he was a
person of the best capacity, and sedulous in business, much lessened his fortunes when in the decline of life, so that, notwithstanding he had added
some estates to those left him by his grandfather,
yet he was obliged to part with many more.   Q
Eliz. permitted him, and Will. Whalley, gent.
to alienate the house and scite of the monastery of
Welbeck, by the name of the manor of Welbeck,
and the two granges Bellers and Hurst, and the
grange of Gledthorpe, and the manor of Norton,
and the grange called Hardwicke-Grange, to
Edw. Osborne, citizen and clothworker, of London, and having first inclosed, he mortgaged, and
in the end was obliged to sell, the lordship of
Sibthorpe, with other lands in Canolston, Hawkes-
worth,

worth, and Flintham, which were only a collateral fecurity with Sibthorpe; nor were thefe, though very great, the only facrifices he made. He had three wives, Ann, daughter of Geo. Horfley, of Digfwell, his fecond was Fra. daughter of fir Hen. Cromwell, of Hinchinbrooke, knt. grandfather of the prot. Oliver, and the third was Jane, daughter of —— Stirap, who re-married to Edw. Coleby. mr. Whalley had only children by the fecond, the protector's aunt; they were, 1. Tho. 2. Edw. one of k. Cha. I.'s judges, and 3. Henry, the judge advocate; whofe hiftories will be given when we have gone through the eldeft branch.

Tho. Whalley, efq. who died in the life-time of his father, he married Mary, daughter of fir Tho. Penifton, knt. fhe re-married to Rich. Draper, of Flintham, efq. by whom fhe had Whalley Draper, married to Rob. Butler, the parents of a fon of both their names. Mr. Tho. Whalley had only 3 children; Penifton Whalley, efq. of whom prefently, Martha, who died unmarried in 1624; and Eliza, married to Will. Ayloft, of Bafingbourne, efq. by whom fhe had no child.

Thomas Whalley, efq. firft coufin to Oliver lord prot.

Penifton Whalley, of Screveton, efq. born in 1624, who, as a minor at his grandfather's death, was under ward to his relation Rich. Draper, efq. he was fufpected, in 1654, of difaffection to Oliver the prot. for which he was ordered up to London, and underwent an examination, but as nothing appeared againft him, he was fet at liberty; however, it occafioned his exclufion from parlement in 1656, at which time he was one of the reprefentatives for Nottinghamfhire, but, in the following year, he fo far regained his highnefs's good opinion, that he was appointed one of the commiffioners of affeffment for his own county, at that time he

Penifton Whalley, efq. 1ft coufin, one remove, to Oliver lord prot.

lived

lived in a very elegant manner, keeping his coach; he survived the restoration, and pleading the hardships he had suffered for the royal cause, he was set down in the catalogue of those who were to have been created a knight of the Royal-Oak, at which time his estate was estimated at 1200l. per annum, which was but inconsiderable to what his ancestors had enjoyed, and even he himself began life with, but this that was left soon dwindled away to nothing: he sold his manor of Screveton, in Nottinghamshire, to Tho. Thoroton, citizen of London, whose son Tho. was recorder of Lincoln, and elder brother of dr. Thoroton, the historian of the county. His moiety of Willoughby he sold to sir Will. Willoughby, bart. But all his sacrifices could not keep him from a prison, for he died in London, confined for debt, attributing all his misfortunes as happening from the judgment of heaven, for his cruelty to mr John James, of Exeter College, Oxford, the ejected minister of Flintham, as he himself expressed, in a letter he wrote to that unfortunate gentleman, declaring himself guilty of a great crime in having been his enemy, and owning that the hand of God was ' justly upon him for it ' Peniston died in 1672, aged 48; he married Marg. daughter and sole heir of Geo. Ireland, eldest son and heir of sir Tho. Ireland, of Beausey, near Warrington, knt. the seat of the Butlers, in Lancashire, descended of an ancient family, seated at Hut, in that county, and dying in oct. 1669, aged 76, was buried at Screveton, where his daughter, mrs. Whalley, laid down a grave stone; in the inscription upon which, his loyalty is mentioned: she herself died sept. 10, 1675, having survived her husband, Mr. Whalley. The issue of Peniston, by this lady, was only two daughters and co-heirs, Eliz born in 1654, and married in 1672 to the rev. Tho. Hall, presented

to

to the rectory of Screveton, in 1674, and Margaret, born in 1656, and was living, and unmarried, in 1672. Mr. Hall obtained, partly by alliance, and partly by purchase, two manors in Colston, with the vicarage of that place, which had long been enjoyed by the Whalley family; but in 1670 Will duke of Newcastle obtained possession by virtue of an extent, but after his grace's death they reverted to the heirs of Peniston, by a decree, I believe, of Chancery. Having taken the eldest branch of this family, I now return to Edw. 2nd son of Rich. Whalley, esq. by Fra. aunt to the prot. Oliver.

Edw. Whalley, esq. was brought up to merchandize, Heath says, he was put apprentice to a woollen-draper, some other writer calls him a broken clothier, a thing almost impossible, when the grandeur and wealth of his family and father are considered; another writer, no more a friend than Heath to him, acknowledges that he was a merchant, so that we may suppose this one of the many misrepresentations of that virulent writer. Whether he was actually engaged in traffic at the commencement of the civil wars, is uncertain; but no sooner did the quarrel between k. Cha. I. and his parlement blaze out, than he (though in the middle age of life) took up arms in defence of the liberty of the subject, and this in opposition to the sentiments of his nearest relations: probably his religious opinions determined him as much, or more, than any other consideration, as he was a rigid puritan: and though the usage of arms must be new to him, yet he early distinguished himself in the parlement service, in many sieges and battles, but in none more than in the battle of Naseby, in 1645, in which he charged, and entirely defeated, two divisions of Langdale's horse, though supported by pr. Rupert, who commanded

Col Edw. Whalley, one of k Cha I 's judges, a maj gen and one of the prot Oliver's lords, to whom he was first cousin.

the

the reserve; for which the parlement, jan. 21, 1645-6, voted him to be a colonel of horse. He also was greatly instrumental in obtaining the defeat of lord Goring, in Somersetshire, and was the commander of the horse at the siege of Bristol, when pr. Rupert surrendered it up; from whence he was sent to prevent the royal garrison in Oxford from marching out of that city, which he having effectually prevented, he was dispatched to Banbury; and, may 9, 1647, they gave him the thanks of the house, and 100l. to purchase two horses, for his brilliant action at that place, which he took by storm, and afterwards marched to Worcester, which city surrendered to him july 23 following· his successful bravery procured him the hatred of the fanatics (who accused him of being a presbyterian) at the head of whom was Hugh Peters, whom he threatened to cane. The commons granted him, feb. 3, 1647-8, for his arrears, at the rate of fifteen years purchase, the manor of Flawborough, part of the estate of the marquis, afterwards duke, of Newcastle, the annual rent of which was 410l. 2s. the overplus of the value, after satisfying the arrears, to be paid into the treasury. mr. Whalley pretended that the marq. of Newcastle's father had purchased it of his father for a small part of its value. Cromwell confided so much in him, that he committed the person of the king to his care, the loyalists have charged him with severity to his royal prisoner, but the monarch himself, in a letter he left behind him, when he made his escape, fully exculpates him from that charge. It is generally supposed that his majesty did not effect an escape through his inattention, but that he was led to attempt a flight by his and Cromwell's contrivance, having frightened the king with an idea that his person was not safe in the army, Charles himself indeed says that it was not the case, but it appears to be fo. He did not always, however, give the king fatisfaction, for when capt. Sayers, june 12, 1647, waited upon his majefty to give him back the enfigns of the order of the garter, belonging to the late pr. of Orange, the king walking backwards and forwards along the room with mr. Sayers, raifed the jealoufy of mr. Whalley, who did not approve of this conference; he therefore interpofed; upon which the exafperated monarch pufhed him away with both his hands, and in indignation of the affront, raifed his cane to the colonel's head, and fome fay, ftruck him, but lord Clarendon fays, the king did not go to that extremity. his lordfhip adds, that the army were far from being difpleafed at his majefty's conduct in punifhing his infolence. He was the abject tool of Cromwell's ambition, perhaps without his own knowledge, who employed him in carrying all the petitions of the army to the parlement, to prepare them for the tragic death of the king, one of whofe judges he was, and the warrant for whofe execution he figned. At the battle of Dunbar, fought fept. 3 1650, he, with Monk, commanded the foot, and greatly contributed to completely defeat the fcotch army; and here he exhibited the greateft proofs of valor, having his horfe fhot twice under him; the laft fhot was fatal to the creature, but mounting another, he followed in the purfuit, though he had received a cut in his wrift. Cromwell left him in Scotland, with the rank of commiffary-general, and gave him the command of four regiments of horfe, with which he performed many actions that gained him great honor.

He continued a fteady friend to his coufin Oliver, after he had raifed himfelf to the fovereignty, and was entrufted by him with the government of the

counties of Lincoln, Nottingham, Derby, Warwick, and Leicester, by the name of major-general, an important office, in which he was so af-
fiduous, that, as he himself says, he did not leave
a vagrant in a whole county. He was one of the
representatives for Nottinghamshire, in the parlements held in 1654 and 1656, the protector made
him commissary-general for Scotland, and called
him up to his other house. This last honor was
so acceptable to him, and he was so fond of it, that
it betrayed him into some improprieties. Col.
Ashfield having spoken very discontentedly of this
new house, in a conversation with him in West-
minster-hall, it so much hurt him, that he even
threatened to cane the colonel, who setting him at
defiance, was, instead of a bastinadoing, complained of to the protector · his highness so highly
valued his relation, as to tell the colonel, that unless he asked pardon, he would cashier him for
speaking disrespectfully to his superior officer, but
he petitioning, that he might have a fair hearing,
the protector consented to it, at least he permitted him to say what he pleased before such officers
as he could depend upon, who adjudged him to acknowledge his fault, and ask pardon of *my lord*
Whalley, but this the resolute colonel absolutely
refused to do. This was at least the second challenge he had received, for in 1647, mr. Murray
sent him a written one, which he declined accepting, and complained of it to the parlement, who
having read it, ordered mr. Murray into custody.
These things are no ways derogatory to his courage,
which was confessedly great, but shews how much
he and his party adhered to their religious sentiments, which strictly forbid their accepting a challenge, it is to be wished that those, who have in
other respects better ideas of religion, would equally abstain from risking their lives about trivial,
unimportant

unimportant difputes, by which they often put themfelves in competition with the moft worthlefs, it certainly is no mark of cowardice to refufe a challenge, when they who dare engage their enemies in the field in the moft gallant manner, do not think it neceffary to accept one.

He was looked upon with jealoufy by the parlement, after the refignation of Rich. the protector, efpecially, as he leaned fo much to the intereft of the army; for this reafon, when the rump was reftored, they took from him his commiffion, this ftill endeared him the more to the army, which, when Monk's conduct began to be dubious, deputed him one of their commiffioners, to agree to terms of peace and amity with that of Scotland, but Monk, who knew his hatred to the royal family, and how much reafon he had to dread their return, abfolutely refufed to treat with him. The reftoration of monarchy foon after becoming vifible, he faw the danger of his fituation, for befides the lofs of the eftate of Sibthorpe, which had been poffeffed by his family, but fold by one of them to the earl, afterwards duke of Newcaftle, of whofe truftees he had purchafed it, when that nobleman was obliged to leave the kingdom, and all his other eftates, efpecially the manors of Weft-Walton, and Torrington, in Norfolk (part of q. Henrietta-Maria's jointure), which he had purchafed, and with whatever other eftates he had he knew would be forfeited, and even his life would be offered up, to the fhrine of that king, whom he had condemned to death, he therefore prudently retired. Sept. 22, 1660, a proclamation was publifhed, fetting forth, that he had left the kingdom, but as there was great reafon to fuppofe, that he and col. Goffe, another of the king's judges, who had married a daughter of his, and had retired with him, were returned, 100l. was offered to difcover either of them,

in

in any of the britiſh dominions, and cauſe them to be brought alive, or dead if they made any reſiſtance. Government was probably miſtaken, in ſuppoſing they had returned, for they arrived july 27, 1660, in America, with teſtimonials from the miniſters of their faith; mr. Tho. Goodwin ſigned his, and mr. John Rowe, and mr. Sethwood, his ſon-in-law's: inſtead of concealing themſelves, they waited upon mr. Endicot, the governor of Boſton, who received them very courteouſly, and they were viſited by the principal perſons of the place, and amongſt others, col. Crown, a moſt loyal gentleman, they that day took lodgings, and reſided generally at Cambridge, four miles from Boſton, and attended all the religious rites of the place on ſundays, faſts, thankſgiving, and lecture days, and were admitted to the ſacrament, as well as private meetings of devotion; they alſo made excurſions to the neighbouring towns, and were frequently at Boſton, where they were once inſulted, but the perſon guilty of the affront, was bound to his good behaviour: their grave, ſerious, and devout deportment, and the rank they had held, procured them reſpect, but, when it was certainly known, that they were expreſsly excepted out of the act of indemnity (which did not arrive there until the laſt day of november in that year), not only they, but thoſe of the government, who had treated them with diſtinction, were juſtly alarmed, however, pity and compaſſion prevailed upon ſome, and they were promiſed protection by a part of the general court, others more prudently adviſed them, to remove to a place of more privacy, and conſequently ſafety the governor, feb. 22, 1660-1, called a court of aſſiſtance, to conſult about ſecuring them, but it was not agreed to, however, finding it improper to continue longer there, they left Cambridge the 26th of that month, and came to New-Haven, march 7, where they were treated with great refpect, by both the minifters and magiftrates of that town, and they flattered themfelves that they were free from every danger, but in a few days news arrived of his majefty's proclamation, which obliged him to abfcond; it was happy for them that they did, as capt. Breedan, having feen them in Bofton, informed the court of it upon his return to England, a warrant was iffued march 8, by the governoi and affiftants, to fecure them, which was fent to Springfield, and other towns in the weftern parts of the colony; yet, they appeared at Milford in the day-time, ard retired in the night to New-Haven, and lay concealed in the houfe of mr. Davenport, the minifter of that town, thus they lived until april 30, about which time they were greatly fhocked at hearing that ten of thofe who had alfo fat in judgment upon the late king, were executed, and that the govtrnor had received a royal mandate, dated march 5, 1660, to caufe them to be fecured: they were now in great danger, as two zealous loyalifts were fent through the colonies as far as Manhados, to feize them, but their friends informing them of it, they had time to withdraw from mr Davenport's to one Jones's, where they concealed themfelves until may 11, when they removed to a mill, and from thence upon the 13th, into the woods, where they met Jones and two of his companions, who, for their greater fafety, humanely conducted them to a place called Hatchet-harbour, where they lay two nights, until a cave, or hole in the fide of a hill, was prepared to conceal them: to this hill they gave the name of Piovidence, wheie they continued from may 15 to june 11, fometimes in the cave, but in very tempeftuous weather, in an houfe near it. They cannot be enough commended for the noble man-

ner

ner in which they acted towards mr. Davenport,
and their other friends, for when the meſſengers
ſent to ſecure them, diſcovered that they had been
at mr. Davenport's, and that he was ſuſpected of
ſtill concealing them, diſregardful of their fate,
and though their three friends were moſt true to
them, they reſolved to go to New-Haven, and acquaint the deputy-governor, mr. Leete, with their
arrival, which they did, but he took no notice of
it: many of their friends, when they ſaw them determined to deliver themſelves up, requeſted them
rot to ſurrender, in conformity more to theſe ſo-
licitations, than to prolong a wretched exiſtence,
they (after ſhewing themſelves in New-Haven,
which ſufficiently exculpated mr. Davenport)
retired, june 24, to their cave in the woods, where
they remained until aug. 19, ſometimes venturing
to a houſe near the cave, and when the ſearch for
them was very much abated, they ventured to go
to the houſe of one Tomkins, near Milford, where
they remained two years, but never ſo much as
vent into the orchard, however, after that time
finding little inquiry after them, they took more
liberty, making themſelves known to ſeveral perſons, in whom they could confide, and each of
them frequently prayed, and alſo exerciſed, i. e.
preached at private meetings in their chamber. In
1664 they were again moſt juſtly alarmed by his
majeſty's commiſſioners coming to Boſton, they
therefore again retired to their cave, where they
continued for 8 or 10 days, but unluckily ſome indians in hunting, diſcovered their bed, &c. in the
cave, and reporting it, they found it expedient to
leave their retreat, wherefore, oct. 13, in that year,
they removed to Hadley, near 100 miles diſtant,
travelling only by night, where mr. Ruſſel, the
miniſter of the place, had previouſly agreed to receive them, here they remained as long as they
                                              lived,

lived ; very few perfons in the colony knowing that
they were there. The time of mr. Whalley's death
is not known ; but it happened fome time before
the year 1679 · the tradition of Hadley is, that two
perfons unknown were buried in the minifter's
cellar, he was no lofer by them, for they conftantly
received yearly remittances from England : thofe
perfons who knew their retreat, made them frequent prefents, Rich. Saltonftall, efq. who was in
the fecret, when he left the country to go to England, in 1672, gave them 50l. and mr. Goffe, in
his journal, mentions feveral other donations of
their friends. Such hardfhips as thefe muft hurt
the feelings of any, how much foever they may
diflike their political fentiments, and they muft
pity the condition of two gentlemen, who had
held the rank of nobles, and poffeffed very great
power, being obliged for many years to live in
conftant fear, often in a cavern, and almoft conftantly confined to a private wretched apartment,
depending upon precarious remittances and bene-
factions, deprived of the comforts of affociating
with their families, friends, and almoft debarred
human converfe. Happily for themfelves, they efteemed each other, mr. Goffe ftrongly defcribes
their mutual regard and friendfhip, under fuch
uncommon misfortunes how much better was
the lot of their brethren, the king's judges, who
efcaped to Switzerland, where they lived refpected
and protected, if we except one or two, who were
affaffinated by the procurement of fome of the
royal family Thefe unfortunates were not without
the only confolation of the miferable—hope, theirs
was as chimerical as fallacious, their greateft
expectations were from the fulfilling of the pro-
phecies, not doubting that the execution of the
judges, was the flaying of the witneffes, and they
were much difappointed, when the year 1666 had

paffed

paſſed without any remarkable event; but they flattered themſelves, that the chriſtian æra might be erroneous: how ſtrangely does fanaticiſm blind the judgment of its votaries, of men of the world, who in other reſpects were well informed and ſenſible! Their greateſt pleaſure was in having conſtant, and the beſt intelligence from England, in other reſpects their comforts muſt have been very circumſcribed; their journal for ſix or ſeven years contains little more than the events of the town, the church, and the families in the neighbourhood: poor ſubjects for men who had held moſt conſiderable places in the victorious army, and ſenate of their relation the prot. Oliver. They were in conſtant affright, though they hoped, that after ſome time, all inquiry would ceaſe: eſpecting them, and they received with much ſatisfaction, the intelligence that they were ſuppoſed to have been killed with other judges in Switzerland nothing probably could have ſupported them through their misfortunes, but, the dread of the horrible puniſhment inflicted upon traitors, and which they would, had they been taken, have experienced in the fulleſt manner, and being held up as the vileſt malefactors, to be inſulted by an enraged populace, for they confeſs that ‘ their lives were miſerable, and ‘ conſtant burdens,’ as they were ‘ baniſhed from ‘ all human ſociety.’ Of mr. Whalley ✝, I ſhall only ſubjoin that his valor, and military knowledge were confeſſedly great, his religious ſentiments wild and enthuſiaſtic, from a merchant's counter, to riſe to ſo many, and ſuch high offices in the ſtate, and to conduct himſelf with propriety in them, ſufficiently evinces, that he had good abilities; nor is his honeſty queſtioned by any,

---

✝ See a further hiſtory of col Goffe, amongſt Oliver the prot's lords at the end of the next volume

which,

which, as one of the king's judges, and a major-general, would lay him open to a very narrow ſcrutiny. Sir Philip Warwick does not ſeem to do him juſtice, when he calls him ‘ a ridiculous ‘ phanatic, as well as a crack-brained fellow; ‘ though he was,’ continues the knight, ‘ a gentle-‘ man of good family .’ however ridiculous he was in his religious ſentiments, there are no reaſons to ſuppoſe his head otherwiſe diſordered

The major-general married the ſiſter of ſir Geo. Middleton, knt. who was as great an enemy to k Cha I. as he was a friend to k. Cha. II. * She died either in, or juſt before 1662, he had ſeveral children, what became of them is unknown, ex-cept mrs Goffe, and John, his eldeſt ſon and heir, who was a coronet of horſe, and who was returned a member of parlement for the town of Notting-ham in 1658-9, and alſo for the borough of Shore-ham, at the reſtoration government owed him 151l 13s. 4d but which, probably, he was never paid : it appears by his ſiſter, mrs. Goffe's letter, that he was gone abroad in 1662.† He married

---

* Sir Geo. Middleton, knt. though one of the ſervants of k Cha J eſpouſed the parlement intereſt, and was made capt. of 1 troop of horſe , not valuing tne lucrative places he then held in the court, he run all the lengths of the diſaffected, and ſubmitted to tne uſurpation of Oliver, but was won by k Cha. II for whom he acted as a ſpy upon the protector, but was de-tected, his perſon ſeized, his eſtates ſequeſtered, he was tried in april, 1656, and condemned , but, through the earneſt en-treaty of his ſiſter Whalley, he was ſpared , and, leaving the kingdom, he more openly ſided with the exiled king, by whom he was highly honored and truſted He had two ſons killed in the prot Oliver's ſervice, in Ireland , another was ſent by his highneſs to Jamaica.

† There was a John Whalley, gent. who, by his will, dated aug 20, 1664, diſpoſed of his eſtates in Bury and Wiſtow, in Huntingdonſhire, to his ſiſter Hampſon and her children, at the diſcretion of his ſiſter Eliz. Wingfield, and couſin John Blew.

the

the daughter of fir Herbert Springate, knt. by
whom he had Herbert Whalley, efq. his eldeft
fon and heir, who, though k. Cha. II granted the
manor the parlement had given to the major-general, to the duke of Newcaftle, to whom it once
belonged, with all the reft of his own lands, forfeited to the crown by any of the purchafers, yet this
Herbert Whalley, efq. was, in 1672, in poffeffion
of fome of the paternal inheritance of the Whalleys, particularly Sibthorpe, which, though forfeited to the crown, and granted to the duke of Newcaftle, was found to have been mortgaged to fir
Arnold Waring (probably a truftee for the Whalley family), and which, through affignments or
heirfhips, became vefted in this Herbert.

Hen Whalley,
efq. judge-
ac meate, firt
coufin to O ver,
lord protector

Henry Whalley, brother of the major-general,
was an alderman of London, probably; he had
been an advocate in the parlement army, and from
the regard his coufin Henry Cromwell, lord-deputy, had for him, was promoted to the office of
judge-advocate of the armies in England and Scotland; before he was fettled in that poft, he, in a
letter to his highnefs the protector, dated from Edinburgh, march 8, 1654-5, intreated a line or two,
to inform him, whether he might promife himfelf
a conftant employment there, or know whether
he was to return, that he might at laft fettle himfelf, his family, and affairs, for the reft of his life;
concluding, ' I chearfully fubmitting to what
' the Lord fhall put into your heart therein '
He continued in Scotland during the remainder of the protectorate of Oliver, and, in the
year 1656, reprefented the fheriffdom of Sel-
kirk and Peebles in the britifh parlement, and
was one of thofe who figned the order for
proclaiming his coufin Rich. lord protector
what befell him after the reftoration I have no
where

where ſeen, nor what family he left, or what became of them.

* The Whalleys, whom I have met with in the hiſtories of
England, during the government of k. Cha. I. the commonwealth, and the prots. Oliver and Rich beſides ſuch as are
given above, are, Cha Whalley, of Cheſhire, eſq whoſe delinquency was diſcharged june 30, 1649, having been rated at
268l 10s. and he reſtored to the good graces of the houſe of
commons, he was member for the city of Cheſter, in 1654,
and one of the aſſeſſors in 1657 for that city, of which he was
recorder, it is reaſonable to ſuppoſe he was not ſatisfied with
the protector's government judge-admiral Whalley, lieut.
Whalley, who ſerved in Hacker's regiment, Rob. Whalley,
quarter-maſter, Will. and Stanhope Whalley, both of Norton, in the county of Leiceſter, eſqrs one of them had an
eſtate of 1000l. a year, and was to have been a knight of the
royal oak, had that title been eſtabliſhed, Peter Whalley,
gent member of parlement, in 1654, for the town of Nottingham, and Henry Whalley, maſter of the company of ſtationers
in 1655, ſeveral, and perhaps all of theſe, are of the major-
general's family —Theſe are ſeveral good families of the
name of Whalley in England, particularly in Lancaſhire, to
whom the title of baronet is entailed upon failure of male
iſſue of the preſent ſir John Whalley Gardiner, bart of
Billeſley, in Warwickſhire, Bernard Whalley, eſq. rebuilt
that church in 1692. The hiſtory of the Whalleys is taken
from Thoroton's antiquities of Nottinghamſhire (a defective
ibſtitute written book), viſitations of that country, ſeveral
lives of Oliver lord prot. various hiſt of Eng. particularly
thoſe of Whitlock, Clarendon, Warwick, and Heath, Thurloe's and Clarendon's ſtate papers, journals of the houſe of
commons, ordinances of the parlement, nonconformiſt memorials the late mr. Hollis's life, Blome's Britannia, baronetages, Reliquiæ Baxterianæ, Hutchinſon's hiſt. of Maſ-
ſachuſſet's-Bay, biſh. Burnet's hiſt. of the reformation, &c.

No. XIII.

*The history of the Dunchs, of Little-Wittenham, allied
to the Cromwells by the marriage of sir Will. Dunch,
knt with Mary, the youngeft daughter of sir Hen
Cromwell, knt. and aunt to the prot. Oliver.*

NUM XIII
Dunchs
Antiquity and
arms
Will Dunch,
efq

THE Dunchs were a very ancient family, and
bore for their arms, fable, a cheveron engrailed, or, between three caftles triple-towered,
argent : Will. Dunch, efq. was auditor of the
mint, both to k. Hen. VIII and k Edw. VI. and
fworn efquire extraordinary of the body of q. Elizabeth, who granted him the manor of Little-Wittenham, near Wallingford, in Berks, where he
fettled. In the 5th year of that fovereign's reign,
he reprefented the town of Wallingford in pailement, and in the 12th year of the fame reign, he
was fheriff of Berks He died may 11, 1597, and
is buried in the dormitory in Little-Wittenham
church, where there is a remarkably elegant monument erected to his memory. This Will. married Mary, daughter of Will. Barnes, of London,
efq and coheir of John Barnes, alfo of London,
efq. porter of the town and caftle of Guyfnes,
in France, and one of the privy-council there *,

---

* J. Barnes, efq was buried in the chancel of Little-Wittenham church, he died in London may 24, 1588, he left
Mary, whofe maiden name was Farington, his widow, but by
whom he feems to have had no child, he bequeathed divers
marks to the poor of the towns of Abingdon and Wallingford,
and the village of Little-Wittenham Near the monument of
J. Barnes is a brafs plate informing the reader, that Marg.
Barnes is buried beneath, who died dec 3, 1568.

fhe

she survived her husband 8 years, and was buried near him, may 13, 1605. The issue of this marriage was 2 sons, Edm. the eldest, and Walter, bred a counsellor at Gray's-Inn, he represented the borough of Dunwich in the parlements held in the 27th and 31st years of the reign of q. Eliz. He died june 4, 1594, aged 42, and is buried near his father; his mother and son placed a brass plate against the east wall of the dormitory, recording his worth, and that he married Deborah, daughter of dr. Ja. Pilkington, bishop of Durham, maternally sprung from the Kingsmills, she surviving him, re-married to sir Ja. Mervin, knt. by whom she had two sons and four daughters, Edmund; Will. who was baptized at Little-Wittenham, may 8, 1594, he succeeded to the estate at Abesbury, Wilts, and married the sister of sir John Cooper, bart he was buried at Little-Wittenham, in may 1597. Deborah, Ruth, Mary, married first to mr. Swayn, secondly, to sir John Philpot, of Compton, Hants, knt. Ann, married to —— Lambert, of Wilts, esq

Sir Edmund Dunch, knt. eldest son and heir of Will was returned a member for Wallingford, in the parlement held in the 13th year of q. Eliz.'s reign, and for Wotton-Basset in the year following, he served the office of sheriff for Berks, in the 29th and 34th years of the same reign, and again in the 1st of k. Ja. I. and in the 21st year of that sovereign, he was returned for Berks, as he was in the two parlements called in the 1st year of the reign of k. Cha. I in which year he seems to have been knighted, and probably did not live long after. He married july 30, 1576, Anna, daughter and heir of Nich Fettyplace, of Kentwood, esq of a most ancient family, and sprung

from

from the kings of Portugal *. she died jan. 19, 1627-8, aged 71, and is buried at Little-Wittenham, where she has a monument. Their issue was, 1. Edm. baptized feb. 1581-2, and buried at Little-Wittenham, april 14, 1595; 2. Sir Will. of whom presently; 3 Walter, baptized may 31, 1584, and died jan. 6, 1644-5, to whose memory his widow, Mary, daughter of ——— Hungerford, esq. out of her dear affection to him, erected a monument in 1659, in the chancel of Newington church, in Oxfordshire †; 4. John,

---

* The Fettyplaces came in with the norman conquest, one of them was gentleman usher to k. Will I. Tho Fettyplace esq as the above Anna's monument says, or John, as the baronetage gives it, married Beatrice, natural daughter of John, k. of Portugal, she first married Tho earl of Arundel; after his death, she became the 2d wife of the great Gilbert Talbot, 1st earl of Shrewsbury, the victorious general of the english forces in France, after whose decease she married John Holland earl of Huntingdon, and lastly, to Tho. or John Fettyplace, esq She had, I believe, no issue by her 1st or 3d husband, by the earl of Shrewsbury she had Ankaret, an only daughter, who died a child, and by mr. Fettyplace, a son, who was the common ancestor of Anna, the wife of Edm Dunch, esq. and the John Fettyplace, esq. created a bart. by k. Cha. II in 1661 It must be observed, that Beatrice was much beloved by her father; for, upon the death of her first husband, the king wrote, 4th k Hen V to sir John Pelham, who was a favorite of that monarch, desiring him ' to shew the lady Beatrice, his ' daughter (being deprived of her husband, the earl of Arundel) ' the same favor he had before shewn to her.' It is observable, that Charlotte, wife of Mr Fettyplace, is daughter of the late vise. Howe. by Charlotte, natural daughter of k. Geo I. and that the natural daughter of pr. Rupert married to an ancestor of lord Howe. The arms of Fettyplace are gules, two cheverons a gent.

† The descendants of Walter became opulent, and ended in the male line in Hen. Dunch, of Newington, in Oxfordshire, whose only daughter and heir, Eliz. married to sir Cecil Bishop, of Parham, in Sussex, bart.

buried

buried at Little-Wittenham, may 20, 1586, aged one year, 5. Sam. Dunch, efq who married Dulcibella, daughter and coheirefs of John Moore, ferjeant-at-law, with whom he had the manor of North-Baddefley, Hants, where his family feated themfelves *, 6. Mary, the eldeft, was baptized fept. 18, 1579, fhe firft married Will. fon and heir of Fra. Winchcombe, of Bucklebury, in Berks, efq. who died july 29, 1614, without having had any child, in the 38th year of his age, and is buried in the chancel of Little-Wittenham church, fhe re-married to fir Edw. Clarke, of Ardington, alfo in Berks, knt. whom fhe furvived 16 years, fpending the remainder of her life in widowhood, ' pioufly towards God, and confcientioufly to man.' fhe died oct. 18, 1646, and is buried near her firft hufband; 7. Elizabeth, who became the 2d wife of John Ifham, of Pitchley, in Northamptonfhire, efq. He died dec. 9, 1626; fhe aug. 6, 1657, and was buried in the chancel of Little-Wittenham church.

Sir Will. Dunch, knt. uncle by marriage to the prot. Oliver, was baptized may 25, 1578, he was member of parlement for Wallingford, in the 1ft year of the reign of k. Ja. I. and was knighted by that monarch in the fame year, at the houfe of Geo. Fortefcue, efq He was cut off at the early age of 33, jan. 22, 1611-12; in the dormitory of Little-Wittenham church, is one of the moft coftly monuments I have feen, erected to perpetuate his memory, it is of various marbles and alabafter, but much fpoiled by paint and gilding; he is reprefented in armour, and below him the effigies of his lady, both recumbent, and as large as life, and the figures of their 4 fons and 5 daugh-

Sir Will Dunch, knt uncle by marriage to Oliver lord prot.

* Vide No. xxxvii in this vol where many of the defcendants of Edm. Dunch, of North-Baddefley, efq. are given.

ters,

ters, kneeling upon the base, except two of their daughters, who are given in their grave clothes. At the top of the monument are the arms of the Dunchs, with a label of 3 points with the crest, and on each side, the arms of the Dunchs impaling the proper arms of the Cromwells, with various other bearings of that family; over his effigies is the following inscription, in letters of gold:

Gulielmo Dunchio Equiti Aurato viro

Famæ integerrimæ fidei Spectatissimæ

Spei expectatissimæ cum magno suorum

Damno et dolore defuncto Janua-

Rii 22°. 1611° ætatis vero suæ 33°.

  Parentes mœstissimi posuerunt.

Hic qui dormit Eques rem spe superavit, et annos

Consilio, Juvenis, Tempore mente Senex

Conjuge qui felix numerosa prole beatus

Qui lumen patriæ qui columenq Domus.

Hunc pietas virtus gravitas celebravit honore

Quas animi dotes fama fuisse refert

Berchia te luget te gens Cromwellia luget

Illam consilio hanc Juvit amore frui

Cum nondum patriæ, naturæ nec sat amicis

Vixerat et domino vixerat ille satis.

He married Mary, daughter of sir Henry Cromwell, knt. grandfather to the prot. Oliver,[*] her ladyship was buried at Little-Wittenham, may 26, 1617: their issue was, 1. Edm. of whom below, 2. Will baptized march 4, 1604-5, 3. Hen. both of whom died, leaving no child, 4. Walter, one of the judges of the King's Bench, he died jan. 11, 1648-9, and is buried in St Peters

* Many parts of the bridal dress of sir Will and lady Dunch, are still preserved in the family, a proof how much they prided themselves upon this alliance.

church

church in Oxford. 5 Dorothy, baptized at Little-
Wittenham, Jan. 5, 1610-11. 6. Mary, married
to Tho. Kirketon, of Thorpe-Mandeville. 7.
Ann. 8. Cath. and another whose name is unknown.

Edmund Dunch, esq. the eldest son of sir Will. Edm. Dunch,
esq created
baron Burnel,
by his first
cousin Oliver,
lord prot
and heir to Edm his grandfather, was born in 1602,
and returned a member for Wallingford, in the
parlements called by k. Cha. I. in the 3d, 15th,
and 16th years of his reign, he was a strenuous
advocate for the liberty of the subject, which occasioned him to suffer very great and severe hardships from the court; for when the book, in which
a list of such sums as several members of parlement had subscribed for k. Cha. I.'s use, was
found after the battle of Naseby, and which his
majesty had written in several parts himself, Len-
thal, the speaker of the long-parlement, addres-
sing himself to the house, said, he had perused the
book, and did not find there his own name, nor mr.
Dunch's, or mr. Whitlock's name, and he believed
the reason was, because the king had taken all from
them, it cannot therefore be wondered, that his acri-
mony was great against that sovereign. In 1641,
he signed the famous protestation; in 1643, he
took the covenant, in 1647, he was one of the
committee for Oxfordshire, to levy money upon
the delinquents' estates, and in 1648, he was one of
the protestors against the propositions for an agreement with the king. In the year 1654, and 1656,
he was returned to serve in his relation Oliver the
protector's parlements for Berks: he was much
beloved and trusted by that sovereign, who appointed him governor of Wallingford-castle, and, as a
further mark of his favor, created him a baronet,
and afterwards, apr. 26, 1658, made him a peer
of the realm, by the title of baron Burnel, of
East-Wittenham, Berks. The late lord Dacre,
having permission to examine the writings in sir

Hen. Oxendon's evidence-room, difcovered the original patent of peerage, a fac fimile of which my moft noble friend the earl of Leicefter has prefented me with, as an embellifhment to thefe volumes. After the decline of the Cromwell family, mr. Dunch retired from the public fcene, which was occafioned by his diflike to an abfolute republic, and from the jealoufy the commonwealth party entertained of him, but when, from the various revolutions that convulfed the kingdom after Rich.'s refignation, he perceived the reftoration of monarchy likely to take place, he again took an active part, and was chofen one of the committee of fafety, in 1659. this procured a good reception for himfelf and his family from k. Cha. II. probably he had fome expectation of having a new patent for his nobility, but if fo, he was difappointed, for he died a private gentleman, and was buried at Little-Wittenham, aug. 4, 1678 He married Bridget, daughter and fole heirefs of fir Anth Hungerford, of Downe-Ampney, in Gloucefterfhire. knt. * which manor was part of her large fortune, at leaft 60,000l. a prodigious fum in the laft century: by this lady he had 3 fons and 2 daughters, 1 Hungerford, of whom below —2. Hermes.—3. Hen. born 1649. —4 Eliz.—and 5. Lucy.

* Sir Anth Hungerford was defcended from fir Tho Hungerford, fpeaker of the houfe of commons, in the reign of k Edw III (being the firft whom we find to have enjoyed that high honor) and from Walter lord Hungerford, knt of the moft noble order of the garter —In the regifter of Little-Wittenham, is this entry The lady Cath died in London, fept. 4, 1697, and was buried there the 10th of the fame month Query. Was fhe the fecond wife of Edm. Dunch, efq whom he left his widow or was it a fifter of his ? The Hungerfords were averfe to the royal caufe in the reign of k. Cha I fir Edw. Hungerford was a parlement colonel, and took Warder-caftle, he had 1500l. per ann out of the lands of the countefs dowager of Rutland ; and her ladyfhip had only 500l. a year.

Hungerford

Hungerford Dunch, efq. born 1639, was member for the borough of Wallingford, at the reftoration, and he was put down in the catalogue of thofe who were to be created knights of the royal-oak, and his eftate is eftimated at 2000l. per ann. though his father was then living. He was return-ed a member for both Wallingford and Cricklade, in the parlement held in the 12th year of the reign of k. Cha. II. but made his election for the latter. He died in London, nov. 9, 1680, and his body was brought down to Little-Wittenham, and bu-ried in the vault on the north fide, upon the 13th of the fame month. He was, like his father, an amiable character. His widow was buried march 26, 1684, in the family vault, in Little-Witten-ham church, fhe is called in the regifter, truly pious, virtuous, and charitable.

Edm. Dunch, efq. fon and heir of Hunger-ford, was born dec. 24, 1657, in Little-Jermyn-ftreet, London, and baptized upon new year's day following: he joined heartily in the revolution, and was conftituted, oct. 6, 1708, mafter of the houfhold to q. Ann, and alfo to k. Geo. I. oct. 9, 1714, he was reprefentative for Cricklade, in the 1ft, 2nd, and 3d parlements of Great-Britain; for Boroughbridge in the 4th, and for Wallingford in the 5th. Mr. Dunch cut off the entail of the Wittenham eftate, and left it to his daughters: he died may 31, 1719, and was buried with his anceftors, june 4th following, his portrait is amongft thofe of the Kit-Cat-club. He married Eliz. one of the two daughters of col Godfrey, by lady Arabella Churchill, fifter to the great duke of Marlborough*, fhe died at Whitehall,

* Lady A. Churchill was maid of honor to the duchefs of York, and became the miftrefs of k Ja. II. by whom fhe had feveral children, fhe afterwards married col. Godfrey, by whom fhe had Charlotte, vifc. Falmouth, and mrs. Dunch.

much

Duncns.

Eliz elder coheiress of Edm Dunch, efq mar to fir Geo Oxenden, ba.t

much in years, and greatly refpected, their iffue was 4 daughters.

1. Eliz. married to fir Geo. Oxenden, of Dean, in Wingham, Kent, bart. member for Sandwich in many parlements; a lord of the admiralty in the reign of k. Geo. I. and a lord of the treafury in that of his late majefty *. The iffue of this marriage was 2 fons, and 2 daughters. 1. fir Hen. Oxenden, the prefent baronet, who married Martha, daughter of fir Geo. Chudleigh, bart. by whom he has had Hen. born in Albemarle-ftreet, in the parifh of St. George, Hanover-fquare, London, may 14, privately baptized there may 20, and chriftened at Little-Wittenham, july 20, 1756, now unmarried; and Ifabella, who died a child 2. Geo. Oxenden, efq who took the name of Dixwell, purfuant to the will of fir Bafil Dixwell, bart. who left him a large eftate at Brome, near Canterbury, which, as he died a bachelor, is now poffeffed by his elder brother fir Hen Oxenden, bart. 3. Dunchabella, who died apr. 6, 1732: and 4. a daughter who alfo died a child.

Harriot, 2nd coheirefs of Edm Dunch, efq mar to Rob duke of Manchefter.

2. Harriot Dunch, married apr. 3, 1735, to lord Rob. Montagu, afterwards duke of Manchefter; fhe died feb. 25, 1755, leaving Geo. the prefent duke, who was born apr. 6, 1737, and married oct. 23, 1762, Eliz. the eldeft daughter of fir Jam. Dafhwood, by whom his grace has 1. Lord Geo. born nov. 11, 1763, and died feb. 24, 1772. 2. Lord Geo.-James, born aug. 28, 1769, and died may 2 following. 3. Will. vifc. Mandeville, born oct. 21, 1771. 4. Lord Fred. born nov. 8, 1774. 5. Lady Caroline-Maria, born aug. 16, 1770, and 6. Lady Anna-Maria, born oct. 30, 1777. My lord duke, when vifc. Man-

* The Oxenden family were attached to the parlement caufe againft k. Cha. I. Sir Ja. Oxenden, knt. and Hen. Oxenden, efq. were committee-men for Kent.

deville,

deville, reprefented the county of Huntingdon, in
the parlement fummoned in 1761; and in that
year, he, with five other lords, eldeft fons of peers,
fupported the train of the prefent king, at his coronation proceffion. the duke is a privy counfellor,
lord-lieut. and cuftos rotulorum, and colonel of the
militia of Huntingdon, high-fteward of Godman-
chefter, collector of the cuftoms outwards of the
port of London, L. L. D. and was lately ambaffador to his moft chriftian majefty.

3. Cath. who died young, and unmarried.

4. Arabella, the 4th and youngeft daughter, married to Edw. Thompfon, of Marfden, in Yorkfhire,
efq. lord of the admiralty, in the reign of the late
king, member in 4 parlements for the city of York,
as alfo one of the commiffioners of the revenue in
Ireland he died in 1742, fhe was buried in Little-
Wittenham church, oct. 18, 1734, as was Arabella her only child, feb. 28, 1734-5. Sir Hen.
Oxenden, bart. and the duke of Manchefter, are
the reprefentatives of the eldeft branch of this
ancient and honorable family; and who through
the Dunchs by females, are defcended from the
kings of Portugal, and a lady who was aunt to
Oliver, and great aunt to Rich. lord protectors,
fometime fovereigns of the britifh dominions.

The feat of Little-Wittenham is ftill ftanding,
but in great decay, it adjoins to the church, and
is one of the refidences of fir Hen. Oxenden, bart.
who purchafed the other fhares of it, and the manor,
from the duke of Manchefter, and mr. Thompfon*.

Cath 3d co-
heirefs of
Edm Dunch,
efq died
young and
unmarried

Arabella, 4th
coheirefs of
Edm Dunch,
efq mar to
Edw. Thomp-
fon, efq

---

* The hiftory of the Dunchs is taken from the vifitations of
the Heralds, the parifh regifter and funeral monuments in Little-Wittenham church, which, in the moft polite manner, were
permitted to be copied by the rev. Hen Carter—(copies of the
epitaphs of the Dunchs would have been given, but they are
fo very long, fo intirely deftitute of merit, and many of them
even of fenfe, that it was thought beft not to tire the reader

with

No. XIV.

Some particulars of the Flemings, allied to the prot. Oliver by the marriage of sir Tho. Fleming, knt. with Dorothy, the youngest daughter of sir Hen. Cromwell, knt. and aunt to that sovereign.

IT is with great concern that I can obtain so very few facts relating to the history of the Flemings, though uncommon pains have been taken to gain the fullest information. Sir Tho. Fleming, knighted by q. Eliz. in 1583,* was born at Newport in the isle of Wight, and was bred to the bar, and very much distinguishing himself, was called to be a serjeant-at-law, afterwards recorder of London, solicitor-general to q. Eliz. and k. Ja. I. lord-chief-baron of the Exchequer, and lastly, lord-chief-justice of England; all which places, the inscription upon his monument says, he executed with so great integrity, justic, and discretion, ' so that his life was of all good men

with them), lives of Ol. lord prot. various hist of Eng- Willis's not parl. Rudder's hist of Gloucestershire, Fuller's worthies; Journals of the house of commons, ordinances of parlement; Rushworth's collections, Mystery of the good old cause, Neal's hist. of the puritans, Sandford's genealogical hist. Le Neve's monumenta anglicana, peerages, and baronetages I cannot but express how much I was obliged by the late lord Dacre, who was pleased to rectify several inaccuracies in the pedigree of this family, and to mr. Longmate. who made several additions to it.

* Sir Fra. Fleming was also knighted in 1583 —Tho. Fleming was called to be a serjeant-at-law in 1594, but was degraded the same year. probably he was a near relation, perhaps a son, of the judge

' desired,

defired, and his death of all lamented.' By lady Mary, who furvived him, whom he married when in the 26th year of his age, and with whom he lived 43 years, he had 8 fons and 7 daughters, of them 2 fons and 5 daughters died in his life-time. Sir Tho the lord-chief-juftice, purchafed the manor of Baddefly, in Hants, of Mr Forfter, but difpofing of it to counfellor More, he purchafed of the earl of Southampton, North-Stoneham, 4 miles from the town of Southampton. Upon his return from the northern circuit at the latter end of the harveft, he gave, what in that part of the kingdom is called a rearing-day, as he ufually did, to which his tenants were invited, and after fpending the day in feftivity, he went to bed in health, but died before morning, aug 7, 1613, at which time he was in the 69th year of his age, and was buried in North-Stoneham church, where there is a monument to his memory.

Of his defcendants I can only fay, that Eliz. one of his daughters, married Rob. Maverell, of Staffordfhire, efq. fhe died aug. 5, 1628, he, feb. 5, 1626-7, and are buried in Blore church. their only child was married to Tho lord Cromwell, vifc. Lecale, and that fir Tho. Fleming, knighted by k. Ja. I. at Newmarket, feb. 27, 1604-5, was his eldeft fon, and who married Dorothy, youngeft daughter of fir Hen. Cromwell, knt. fo that fhe was aunt to the prot. Oliver. His fon and grandfon, of both his names, poffeffed his eftate. the father, fon, and grandfon, are all buried in the church of North-Stoneham with the lord-chief-juftice.

Sir Tho Fleming, knt uncle by marriage to Oliver lord prot

The Flemings joined their family connections, in oppofing k Cha. I. Three of them diftinguifhed themfelves during the civil war. capt. Chriftopher Fleming, adjutant-general of horfe, fell in their fervice at the fiege of Oxford, in

Capt Fleming, coufin to the prot Oliver

1645,

1645; his death was occasioned partly by exceeding his orders, from eagernefs to attack the enemy, and partly by the reftivenefs of his horfe, which carried him amongft the enemy, where he received a mortal wound in his belly, by a fhot from the adverfe party. Col. Fleming, another of the family, was appointed in 1647, by gen. Fairfax, for his gallant actions, governor of Pembroke-caftle; but Mr. Poyer, who had been mayor of that place, refufed to deliver it up to him, for which reafon the parlement made an ordinance to fettle the difpute, but mr. Poyer abfolutely declined the award, and withftood both the parlement and their army; and, in 1648, routed col. Fleming, killing and taking moft of his men, and fuftained a fiege, where he fhewed the utmoft bravery and refolution, nor did he fubmit until lieut.-gen Cromwell was fent againft him, nor then, until he had expended his provifion and ammunition.

Col Fleming.

The third perfon was fir Oliver Fleming, knt [*] firft coufin, I fuppofe, to the prot. Oliver: he was appointed mafter of the ceremonies to the parlement, nov. 2, 1643, occafioned by a meffage from the lords to the houfe of commons, defiring their concurrence in an ordinance for him to execute the place of mafter of the ceremonies, and to receive the profits belonging to that office. the commons, in compliance with this meffage, having ftated that there were feveral ambaffadors, and other public minifters from foreign ftates refiding in the kingdom; and that the ordinary way of introduction, and paffing of all other public civilities were neglected, for the want of a mafter of the ceremonies, ordained (jointly with the lords in parlement affembled) that ' fir Oliver Flem-

Sir Oliver Fleming, knt mafter of tne ceremonies

---

[*] Sir Oliver Fleming does not occur amongft Whalkley's catalogue of knights made by k Cha I though there is great reafon to fuppofe him fo created by that fovereign

' ing,

' ing, knt. a perſon of great experience and in-
' tegrity in public affairs, be authorized and
' enabled to execute that place with enjoying
' ſuch allowance, rights, and privileges, as hath
' at any time, or doth belong to any maſter of the
' ceremonies,' and in the year following he was
ordered by the parlement to attend upon the
prince electro Palatine, who came into England.
Sir Oliver was confirmed in that office by the
commonwealth, and alſo by his relations the
protectors Oliver and Rich. He was no great
credit to the party who employed him, as he was
greatly involved in his circumſtances, owing very
conſiderable ſums abroad, where he had reſided:
Mr John Pell, the protector's reſident in Switzerland, in a letter to mr. ſecretary Thurloe,
dated from Zurich, ap. 1, 1656, ſays, that it
was almoſt a year ſince he had given notice, that
one Geſner, a citizen of that place, was coming
to London, to call upon ſir Oliver for ſome money lent to him whilſt he reſided there, and that
moſt of the other creditors were men of principal
note, he that was his landloid was then one of the
two burgo-maſters, and another who was alſo a
principal creditor, was a near kinſman of the firſt
ſecretary of ſtate, by theſe, he continues, it was
not difficult for the poor creditors to have their
buſineſs propoſed in the ſenate; they complained
to him that mr. Geſner had been almoſt a year
in London, and though he had once ſpoken to the
protector, yet he had not obtained any money whatever from ſir Oliver, wherefore the ſenate themſelves reſolved to write to his highneſs, and had
ſent the principal ſecretary to him, to requeſt he
would accompany it with one from himſelf, but
it is highly probable, that the creditors had very
little ſatisfaction during the government of the
protectors. At the reſtoration he loſt his place by

ſir

fir Cha. Cotterell, knt. refuming that place which he had held in the reign of k. Cha. I. M. Bourdeaux, the french ambaffador, accufed him in 1656, upon his return into France, to mr. Lockhart, his highnefs's ambaffador, with being a penfioner to Spain; to which mr. Lockhart replied, he believed, that if either the french or fpaniards did entertain penfioners there, they would endeavour to beftow their penfions upon perfons better interefted at court than he was: but it appears from Whitlock, that he had fome influence with the elder protector, whom he perfuaded to receive the fwedifh ambaffador when he had been kept fo long, that he was going to abruptly leave the kingdom. To this fhort relation of this family, I fhall add, that the feat of Stoneham, with its extenfive park, is one of the moft elegant in Hants; the fummer-houfe, called Belvidere, near the road, commands a very rich and diverfified profpect on every fide; and no landfcape can be finer. The feat and eftate is now enjoyed by John Willis, efq. who has changed that name for Fleming; he reprefents the borough of Southampton in the prefent parlement, and married a fifter of Lucy Knightly, of Faufley, in Northamptonfhire, efq *

* The above particulars of the family of Fleming are taken from materials fent me by Lancelot Brown, efq the rev mr Breedon, rector of North-Stoneham, the rev. Sam. Gauntlet, and other friends, with Thurloe's ftate-papers, Whitlock's memorial, Sprigg's England's recovery, Chronica Juridicialia, &c. It is moft unfortunate that the regifter of North-Stoneham is very defective, the old ones are loft, what remains commences in 1640, the only item it contains is, that july 2nd, 1651, Edw Fleming, efq married to mis Cath. Hooper.

No.

No. XV.

Some observations upon the Bromley family, with whom sir Oliver Cromwell, the prot. Oliver's uncle, allied himself by his first marriage.

THE Bromleys are of very ancient date in Staffordshire, being seated there so early as the reign of k. John. Sir John Bromley, knt. distinguished himself in the wars in France, in the reign of k. Hen. V. particularly in recovering the standard of Guyen, in the battle of Le Corby, won by the french, for which he was knighted, received lands of great value in Normandy; and, as a perpetual memorial of his gallantry, the standard of Guyen was given him for a crest, viz. upon a wreath of the colors a demy lion rampant, sable, issuing out of a mural crown, or, holding a standard, vert, charged with a griffin-passant, or, the staff proper headed argent. I mention this the rather, because the crest of the Bromleys, in the window of Hinchinbrook, is so totally different, and is the same as that given upon sir Tho. Bromley's monument in Westminster-abbey, as appears by Dart, but the lord Montforts use that given them by k. Hen. V. and the same is upon the shield of arms under the mezzotinto plate of Will. Bromley, esq. member of parlement for the borough of Warwick, and speaker of the house of commons in the reign of q Ann, to whom he was a privy counsellor *.

NUM XV.
Bromleys.
Antiquity.
Sir John Bromley, knt.

---

* The heralds, I am informed, made a distinction of the lord Montforts arms from the ancient ones used by the Bromleys,
by

NUM XV.

Bromleys.

Sir Thomas
Bromley, knt
lord-chancel-
lor of England.

Sir Tho Bromley, lady Cromwell's father, died lord-chancellor of England, april 12, 1587, ' to ' the grief of all good men.' He married Eliz. daughter of sir Adrian Fortescue, knt. of the Bath, by whom he had four sons, 1. sir Hen. Bromley, knt. 2. Tho. 3. Geo. and 4 Edw. and four daughters, 1. Ann, married to Rich. Corbet, of Stoke, in Shropshire, father of the first baronet, created 3rd k. Cha. I. 2. Meriel, married to John Lyttelton, of Frankley, in Worcestershire, esq. who, from the greatest affluence, was reduced to the greatest indigence, by joining with the earl of Essex, the favorite of q. Eliz. and was meanly deserted and insulted by his friend, sir Walter Raleigh.—K. Ja. I. restored Tho. his son and heir, to a great part of the family estates, and created him a baronet: he was ancestor of the two late lord Lytteltons, dr. Lyttelton, bishop of Carlisle, and the present lord Westcote: this affinity to the Cromwell family, is the reason assigned why the copy of the prot. Oliver's portrait, by Jarvis, is hung in the gallery of lord Westcote's seat, at Hagley *. The 3rd daughter of sir Tho. Bromley, was married to sir Edw. Greville, of Milcot, in Warwickshire, knt. of the family of the lords Brooke, now earls of Warwick, and 4. Eliz. the youngest, to sir Oliver Cromwell. Henry Bromley, esq. a descendant of the lord-chancellor, was created lord Montfort, baron of Horse-Heath, in Cam-

by obliging the first nobleman of that title to bear gules, and or dove-tailed instead of indented; which was the first time, it is supposed, that the term was known in heraldry.

- The Lytteltons were great sufferers for their attachment to the royal cause in the last century: their elegant seat at Frankley, with all its valuables, was destroyed by pr. Rupert, to prevent its falling into the hands of Cromwell.

bridge-

bridgeſhire, and took his ſeat in the houſe of lords, may 9, 1741, and died jan. 1, 1755. He was ſucceeded by Tho. his only ſon, the preſent lord Montfort *.

No. XVI.

The hiſtory of ſir Horatio Palavicini, and his deſcendants, allied to the protectoral houſe of Cromwell, by ſeveral marriages.

AS the Palavicini were by ſeveral inter-marriages ſo cloſely allied to the protectoral houſe of Cromwell, I ſhall be rather particular in giving their hiſtory, eſpecially as it is little known. This family has been long, and is ſtill conſpicuous in Italy, many of the branches of which are ſcattered in the various ſtates of that country; the eldeſt of them at Parma, from whence the others derive themſelves. They are mentioned in the annals of Genoa, as filling the firſt poſts of that commonwealth †. Signior Horatio Palavi-

---

* Theſe remarks of the Bromley family are taken chiefly from the peerage, and given to ſhew, that ſir O. Cromwell, knt of the Bath, uncle to the plot Oliver, was connected with few families but what were, like himſelf, loyal to k Cha I.

† Will marquis Palavicini, was ſet over Genoa, with the title of regent, in 1353, by its lord John Viſconti, duke of Milan; as was John-Scipio Palavicini, by Galeazzo, duke of Milan, in 1476. Nich. Palavicini was general of the genoeſe army in Corſica, in 1555. Auguſtine Palavicini was elected biennial doge of Genoa, july 13, 1637. The marq. Palavicini was ſent envoy extraordinary from the republic of Genoa, in 1685, to congratulate k. Ja. II. upon his acceſſion to the britiſh throne.

cini of this family, was born in Genoa; but leaving Italy, went and refided in the Low Countries, where he married a very mean perfon: but, as his father was then living, he did not think it prudent to acknowledge her as his wife, fhe dying, he married a perfon of fafhion in that country; fome time after his father died, when he came and fettled in England. Q Mary I. who was then feated upon the throne, had re-eftablifhed the romifh fuperftitions, to whom he was recommended *; her majefty appointed him collector of the papal taxes to be gathered in this kingdom. At the death of that bigotted princefs he had a very large fum of money in his hands this was too great a temptation for his honefty to withftand; he abjured the religion of Rome, and retained the treafure due to the pontiff Such perfons, though every way deteftable, are too ufeful to princes to be openly defpifed: fo

throne. Jerome Palavicini was appointed governor of Corfica, and the family have given generals and ftatefmen to feveral italian powers, and they have frequently received red hats, the moft celebrated cardinal of the name died very lately. It is pretty fingular, that the prefent head of this family, the old marq. Palavicini, is the only one of the old nobles who continues to frequent the Exchange, for, though the nobles in Genoa, both old and new, chiefly are merchants, yet they feldom converfe with other traders, except upon bufinefs of commerce, the people, difgufted with this haughtinefs, have quitted the portico, and ftand in the open ftreet to tranfact their affairs, to oblige the nobles to come thither, this fo hurt their pride, that they now fend their agents.—The arms of Palavicini are checky of nine, or and azure, upon a chief of the firft, a ftaccado of the firft couped fable, this makes the coat a rebus, becaufe the ftaccado, or dam made with wooden pales faftened together, are called Pali Vicini.

† Rango Palavicini was a fervant of k. Edw. VI. and had a grant, in 1551, of 250 l. during pleafure probably through his relationfhip and recommendation, fir Horatio procured preferment in England.

wife

wife a fovereign as Elizabeth, knew how to make
a proper ufe of fuch a character; and therefore,
inftead of driving him from her dominions to
enrich thofe of an enemy, or troubling him about
money, which it was eafy for him to conceal, and
impoffible for her to afcertain, not only afforded
him her protection, but gave him marks of her
favor. nov. 2, 1586, fhe gave him a patent of
denization; and, in the following year, honored
him with knighthood: in 1588, he fitted out and
commanded a fhip againft the fpanifh armada.
His portrait is given in the tapeftry in the houfe
of lords, amongft the patriots and fkilful commanders, that refcued England from a threatened
flavery. It is obfervable, that mr. Granger has
wholly omitted mentioning him. The queen
employed him in 1591, in negotiating with the
german princes, with whom fhe kept up a clofe
correfpondence, and allowed feveral of them annual penfions; by his addrefs in procuring their
making great levies of foldiers for the ufe of the
dutch, againft the tyranny of k. Phil. II. of
Spain, and by fupplying the exigencies of ftate,
with that money which he had defrauded the
public of, he ftill further ingratiated himfelf in
the favor of Elizabeth, and evinced to her majefty the importance of retaining him in her fervice.

He had taken fo much pains in improving his
fortunes, that his riches became (for a private
perfon) almoft immenfe, fo that upon him hung
the fate of kingdoms, but they that bought his
friendfhip, purchafed it at a very high price—an
ufurious intereft. In 1587, he raifed (at the defire of q Eliz.) 101,560 french crowns, for the
ufe of the gallant k. Hen. IV. of France to enable his majefty to raife an army in Germany, to
be

be commanded by the baron Dolma.   The dutch
were, in some measure, obliged to him for their
independency, and for freeing them from a gal-
ling yoke, the money our queen advanced for them
being raised by him: the monstrous usury she paid
for this money, made her often uneasy ; and, in 1595,
she demanded the re-payment of it, particularly,
and insisted, that commissioners should be appointed
to enter into some plan, how the whole money
dispersed in their cause, and due to him, might
be paid: after much altercation and high words,
it was agreed, in 1598, by the earnest desire of
the dutch, that ' for the money due to Palavi-
' cini, the queene should have her entire right
' against Brabant and Flanders, and the rest of
' the provinces confederate.' Sir Horatio died
july 6, 1600, was buried in the church of Baberham, in Cambridgeshire, july 17, and his
funerals were kept aug. 4 following. He resided
chiefly at Baberham, a seat built by himself, with
piazzas, in the italian style, he had likewise two
considerable manors in Essex, and probably several in other counties ; but yet, we may suppose,
the principal part of his fortune was in money.
The following epitaph was written upon him :
Mr. Walpole says, it was in manuscript, in the
possession of sir John Crew, of Worthington, a
great antiquary and herald :

Here lies Horatio Palavezene,
Who robb'd the pope, to lend the queene :
He was a thief, a thief! thou liest ,
For whie ? He robb'd but antichrist.
Him death wyth besome swept from *Babram*,
Into the bosom of oulde *Abraham*
But then came Hercules with his club,
And struck him down to Belzebub *.

* It appears by the Bodleian catalogue that there was published in London, in 1600—' Album seu Nigrum amicorum in
' obitum Horat. Palavicini.' A book I could never meet with.

Sir

Sir Horatio was every way diftant from amiable, but he poffeffed the beft abilities: lord Arundel mentions him firft amongft the experienced per-fons in England, to whom he refers the queen's minifters, to affure them that he had committed no crime in accepting of the title of count of the empire, without her majefty's permiffion, for which he was then under confinement: mr. Walpole men-tions him as an arras painter. Sir Horatio's firft marriage I have never feen mentioned; his 2d was with Ann, daughter of Egidius Hooftman, of Antwerp*. This lady was alfo made a denizen, in 1593; fhe re-married, july 7, 1601 (exactly a year after her firft hufband's death), to fir Oliver Cromwell, knt. of the Bath: never did any lady marry two fuch oppofites, the extremeft mifer, and one of the moft unbounded expences. By his firft wife, fir Horatio had only one fon; by the laft, feveral.

1. Edw. Palavicini, efq. the only fon of fir H. Palavicini by the firft marriage, was, to pleafe his mother-in-law, declared illegitimate, and by his father's will, difinherited; thus injured, he endea-voured to right himfelf, though unwarrantably, by petitioning k. Ja. I. to do him juftice, as eldeft fon and heir, born in wedlock, and charging both his father, and his brother Toby, with defrauding q. Eliz. and his majefty, of many thoufand pounds; but when the matter was referred to fir Hen. Spelman, and others, the brothers chofe to come to a compromife, which put a ftop to any further examination.

Edw Palavi-cini, efq eldeft fon of fir Horatio Palavicini, knt.

* Cornelius Hooftman, a native of the Low-Countries, was knighted, june 29, 1609, at Greenwich, by k Ja I. who in 1611, made him a denizen, the patent expreffes his worth, and the gentility of his family, and that he deferved the privilege granted him from his fervices.—Probably he was a brother to lady Palavicini.

2. Sir Hen. Palavicini, knt. was a minor at the time of his father's death, and was put in ward to the then secretary of state: sir Henry married at Huntingdon, april 10, 1606, Cath. daughter of sir Oliv. Cromwell, knt. of the Bath (2nd husband to his mother lady Palavicini) · she died in the year 1613, and is buried in Huntingdon; he oct. 14, 1615, without issue.

3. Sir Toby, or Tobias Palavicini, knt. was born may 20, 1593, and baptized the same day, at Baberham: the estates of his brother sir Hen. in the counties of Cambridge and Essex, together with the abbey, and impropriation of Westacre, purchased of sir Tho. Cecil, with many other estates, came to him upon the death of sir Henry; and he made great additions by purchasing a great part of Great and Little-Shelford, in Cambridgeshire, which had been the possession of the Freville family, one of whom sold them to Jos. Banks, esq. Here he built a mansion-house in the same style as his father's at Baberham; but just as it was completed, he disposed of it to John Gill, of Gillingham, esq. and he soon after squandered the rest of his property away with as great indifference as his father had procured it by rapacity; which brought him into such difficulties, that he was obliged to procure an act of parlement in 1624, to enable him, ' to sell ' lands for payment of debts, and preferment of ' children.' His profusion had necessitated him to dispose of Westacre, with the impropriation, which was purchased of alderman Burham, but this was not sufficient to discharge the many debts he had contracted; estate went after estate, until there was no more that he could dispose of, and being still in debt, to avoid his creditors he threw himself into the Fleet prison, whether he ever regained his liberty is unknown. His lady was Jane
Cromwell,

Cromwell, fifter of his brother's wife, and he married her upon the fame day, and at the fame place as fir Henry was married: lady Jane was buried within the communion rails of the chancel of Cheping-Ongar church, over her remains is a black marble flab, with the arms of Palavicini, impaling thofe of Cromwell, and under it this infcription: ' Hic ' jacet Jana D. Oliveri Cromwelli Hinchinbro-' chienfis e fedibus Huntingdonienfis Equitis Bal-' nienfis filia, uxor Tobiæ Palavicini armigeri ex ' illuftri nominis illius in agro Cantabrigienfi fa-' milia oriundi ad quadragefimum ætatis ann. et ' ferme tertium p. tintgens quod mortale fuit in ' illa officio vitaque functa in hoc pulvere depofuit ' Martii 24 Annoq. Chrifti 1637.' The iffue of this marriage was three fons and a daughter, Horatio, baptized fept. 1, 1611; he was buried near his mother, with this honorable memorial. ' Here ' lies the body of that truly noble and religious ' gentleman Horatio Palavicini, efq. who died ' may 6, 1648, aged 36.' Tobias, baptized july 14, 1612, and buried nov. 6, following, James, baptized dec. 3, 1620; and Eliz. baptized oct. 20, 1618, and buried may 23, 1630 *.

4. Baptina, the only daughter of fir Horatio, was baptized at Baberham, fept. 22, 1594, fhe became the wife of Hen. Cromwell, efq eldeft fon and heir of fir Ol. Cromwell, knt. of the Bath.

Baptina, only daugh. of fir Horatio Pilavicii i, knt. mar to Hen. Cromwell, efq.

This family, which rofe fo rapidly by extortion and fraud, is now unknown in England. The magnificent feats at Baberham, and Little-Shelford, in Cambridgefhire, are now no more†, and no traces

---

* The baptifms and burials of fir Toby Palavicini's children are taken from the regifter of Baberham.

† Baberham has been poffeffed by the baronet Bennet family, the Alexanders (who took the name of Bennet) jointly with the Mitchells, fince then by the Jones's, and it is now the eftate and feat of general Adeane There was the ftory of Mutius

of their ever having existed, are now remaining at those places, except in the registers of the former: the fate of Westacre has been seen, the manors of Cranbrooke, and Little-Ilford, in Essex, have as long been enjoyed by strangers, and all the vast personalty was dissipated before any of the estates—Such is the precarious tenure of wealth in families, especially when gained by injustice, extortion, and usury*.

Scævola, very finely expressed, upon the chimney-piece in the hall of the old seat, with the arms and initials of sir Toby Palavicini, which at the taking down of the seat was sold to a gentleman in Kent, or Essex. The seat at Shelford was taken down so late as 1750; upon the loggia, in the center front, was the Palavicini's shield of arms. Will Ingle, esq the present owner of the manor, built a seat upon the scite of that erected by sir Toby.

* The history of the Palavicini is taken from the hist. of Nepotismo, revolutions in Genoa, various other foreign writers, Pointer's chronological hist. of Engl. Rymer's fœdera, sir H. Spelman's hist. of sacrilege, Stow's chron. Brown and Camden's hist. of q. Eliz. Sydney's letters, mr. Walpole's anecdotes of painting, Bowyer's life, mr. Salmon, and mr. Morant's hist of Essex, Pedigree of the Cromwells, Pine's tapestry of the house of lords; Boyer's treatise of honor, with various foreign heraldic writers, &c. together with the register of Baberham, extracts from which the rev. E. Bradford, the rector of that church, most politely communicated to me.

No. XVII.

The history of the Ingoldsbys, allied to the Cromwells by the marriage of sir Rich. Ingoldsby, knt. with Eliz. daughter of sir Oliver Cromwell, knt of the Bath, and also first cousin to Oliver lord protector.

THE Ingoldsbys were originally of Lincoln-shire, and took their name from a manor in that county; they had resided at Lenthenbo-rough, in Bucks, for several generations *.

Sir Rich. Ingoldsby, of Lenthenborough, knt. was, by an inquisition taken upon the death of his father, Fra Ingoldsby, esq. in 1634, found to be his eldest son and heir; he inclosed his lordship of Lenthenborough, and procured a licence from k. Ja. I. to make a park there, in the 3d year of that

NUM XV.

Ingoldsbys Antiquity

Sir Rich. Ingoldsby.

— The Ingoldsbys seated themselves at Lenthenborough by purchase, in the reign of k Hen VI. From an old vellum book, which sir Rich. Ingoldsby shewed at the visitation of Bucks, in 1634, to the heralds, it appears, that they derive their origin from the ancient possessors of Ingoldsby and Skinnard parishes, in Lincolnshire sir Roger Ingoldsby was lord of those parishes about 1230, and had two sons, John and Roger, of which, John the eldest dying without issue, was suc-ceeded by his brother Roger, father and grandfather of other Rogers, the latter of these married the daughter of —— Kelby; Tho his son and heir, by the daughter of — Freme, was father of Ralph and John Ingoldsby, joint purchasers of Lenthenbo-rough, Ralph, the eldest, received a commission from k. Hen VI. anno 1448, to provide ships for the defence of Aqui-taine, in France, as in the patents appear, John was, in 1462, constituted a baron of the Exchequer, which office he held un-til 1468. This last Ralph married Agnes, daughter and heiress of Will Bardwell, by whom he had Rich. who married the daughter of John Elmes, esq. by whom he was father of Rich. Ingoldsby, who, by the daughter of John Greenway, of Dinton,

N 3
Bucks,

reign, he was sheriff of Bucks*; he was buried at Buckingham, aug. 28, 1635: by Eliz. daughter of Will. Palmer, of Waddeston, Bucks, esq. he had 1. Sir Rich. of whom below. 2. Dorothy, baptized july 12, 1582, and married thrice, first may 28, 1602, to sir Christopher Pigot, of Dodders-hail, Bucks, knt. and lastly, to Maximilian Petty, esq. she was buried at Lenthenborough in 1643. 3. Agnes, married to Rich. Serjeant, of Dinton, Bucks, esq. from whom came a numerous family: And 4. Martha married at Lenthenborough, may 18, 1637, to John Pessey, esq

Sir Rich. Ingoldsby, eldest son, and heir of sir Rich. was knighted by k Ja. I. oct. 22, 1617, when that monarch was at Hinchinbrook, the seat of his father-in-law, sir O. Cromwell, knt. of the Bath, whose daughter Eliz. he had married. both himself and his lady were strenuous on the parlement side, in the dispute between k. Cha. I. and his subjects, which must have given very great uneasiness to the loyal sir O. Cromwell. The near relationship between him and Oliver lord protector procured him much respect, and to his interest, probably, he was very much attached; he was buried at Buckingham, by his ancestors, dec. 20, 1656†, which place he appointed for his sepulture,

Bucks, esq. justice of peace in the reign of k Hen. VIII left Francis, who was born in 1579, and was buried at Buckingham, which Fra married twice, first a daughter of Will. Sanders, of Welford, in Northamptonshire, esq. and, secondly, the daughter of ―― Crispe, esq and widow of ―― Dormei, by the former he had sir Rich. in whom this pedigree commences, by the latter Fra. who had a son named John The arms of the Ingoldsbys are ermine, a saltire engrailed, sable.

* In the pedigree sir Rich. is only styled esquire, but by Fuller in his worthies, knight.

† The family of Ingoldsby buried their dead in a large vault, in the great cross ayle, called Poulton's ayle, in the church of Buckingham, but there is no memorial of any of them in that church.

by

by his will dated july 14, 1656, and proved jan.
14 following, by it he bequeathed all his goods and
chattels whatfoever, both real and perfonal, to Eliz.
his dearly beloved wife, whom he makes fole executrix, and mentions no other perfon in his will:
his widow was buried near him may 2, 1666, by
her he had the numerous family of 8 fons and 3
daughters. 1. Fra. Ingoldfby, efq. baptized aug.
14, 1614, he refided at Lenthenborough, enjoying the family eftate. in the parlements called by
the prot. Oliver, in 1654, and 1656, he reprefented the county of Bucks, as he did alfo in that of
1658-9, called by the younger protectoi, but he
was fo well received by k. Cha. II. at the reftoration, that he was one of thofe put down in the catalogue, to have had the new title of knight of the
royal-oak. his eftate is marked there as 1000l.
per ann. but by the extravagance and folly of himfelf and his wife, he foon diffipated his fortune,
and after difparking the ground his grandfather had
enclofed, and mortgaging the whole of his eftates,
for as much as it was poffible, he went to London,
about 1673, and was admitted in 1679, a penfioner at the Charter-houfe, where he died, oct. 1, 1681.
By Lettice, daughter of Crawley Norton, of
Offley, Herts, efq he had 3 fons and 5 daughters.
Fra -Rich. baptized apr. 23, 1652; Edw. baptized
fept. 3, 1660; Ellen, born in 1649; Ann, born in
1650, Lettice, baptized apr. 9, 1654, Martha, baptized july 11, 1662, and Eliz. all of whom, except
Edw. who it is fuppofed died young, were left deftitute by the imprudence of their parents. 2 Sir Rich.
Ingoldfby, knt. whofe life is given in a future page.
3. Sir Oliver Ingoldfby, knt. born in 1619, a
gallant officer in the parlement army: he was flain
at Pendennis. 4. John Ingoldfby, efq born in 1621:
by what falls from Wood, in his hiftory of his own
life, this John was an officer in the parlement army,
and had a regiment, with which he was at the fiege of

Drogheda, in Ireland, and buried Wood's brother, who died in that service: mr. Ingoldsby died at sea. 5. Sir Hen. Ingoldsby, bart. born in 1622, he was first an officer in the army of k. Cha. I. afterwards captain, and then a colonel in the parlement service, he went into Ireland, where he was very useful to his party, but if we believe lord Clarendon, he performed actions that disgrace humanity, the barbarities exercised 'n Spanish-America not exceeding his; a relation of them is too dreadful to mention, but that noble and elegant historian, must be read with an excess of caution. Sir Henry was returned a member of parlement for the counties of Kerry, Limerick, and Clare, in 1654, 1656, and 1658-9. Upon Rich. the protector's resignation, he passed over to Ireland, to give timely notice to Hen. Cromwell, the lord-lieut. to put himself upon his guard; and returning into England, he besieged and took Windsor-castle, which the republicans had filled with all kinds of arms and ammunition, and kept it for the king's use. It is singular that he was created a baronet, by the prot. Oliver, his relation, march 31, 1658, and by k. Cha. II. aug. 30, 1660. Sir Henry died in Ireland, 1701, one of the oldest officers in the army, he was succeeded in his title by sir Geo. his eldest son, who married Mary, daughter of sir Peter Stanley, bart. by whom I think he had 2 children; sir Will. Ingoldsby, bart. who married Theophila, daughter of sir Kinsmill Lucy, bart. but died without male issue, apr. 25, 1726, and his lady july 30, 1721. Ann, married to sir F. Blundel, bart. their issue was Ann, married to lieut.-general Echlin, sir Will Blundel, bart. neither of whom had any child, and Montagu Blundel, bart created by k. Geo. I. baron Edenderry, and visc. Blundel, both in Ireland *

* There appears to have been also an irish baronetage in the family of Ingoldsby, as the historical register says, dec 23, 1724, sir Ja. Ingoldsby, a bart of Ireland, married mrs Delaune.

6. Geo. Ingoldſby, eſq. 7. Tho. Ingoldſby, eſq. born feb. 29, 1624-5, he was a captain in his bro-ther, ſir Rich.'s regiment, and I think in Alured's, in 1659. 8. Will. Ingoldſby, born in 1627: I can ſcarce ſuppoſe that he was the perſon of thoſe names who was ſequeſtered, in 1643, from the rectory of Watton, Herts. One of theſe brothers was wound-ed in the ſtorming of Briſtol, in 1645, and another was mortally wounded alſo in the parlement ſer-vice 9. Eliz. born in 1618, who died unmarried. 10 Sarah, who alſo died ſingle. 11 Ann, born in 1626, ſhe married to ſir Edw. Chaloner, knt. a relation of the two brothers, judges of k. Cha. I *.

launc. Theſe perſons alſo ſeem to be of this family. Sir Cha. Ingoldſby, a judge of the Com.-Pleas temp k Ja II. who died aug 4, 1719, and Rich. Ingoldſby, eſq. one of the lords juſ-tices general, and general governors of Ireland, lieut.-gen. and commander in chief of the forces of that kingdom, who died at Dublin, jan. 11, 1711-12, and was buried in Chriſt church, in that city, feb. 2 following.

* The Chaloners are an ancient and knightly family, of Giſ-borough, in Yorkſhire, where the principal line ſtill continues, but a branch of them ſeated themſelves at Steeple-Claydon, Bucks, they were no leſs celebrated for letters than arms · ſir Tho. Chaloner wrote an hiſtory of the emp. Cha. V.'s attack upon Algiers, which he himſelf aſſiſted at, and ſaved his life by ſwimming with his ſword in his mouth from his ſhip, which was blown up, to another the duke of Somerſet knighted him for his valor in Muſſelborough-field, he was afterwards q. Eliz. ambaſſador to the emp. Ferd. I and to k. Phil. II. of Spain, in whoſe dominions he remained four years, and wrote in that time his five books, de republica Angloium inſtauranda. he died in 1566, and was magnificently buried in St. Paul's church in London, Cecil, lord Burleigh, walking chief mourner his ſon, ſir Tho. Chaloner, knt was tutor to Hen. pr of Wales, and was a learned author. By Eliz daughter of ſir Will Fleetwood, knt recorder of London, he had ſeveral children, three of the ſons were, ſir Will. created a baronet by k. Cha II Tho. one of k. Cha I.'s judges, who was as profligate as Harry Marten Cromwell, when he ſo abruptly diſſolved the long-parlement, called him a drunkard, he was an author, and if Wood is to be credited,

by ſir Edw. ſhe had Ann, born in 1654, and Edw. in 1660. 12. Mary, born in 1629; ſhe married major Read, who was wounded in the parlement ſervice, at the taking of Briſtol in 1645.

Sir Rich. Ingoldſby, knt. of the Bath, ſecond ſon of ſir Rich. made ſo conſpicuous a figure in the civil wars, that it would be unpardonable not to ſpeak particularly of him. He was early attached to puritaniſm, and an enemy to both the court and the hierarchy: upon the breaking out of the wars between the king and the parlement, he obtained a captain's commiſſion, in his relation Hampden's regiment, in 1644, he was obliged to ſurrender himſelf to the king's officers; regaining his liberty, he was raiſed to the rank of a colonel of foot, and ſoon afterwards of horſe, and appointed one of the parlement committee for Bucks He performed many gallant ſervices for the cauſe in which he embarked, this, and his alliances made him greatly truſted, the city of Oxford was committed to his care, the government of which was a very important poſt, as it was the chief reſidence of loyalty. He was named a commiſſioner

credited, a very inferior one, and James, who was alſo one of k. Cha. I.'s judges, he was an eminent antiquary. Tho. died at Middleburg, in Zealand, in 1661. James put an end to his life in 1660, for fear of falling into the hands of k. Cha. II. See the lives of all theſe writers in Wood's athen oxonienſes, in which are many curious particulars of them —Of this family were dr. Edw. Chaloner, principal of S.. Alban's Hall, Oxford, chaplain to k. Ja. I. and k. Ch. 1 who died of the plague in 1625-6, aged 34, and dr. Luke Chaloner, another great divine, who bequeathed his only daughter Phebe, to dr. Uſher, afterwards archb of Armagh, the young people fulfilled the will of the deceaſed, ſhe was a great fortune, and lived with the archb 40 years, and mr. Chaloner, a citizen of London, of good wealth and credit, who was executed for joining with the poet Waller, in the plot to force both the king and parlement to give their bleeding country peace.

of

of the high court of juſtice, erected for the for-
mal trial of the ſovereign, but he did not attend
any of the ſittings, though he ſigned the warrant
for executing that miſerable prince.   He was one
of the repreſentatives in the long-parlement, but
he did not ſit until the king's death.   In 1650, he
was ſent by the parlement into Ireland, where he
was very ſerviceable, and performed many gallant
actions, particularly in defeating col. Grace, who
commanded 3000 iriſh*.   Upon his return into
England, he was elected a member of the council
of ſtate.

Upon his couſin Oliver's aſſuming the title of
protector, he was made one of his chief confidents;
he ſat as one of the members for Bucks in 1654,
and 1656, in this year he was appointed governor
of Oxford caſtle, and in the following, raiſed by
his highneſs to be one of the lords of the *other houſe.*
As he was of a ſprightly humour, he rendered
himſelf particularly agreeable to the prot. Rich.
who was himſelf alſo of a cheerful diſpoſition,
though ſurrounded by men of auſtere diſpoſitions,
and mortified looks†: he deſerved all Rich.'s regard, for he would have run very great riſks to
have ſerved him, but he found it impoſſible to ſtem
the torrent.   When the government was intirely
gone from the hands of the Cromwells, into thoſe
of the republicans, he was appointed one of the
council of ſafety, his ſole aim at this time was

---

* It is obſervable, that col. Grace, almoſt immediately after
his defeat by col. Ingoldſby, was obliged to ſurrender to col.
Zanky, who inhumanly ſhot ſeveral of the officers, for what
ought to have endeared them to him—making a brave reſiſtance,
—but, ſays Zanky, they fell off from the cauſe of God, and
the commonwealth. The prot Oliver, with more humanity,
reſtored col Grace to his eſtate, as ſoon as himſelf was clothed
with power, which was a ſad offence in the eyes of Ludlow.

† Vide life of the prot. Rich. given in vol. I.

making

making himſelf acceptable to the king, whom he diſcovered would ſoon be reſtored: Monk ſo well knew his ſentiments, that he gave him Rich's regiment, and the ſoldiers received their old commander with particular pleaſure, they having juſt before deſerted from mr. Rich to him. He had ſoon an opportunity of recommending himſelf to the exiled king, by defeating, and taking priſoner, general Lambert, who had eſcaped from the Tower; and this arduous taſk he performed at the deſire of Monk, though he had only three days allowed him to collect his regiment, which was diſperſed in Norfolk and Suffolk, but he aſſembled them before the time, and accompliſhed the ſervice, by bringing Lambert back a priſoner to London, whoſe eſcape had alarmed the whole kingdom.

It is not probable that he ſhould do all this without ſome previous terms with his baniſhed maſter; when he ſtood in the predicament of his royal father's murderer, and conſequently devoted to certain ruin, whatever his ſubſequent ſervices might be, unleſs mercy was extended to him, Lord Clarendon declares, that he made no ſtipulations whatever; but ſays, that he told mr. Mordaunt, that ' he would perform all ſervices ' he could, without making any conditions, and ' be well content that he' (the king) ' ſhould take ' off his head, if he thought fit; only deſired that ' his majeſty might know the truth of his caſe.' On the contrary, Ludlow aſſures us, that ' he ' had his pardon granted before the reſtoration,' and he was very likely to know. To ſave appearances, however, he declared, that he was compelled by Oliver, afterwards prot to ſign the fatal warrant for k Ch I.'s execution the circumſtances of the fact, he ſtated thus: Having ſome buſineſs with an officer, who was in the painted

chamber,

chamber, he went to him, where the king's

judges were affembled : Cromwell feeing him,
laid hold of him and faid, ' Though you have
' efcaped me all the while before, you fhall now
' fign that paper as well as they,' but when he
difcovered what it was, he refufed with much
paffion, upon this Cromwell, and others, pulled
him to the table, and Oliver, putting the pen between his fingers, wrote ' Richard Ingoldfby,'
he making all the refiftance in his power, and he
declared, that if his name was compared with
what he had wrote, it would be immediately feen
that it was not his hand-writing. the warrant was
not found until many years after, or it would
have been feen, that his name is very well written,
and much unlike Cromwell's hand-writing but,
how came fir Rich 's feal of arms to it ? was his
watch, to which it was appendant, forceably
taken out of his pocket ? but how was it that he
and his regiment petitioned to bring k. Cha. I.
to a trial, that he might be punifhed for the vaft
effufion of Britifh blood ? However it was, his
fervices deferved his pardon · perhaps his greateft
commendation is, that Hen Cromwell, lord-lieut.
of Ireland, calls him honeft Ingoldfby.

He was the only one of the regicides that had
any favor fhewn them by k. Ch II. (except fav-
ing their lives, and that generally at the expence
of perpetual imprifonment), but he had not only
an entire pardon, but was created a knt. of the
Bath by that fovereign, previous to his majefty's
coronation · he prefented to the throne, dec. 19,
in that year, a moft loyal and dutiful addrefs in
behalf of himfelf, his officers, and the foldiers of
his regiment upon their being difbanded at Northampton. Little credit is due to what bifh. Parker relates, that he was to have joined, in 1662-3,
with the republicans, as he neither liked them

well

well enough, nor would they have truſted him: he was too ſenſible of the favor and protection he had found, to venture the loſs of it, by any chimerical project in behalf of men whom he had always oppoſed. He reſided at Waldridge, in the pariſh of Dinton, near Ayleſbury, which he had purchaſed in 1651 ✳: he ſerved in the parlements called by k. Ch. II. in his 13th, 31ſt, and 32d years of his reign, as one of the members for Ayleſbury. Sir Rich. was buried in Hartwell church, ſept. 16, 1685: he married Ann, daughter of ſir Geo. Crooke, one of the juſtices of the King's Bench, and widow of Tho. Lee, of Hartwell, eſq. Lady Ingoldſby was buried at Dinton, may 7, 1675, their iſſue was a ſon and a daughter. 1. Rich. of whom below, and, 2 Jane, married to John Marriot, of Aſcot, in Glouceſterſhire, eſq.

Rich. Ingoldſby, eſq.

Rich. Ingoldſby, eſq. only ſon and heir of ſir Richard, married Mary, only daughter of Will. Colmore, of Warwick, eſq †. He died april 14, 1703, in the 49th year of his age, ſhe was buried near her huſband in Dinton church, june 2, 1726: they had 7 ſons and 7 daughters. 1. Rich. buried at Dinton, dec. 26, 1686, when very young. 2. Will. born in 1680, and buried at the ſame place in his infancy. 3. Tho. of

---

✳ The virulent Wood pretended, that it was ſuppoſed, that ſir R Ingoldſby ſold Lenthenborough to mrs Ellen Gwynn, for the uſe of her natural ſon by k Cha. II. but there is not the leaſt foundation for ſuch a ſurmiſe, ſir Rich was never in poſſeſſion of that eſtate · his brother ſold it to his ſteward, mr Will. Robinſon, who died in 1696.

† Mr. Colmore was one of the parlement committee for Warwickſhire. I have ſeen a paſs granted by him for a perſon to travel from that county to London he died feb. 9, 1674-5: and is buried in the church of St. Mary, in Warwick this family was ſeated at New-hall, then near, but now in, Birmingham, a very conſiderable part of which town they now poſſeſs.

whom

whom below. 4. Rich. who was living in 1713.
5. Hen. died an infant, and was buried at Dinton. 6. John, buried in that church feb. 20,
1696-7. 7. Unknown. 8. Eliz. died an infant,
and was buried with her brothers who died young.
9. Frances, living and unmarried in 1713. 10.
Ann, alfo died in her infancy, and is buried at
Waldridge. 11. Henrietta, living and unmarried in 1713. 12. Jane. 13. Sarah, both of
whom died children, and are buried at Dinton:
and 14. Letitia, buried at Dinton, dec. 4, 1711.

Tho. Ingoldfby, efq. the eldeft furviving fon Tho Ingoldfby,
and heir of Rich. Ingoldfby, efq. was born in efq.
1688, he was fheriff of Bucks, 7th k. Geo. I. and
elected, in 1730-1, a member of parlement, as one
of the reprefentatives for Aylefbury: his wife was
buried in Dinton church, may 23, 1741, by whom
he had,

Rich. Ingoldfby, efq. his eldeft fon and heir, Rich. Ingoldfby,
alfo feated at Waldridge, likewife fheriff of the efq.
fame county his father had been, and one of the
members of parlement for Aylefbury. he died in
the latter end of the year 1768. The fecond fon
of Tho and brother of this laft Rich. was a
brigadier-general in the army · he was buried at
Hartwell, dec. 18, 1757. a daughter of whom I
think was married to John-Lenox-Naper Dutton,
efq father of the prefent lord Sherborne *.

* The hiftory of the Ingoldfbys is taken from Brown Willis's M S hift of the parifh of Dinton, his furvey of the town,
&c. of Bucks, which has been publifhed Information communicated by the rev. mi. Cook, rector of Dinton, and the
rev. mr. Jones of the fame place, Vifitations of Bucks, in
1634, with additions to it, fent me by mi. Longmate, Fuller's
worthies, various hift. of Engl. lives of Oliver lord prot.
peerages, baronetages, Clarendon's ftate papers, Gray's reply to Neale's hift of the puritans, hiftorical regifters for
1719, 1724, &c. Sabin's hift of St Mary's church in Warwick;
Kennet's hift. regifter, and chronicle of Englifh affairs, &c.

No.

No. XVIII.

The hiftory of the Steward, or Stuart family, the anceftors of mrs. Cromwell, wife of mr. Rob. Cromwell, and mother of the prot. Oliver.

NUM. XVIII

Stewards.
Antiquity.
Banquo.

Fleance.

Walter.

Alexander,
lord-nigh-
fteward of
Scotland

MRS. Cromwell was defcended from the royal houfe of Stuart, which ruled for many years the kingdom of Scotland, and has given feveral kings to England. Banquo, thane of Lochabar, and the chief officer of the crown, was affaffinated, with his three fons, by Macbeth, the tyrant of Scotland, as it is faid to evade the prediction that his race fhould fucceed to the fcottifh throne.   Fleance, another fon of Banquo, fled into Wales to avoid the fame fate, where he found protection, and had Nefta, daughter of Griffith Llewellin, prince of Wales, given in marriage to him: Walter, eldeft fon of this marriage, having killed a perfon in the welch court, fled into Scotland, where the fovereign received him as a perfon whofe anceftors had fuffered much for the royal family, and created him lord-high-fteward of Scotland, making that office hereditary, and by this means the family received their fir-name, in the fame manner as the Botelers, or Butlers, and the Chamberlains did in this king-dom.   Alexander, lord-high-fteward of Scotland, had 3 fons and 2 daughters: 1. John, or James, alfo lord-high-fteward, who left that office to his eldeft fon Walter, who marrying Margery, eldeft daughter of Rob. Bruce, king of Scotland, and heirefs to her brother k. David II. his eldeft fon Rob. became k. of Scotland, in which line the

crown,

crown ever afterwards continued, fo long as it was
a feparate kingdom, and until k. Ja. VI. of the
firname of Stuart fucceeded to the Englifh throne;
2. Sir John Stewart who was killed at the battle
of Falkirk in 1298. By marrying the daughter of
fir John de Bonkill, he made the place of that
name his refidence: he had 7 fons, from whom
many families in Scotland are defcended, and
feveral of which have been ennobled *. 3 Andrew,
of whom below. 4. Eliz. married to Will. Lord
Douglafs. 5 Margaret a nun.

Andrew Steward of Dundavale, efq. the young- Andrew
eft fon of Alex. married the daughter of Ja. Bethe, Steward, of
by whom he had, Dundavale, in Scotland.

Sir Alex. Steward, firnamed the Fierce; Sir Alex
who in the prefence of Cha. VI. k. of France, Steward, the
encountering a lion with his fword, and that Fierce.
breaking, he feized a ftick, and with it killed
the creature, which fo much pleafed his majefty,
that he immediately gave in addition to his arms,
(which were or, a feffe checky argent and azure)
a lion rampant gules, over all a bend reguled or.
Sir Alex. had 2 fons, Will who was flain in the
battle of Varnoile, in Picardy, and,

Sir John Steward, knt who fettled in England, Sir John
and was the founder of the firft family of the Steward, knt.
name of Steward, or Stuart, in this nation;
the occafion of his fettling himfelf in this
kingdom was fingular; he was one of the attendants of Ja. pr. of Scotland, afterwards k.

* From fir John Stewart of Bonkill, defcended the Stewarts,
barons Darnley, created earls and dukes of Lenox. Hen. the
eldeft fon of Matth. 5th earl of that title, enjoyed the marriage
crown of Scotland, with the beautiful and unfortunate q. Mary
(k Cha II. enjoyed the hereditary eftates of the laft duke
of Lenox, as next heir-male). The earls of Angus, Bleffing-
ton, and Caftlemilk (now extinct), and the prefent earls of Galloway and Traquair, the baron Blantyre, and the baronet
Stewarts of Goodtrees, and Allanbank. Thefe families write
their names, and bear their arms with fome variation.

NUM XVIII

Stewards.

Ja. II. at the time he was paffing into France, that he might avoid the fate of his brother, who had fallen a victim to the ambition of his uncle; but, in the voyage, the veffel was driven upon the englifh coaft, and the prince was detained in England, contrary to every principle of honour, fir John did not defert his mafter, but continued conftant to the royal captive, and with his leave remained ever afterwards in this kingdom, for having obtained the regard of k. Hen. IV. who not only took him into his fervice, but knighted him in the 10th year of his reign, at a tournament held at Smithfield, he afked and obtained from Joan, queen to k Ja. II. Mary Tollemache, maid of honour to her Majefty, the iffue of this marriage was,

Sir John Steward, knt

Sir John Steward, who was knighted by the gallant k. Hen. V. at the eve of his queen's coronation, at which he officiated as fewer *, he married the daughter of fir John Keyriell, or Kyrriel, knt. by whom he had Tho. Rob. and Magdalen.

Tho Steward, efq

Tho. Steward, efq. the eldeft fon of fir John, fettled at Swaffham-Market in Norfolk, was a famous mariner: he married twice, 1ft, the daughter of fir John Hamerton, knight, the eldeft fon of which marriage was,

Richard Steward, efq

Richard Steward, efq. who by the daughter, and heirefs of John Borelev, left Nich Steward, of Well, in Norfolk, efq. who, by Cicily, daughter and heirefs of —— Bafkerville, efq. had 6 fons and a daughter: three of the fons were founders of different branches of this family. 1. Rob. from whom defcend the Stuarts or Stewards of Well, and other places in Norfolk. 2. Nich. from him defcended the mother of the prot. Oliver; his life is given hereafter. 3. Rob.

* Sir John Steward had an elder brother alfo named John, and a fifter of the name of Candora.

who

who was the laſt prior, and 1ſt dean of Ely: dr.
Steward was remarkably attentive to his family,
and by joining with the chapter of Ely, in granting to his brothers various leaſes of lands, cauſed
them to ſettle in Cambridgeſhire. dr. Steward
died ſept. 22, 1557, and was buried in the cathedral of Ely, where there is a moſt magnificent
and elegant monument erected to his memory:
he left a curious pedigree of his family. 4 Simeon*,

* Simeon Steward, eſq had 8 ſons and 2 daughters. ſir Mark,
the 3d ſon, was ſeated at Stuntney in Cambridgeſhire, he died
july 23, 1603, aged near 80; he is buried in Ely cathedral, over
his remains is placed a moſt coſtly monument, adorned with an
atchievement of 23 quarterings, the bearings of the Steward
family, and of the heireſſes both ſcotch and engliſh, with whom
they had married. SirMark ſurvived all his children by his lady,
Ann, coheireſs to her father Rob. Huick, chief phyſician to q.
Eliz except Mary, married to ſir Will. Foſter, of Aldermar-
ſton, Bucks, knt and ſir Simeon Steward, alſo of Stuntney, knt.
who received his education at Trinity-hall in Cambridge, as
his father had ſir Simeon placed in his chamber this diſtich:
    Francorum Carolus voluit ſic ſtemmata ferri
    Singula cum valeant, ſunt meliora ſimul.
A ſentence often uſed by this family, their mottoes alluſive
of the ſame were 'Premendo ſuſtulit,' and 'Ferendo vicit.'
By Grace, daughter of Edw. St. Barbe, of Aſhington, in So-
merſetſhire, eſq he had Rob. his eldeſt ſon, who inherited a
leaſe of the rectory of Stuntney; he married Mary, daughter of
ſir Tho Rereſby, knt. their eldeſt ſon and heir was, Tho. Steward, of the ſame place, eſq. who is called couſin by Hen.
Cromwell, lord-deputy, and to whom he did a kindneſs, he had
a renewed leaſe of the rectory of Stuntney, for the lives of his
ſons Simeon and Tho the family continued leſſees of Stuntney
rectory until the beginning of this century —Nich. Steward,
the 8th ſon of the firſt mentioned Simeon, and the younger
brother of ſir Mark Steward, was L. L. D. he died june 1, 1633,
and is buried in St. Martin's-in-the-fields, London by Fra.
daughter and heireſs of John Baker, of Cambridge, eſq. he had
3 ſons and 5 daughters, Simeon his eldeſt ſon and heir, by
Dorothy, daughter of ſir Rich Ingoldſby, of Lenthenborough,
Bucks, knt. and widow of ſir Chriſtopher Pigot, knt had ſeveral children, the eldeſt ſon was ſir Nich. Steward, of Hartley-Mauduit, created a baronet.

O 2   ſeated

seated at Lackenheath in Suffolk, but afterwards probably of Stuntney in Cambridgeshire; which manor, with those of Barton-Parva and Undeley, he received by grants from k. Edw. VI. to hold in capite, by knight's services. He married Jane, daughter and coheiress of Edw. Bestney of Soham, in Cambridgeshire, esq. by whom he was progenitor of the knightly family of the Stewards of Stuntney, and the baronets of Hartley-Mauduit, Hants. 5. John. 6. Tho. 7. Agnes.

Nich Steward, knt.

Nich. Steward, of Ely, esq. 2nd son of Nich. resided at Ely, he received, sept. 26, 1548, jointly with his son Will a lease of the rectory of Ely, called the Sextry, granted to him by dr. Steward, his brother, and the chapter of Ely, for 21 years, commencing from the annunciation in 1563. He was buried in the cathedral church of Ely. By Eliz. daughter of ———— Lucas, of Well, esq. he had,

Will Steward, esq. maternal grandfather of the prot. Oliver.

Will. Steward, also of Ely, esq. who possessed a very considerable landed estate, and enjoyed many other ecclesiastical lands, under leases granted by the dean and chapter of Ely, besides the rectory his father had, and which in 1565 was renewed to him for 61 years. Like many others of his family, he was proud of the honour of descending from the same origin as that upon the throne, and as a memorial of this circumstance, he had his descent represented upon glass, in the middle compartment (which is 9 inches by 6 inches and an half) is painted sir Alex. Steward in armour, standing with a knotted, or ragged staff, or club, in the action of striking a rampant lion, his paternal shield of arms is appendant upon his breast, another coat, with the addition of arg a lion rampant gules, over all a bend reguled or, placed upon the fesse, is held out to him from the clouds by a dexter arm, cloathed with the french

arms,

arms; in the back ground is a town and castle:
the whole is inclosed in a border about 3 inches
wide, which gives Banquo the patriarch of the
family, sitting upon the ground, with a tree spring-
ing out of his body, with these figures, arms, and
names, resting upon its branches in this order,
Fleanchus, Walterus, Alanus, Alexander, who
first bears the arms, arg. a lion rampant gules,
over all a bend reguled or, and which is continued
alone by the following 7 persons, Walter, Alexander, Andrew, Alexander, Johannes, Johannes,
Thomas, Ricardus, who reassumes the more ancient arms, or a fesse checky arg. and azure, Nicholas, Nicholas, Gulielmus, with the date above,
1574 · this invaluable painting upon glass is now
possessed by my most obliging friend, the rev. Rob.
Master, F. A. S. Will. was buried in the cathedral of Ely, march 10, 1593-4, he married
twice, 1st. Mary, daughter of ——— Fulnetby, in
Lincolnshire, esq. and 2ndly, Cath. daughter of
Tho. Payne of Castleacre, in Norfolk, esq. by
the former he had Mildred, Ann, and Barbara;
by the latter, sir Tho. * Cath. Eliz. and Eleanor.
I have very great reason to suppose, that all these
children died young, or unmarried, except sir Tho.
and Eliz. of the former I shall speak in a future
page. Eliz. married twice, 1st. Will. Lynne,
gent. son and heir apparent of John Lynne,
of Bassingburne, in Cambridgeshire, esq. † who
died july 27, 1589, in the 27th year of his
age, and was buried in the cathedral of Ely,
as appears by this inscription: Hic inhumatus jacet optimæ Spei Adolescens Gulielmus Lynne

NUM XVIII.
Stewards.

Eliz. married,
1st, to W
Lynne, gent.
2dly, to R
Cromwell,
esq by whom
she was mo-
ther to Oliver
lord prot

---

* Some give sir Tho. Steward by the 1st marriage
† The Lynnes bore for their arms gules, a demy lion arg.
within a border or, pelletty.

Generosus,

Generosus, filius & hæres apparens Johannis Lynne de Baffingborne in Co. Cantab. Arm. qui quidem Gulielmus immatura morte peremptus in ipsius Ætatis flore 27 agens Annum, 27 die Julij A.D 1589, non sine summo omnium dolore, ex hac Vita placide migravit, uniquam relinquens filiam Catherinam scilicet, quam etiam 17 die Martij sequentis præpropera mors eadem Naturæ lege natam sustulit, simulque jam cum Patre æterno fruitur gaudio---Posuit amoris ergo moestissima illius Conjux Elizabetha filia Gulielmi Steward de Ely Armigeri   After remaining a widow about a year, she again married to Rob. Cromwell, esq. by whom she had Oliver Cromwell, lord protector of England, &c and several other children

Sir Tho. Steward (or, as he generally wrote his name, Stewarde; but he usually spelt his words with an e final), the only brother of the prot. Oliver's mother, was knighted by k. Ja. I. at Windsor, in sept. 1604, he possessed very considerable estates from his father, together with leases of the rectory of Ely, called the Sextry, as also the tythes of the parishes of Trinity and St. Mary in Ely but having neglected to repair the wall of the cemetery of Trinity church, which, as lessee of the tythes of that rectory, it was thought his province to do, the ecclesiastical court proceeded against him, whilst he was absent upon a visit at Emneth. The concern this gave sir Tho. and his amiable disposition, is so obvious in a letter he wrote upon this subject, that I shall make no apology for giving it entire. ' Sir, I doe heare a Report (which I ' knowe not whether I should credit or noe) that ' in defaulte of appearance at the spiritual court ' holden at Ely upon the xith daye of December ' last past, I should be suspended, wch I take the ' more grievously in regard that I hope I have not ' so lived as that I should be justly charged to be ' a con-

' a contemner of the authoritie of the Prince ey-
' ther ecclefiaftical or civille, & befides for that
' I cannot conceive any caufe wherefore I fhould
' be afcited to appear at the Court, unlefs it
' fhould be about the Church Wall belonging to
' Trinity parifh (wch I thought I had above a yeere
' fince fatisfied you, that it did not belong to me
' to repayre, but unto the Paryfh) nevertheleffe
' if that be the caufe, although I fuppofe it to be
' a charge I ought not to undergoe, yet I do fo
' much hate contention and reverence your eccle-
' fiaftical Authoritye, as I will be readye to obey
' any fuch order, as you fhall thinke fitte to fet
' downe.   The wch if the Froft had not hindered
' the conveyinge of Letters, you fhould have beene
' certified from me before the f^h day of appear-
' ance, for I had written Letters to Tho. Darnell
' of Ely, to talke with you about it, and to have
' made you privie to my readineffe to obey any or-
' der that you in confcience fhould fett downe.
' Thus indicating that if the report of my being
' fufpended be true, I may underftand both the
' caufe wherefore it is, and alfoe may enjoye your
' lawfull favour to have it remitted, I committ
' you to God his merciful protection.   Enmeth,
' this 30th of December, 1608, your loving frende
' to ufe, Tho. Stewarde.'——' I am the more
' greeved in that where (as) I purpofed to have
' (uppon newe yea(r)es day next) receyved the fa-
' crament.   I find by this occafion myffelfe difap-
' poynted, and in fome fort made unfitt to receyve,
' in regard of the unkindneffe wch I take to heare
' myfelfe to be foe unkindly dealt withall.' ' To
' the right worfhipfull mr. Doctor Gayer at his
' houfe in Cambridge, give thefe wth fpeed.' This
letter had the defired effect; the court fees, 5s. 11d.
were paid, and the wall complained of, engaged
to be repaired . his conduct fo much pleafed the

dean

dean and chapter, that, oct. 25. 1610, the leafe
of the rectory, called the Sextry, was renewed, to
hold during the lives of himfelf, his lady, Rob fon
and heir apparent of fir Simeon Steward, of Stuntney,
knt. and of Oliver (afterwards prot.) eldeft fon of
Rob. Cromwell, of Huntingdon, efq. and the
furvivor of them. He had alfo a leafe of Paradifc-
clofe, in Ely, dated july 18, 1611, to hold during the lives of Rob. the fon of Edw. Trincham,
of Outwell, in the ifle of Ely, efq Tho. fon of
John Chinnerye, of Ifleham, in Cambridgefhire,
gent. and Robina, daughter of Rob Cromwell, of
Huntingdon efq. and the longeft liver of them

It muft have been very diftreffing to fir Tho.
to have his nephew, Cromwell, entertain fuch different civil and religious fentiments to himfelf, and
this diflike to a character fo oppofite to his own,
muft have been heightened by Oliver's endeavouring to obtain from his majefty k. Cha. I. leave to
be committee of his perfon and eftates, as one incapable of managing them , but which was rejected as unreafonable, as he was fully competent to
take care of himfelf and his property ; yet this amiable knight was not only reconciled to him after
this behaviour (which nothing can excufe), but
he made a will in his favour, probably through the
perfuafion of, and from the regard he entertained
for his fifter, mrs. Cromwell. Before I ftate the
particulars of his will, I fhall obferve that he
greatly interefted himfelf in the affairs of Ely,
where he was very popular, and his name frequently occurs in the records of that city ; he was
a principal in procuring a charter granted by k.
Cha. I. jan 16, 1633-4, to incorporate truftees
to a charity left by a perfon of the name of Par-
fons, in which he (with the bifhop, dean, and feveral others) was named one of the firft governors,
with power to elect new feoffees upon the death
of

of any ecclefiaftical or lay perfon, or the removal
of any of the latter from Ely. he was fo fond of his
native place, that he left a legacy to that city.
Sir Tho. made his will jan. 29, 1635-6, in which
he is defcribed as then of Ely, by this will he appoints his trufty and well beloved in Chrift, Humphry Steward, efq. (being executor, with him, of
the will of Nich. Steward, L. L. D.) his fole executor, he requefted to be decently buried in the
cath. church of Ely, in the tomb or grave of his
grandfather. he gave to his fifter, Eliz. Cromwell, widow, an annuity of 30l. which he charged
upon his manor of Bernes or Barnes*, and other
his freehold meffuages and lands in Elme and Emneth, within the ifle of Ely, and in the county of
Norfolk, he bequeathed to his brother-in-law,
mr. Rowland Poole, and Mary his wife, and the
furvivor of them 10l. per ann. payable out of the

* The gentleman who fent me the extracts from fir Tho.
Steward's will, wrote the manor which fir Tho. Steward left his
nephew Cromwell, Vernes or Varnes, but another friend of
mine, Mr Mann Hutcheffon, of Wifbech, fuggefted to me,
that it was not Varnes (no fuch manor being known in that
part of the kingdom,), but Barnes, New-Barnes lying within
a mile and an half of Ely, and is conftantly held under the dean
and chapter of that fee, who ufually fet it for three lives.
I thought at firft this probable, becaufe the manner of
making the fmall b and the v, is not much unlike, but as it is
called a freehold manor, I afterwards thought he had miftaken
it, though a perfon of great knowledge, and efpecially in matters of this kind, but, whilft this fheet was printing, I was fully
convinced that I erred in judgment, by a letter lord Sandwich
honored me with, dated fept 3rd, 1786, in which his lordfhip
was pleafed to remark, ' I cannot fay I think your reafoning
' about Varnes is by any means conclufive, though Barnes is
' an ecclefiaftical eftate, and has been fo probably time im-
' memorial, yet it has always been in my memory leafed out,
' on a freehold leafe, with the manorial privileges I have been
' there more than once when mr. Harknefs had it, and he
' confidered himfelf as much mafter and lord of the foil
' (whilft any of his three lives were in being) as he certainly
' was, as if the original fee-fimple had been in him.'
                                              manor

manor of Barnes, which manor, with his lands in Elme, and Emneth, he devised to Humphry Steward, esq. in trust to pay debts and legacies, remainder to his nephew, Ol Cromwell, in fee, and also a variety of leases of lands, and the rectory of the Holy Trinity, and the blessed Mary the Virgin, in the town of Ely, and the chapel of Cheltisham, with all their rights, to Humph. Steward, esq. in trust for payment of debts and legacies, and afterwards to his nephew, O. Cromwell, during the remainder of their several terms, he also left these bequests: to his cousin Arthur Needham, 20l. to his cousin, Rob Orwell, and his wife, each 5l. to his cousin Austin Brograve, 20l. to the poor of Ely workhouse, 20l. to his executor, 100l. and to the eldest son of his nephew Oliver Cromwell, 5l. all these legacies were to be paid within one year of his death, sir Tho. also mentions that his father Will. Steward, esq. by his will, entailed several messuages and lands in Ely, &c. &c with several remainders, and it having pleased God to give him no male issue, he had neglected to cut off the intail, out of especial affection to the persons in remainder, though by such a conduct he had omitted, and lost such advantages as he might have had by the laws of the realm.   Sir Tho. was, according to his desire, buried in the cathedral of Ely, jan. 30, 1635-6, surviving his lady Bridget only a few days, she having been buried there the 12th of the same month, she was the daughter of John Poole, of Poole, in Cheshire, esq. ancestor of the baronets of that place and name, to whom sir Tho was married at Stuntney, march 8, 1592, but by whom he never had any child.

Miss Cromwells have a portrait of a knight of the name, whom they suppose was uncle to the prot. Oliver; but as they call him sir Rob and say he was a general in the army, and that he is represented

reprefented in armour, 1 fhould fuppofe it was
fir Rob. Steward, a commanding officer in Ireland againft the irifh rebels, in the parlement
fervice, for the Stewards fettled in England
(though of the fame family as the Stuarts upon
the throne) were much divided in political fentiments. Sir Rob. Steward, knighted by k. Ja. I.
with fir Will. Steward, at Royfton, oct. 23, 1613,
were officers in the army of k. Cha. I. in Ireland,
when the rebellion firft broke out in that kingdom, in 1641, but they ferved the long-parlement, as well before, as after the king's death,
in the Irifh wars. fir Rob. particularly diftinguifhed himfelf, but upon fome mifunderftanding
with fir Cha. Coote, under whom at that time he
ferved, he was fent into England, however,
though fir Cha's conduct was approved, fir
Rob. was again employed. Sir J. Steward, and
feveral others of the defcendants of fir John
Steward, who firft fettled in England in the reign
of k. Henry IV. declared againft k. Cha. I but
others, on the contrary, were greatly attached to
the royal caufe; Nich. Steward, efq. of Hartley-
Mauduit, Hants, for his loyalty, was fined by the
parlement 1400l. as was Rich Steward, of the
fame place, efq 127l. in reward to the former,
Cha II. created him a baronet, and appointed
him one of the chamberlains of the Exchequer;
and Hen Steward, of Norfolk, efq. for his attachment to the intereft of the crown, was put
down for a knight of the royal oak, his eftate
was eftimated at 1000l. per ann.

Having now gone through the hiftory of the
Stewarts from whom the prot. Oliver maternally
defcended, I cannot refift the temptation of fhewing the degree of relationfhip between k. Cha. I.
and his fuccefsful antagonift Oliver, afterwards
lord protector, as it has never been before attempted.

Alexander

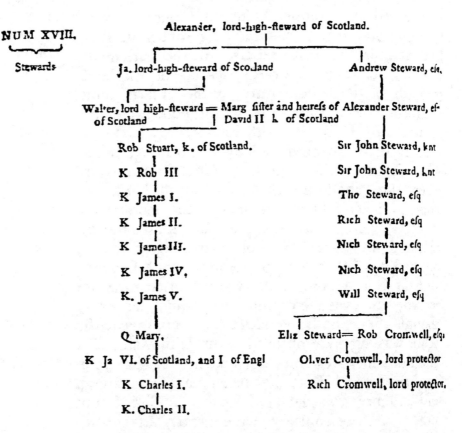

By this table of defcent it appears, that k. Cha.
I. and Elizabeth wife of mr. Rob. Cromwell, the
mother of the protector Oliver, were eighth coufins; k. Ja. I. and that protector were ninth
coufins; and k. Cha. I. and Oliver were ninth
coufins, one remove; and confequently k Cha I.
and the protector Richard were tenth coufins. It
may be obferved, that the royal line as conftantly
marrying at a very early age, had got one defcent
of the younger branch, from whom mrs. Cromwell, Oliver's mother, derived her birth, a thing
very common, owing to a caufe too obvious to
be mentioned *.

* The hiftory of the family of Steward is taken from a variety of materials fent me from the records of Ely, by feveral
friends: vifitations of Cambridgefhure, mr. Bentham's hiftory

No. XIX.

*Some particulars of the Whitstones, allied to the pro-
tector Oliver, by the marriage of Roger Whitstone,
esq. with Cath. a sister of his highness.*

THE Whitstones are of an ancient family, NUM XIX.
seated in Lincolnshire, they bore arg. a
lion rampant sable, on a canton gules, a cinque- Whitstones.
foil ermine   Francis Whitstone, of Peterborough, Fra Whitstone,
esq died april 6, 1598, and was buried in the esq.
chancel of the church of Bernack, in Northamptonshire *, but upon the borders of Lincolnshire;
upon this monument he is represented kneeling, with
his three sons behind him, and his wife on the left-
hand, in the same position with her three daugh-

tory of Ely cathedral, Bloome's britannia, MS catalogue of
k Ja I's knights, Walkley's knights of k Cha. I. Goodwin's
history of the reign of k. Hen. V and several general histories
of England, Whitlock's memorial, Thurloe's state papers,
baronetage, genealogy of the house of Stuart in all its branches,
catalogue of the loyal lords, knights and gentlemen, who compounded for their estates during the civil wars, and many
curious particulars obligingly communicated to me by various
friends

* Probably Fra. Whitstone, esq. was connected with Ber-
wick, from his father's marrying an heiress of that place, as
there is a handsome monument in that church which has a
shield of arms, baron and femme, each of four quarters, baron,
1st and 4th, a cheveron inter 3 escallop shells; 2d and 4th, a
label, with a fesse charged with 3 —— Femme 5th and 8th,
a bear rampant muzzled, 6th and 7th, three fishes, the colors
are not distinguishable.   These, and the other armorial bearings mentioned in this life, were sent me by a gentleman who
acknowledged his little skill in heraldry, which pleads for
omissions, or any mistakes in that particular.

ters

ters also behind her ; near him is a shield of four quarterings, viz. 1st and 4th Whitstone, 2nd arg a bear rampant sable muzzled, and 3rd argent 3 haddocks (or some fishes of that shape) proper, in an orle engrailed gules : upon the left side is the arms of his wife, gules five lozenges in sesse, ermine, and upon the top of the monument is a shield of arms baron and femme, as above . the inscription is :

Hic jacet mr. Franciscus Whitstones Armig.
Peterburgensis olim Civitatis Incola
Generos'.   Juris-consult. Justiciarius
Et quod omnem Mundi fastum superavit
Vir vere fidelis, et religiosus.
Sed evanuese Genus, Jus, Justitia
Genus in Sepulchrum, Jus in Silentium,
Justitia considit ad pedes misericordiæ
Sola illi virtus in cælo superest.
Obiit Anno Domini 1598, Aprilis 6.

Rob Whitstone, esq
The eldest son of Fra. most probably was Rob Whitstone, of Bernack, esq. who published his last will, april 6, 1626, and which was proved july 19 following, wherein he requested his body to be buried in the north chapel of Bernack church He possessed the manor of Tollington, in Lincolnshire, near Bernack, and also estates in Bristol and Pilsgate he mentions in his will his godson, Wm. Underwood, of Whittlesea. Robert had one son and two daughters, by Cath. his wife (probably sister of mr Michael Pickering, as mr Whitstone, in his will, calls him his brother-in-law). 1 Jonas 2 Ann, married to Rich. Heron, of Maxley, in Lincolnshire, and 3. Fra. who was married to Allen King, of London, whom she survived.

Jonas Whitstone, esq
Jonas, the eldest son of Rob was the father, there is every reason to believe, of Roger Whitstone, who married Cath. the prot. Oliver's sister.
Roger

Roger Whitſtone was bred to the ſword, and ſerved in the britiſh forces in the pay of Holland at what time and place he died, is uncertain; but it was before the exaltation of Oliver to the protectorſhip, and moſt probably abroad. From what has been mentioned, it appears, that the Whitſtones were at leaſt well acquainted with the Underwoods of Whittleſea, in Huntingdonſhire, where I apprehend Roger had an eſtate, and ſettled, it is not far from Bernack, though in a different county. The iſſue of Roger by Cath. daughter of Rob. Cromwell, of Huntingdon, eſq and ſiſter to Oliver, afterwards lord protector, was three ſons and two daughters: 1. Henry, whom I ſuppoſe born in England; 2. Tho Whitſtone; 3. Rich. who married Cath. a foreigner, 4. Cath. and 5. Levina, of whom hereafter All theſe perſons, except Hen. the eldeſt ſon, were naturalized by Oliver's parlement, in 1656. It is highly probable that both Tho. and Rich retired to the continent again at the reſtoration. I ſhould ſuppoſe that they were both bred to the ſword.

Henry Whitſtone, of Whittleſea, eſq followed his father's profeſſion· he bore arms under both the government of the commonwealth, and during the government of his uncle Oliver: april 15, 1652, he took a veſſel belonging to the ditch, with whom England was then at war· in dec 1655, he was engaged to ſurvey the fenny country round his ſeat, probably to drain the marſhy counties, for though Oliver, when a private man, oppoſed that plan, becauſe adopted by the court, and obnoxious to the people, yet, when he became a ſovereign, he acted the part he had ſo openly condemned in Charles, as knowing it was of public utility. Mr. ſecretary Thurloe, in a letter to col. Underwood,

NUM XIX.
Whitſtones
Roger Whitſtone, eſq brother-in-law to Oliver, lord prot

Hen Whitſtone, eſq.

4   dated

dated from Whitehall, dec. 17, 1655, says, that as he has no great judgment in the business of surveying, he must rather refer himself to capt. Whitstone, than accept of his reference to himself; he thinks 4 l. per 1000 (acres) not unreasonable for the inclosed lands, consisting of small pieces, but somewhat may be abated for the fens and marshes, which lie in great proportions together, and under water; but he desires him to prepare for the work, and hopes they shall not differ; he also requests to know when he can begin, and what his thoughts are upon the whole, as he trusts that he shall soon put the bailiwick into a good way of reformation.

His name occurs, nov. 28, 1656, as captain in the ' list of officers and soldiers, in the troop ' of col. Fra. Underwood, in the isle of Ely,' probably in the militia. In the war undertaken by the elder protector against the spaniards, he served under Stokes, admiral of the fleet in the Mediterranean, and was employed by him to command a squadron with the french, june 15, 1658, but he behaved so little to the satisfaction of the admiral, that he sent him home with others, under an arrest, and apologized to Thurloe, by letter, ' for having put any disrespect ' upon one so nearly allied to his highness,' and desired the secretary to acquaint him, ' that he ' had shewed little regard to the protector's and ' *his* own interest.' A court-martial of the admiralty was appointed to try him, at which all the commissioners of the admiralty were to assist, with many other officers and gentlemen, the quorum not to be less than fourteen. As Oliver's death immediately followed, and the disturbances soon after succeeded, perhaps his trial never took place. After the restoration he retired to Whittlesea, and died almost immediately

after,

after; he was buried there. Elizabeth, his widow, made her will, march 17, 1660-1, in which
she mentions her seven children, and her sister
Hunt, she left Fra. Underwood, esq. supervisor,
the executor, Abigail Underwood is one of the
witnesses to it. The children of Hen. and Eliz.
Whitstone, were, 1. John, 2. Christopher; 3.
George, 4. Tho. of whom below; 5. Hen. 6.
Eliz. and 7. Agnes.

NUM XIX
Whitstones.

It is probable, that the three eldest sons died
young, leaving no child, as Tho. the fourth
quitted the woollen drapery business, to which he
was brought up, and settled at Whittlesea, St.
Mary, in the isle of Ely, upon the estate of his
ancestors, valued at 200l. per ann. and rebuilt
the mansion-house. He resided here with great
reputation, occupying his own lands, was an acting justice of the peace, and one of the quorum
for the isle of Ely, and also a captain of the
militia· he died nov. 11, 1733, aged 76; and
was buried in the high church there. Mr. Whitstone married Barbara, daughter of Tho. Taylor,
of Fakenham, in Suffolk, esq. she died aug. 20,
1719, aged 56, and is buried in the same church,
as was also her husband their issue was four sons,
and four daughters, 1. Tho. of whom below, 2.
Fra B. D. rector of Woodstone, in Huntingdonshire, and fellow of St. John's college, in
Cambridge, he was born march 23, 1687-8, and
died unmarried, jan 25, 1729-30. His piety,
benevolence, and orthodox faith, with his other
virtues, are mentioned in a long latin inscription
upon his monument in Whittlesea church, which
gives his arms, with the quarterings I have before mentioned as borne by this family, with a
crescent as a difference, and this significant
motto. Pio evangelio, rege & patria. 3. Hen.
baptized sept. 8, 1689. 4. Reynold, baptized

Tho Whit-
stone, esq.

ſept. 18, 1694, of whoſe hiſtory I can obtain no intelligence; 5. Barbara, who died an infant, april 17, 1686, 6. Eliz. died unmarried ſept 18, 1607, aged 23, and 7. Barbara, baptized oct. 5, 1690; ſhe died unmarried apr. 22, 1751. Mrs. Bouchier, of Peterborough, remembers an old lady living at Warrington, of the name of Whitſtone, who prided herſelf exceedingly upon her relationſhip to the Cromwells, this, perhaps, was the perſon, 8. Mary, baptized march 7, 1691, ſhe married ——— Ablett, a perſon inferior to herſelf, by whom ſhe had no iſſue.

Tho. Whitſtone, eſq was baptized feb. 2, 1686-7; he received his education at St John's college, in Cambridge, and had a grant of the Mitre-Tavern, from the univerſity, which he leaſed out many years, he reſided upon the family eſtate at Whittleſea, where he was buried with his anceſtors, he died about 30 years ſince· he married twice, firſt, Ann, daughter of Geo. Underwood, eſq ſhe is buried in the chancel of the other church in Whittleſea, with her own relations; ſecondly, Suſanna, daughter of the rev. John Balderſtone, D. D. maſter of Emanuel college, Cambridge, and prebendary of Peterborough, ſhe was born nov. 28, 1683, and died oct. 22, 1728, and was buried with the Whitſtone family; by neither of theſe wives mr. Whitſtone had any children.

Having taken all the Whitſtones that I have been able to trace (for there is now a mean perſon of the ſame name, and probably of the family, at Whittleſea), I return to Levina, the daughter of Roger Whitſtone, eſq. by Cath. ſiſter of the prot. Oliver, ſhe was married feb 7, 1655-6, to major Rich. Beke, deſcended of an ancient and knightly family in Buckinghamſhire: the marriage ceremony was performed at Whitehall,

hall, in a very pompous and magnificent manner, the protector, and feveral nobles gracing it
with their prefence, as may be feen in the following item, no. XI. given in Peck's defiderata cu-
riofa, dated feb. 7, 1655-6, and which is called
an original (once mr. Oudart's) and then in the
hands of the editor, it runs thus: ' Thefe are
' to certifie whom it may concern, that upon the
' xii day of January MDCLV. it was defired by
' Richard Beke, Gent. (the fonne of Henry Beke,
' deceafed, and Frances his wife, now Inhabitants
' of Yorke, & Levina Whetftone, Spinfter, the
' daughter of . . . . . Whetftone & . . . . his Wife,
' late Inhabitants in the Netherlands) that Pub-
' lication fhould be made of their Intention of
' Marriage in the publique Meeting Place in the
' Parifh church of Martins in the Fields, in the
' county of Middlefex. Accordingly, in obedi-
' ence to an Act of Parliament commandinge
' me thereunto, I made publication in the pub-
' lique Meetinge Place in the Parifh Church of
' Martins, &c. of the Intention of Marriage of
' Richard Beke & Levina Whetftone, both of the
' Parifh of Martins afoiefaid, upon three feveral
' Lordes dayes, at the Clofe of Morninge Exer-
' cife; namely, upon the xiii. xx and xxvii dayes of
' January, MDCLV. All which was faithfully
' performed according to the faid Act without
' Exception.
    ' In Witnefs whereof I have hereunto fett my
' Hand, the vi day of February, MDCLV.
                ' William Williams, Regifter of the
                  ' Parifh of Martin in the Fields.'
    ' (Then follows the Name Hen. Scobell)
    ' This marriage was folemnized on Thurfday
' the vii. of Feb. MDCLV. at Whitehall, in pre-
' fence of his Highnes the Lord Protector, the
' Lord Prefident, Lord Deputy of Ireland, Ed-
' mund

‘ mund Sheffield, Earl of Mulgrave, & many
‘ others.’

This mrs. Beke is mentioned by lord Fauconberg in the poſtſcript of a letter to his brother-in-law, Henry Cromwell, lord-deputy of Ireland, in which his lordſhip tells Henry, that their ‘ ſhee
‘ coſen Beake is out of all hopes of lyfe,’ and it
is moſt probable ſhe. died at that time, leaving no
child. Major Beke, though mentioned as an inhabitant of York, was a native of Buckinghamſhire, of which his father, Hen. Beke, eſq. was
ſheriff, 20th k Cha. I. and alſo one of the parlement committee for the ſame county: however it
is probable that the major either had an eſtate in
Yorkſhire, or ſome military appointment in that
part of the kingdom, as he was named a viſitor
of the college erected by the protector Oliver, at
Durham, his highneſs Richard had a great regard for mr. Beke, giving him the command of
his life-guard, and knighting him: at the revolution he came into favor, was a colonel in the
army, and many years in the commiſſion of the
peace, and alſo a commiſſioner of appeals. he
repreſented Ayleſbury once, and Wendover twice,
in the parlements of k. Will. and q. Mary, he
died nov. 29, 1707, aged 78, and was buried in
the church of Dinton, in Buckinghamſhire, in
which pariſh he had a ſeat. Colonel Beke married to his ſecond wife, Eliz. third daughter of ſir
Tho. Lee, of Hartwell, in Bucks, bart ſhe died
may 20, 1737, aged 74 years, and is alſo buried
in. Dinton church, by this wife he had iſſue three
daughters, 1. Ann, married to Mark Antonie, eſq.
2 Eliz. who died young, and Mary, married to
John Baynes, eſq. ſerjeant-at-law .

× The hiſtory of the Whitſtone family is taken from extracts
of the regiſters, and from the funeral monuments belonging to,
and in the churches of Beinack and Whittleſea, St. Andrew,
which,

No. XX.

*The life of colonel John Jones, who married Cath.
sister of the prot. Oliver, and widow of Roger
Whitstone, esq. one of k. Cha. I.'s judges, and a
lord of Oliver the protector's other-house.*

COLONEL Jones has received excess of admiration and respect, as also the full weight
of hatred and contempt, just as party prejudice
has suggested: the republicans venerate him as one
of their most virtuous patriots, a second Brutus,
the puritans, as one of the choicest of their saints,
and the royalists, as the foremost of incendiaries,
and the most implacable of enemies; their regard
and detestation of him is so great, as to prevent
the discovering truth, and it is with difficulty that
impartiality can believe it the same person that
such opposite characters are given of, nor is it his
character only that they so greatly vary in, his
identity seems to be lost also in the description of
his original fortune and situation in life. The
cavaliers say, he was a mean person of Wales, and
designed for trade, but from some cause (which
they do not explain) he became a servant to a

NUM. XX.

The life of
John Jones,
esq raised by
his brother-
in-law, Oliv.
lord prot to
be one of his
lords

which, with various other particulars, were communicated to
me by several friends. Journals of the house of Commons;
Thurloe's state papers, Peck's desiderata curiosa, Willis's
not. parl and mr Hutchinson's 1st vol of the hist. of the bi-
shopric of Durham —There is a family of the name of Whitstone, seated at Woodford-row, in Essex, whose arms are the
same as those of Lincolnshire, but another family of the same
name, also residing in Essex, bear gules, a lion rampant argent, on a canton or.

P 3   gentleman,

gentleman, and was afterwards in the same capacity to fir Tho. Middleton, lord mayor of London, and in which he continued many years, and that he perfuaded his mafter to declare againft the king, and occafioned fir Tho. to become one of the moft active perfons for the parlement caufe. On the contrary, the republicans difplay him as a gentleman of North-Wales, of a competent eftate, and though it muft be fuppofed many perfons, in a civil war, from the meaneft beginnings, raifed themfelves to power and riches, yet there is no reafon for fuppofing that col. Jones was one of the number, probably, he was a gentleman by birth, but had only a fmall paternal inheritance, this I think the more reafonable to fuppofe, as mr. Pennant, in his journey to Snowdon, fays, that he was born in an ordinary houfe, called Maes-y-Garnedd, however, in the diftractions of his country, he greatly augmented his fortunes, as to his fervile ftate, I look upon that as a miftake, or mifreprefentation, for it is acknowledged, that the firft poft he had in the parlement army (into which he went upon the commencement of the civil war) was a captain of foot, and he was returned a member for Merionethfhire, in 1640. his reducing the ifle of Anglefey to obedience, procured him the greateft refpect, and the particular regard of the long-parlement, as his infolence to the neighbouring gentry occafioned their diflike of him, and their defcendants ftill fpeak of it with warmth.

None were more implacable againft the king, he not only fat in the high court of juftice at that unfortunate monarch's trial, but figned the warrant for his execution· upon erecting the commonwealth, he was conftituted one of the commiffion ers for managing the civil affairs of Ireland, in which his conduct is varioufly reprefented, Ludlow

low fays, he acted with great diligence, ability, and integrity, for feveral years, and diftinguifhed himfelf in bringing to juftice thofe who had been concerned in the maffacre of the englifh proteftants his enemies, on the contrary, affirm, that he executed his office of commiffioner with great tyranny, perfecuting all that were of contrary principles, reviving old laws concerning brewing, punifhing innkeepers, and thofe who frequented public houfes, not fuffering any one to enjoy any employment under government, who had ever been in fuch a place, fo that going into a tavern or a church, were crimes equally dangerous and punifhable: his feverity was certainly highly unpopular, and only pardonable from the wretchednefs of his narrow mind, and that fanaticifm that could make him prefer his favourite chaplain Patients, who had been a flocking-footer, in London, to the regular clergy, poor Patients was appointed to expofe himfelf before Jones and the council in Chrift-church, Dublin, every funday.

Upon his recal from Ireland, Oliver endeavoured to gain him to his intereft by giving him his fifter Catherine in marriage, ' who had,' fays Heath, ' as many females to beftow as a cardi-'nal.' This lady was the widow of Roger Whitftone, efq. an officer in the pay of Holland, and though he was a moft rigid republican in his principles, he accepted places of honor and profit from his brother-in-law, the protector, and, in 1656,

---

' Heath's chronicle the author of which book, according to his ufual inaccuracy, hints that Jones was married to the prot Oliver's fifter before the king's death, and on that account Cromwell knew he could depend upon him. But from the character and principles of Jones, he wanted no inducements to confent to what was the darling wifh of his heart, to deftroy the king and monarchy, and in their ftead erect a commonwealth

he

NUM XX

The ufe of John
Jones, efq &c.

he was returned for the counties of Merioneth and Denbigh, but made his election for the former, he was afterwards called up to his house of peers, however, this was rather a bribe to keep him quiet, than from any regard Oliver had for him, as it appears he was conftantly fufpected of fiding with the commonwealth party againft the intereft of the Cromwells, and it was for that reafon that he was removed from Ireland, for Henry Cromwell, lord-deputy, wrote to Thurloe, march 8, 1653-4, that he was highly diffatisfied, though he was more cunning and clofe in hiding his fentiments than Ludlow.

When the long-parlement was reftored, he was deputed by them one of the eight perfons who compofed the council of fafety, until a council of ftate could be appointed, and when that took place, he was named one of the members. Upon may 7, 1659, he was fent with three others to govern Ireland, and Ludlow, upon his leaving that kingdom, committed the army to his care, with the confent of the council, which office, that gentleman acquaints us, he accepted with modefty and gratitude, and promifed to apply himfelf with all fidelity in the difcharge of it. He did not long continue there, for, in january 1660-1, he and his colleagues were accufed of high-treafon; the charge againft him was, that he had taken part with the army againft the parlement· to anfwer which, he was fummoned before the new council of ftate, where he was obliged to fign an engagement, to give no difturbance to the then government.

He had rendered himfelf very obnoxious to his majefty k Cha. II from his known attachment to a republican form of government, as well as his being one of the inftruments of his father's ignominious death, thefe caufes, with the influence

he

he had in the army, and perhaps his relationſhip to the Cromwell family, made it determined that he ſhould be one of the ſacrifices offered up to the manes of the murdered king. His conduct had certainly been very imprudént, for, as the king's return was foreſeen ſome time before it happened, he might be ſure that he was too odious to the ſon of k Cha. I. to eſcape puniſhment, yet, he neithei left the kingdom, nor took care to ſecure his concealment, for he was taken up in London, at a little diſtance from his own lodgings, when he was refreſhing himſelf by an evening walk, and immediately committed to the Tower. With many other gentlemen concerned in the death of the king, he was tried, oct. 12, 1660, and knowing mercy would be denied, he pleaded guilty: his behaviour throughout that diſtreſſing ſcene, was more proper than any other of thoſe who afterwards ſuffered. On the 16th of the ſame month, he was with colonel Sciope, mr. Scot, and mr. Clement, drawn upon ſledges from Newgate to Charing-Croſs, where they underwent the full of that dreadful ſentence, which our laws have pronounced againſt tiaitors, and which was too inhuman even for the feelings of the callous heart of the execu-tioner to ſupport himſelf under, for he was ſo overcome with the horrors of his office, that he was obliged to leave col. Jones to his boy.

His conduct after condemnation, and to the laſt, ſhewed a mind far from being depreſſed by misfortunes, but rather rejoicing and glorying in them, miſtaken zeal was eminently diſplayed in all his actions: he looked upon himſelf as a martyr (a term ſadly profaned in the laſt century) to religion and civil liberty: yet he ſeemed by ſome expreſſions, to acquieſce in the juſtice of the ſentence, for, ſpeaking of thoſe that were gone abroad to avoid his fate— ' O deai hearts ' (ſays he)

NUM XX.

The life of John
Jones, efq &c

he) ' in what a fad condition are our dear friends
' beyond fea, where they may be hunted from
' place to place, and never be in fafety, nor hear
' the voice of the turtle ! how much have we got-
' ten the ftart of them, for we are at a point, and are
' now going to heaven.' After condemnation, when
he obferved one of col. Scrope's children weeping, he took her by the hand, and faid to her, ' You
' are weeping for your father, but fuppofe your fa-
' ther were to-morrow to be king of France, and
' you were to tarry a little behind, would you
' weep fo? Why he is going to reign with the
' king of kings in everlafting glory ' And, fpeaking
to a friend that was to have accompanied him to
Ireland, ' Ah ! dear heart,' fays he, ' thee and I
' were in that ftorm together, going to Ireland,
' and, if we had gone this journey then, we had
' been in heaven to have welcomed honeft Harri-
' fon and Carew, but we will be content to go
' after them, *we will go after.*' He would take
heaven by ftorm, and as he went to execution, he
compared his fledge to Elijah's fiery chariot, only
it went through Fleet-ftreet: at the gallows, he
vindicated himfelf from intending murder, in the
part he acted in the king's trial and execution,
and confequently, that that monarch was legally
put to death, which was impoffible, but it is obvious, that k. Cha. I's death was murder, becaufe
our laws exculpate majefty from punifhment, and
even declare it cannot do wrong, but, fubftracted
from this confideration, the parlement did not,
nor could condemn that prince, for a parlement
muft confift of a fovereign, the peers, and the
houfe of commons, the two firft branches then
did not act, and the latter were not then in a capacity, fuppofing that they had the power, for
they had expelled many of the members, which
reduced them to a fmall number, and only 46

2   were

were prefent when the king's trial was voted, and
but 26 gave their affent.—To thefe remaiks may
be added, though unneceffary, that the houfe of
commons never was a court of judicature. Colonel Jones likewife faid, that ' I muft confefs I very
' freely acquit his majefty, confidering what he
' doth in this cafe, is the part of a loving fon to a
' father, efpecially, the judges telling him that
' it is the law and (continued he) I conceive
' that the court did nothing, but what they, to
' then beft underftandings, judged right as to law.
' Therefore, I freely acquit the court, though there
' was not enough faid to fatisfy fuch a poor crea-
' ture as I am, in fo great and deep a point as this
' was.' If we believe Ludlow, ' the gravity and
' graceful meen of thefe aged gentlemen, accom-
' panied by vifible marks of fortitude and internal
' fatisfaction, furprifed the fpectators with admira-
' tion and compaffion !' It muft be obferved, that
the pailement that invited the king to return to the
throne of his anceftors, was very fanguinary, and
would have fpared but few that had particularly
diftinguifhed themfelves during the ufurpation,
had the king acquiefced, but much to his majefty's honor, he feemed averfe to the few that died
on account of his father's murder, and mr. Jones
vas the only facrifice that was made, who was allied to the Cromwell family (at leaft nearly fo), and
who by his conftantly oppofing that intereft, could
fcarcely be faid to be one: the act of indemnity
was certainly both merciful and prudent —Probably col Jones had no iffue by the widow of mr.
Whitftone we have feveral of the name of Jones,
who, it may be fuppofed, were nearly allied to
mr Jones They were col. Philip Jones, who
was a privy counfellor to both the protectors, and
one of Oliver's lords · fee his life amongft them.
Ira Jones, of Beddington, in Surry, gent. and
                                                 his

NUM. XX
The life of John
Jones, esq &c

his brother, mr. ———— Jones, an apothecary of Newton-Toney, who were tried and condemned at the assizes held at Exeter, april 18, 1655, for being engaged with col. Penruddock, for conspiring against the protector, and were pardoned on account of the family connection of the Jones's with the Cromwells : the former of them was a married man, as appears from a letter, written from Exeter gaol, june 2, 1655, to Thurloe, and in which he also almost humbly solicits mercy, and desires his honor would do him the favor of stating his real case to his highness, and speaks of the cruelty of his enemies, who have charged him with having been an highway-robber ——Sir Henry Jones, knighted by the prot. Oliver, at Hampton-Court, july 17, 1658   dr. Henry Jones, who was scout-master-general of the army in Ireland, during the protectorship of Oliver. These Jones's are mentioned in Thurloe's state papers, as are three Henry Jones's, who signed a petition of the officers in Ireland, in behalf of the Waldenses, oppressed by their sovereign, the duke of Savoy, on account of religion   Will. Jones, who sent a letter of intelligence to the prot. Oliver, from Paris, march 17, 1657-8, and Humphry Jones, of London, to whom col. John Jones assigned the care of his letters *.

* The life of col John Jones is chiefly taken from lives of the prot. Oliver, Thurloe's state papers, the trials of the regicides, and mr. Pennant's journey to Snowdon.

No.

No. XXI.

*The life of col. Val. Wauton, who married Margaret
the daughter of mr. Rob. Cromwell, and fister of
Oliver, lord protector.*

VALENTINE Wauton, esq. was descend- NUM. XXI.
ed from a knightly family, seated at Great- Wautons.
Stoughton, in Huntingdonshire, which manor, Antiquity.
with other considerable estates, they had long enjoyed from marrying the heir-general of sir Adam
de Cretings, of Cretingsbury, who distinguished
himself in the wars of k Edw. III. in France;
John de Wauton, or Waweton, was a knight of
the shire in the parlements held in the 43d, 46th,
and 47th years of that king's reign, and in the 1st
and 5th of k. Rich. II.'s, as was Tho. Wauton,
or Wawton, in the 20th of the same reign, and
in the 2d of k. Hen. V. A descendant, no doubt,
of this family, was

Tho. Wauton, of Great-Stoughton, esq. who Tho Wauton,
died dec. 29, 1555, and from the inquisitio post esq.
mortem, taken at Huntingdon, may 9, in the 2d
and 3rd years of the reign of k. Phil. and q.
Mary I. it appears that he had three sons, 1.
Tho. 2. Will and 3. Gilbert.

Tho the eldest son and heir, died in his father's Tho Wauton,
life-time, leaving by Eliz. 2 sons; 1. Geo. heir esq.
of his grandfather, then aged 15 years, 8 months,
and upwards, and 2 Tho

Sir George Wauton, knt possessed the manor Sir Geo Wau-
of Great-Stoughton, valued at 50l. ab antiquo. ton, esq
Cretingsbury in SS. parva ac alibi, held of the
bishop of Lincoln, of his manor of Bugden, by a
                                        fourth

fourth part of a knight's fervice : he was knighted by k. Ja. I. in 1604   There was a particular friendſhip between ſir Geo and ſir Oliver Cromwell, uncle to the protector Oliver, who, to per petuate the regard he had for the memory of ſir George, erected a magnificent painted monument in the ſouth ayle of Great-Stoughton church, which repreſents the defunct in armour, his head reſting upon a cuſhion ; his feet againſt an helmet, the tablet upon which the figure lies, is very high, and is ſupported by two male ſtatues ſtanding upon very elevated pedeſtals, over the effigies of the deceaſed, are his creſt and arms ; the former is a plume of feathers arg and ſable, ſet upon an helmet ; the latter is, 1. argent in the dexter point, an annulet ſable, and a chevron of the ſecond, 2. gules, a lion rampant argent, crowned or ; 3. argent three mullets gules, and a chevron of the ſecond, 4. ſable on a bend murry, three goats argent, and underneath is this inſcription :

Georgius Wauton Eqves Auratus.
Egreſſus ex hac vita quarto nonas ivnij,
Anno parte ſalvtis milleſimo ſexcenteſimo
Sexto, Etatis ſve ſeptuageſimo ſecundo
Sub ſpe melioris reſurrectionis.
Hoc eſt conditvs monvmentv. qvod
Olivervs Cromwell miles de le Bathe ;
Amicos optimos, optimo amico in mutvi.
    Amoris vereque gratitudinis
Teſtimonivm per ſolvtis ante ivſtis
    Funebribvs poſvit et locavit
Anno   Ante dicto *.

* There is an ancient tomb and grave-ſtone, that have had braſs plates upon them, near the monument of ſir Geo Wauton, probably they belong to the family   the Wautons were benefactors to the church, we may ſuppoſe, as their arms were anciently in the windows ; had the old regiſters of the church
been

Valentine Wauton, efq. was probably either a defcendant of fir Geo. or of that branch of the family that was feated at Sepath, in Cambridge- fhire, which manor, rectory, and water-mill, was the property of Tho. Wauton, efq. then of the age of 50 years· he fucceeded to them and two tene- ments, in the parifh of St. Mary of the Arches, and one tenement in Mark-lane, in the parifh of St. Olave, both in London, by the death of his brother John Wauton, efq. who dying aug. 5, in the 34th year of q. Elizabeth's reign, left no iffue by Maria his wife· this is probably the Tho. who was knighted by k. Ja. I. at Whitehall, july 23, 1603 If, however, Valentine was of this branch of the family, the elder line had become extinct, for he poffeffed Great-Stoughton: the friendfhip that was between his family and that of Cromwell, we may doubtlefs determine was the caufe of the alliance between him and Margaret, the protector Oliver's fifter, a circumftance as productive of emolument to him, in the commencement of the civil war, as it was ruinous to him at the reftoration.

He was returned a member of the long-par- lement for the county of Huntingdon, but not at its commencement, and he took the covenant, as foon as the civil war broke out, he joined the parlement, and was a ftrenuous partizan in their quarrel. In 1642, he prevented, in a great mea- fure, the plate of the univerfity of Cambridge going to his majefty then at York, and for which the parlement gave him, with his brother-in-law

been in being, I fhould have probably obtained ftill further information of this family, but they are deftroyed.—There is fome contradiction in the dates of the inquifitio poft mortem, and the infcription upon fir Geo. Wauton's monument, but the former is very erroneous, Cretingfbury is written Cre- tingfburgh, and Bugden, Brugden.

Cromwell,

Cromwell, an indemnity : in the following year he was taken prisoner by the royal army, and was confined at Oxford, during his captivity he petitioned the parlement to procure his exchange, and they directed the lord-general to procure his enlargement, for col. sir Tho. Lemsford, their prisoner at Warwick-castle; in consideration of his services, they promoted him in 1646, to the rank of colonel, the following year he was made a commissioner for preventing scandalous persons receiving the sacrament. He was of the strictest republican principles, this blinded his judgment so far, that he promoted as much as possible the death of the king, his name occurs in almost every public and private sitting of the commissioners of the high-court of justice, erected for trying the king, and his hand is also to the warrant of his execution *, this, with his relationship to Cromwell, procured him many places of consequence, and which his abilities and services in the cause deserved : he was one of the council of state in the years 1650, 1651, and 1652, and governor of King's-Lynn, and Croyland, with all the level in Ely, Holland, and Marshland. Walker, in his history of the independents, says, that Boston, King's Lynn, &c. were able to support 40,000 men, besides its own native inhabitants; and that it might be laid under water at pleasure. he adds, ' there are but three passes to enter it over ' three bridges, upon which they have, or may ' build forts, for their defence, and may from ' thence invade the adjacent country at pleasure,

---

* Col. Wauton is called Walton, by all our historians, also in the register of his marriage, and the birth of his children, yet he generally wrote his name Wauton, and it appears so in the death warrant of the king, and it is spelt so in the commission impowering the high-court of justice to act, but I have seen a letter of his to col. Fra Underwood, dated from Whitehall, jan. 1652-3, signed Walton.

' being

' being themſelves free from incurſions, or they
' may, if they liſt, break down the ſaid bridges.
' Theſe places (already ſtrong by nature) they
' daily fortify by art, for which purpoſe, great
' ſums of money have been ſent to him (Wauton)
' and *much arms, powder*, ammunition, and ord-
' nance from Windſor-caſtle. Here (when all
' other helps fail) *the godly mean to take ſanctuary*,
' this ſhall be their *retreat*, from whence they
' draw the whole kingdom *to parley upon articles*
' *of treaty, and enforce their peace from them at laſt*.
' Theſe are the ſtratagems of the godly. Theſe
' are our *ſaints*, no where canonized, but in the
' devil's calendar.' Heath in his chronicle calls
mr. Wauton, *governor of Linn*, and *Baſhaw of the
iſle of Ely*. His ſentiments of government occaſioned his being greatly diſſatisfied at Oliver's
aſſuming the protectorſhip, and he lived during
Oliver's government in retirement and diſcon-
tent, almoſt unnoticed by the protector, except
by having his conduct narrowly watched, leſt he
ſhould join with Ludlow, and other republican
malcontents, to diſturb his government, but I
find his name among the aſſeſſors for Huntingdonſhire, in 1657· the protector could not with
decency have done leſs than name him one for the
county he reſided in.

Upon Richard's ſucceeding to the protectorial
dignity, he came to admiral Edw. Montagu at
Hinchinbrook, ' to take off prejudices, and let
' him know that his principles were not ſuch as
' they might be repreſented, and that he was firm
' to his highneſs, and not a commonwealth go-
' vernment, and in diverſe other particulars diſ-
' courſed very orthodoxly.' However, colonel
Wauton's principles were too well known for him
to be truſted, ſo long as the feeble Richard preſided at the helm, but no ſooner was he dethroned,

than he emerged from his neglected situation, and joined in the bustle of the times, declaring for the parlement against the army, which so ingratiated him into their favor, that they appointed him, oct. 12, 1659, one of the seven commissioners for governing all the forces. in this post he acted with great spirit, and with sir Arthur Hasilrigge and col. Morley, secured Portsmouth for the parlement, in opposition to major-general Lambert, for which he received the thanks of the house. At the close of the same year he was appointed one of the three who were to nominate all officers to regiments : in january 1660, he was made colonel of Morley's regiment, in the following month, he was joined with general Monk and three others, for governing the army, and he was also appointed one of the 21 commissioners for managing the affairs of the Admiralty and Navy.

Perceiving that Monk's design was to restore the exiled monarch, he prudently retired to the continent, of which the parlement were informed, may 21, 1660, he became a burgess of Hanau, in Germany, where he received protection. he left that place, as fearing, that, like some of the other judges of the king, he might be delivered up to his majesty's agent in Holland, a fate he narrowly escaped. The close of his life was spent in the greatest privacy in Flanders, or the Low-Countries, under a borrowed name, and in the disguise of a gardener, and which was continued until near the time of his death, when being very ill, and foreseeing it would end in his dissolution, he discovered himself, and desired, that after his death, his near relations in England might be acquainted with it. He died in Flanders, in 1661, probably occasioned by disappointment, anxiety and dread of a violent and ignominious death.

Mr.

Mr. Wauton was a confiderable fufferer by the reftoration : for the real eftates that either he inherited from his anceftors, or had procured, were fure to be loft to him, and his family, amongft the latter, was Somerfham, in the county of Huntingdon, with the park, chace, and five manors, together with half the manors of Crowland, and Spalding, which were part of the dowry of the queen mother Henrietta-Maria, and granted to him in fee-fimple, in nov. 1649, in fatisfaction for 2132 l. 6 s. then due to him for monies advanced for the ufe of the commonwealth. He very greatly improved Somerfham, by erecting decoys, &c. but immediately before the reftoration, the common people, to exprefs their diflike to him, broke in, and totally deftroyed them. There is an anecdote of mr. Wauton, which is much to his honor : having received many kindneffes from dr. Tho. Laurence, head of Baliol-college, and Margaret-profeffor, when a prifoner, at Oxford ; he procured Coln, a fmall chapelry to the church of Somerfham, to be made a rectory, by getting the tythes annexed to it, and giving it to the doctor, who was then in great diftrefs, having been ejected from his preferments, for his loyalty *. Col. Wauton married twice, firft Margaret, Oliver the protector's fifter, by whom he had four fons and one daughter : 1. Geo. baptized july 20, 1620, at the church of St. John the Baptift, in Huntingdon, he died an infant. 2. Valentine, baptized fept. 16, 1623, at the fame church. 3. Geo. born feb. 20, and baptized may 10, 1624 ; probably it was him who was wounded by a fhot in the knee, in

---

* Dr. Lawrence was appointed by k. Cha II to an irifh bifhopric, but this unfortunate and worthy divine died before the reftoration of his royal mafter.

1644, whilft fighting for the parlement, and who was an affeffor for Effex in 1647, he might marry and refide there, or have fome place of truft in that county. 4 Robert, who was a mercer, and citizen of London; he ferved part of the prot. Oliver's funeral, the black cloth which he fupplied for that ufe, came to 6926l. 6s. 5d. but the parlement at the reftoration, would not allow the debt, fo that he loft the whole of it; which was the ruin of himfelf, as well as feveral clothiers, whofe goods he had upon credit *. He married a daughter of col Pride, one of Oliver's lords. 5. Anna, baptized alfo at St. John's church, in Huntingdon, may 22, 1622; and perhaps other children. Ralph Wauton, a lieut. in Monk's regiment, who was killed in Scotland, was perhaps another fon of col. Wauton. Fortune, his widow, petitioned the houfe of commons, in 1651, to confider her cafe. I have not feen any account of the death of Margaret, his firft wife, but we may fuppofe fhe died fome years before him, perhaps prior to her brother's advancement to the fovereignty, as mr. Wauton, after her death, married the daughter of a gentleman whofe name was Pimm, or Pyme, of Brill, in Bucks, and the widow of another gentleman, alfo of the fame place, named Auftin. At the reftoration fhe retired to Oxford, and lived in a mean manner, in Catftreet, fhe dying there, nov 14, 1662, was buried in St. Mary's church, in that city †.

---

* Amongft others that loft their money by ferving Cromwell's funeral, were mr Hampden (probably a near relation to John Hampden, efq, the patriot), his bill amounted to 5000l Fofter who alfo failed, his debt was 1500l. and Hexmour's was likewife 1500l

† The life of col. Wauton is taken from contemporary hiftorians, Journals of the houfe of commons, Thurloe's ftate papers,

No. XXII

The history of the Sewster family, allied to that of Cromwell, by the marriage of Ann, sister to the elder protector, with John Sewster, esq

THE family of Sewster were of no long standing in Huntingdonshire, to which county they came from that of Cambridge, they bore argent a chevron, between three boars' heads coupt sable, tusked or, and for a crest a Cupid blinded, shooting, with a sheaf of arrows. Will. Sewster died in the second year of the reign of k. Henry VIII. Will his son and heir, was of Grantchester, in Cambridgeshire, he died July 14, in the 36th year of the same reign; mi. Sewster had one son and two daughters, 1. John, of whom below; 2. ——, who was married to —— Goswick, and, 3. Winifred, married to John Ward, son of a father of both his names

John Sewster, esq. attorney of the court of Wards, died in the 37th year of the reign of k. Hen. VIII. having survived his father only one year; by Eliz. daughter of Nich. Harding, sister to John Harding, a pensioner, he had

Marginal notes: NUM XXII. Sewsters. Antiquity Arms. Will Sewster, esq. John Sewster, esq.

papers, Cole's escheats, preserved in the Brit. museum; Baker's MS register of St. John's church, Huntingdon, Prynne's brevia parliamentaria, hist of the regicides, life of O Cromwell, prefixed to Green's play of that protector—(the historical facts are collected by no mean hind), and England's confusion, or a true and impartial relation of the present actings at Westminster, under the mask of the *good old cause*, written by one of the *few* englishmen that are left in England.

NUM XXII
Sewſters.

one ſon and four daughters, 1. Will. his heir, of whom hereafter; 2. Winifred; 3. Margery, married to John Lynne, of Baſingborne, in Cambridgeſhire, eſq by whom ſhe had iſſue five ſons and four daughters, Will. the eldeſt ſon of this marriage, was the firſt huſband of the prot. Oliver's mother, which moſt probably might lay the foundation for an alliance between the Sewſter and Cromwell families, 3. Elizabeth; 4. Agnes, who was married to dr. Waller.

Will Sewſter, eſq

Will. Sewſter, of Steeple-Morden, in Cambridgeſhire, eſq. married Eliz. eldeſt daughter of Rob. Allington, eſq (who, ſurviving him, remarried Edw. Talkorne, by whom ſhe had John Talkorne, and Tho. Talkorne.) Mr. Sewſter left Giles, his ſon and heir, and Eliz. both unmarried in 1619, and I apprehend another ſon named William. I ſuppoſe Giles * to be the father of ſir Rob. Sewſter, of Great-Ravely, in the county of Huntingdon, who was knighted by k. Cha. II. Fra his daughter and ſole heireſs, took this eſtate (the annual value of which is about 500l.) to ſir Algernon Payton, of Doddington, in the iſle of Ely, in Cambridgeſhire, bart. by whom ſhe had ſir Sewſter Peyton, bart. maſter of the buck-hounds to q Ann, anceſtor of the preſent baronet, who poſſeſſes the eſtate of Great-Ravely, but the ſeat, by ſome timber taking fire in one of the chimneys, was burnt down in 1762. †

* Mrs Sewſter, of Ravely-Magna, who was buried at Upwood, the adjoining pariſh, apr 30, 1640, was probably the wife of Giles Sewſter, eſq

† Sir Hen Peyton, bart. was ſeated at Wicken, in Cambridgeſhire, was cuſtos rotulorum of that county, but diſplaced by the duke of Buckingham, which ſo diſobliged him, that he ſided with the pariement againſt k Cha I and publiſhed a vindication of the violent death of that ſovereign, intitled, ' The divine cataſtrophe of the kingly family of Stuart ' Sir Hen publiſhed many other tracts, he died before the reſtoration.

Will.

Will. Sewster, gent. whom I apprehend was the youngeft brother of Giles (the father of fir Rob Sewster, knt.) and was probably the father of,

John Sewster, of Wiftow, in the county of Huntingdon, efq.* who married Anna, the fifter of Oliver lord protector; he was the leaft diftin-guifhed of any of the brothers-in-law of that fo-vereign, owing, no doubt, to his being averfe to a public life, and perhaps not capable of it, this is the more probable, as the elder protector had a particular regard for this family, and pro-cured one of his daughters a moft honourable al-liance. Mr. Sewfter was buried at Wiftow, feb. 15, 1680-1, at a very advanced age: by Anna, Oliver's fifter, his only wife, he had 2 fons and 4 daughters, 1. John, of whom below; 2. Rob. Sewfter, efq. who refided at Wiftow, where he was buried, dec. 22, 1705 †, 3. Lucy, baptized nov. 26, 1631, and alfo buried at Wiftow, may 8, 1654; 4 Robina, who became the wife of fir William Lockhart, knt. the celebrated ambaffador to France, from Oliver and Richard, lords pro-tectors, from the commonwealth, and from k. Cha. II. 5. Cath. baptized apr. 30, 1642, and buried at Wiftow, oct. 28, 1642, and, 6. Anna, born may 8, 1644, and baptized the 15th of the fame month, fhe was alfo buried at Wiftow, —— 22, 1647.

John Sewfter, of Wiftow, efq. the eldeft fon and heir of John, by Anna, the fifter of the prot.

* Will Sewfter, gent whofe daughter Eliz. was baptized at St John's church, in Huntingdon, mar. 23, 1630, was pro-bably a near relation of the above John Sewfter, efq perhaps a brother.

† Rob. Sewfter, efq 's birth or baptifm is not mentioned in the regifters of Wiftow, but his burial is, there are memoran-dums ftill remaining of fir Will. Lockhart, which mention his lady's youngeft brother, Rob. Sewfter, efq. Wood alfo fpeaks of him in the hiftory of his own life.

Q 4   Oliver,

NUM XXII.

Sewfters
Will Sewfter,
efq
John Sewfter,
efq brother-
in-law to Oli-
ver lord pro-
tector

John Sewfter,
efq nephew to
Oliver lord
protector.

NUM XXII

Sewſter.

Oliver, was baptized june 9, 1638, and was buried at Wiſtow, june 13, 1680, a few months preceding his father's death　by Jane, his wife, (who was buried at Wiſtow, apr. 28, 1667) he left only two daughters, his co-heireſſes, 1. Eliz. married to Tho. Rayner, of St. Ann's pariſh, in Weſtminſter, goldſmith, who was living in 1715, but it is unknown whether there was any iſſue of this marriage, and, 2. Mary, who was the ſecond wife of mr Will. Goſling, of Wiſtow, by whom ſhe had no child, mr. Goſling, a grandſon of mr. Will Goſling, by his firſt marriage, is poſſeſſed of a portrait of the ambaſſador Lockhart, and ſeveral other family pictures, once mr. Goſling's, but are now the property of mr. Cowling, of Fenny-Stanton; one of them is called the portrait of the prot. Oliver, perhaps for no other reaſon, but becauſe the perſon is repreſented as a general, what is ſingular, the truncheon is in the left hand, but, the contour of the face, and the colors of both the hair and eyes are different to thoſe of the elder protector. Another portrait, moſt probably is properly appropriated to mr. Sewſter, the brother-in-law to the great Cromwell, he is given young, with a fair complexion, the noſe long and aquiline, eyes full and dark; the mouth very ſmall, his hair brown, and no beard, the countenance expreſſive of his character, ſerious and inſipid, the dreſs is a grey veſt, with a black cloak over it, and a large band　Another portrait is very ſingular, it is called the prot Oliver's porter, it has the appearance of a madman, his complexion is weather-beaten, his hair grey and ſtanding in all directions, with a wild, ferocious look, he has a large club in his hand. this poor creature fell a victim to the fanatic enthuſiaſm of the times, which depriving him of his reaſon, he died in Bedlam, where he had been confined

many

many years; but what appears almoft incredible, N U M XXII.
he was, during that time, refpected by the populace both as a faint and prophet *.

No. XXIII.

*Life of the ambaffador, fir Will. Lockhart, allied to
the family of Cromwell, by his marrying Robina,
the daughter of John Sewfter, efq. by Anna, his
wife, fifter to Oliver lord protector.*

THE Lockharts are of an ancient and knightly family in Scotland, where they have much
diftinguifhed themfelves by their attachment to
their country and its fovereigns. They are fuppofed to have had originally the name of Locard;
but fir Simeon, or Simon Locard, having been
deputed with the earl of Douglas, to carry over
the heart of k. Rob Bruce to the Holy-land, did,
to perpetuate the memory of fo honorable an
employment, change the fpelling of his name
to Lockhart, to intimate that he was intrufted
with one of the keys of the padlock that was af-

---

* The hiftory of the Sewfter family is taken from the vifitation of Cambridgefhire, by Hen. St George, Richmond herald, in 1619—the regifters of Wiftow, Alconbury, St. John's
in Huntingdon, and Upwood, with fome information communicated by lady Bickerton, mis. Lockhart, Launcelot Brown,
efq. and other friends There was a worfhipful family of the
Sewfters, feated at Afhwell, in Herts, where they poffeffed
very confiderable property in the reign of q. Elizabeth.

fixed

NUM XXIII
Locknarts

fixed to the box which contained the heart of that brave king; at the fame time he alfo made the addition of a human heart within the bow of a padlock, to his armorial bearings, with the motto Corda ferata fero : to enable him to defray the expence of his journey, he borrowed a fum of fir Will. de Lindfey, prior of Ayre; and for fecurity, granted him a bond, dated in 1323, for 10 pounds of filver per annum, during his life, and alfo gave fir Will. an enfeoffment upon his lands of Lee and Cartland, which ftill remain to the family· it is obfervable, that the Douglas's have alfo an augmentation to their arms, of an heart crowned, in remembrance of this fepulchral employment*.

Sir A. an
Lockhart, knt.

A defcendant of fir Simeon or Simon, was fir Allan Lockhart, of Lee, who behaved himfelf gallantly at the battle of Pinkey, where he loft his life. His fon, fir James, who alfo inherited Lee, was defervedly in great favor with k. Ja

S - Ja Lock-
hart, knt.

VI. Sir James, fon of the laft knight, was one of the fenators of the college of juftice, in the reign of k. Cha. I. and was for the fignal fervices he rendered that prince, and his fidelity towards his caufe, forfeited and imprifoned in the Tower of London; as he was alfo again, juft preceding

____

* The family have a ftone, which they call the Lee-penny, and fay that fir Simon had it from the wife of a faracen chief-tain or prince, in ranfom for her hufband, its fuppofed vir-tues are, curing all diforders of cattle, and the bite of mad dogs, both in man and beaft, it has been in great repute in Scotland, and they fay that people have come out of England for the water that the ftone has been in, and that it has been borrowed upon bond, a large fum of money being the for-feiture if the ftone was not returned, and that the family have been put in the ecclefiaftical court for fuppofed witchcraft, re-fpecting it. in fact, the hiftory of its efficacy would fill many pages, but as moft probably it would find little credit on this fide the Tweed, I fhall omit faying any further of it.

the

the reſtoration, which event gave him his freedom,
when k. Cha. II. appointed him lord-juſtice clerk
of Seſſions, in which office he died. Sir James
married Martha Douglas, daughter of a gentleman
of that name, of Mordington, of the court of
Seſſions, and nearly related to the great Douglas
family, by her he had 5 ſons, 1. ſir James, a
colonel of horſe at the commencement of the civil
wars; he was killed on the royal ſide, in a battle
fought near Aberdeen, as was alſo col. Rob. the
2d ſon, a few days after, the 3d ſon was ſir Will.
whoſe life I mean particularly to treat of; the 4th
ſon was that great oracle of the law, ſir George
Lockhart, of Carnwath, the 5th and youngeſt ſon
of ſir James, was ſir John Lockhart, knt. and as he
is called ſir John Lockhart, brother-german of
the ambaſſador, probably he was of a ſecond
marriage. The lives of him and ſir Geo Lockhart, with their deſcendants, ſhall be given after I
have gone through the hiſtory of their eldeſt ſurviving brother, ſir William.

Having conciſely given ſome relation of the
family of Lockhart, I now proceed to the life of
the moſt celebrated perſon it gave exiſtence to,
and perhaps few families in Britain have given a
character ſo every way eſtimable. Sir Will Lockhart was born in 1621, and ſent very young for
education to Lanark, an adjacent town to Lee,
at this early age he was not without his adventures: the pedagogue that preſided over the
ſchool, as too frequently happens, was the tyrant
of his pupils, and ſir Will. having committed
ſome trivial fault, fearful of experiencing the
effects of his cruel treatment, eloped and hid
himſelf in the woods of Clyde, near his father's
ſeat, here he lived the life of a refugee, or outlaw, for ſome time, ſubſiſting only upon what
his father's tenants brought him. Sir James,

who

NUM XXIII.

Lockharts.

Sir Will.
Lockhart, knt.
ambaſſador to
the court of
France, from
his uncle the
prot Oliver.

NUM XXIII

Lockharts
Sir Will
Lockhart, knt
ambaffador to
the court of
France, from
his uncle the
proc Oliver.

who was then at court, being informed of the tranfaction, fent to have the whole country raifed, with the preceptor at their head, that his fon might be taken, and delivered up to chaftife-ment. Finding himfelf furrounded on all fides, and in defperation at the treatment he might ex-pect, he refolved to take the only methods poffi-ble to efcape, which was to throw himfelf from the precipice he was driven to, and though many fathoms deep, he took the defperate leap, but by providentially falling into a fmall water, running from the river Moufe, he received no material injury, when purfuing his way to Edinburgh, and thence to Leith, he concealed himfelf there, and from that place he paffed over into Holland, at this time he was no more than 13 years of age, yet being tall and of a lufty make, he entered into the fervice of the States, where he remained unknown to any, until the following year, 1634, when hearing that his uncle, fir Geo Douglas, was fent ambaffador extraordinary from k. Cha. I. to the courts of Sweden and Po-land, to endeavour to eftablifh a peace between the two crowns, and thinking this a moft happy opportunity to obtain his return, and the favor of his father, he drew out his pafs, and went on foot with his friend and countryman, afterwards general Harry, or Hairry, to Dantzick, where fir George then was it was fome time before he could gain credit, or be received, owing to the ragged forlorn fituation he appeared in; but at length having convinced his uncle, he was treated with every tendernefs by him, but unfor-tunately the ambaffador dying at Damin, in Po-merania, in 1636, he was left in a foreign clime without a friend, however, he attended the re-mains of his uncle into Scotland, acting the part

of

of chief mourner, in the magnificent funerals that were given to his remains.

His return to his father's houfe was far from affording him happinefs, fir James could not forget his abfenting himfelf both from him and his country, nor had fir William's tafte for travelling been fatisfied with the hardfhips that he had experienced, he therefore again determined to retire to the continent, which he foon did, without either the leave or knowledge of his family, nor did his father keep the leaft intercourfe with him by letter, but, through the care of his mother, who fecretly remitted him money by Bailie Lockhait, of Edinburgh (father of fir Will. Lockhart, folicitor to k. Will. III.) he was enabled to remain fome time at Boury *, where he perfected himfelf in thofe ftudies that qualified him for thofe fingularly high ftations he afterwards difcharged with fo much honor to himfelf, and fatisfaction to his employers, even then the love of learning, great at it was, could not take him from what was ftill more the bent of his purfuits, he therefore entered a volunteer in the french army; and his having nothing to truft to but his own merit, gave a ftill higher fpur to his vigilance and gallantry, fo that he diftinguifhed himfelf fo much, that when the queen-mother was apprized of his worth, and that he was a fcotch gentleman, fhe fent him a pair of colours by a perfon of honor; this prefent, in his then fituation, was fo acceptable, that he took an opportunity of repaying the

NUM XXIII.

Lockhaits
Sir Will.
Lockhart, knt.
ambaſſador to
the court of
France, from
his uncle, the
prot Oliver

---

* I know of no fuch place as Boury, there is Bondry, in Switzerland the memoir fiom which great part of the life of fir Will Lockhart is taken, makes ftrange miftakes in the names of perfons and places, it is extiemely ill written, but its authenticity compenfates for its inelegancy. It evidently was written in a great meafuie to apologize for fii Wiliam's receiving employments during the Ciomwell and republican governments.

messenger

NUM XXIII

~~~~

Lockharts

Sir Will Lock-
hart, knt am-
baffador to the
court of France,
from his uncle
the prot. Oliver

meſſenger when his better fortune enabled him to
do it, for, ſeeing this gentleman amongſt the attendants, upon his firſt audience at the court of
France, he, recollecting him, ſaid, ' Sir, I never
have nor can be ſo happy as you once made me.'
To which the other replied, ' If I have been ſo
' happy, it is an honor I do not remember.'   Sir
William having put him in mind of what had
happened, the gentleman recalling the circumſtance, ſaid, ' I am extremely pleaſed to ſee your
excellency ſo deſervedly elevated; as to myſelf,
I remain in the ſame inconſiderable poſt I enjoyed at that time,' whereupon ſir William aſked
and obtained for him a better; ſir Will. roſe
afterwards to be a captain of horſe in the french
ſervice; when he had been in this ſituation ſome
time, he was ſolicited by lord Will. Hamilton,
earl of Lanark, and afterwards duke of Hamilton, to reviſit Scotland, and as that nobleman's
family and the Lockharts had been immemo-
rially in the habits of friendſhip, his lordſhip's
arguments prevailed. Sir Will. found his native
kingdom rent into diviſions by the impolicy of
his ſovereign, and the turbulence of his countrymen, he took the part of the latter, and became
a lieutenant colonel in the regiment of the earl of
Lanark, a ſituation the more pleaſant, as that
nobleman had the greateſt friendſhip and regard
for him, and which was ever continued to him.
Sir Will. was introduced to his majeſty when he
had ſurrendered himſelf to the ſcotch army as it
lay before Newark, Charles was ſo ſenſible of
his merit, and anxious to win him to his intereſt,
that he conferred the order of knighthood upon
him, and diſpatched him to his friend, the duke
of Hamilton, in 1646, to procure the beſt terms
poſſible for the marquis of Montroſe, whoſe ſuc-
ceſſes had greatly exaſperated the ſcotch nation,
and

and for whose safety his majesty was under the
greateft care A perfon could not be more highly
acceptable to both parties, and confequently fir
Will. upon a conference with his grace, eafily fettled fuch terms as the juncture of affairs made abfolutely requifite and neceffary for the marquis
to accept.

NUM XXIII.

Lockharts
Sir Will Lock-
hart, knt am-
baffador to the
court of France,
from his uncle
the prot. Oliver.

In the following year, when the fcotch had
voted to affift their fovereign, then a prifoner in
the ifle of Wight, both fir Will. and his father entered into the fervice with the greateft zeal, and he
himfelf was appointed colonel of a regiment under
his friend the earl of Lanark. Before the fcotch
army had their marching orders, he was difpatched with fome regiments of horfe under his command, in conjunction with col. Turner, and they
had alfo five or fix regiments of foot, with thefe
they were to protect the weftern borders and Car-
lifle, and likewife favor the royalifts in England :
whilft col. Turner lay at Dumfries, he marched to
Annan, which fo alarmed Lambert, that he drew
off his forces from the north, leaving fir Marmaduke Langdale under no reftraint in ferving his
majefty in the northern counties of England ; but
unfortunately for the expedition, the duke of Hamilton, who commanded the main army, was totally defeated at Prefton, in Lancafhire; this,
however, gave fir Will. an opportunity of fhewing
his military knowledge, for, with the utmoft management, he brought up the rear, by conftantly
wheeling about, and fkirmifhing with the purfuing
army, efpecially the horfe, this was the more neceffary, as general Middleton had, by miftake,
marched to Prefton with their cavalry, almoft immediately after his friends were defeated, at
length, by great generalfhip, fir Will. made good
his retreat to Wigan, which was feven miles, where
he joined the main army, though in his retreat

he

NUM XXIII

Lockharts
Sir Will Lock-
hart, knt. am-
baffador to the
court of France,
from his uncle
the prot. Oliver.

he had been conftantly attacked by the victorious
party; but the following night, in marching to
Warrington, the army fell into the greateft confufion, from receiving a falfe alarm, to extricate
them from their fears, fir Will. and his colleague
did all that was poffible; but one of them receiving a wound, and the other being trod under foot,
they, with difficulty, efcaped the prefent danger,
but it was only to fall into another: for the whole
country being poffeffed by the enemy, they were
obliged to fubmit: fir Will. was deputed with col.
fir J Fowlis and fir J. Turner, to agree upon
terms with Lambert, when they were conftrained
to furrender themfelves prifoners of war, as well
the general officers as others, but they were to be
protected from every infult and affront; what,
however, was the moft injurious to them as foldiers, they were obliged to furrender their arms·
fir. Will. was fent a prifoner, in confequence of
thefe terms, to Newcaftle, where having remained
for more than a year, he obtained his liberty at the
expence of 1000l. fterling. he retired into Scotland, and remained there until the royal caufe
was revived by the fcotch voting the recall of
k. Cha II. and refolving that they fhould efpoufe
his caufe, and right him with their fwords, fir
Will. was appointed general of the horfe by the
committee of eftates, who modelled the army, and
he acted as fuch when his majefty arrived in Scotland, but the duke of Argyle, who was then all
powerful, could not bear the idea, that fo high an
office fhould be difcharged by the friend of his
rival, the duke of Hamilton, and therefore never
ceafed importuning the king, until he obtained
lieut.-general Bailie and lieut.-general Montgomery to be joined in commiffion with him, this
was againft the king's idea, but he could not at this
time prevent thus far acquiefcing in the duke of
Argyle's

Argyle's folicitation, fir William remonftrated in the most pointed manner at such a procedure, as well from the impolicy of it, as its being derogatory to his honor to accept a joint commiffion after he had been alone named; the king felt the weight of these arguments, but he had it not in his power to right fir William, whose high fenfe of honor would not permit him to act, wherefore throwing up his commiffion, he withdrew to his feat, and came no more either to the court or to the army; yet his regiment was not difpofed of, but his relation and friend mr. Ja. Crawford, of Ardmillan, his lieutenant, was permitted to command it.

NUM XXIII.

Lockharts

Sir Will Lockhart, knt ambaffador to the court of France, from his uncle the prot. Oliver.

After the battle of Dunbar, when the duke of Argyle's intereft was leffened, though neither Bailie or Montgomery were raifed to the office that duke had intended them, yet fir William was not reftored to it, however, he did not refent this, more than merely declining ferving in a lower rank than he before had held, for when his majefty paffed in his march into England, within a few miles of his feat, his grace of Hamilton making him a vifit, prevailed upon him to go and offer k. Charles his fervice, as a volunteer in whatever fituation he fhould be pleafed to command. When he came to his majefty, who was on foot at Lanark muir, he was received with the moft flattering refpect by a detachment of his own regiment of horfe, which then guarded the king; for they no fooner faw their commander than they fhouted with loud huzzas, at which Charles, when he underftood the meaning, was greatly difpleafed that fuch regard fhould have been fhewn to one who had declined his fervice. his majefty's refentment overcame his prudence, for not weighing how much he ftood in want of fuch a commander as fir William, he would not permit him to kifs his hand, when

NUM. XXIII

Lockhart's.
Sir Will Lock-
hart, knt am-
baffador to the
court of France,
from his uncle
the prot Oliver

the duke of Hamilton prefented him, but turning away, took no notice whatever of him His
grace made every apology for what was not in his
power to have prevented, fir William moft readily
excufed this in the duke, but he could not re-
concile the king's behaviour, for whofe caufe
both his father and himfelf had fuffered fo much
both in blood and fortune; he therefore exclaimed with an oath, that ' no king upon earth fhould
' ufe him in that manner.'   The battle of Worcefter decided the fate of the throne of Britain,
between the contenders Oliver and Charles, the
event of this fatal battle was a fecond banifhment
to the one, and ' a crowning victory to the other,'
but fir William's regiment, under his lieutenant,
who was raifed to the rank of colonel, diftinguifhed themfelves extremely by their bravery, fo
that the lofs of the battle in no wife was occafioned
by them; for it was indifputably one of the beft
corps in the army, as moft of the officers and vo-
lunteers were fir William's near relations, and as
he had ten or twelve aunts married in the weftern
counties, it afforded his troops great advantages
in that part of the kingdom.   After remaining
for two years without interefting himfelf in the
caufe of a ruined party, unable longer to fuftain
the tedium of a total inactivity, he determined to
travel, for which purpofe he came to London,
as well to vifit his father, ftill a prifoner in the
tower, as alfo to folicit permiffion to leave the
ifland, for he thought it not prudent to retire without, for fear of confifcation.   Oliver, the protector
knew his merit, and as the brilliancy of all his
actions, that did not immediately depend upon
himfelf, was owing to fitting men for places, and
not places for men, fir William was received in the
moft flattering manner, and he had offers of the
greateft, and moft beneficial nature given to him
nc

nor did the protector fail setting before him the
total ruin of the party he had heretofore espoused,
and how little reason he had to serve a family, by
whom he had suffered so much, and whose returns
had been so ungracious : these reasons made a
suitable impression upon a mind whose activity
courted business, and whose ambition could not
otherwise be satisfied, and perhaps the reflection
that himself and his family had received nothing
but misfortunes for their loyalty, and himself
insult, added no little weight . such powerful
stimuli were irresistible, he yielded to Oliver's arguments, and resolved to be as obedient a subject to him, as he had been to the Charles's : the
protector, to bind him still further to his interest,
and to shew the value he had for him, as sir William was a widower, proposed his marrying
miss Robina Sewster, his highness's niece, but
an unexpected obstruction retarded the marriage,
the lady was pre-engaged, however, sir William
was either so much attached to her, or so impa-
tient to become the nephew of the sovereign of
the british empire, that he insisted upon his rival's either resigning the fair prize, or leaving
their pretension to the decision of the sword : the
lover, though fond of the lady, was yet more attached to his own personal safety, and therefore
resigned his claim to sir William, who obtained
miss Sewster's hand in april 1654.

The first mark of protectorial favor that he
received, was being declared a scotch judge, one
of the trustees for selling the forfeited estates of
the royalists in that kingdom, and appointed one
of his highness's privy counsellors there, he was
also named a colonel in the army, and served as
one of the members for Scotland in the first parlement called by Oliver, and in 1654, and 1656,
he was a member for the sheriffdom of Lanerk,

NUM XXIII

Lockharts
Sir Will Lock-
hart, ambassador
to the court of
France, from his
uncle the prot.
Oliver

NUM. XXIII

Lockharts

Sir Wil Lock-
hart, knt ar-
baffador to the
court of Franc.,
from his uncle
the prot. Oliver.

in that kingdom ; and as his highnefs was in want of nothing more than proper perfons to reprefent him in foreign courts, he appointed him his ambaffador to the moft powerful prince then in Europe, Lewis XIV. king of France, not only from the elegance of his manners, and his knowing the language and country, but becaufe of the great reach of his capacity . this was, perhaps, the moft fplendid poft Oliver had to difpofe of, during the whole of his government, and required the ableft, as well as the moft accomplifhed perfon about his court to fill; in fine, fir William was every way qualified for the embaffy, the commiffion for which paffed, dec. 30, 1655, with full powers to act in all things as he fhould judge moft proper, nor was there any limitation in his allowances, fir William therefore outfhone all the other ambaffadors at that gay court, and alfo very far exceeded them in confequence, both from the fovereign he reprefented, and his own intrinfic merit. Oliver, himfelf, ftrongly infifted that the britifh ambaffadors fhould be received in every refpect with equal honors as they had during the monarchy, faying, that this refpect had not been paid them becaufe the kingdoms were governed by princes, but was owing to the puiffance of the nations over which thefe fovereigns had prefided. Oliver never fhewed his judgment more than in felecting fir William for this employment, as he not only proved one of the greateft, and moft able negociators that Britain has ever produced, but as brave and expert a commander . he engroffed the whole of cardinal Mazarine's confidence, and eclipfed the confequence of all the other ambaffadors at the gallic court ; he even overcame the cardinal in all his political fchemes, which he obliged him to give up to promote thofe of his highnefs the protector, France panted for peace, Oliver's wifhes and policy was to keep alive the war

between

between that crown and Spain, sir William quashed the treaty carried on for a peace, and bound the french to the intereft of England so far, that they not only agreed to join her in a war with Spain, but also that the royal family of Stuart should not be protected by France, nor any affistance given to them or their adherents. France even ftipulated, to oblige the exiled king and all the princes of the blood to retire from her dominions, protection being only given to Henrietta-Maria, the queen-mother, whom, as a daughter of France, it would have been indecent to have banished, but she and her houshold had so little to support themselves upon, that she was neceffitated to undergo the moft humiliating mortifications, and the princefs, her daughter, was obliged to remain in bed to keep her-felf warm, as no fuel was allowed for her apart-ment: this treaty was figned, march 25, 1656, one article was, that feveral towns belonging to Spain should be feized, and Dunkirk, one of them, should be kept by England, if the confederate forces were fuccefsful, and the others by France, the treaty was to continue one year, during which time neither of the parties were to make peace without the confent of the other.

NUM. XXIII.

Lockharts Sir Will Lockhart, knt ambaffador to the court of France, from his uncle the prot. Oliver.

Sir William's dexterity in the management of this negociation, was so acceptable to the protec-tor, that, july 29, 1656, he gave him a grant of the office of keeper of the fignet of Scotland, ade-quate to fecretary of ftate, during his life, re-mainder to Cromwell Lockhart, his eldeft fon by his lady Robina, with remainder over to Julius Lockhart, the fecond fon by the fame lady, with power to execute the fame by themfelves. or their fufficient deputy or affignee, in as full and ample manner to all intents and purpofes, as Will. earl of Lothian, or any other officer that had held the faid office ever enjoyed, and this is mentioned

R 3

exprefsly

exprefsly for the purpofe of maintaining lady Robina and her children, fo earneft was the protector to provide for every part of his numerous relationfhip; to this grant (which is ftill in being)
is Oliver's great-feal appendant, and in the beginning of it is his highnefs portrayed, not in armour, as in fir William's commiffion appointing
him ambaffador, but in his robes of ftate, lined
and bordered with ermine: he was alfo nominated
one of the lords of the other houfe, but he never
fat in it, owing to his being conftantly employed
abroad during the cromwelian governments. Sir
William's whole conduct was fo pleafing to his
fovereign, that he conftituted him commander in chief of the forces, that were to act jointly
with the french againft Spain. France, according to the policy with which fhe always governs,
endeavoured to make England only the inftrument of her ambition, to obtain acquifitions from
Spain, Montmedi and St. Venaul yielded to the
united arms, but France kept poffeffion of both
places, fuch a procedure was not calculated to fatisfy either the protector, or his reprefentative,
who after properly dwelling upon the breach of the
treaty, threatened to join Spain to obtain fatisfaction, faying, ' his highnefs knew where to obtain
' a more punctual friend.' this was fufficient to
teach the cardinal of France, that no further liberty muft be taken, Mazarine therefore refolved,
though the feafon was far advanced, to do fomething to fatisfy the protector, and accordingly determined to obtain Mardyke, writing to his fovereign, that ' nothing can be of more fatal confe
' quence to France than the lofs of Cromwell's
' friendfhip, and the breach of the union with him,
' which certainly will be broken if fome ftrong town
' is not taken and put into his hands,' fo effectually
had

had fir William urged the abfolute neceffity of complying with the protector's demands Mardyke
therefore was invefted, and the fiege carried on fo
vigoroufly, that it was delivered to major-gen.
Morgan in a few days, with the confent of the moft
chriftian king; and it was immediately fo well forti-
fied that all the attempts of Spain, affifted by the
duke of York at the head of a body of 2000 englifh loyalifts, could not obtain it again, however,
the allies were difappointed, and defeated in their
attack upon Oftend. Oliver's joy was very great
for obtaining Mardyke, yet the acquifition of that
town was not fufficient of itfelf to fatisfy him, and
the cardinal was obliged to pledge himfelf to do
what had been his wifh to evade, to undertake
the fiege of Dunkirk the next fpring, and which
was to be put into the hands of his highnefs, accordingly the next campaign was begun by the 6000
immortal englifh troops, as a writer calls them, under fir William and major-gen. Morgan joining the
french army, who laid fiege to Dunkirk, which the
fiench wifhed to abandon, from finding that the
fpanifh general don John of Auftria, with the
prince of Conde, the prince de Ligny, and the
dukes of York and Gloucefter, with 30,000 men,
were advancing to its relief, Lewis XIV. and his
cardinal-minifter, were perfuaded to retire to Calais, leaving all to be determined by a council of
war, in the firft that was held, it was agreed to
raife the fiege if they were attacked, but in the
next, where fir William and general Morgan were
prefent, this refolution was exceedingly oppofed by
them, and the latter reminded them how great
' the difhonor would be to the crown of France to
' have fummoned a place, and broken ground be-
' fore it, and then raife the fiege, and run away.'
This, with their menacing that if the fiege was
raifed the treaty with England was at an end, put

R 4   a total

NUM XXIII

Lockharts.
Sir Will. Lock-
hart, Knt, am-
baffador to the
court of France,
from his uncle
the prot. Oliver.

NUM XXIII.

- Lockharts Sir Will Lockhart, Lnt. ambaffador to the court of France, from his uncle the prot. Oliver.

a total ftop to all further deliberation, and it was determined that the fiege fhould be carried on at all events. Sir William and marfhal Turenne unwilling to be attacked in their trenches, leaving a body of troops under the duke de Richlieu, advanced with the main body, the marq. de Crefpi commanding the right wing, and fir Will. the left, when pofting themfelves advantageoufly, they waited the approach of the fpaniards, the englifh, however, anxious for action, having with great difficulty climbed up a fandy hill, attacked the fpanifh foot, and after a fharp refiftance, obliged the enemy to give way, when they purfued them to the main army, where the englifh were in danger of being overwhelmed by the horfe and foot, the french giving them no manner of affiftance, until major-general Drummond, a fcotch volunteer, rode up, and upbraided them with their treachery and negligence; when difpatching a body of cavalry to their aid, it fo revived the courage of the englifh, that they defeated the enemy, killing 1200, many of whom were englifh, the partizans of the banifhed king; the main body of the french army now came up, and had the fatisfaction of affifting the victorious englifh in taking prifoners. At the end of the purfuit, marfhal Turenne, with about 100 officers, came up to the englifh, and embracing the officers, faid, ' they never faw a more glorious ac-
' tion in their lives, and that they were fo tranf-
' ported with the fight of it, that they had not
' power to move, or do any thing.' The victory being decifive, the conquerors marched againft Dunkirk, a noble defence was made by its governor, the marquis de Leda, whofe death occafioned the garrifon to furrender fooner than otherwife they would. The french monarch, confcious of the importance of the place, knowing how danger-

ous

ous it would be in the hands of England when at
war with France, and defirous himfelf to poffefs
it, endeavoured to evade the treaty; the place
was furrendered to Turenne, who took poffeffion
with a body of french troops, the k. of France
and the cardinal at the fame time entered the
place, and amufed themfelves with the idea of
having obtained fo precious a morfel from Spain
at the expence of the blood and treafure of England, giving nothing but idle apologies to our
ambaffador and general, who in the moft pointed
manner expreffed the violation of the treaty, and
the refentment his mafter muft feel for his
wrongs Oliver, however, difappointed all their
gay profpects, and invigorated again the mind
of fir William; for his highnefs knowing the duplicity of his eminence, the cardinal, and how
little reliance ought to be placed upon his word,
had opened a fecret correfpondence with the
french fecretary of the council of war, who, by a
bribe, difclofed the fecrets of the cabinet, which,
as Cromwell immediately knew, fo he acted with
his ufual promptitude to evade the fchemes of the
crafty cardinal, by difpatching a meffenger inftantly to fir William with written inftructions for
his conduct, the ambaffador-general immediately,
in compliance with them, pofted his army upon an
eminence, detached from the french, and in fuch
a manner that they could not be furprifed, then
taking his watch in his hand he repaired to the
cardinal, and demanded in a peremptory manner,
a written order for his being put in poffeffion of
Dunkirk, which if it was not complied with in
an hour, he had orders to acquaint him, that his
mafter looked upon the terms of the treaty as violated, and confequently made null, and in that cafe
he fhould retire to his camp, and take his meafures accordingly, which would then be to difpatch

an

NUM. XXIII

Lockharts
Sir Will. Lock-
hart, knt. am-
baffador to the
court of France,
from his uncle
the prot. Oliver

an expreſs to don John, the ſpaniſh general, to acquaint him, that he was ready, and prepared to join his forces to his, to act in conjunction againſt the arms of France. The cardinal thought this only an high mode of expreſſing himſelf, and aſked my lord ambaſſador in banter, whether his excellence had ſlept well the preceding evening, or whether he was yet entirely awake? The ambaſſador aſſured him of both, and coldly drew out his inſtructions in the hand-writing of the protector: the aſtoniſhed cardinal, who knew Oliver's deciſive manner of acting, and which was above all the fineſſe of his arts, began now to liſten with the utmoſt attention; and endeavoured, but in vain, to ſoften the peremptory demand of the ambaſſador, who, with the utmoſt coolneſs replied, that he ſhould be obliged to religiouſly obey the injunctions of his maſter, his eminence perceiving his firmneſs, was obliged to comply, and give up the place, within the allotted time: wherefore the french troops again evacuated the town, and ſir William and his forces took poſſeſſion of the place in the name of his highneſs the protector, he himſelf having the honor to receive the keys in perſon from Lewis XIV *. who in return for Dunkirk, received Mardyke: thus did the engliſh gain the poſſeſſion of Dunkirk, with ſcarce any expence of men or treaſure, and whoſe worth was little inferior to Calais, for it equally gave the engliſh the command of the channel: but that invaluable jewel was ſhamefully bartered away by k. Cha. II. for a ſum of money to ſupport his gallantries. It

---

* This is a much more probable relation of obtaining Dunkirk, than that given by the author of the hiſtory of England during the reigns of the Stuarts. And the Lockhart family muſt certainly have the beſt information of this tranſaction from ſir William himſelf.

would

would be unpardonable not to ftop here to com-
mend the conduct of fir William, who acted both
in the capacity of ambaffador and general during
this important bufinefs. Lord Fauconberg, in a
letter to Thurloe, dated may 29, 1658, fays, that
the duke de Crequi, chevalier Grammont, and
other illuftrious perfons, had vifited his lordfhip,
and ' that they infinitely efteemed my lord Lock-
' hart, for his courage, care, and enduring the fa-
' tigue of the camp beyond all men they ever
' faw, thefe,' continues his lordfhip, ' were their
' own words:' nor muft fo fair an opportunity
efcape of doing that ample juftice to the valor of
my countrymen, which foreigners were lavifh in
commending, for don John was fo aftonifhed at
their intrepidity and defperate valor, that he exclaimed, he was beaten by 'raging wild beafts, rather
' than men:' and the great Conde declared, ' he
' had never feen fo gallant an action as that day's
' performance by the englifh was.' This important
place which fir William's good conduct had obtained, was entrufted to his care, yet, though he
had the government of it, and was declared general
of all the englifh forces in France, his civil department as ambaffador was ftill continued to him, he
took vaft pains to fecure and ftrengthen Dunkirk, by making various additions to the fortifica-
tions, efpecially the citadel, nor did he neglect
his other employment, but continued during Oliver's protectorate, to have the fame fway in the
court of France, and it is certain, no ambaffador
ever knew the french court better, nor was more
feared and courted than him, both from the dread
that nation ftood in of Oliver, as well as their fen-
fibility of the merit, attention, and watchfulnefs of
his reprefentative. this was obvious to all Europe,
from the abfolute command he bore in the french
court, where he not only protected the englifh
merchants

NUM. XXIII.

Lockharts.

Sir Will Lock-
hart, knt am-
baffador to the
court of France,
from his uncle.
the prot Oliver

NUM. XXIII.

Lockharts.

Sir Will. Lock-
hart, knt. am-
baſſador to the
court of France,
from his uncle
the prot. Oliver

merchants in the moſt determined manner from
all attempts to injure them, either at ſea or in their
connections with the mercantile towns of France;
but by protecting the proteſtants in that kingdom,
and obliging the haughty and bigotted Lewis to
procure the ſame indulgence for them in Pied-
mont, from their cruel and tyrannic ſovereign,
the duke of Savoy.

Sir William was continued in all his employments by the protector Richard, but upon his reſignation, he acquieſced in the reſtoration of the
republic, partly, we may ſuppoſe from intereſted
motives, and alſo from policy, as knowing he had
too much offended majeſty, to be eaſily pardoned,
beſides, he might entertain no ſmall prejudice
againſt the perſon of the exiled king, from whom
he had received ſo great a ſlight; from ſome, or
all theſe reaſons, he not only ſubmitted to the
powers then in being, but received a renewed commiſſion, dated july 4, 1659, conſtituting him ambaſſador extraordinary to Lewis XIV. with plenipotentiary power, ſigned by the ſpeaker Lenthall,
and appendant to it is the great ſeal of the reſtored
commonwealth: ſo conſiderable a perſon as ſir
Will. was highly prized, the parlement took every
means of gratifying him; all his great poſts were
continued to him; nor did he ſeem ungrateful for
theſe favors, for Dec. 31, following, he wrote a con-
gratulatory letter to the ſpeaker, Lenthall, upon the
parlement's re-entering upon the exerciſe of their
authority, and promiſed to give up himſelf entirely
to be diſpoſed of by them as became him, declaring that he really was, without reſerve, their moſt
faithful and obedient ſervant, and that he had, to
expreſs his joy for their re-poſſeſſing their power,
cauſed the great guns, both by ſea and land, to
be fired; and alſo declared his admiration of God's
providence, in bringing them back, which was
almoſt

almoft miraculous, and likely to be attended with
happinefs to the three nations. The parlement was
fo pleafed with thefe expreffions of attachment,
that they fent him and the other officers, a letter
of thanks.   During his government at Dunkirk,
whilft he was abfent in England upon fome particular bufinefs, a fpecial meffenger waited upon
him to acquaint him, that the garrifon had muti-
nied, another meffenger alfo came to inform him,
he was wanted at court: without returning any anfwer to the latter, he inftantly fet off for Dunkirk,
and was obliged to fcale the wall, which he did
before he was noticed by the centinel, and marching immediately to the parade, where all the officers were affembled together, he fingled out the
ringleader, of whofe conduct he had been previoufly informed, and drawing his fword, fheathed
it in the culprit's body, who fell dead at his feet;
then turning to the others, he faid, ' Gentlemen,
' return to your duties, and you will all be for-
' given.' Thus, by a defperate ftroke, he faved
this place, and having made the proper difpofitions
in the garrifon, immediately returned to London,
and made an apology for not having attended fooner
the command he had received from court.

The parlement was extremely fenfible of his
merit, and appointed him their plenipotentiary to
attend the treaty of the Pyrenees, where he ferved
his mafters fo ably, that though Britain was convulfed with faction and anarchy, yet k. Cha. II.
who came to St. John de Luz (a fmall town upon
the frontiers of France and Spain, where the treaty
was held), could not obtain of don Lewis de Haro,
the fpanifh ambaffador, permiffion for the duke of
Ormond to deliver any meffage to him, but only
to fpeak to his excellency accidentally as he paffed
along; and cardinal Mazarine went ftill further,
for he declined taking the leaft notice of the king,

or

NUM. XXIII.

Lockharts
Sir Will Lock-
hart, knt. am-
baffador to the
court of France,
from his uncle
the prot. Oliver.

NUM. XXIII

Lockharts.

Sir Will Lock-
hart, knt. am-
baffador to the
court of France,
from his uncle
the prot. Oliver.

or his ambaſſador, telling his grace, that France was not in a capacity to break with the common-wealth, and confequently could do nothing but compaſſionate his maſter; on the contrary, the cardinal received the engliſh plenipotentiary in the moſt pompous manner, ſending his coaches and guards a day's journey to receive him, and gave him his right hand, which he refuſed to crowned heads.

After the peace was concluded, he went to Dun-kirk, and from thence paſſed into England, and took all imaginable pains to penetrate the deſigns of general Monk, but as he ever perſiſted in pro-teſting in the moſt ſolemn manner to be true to the commonwealth, and an enemy to the royal family, ſir William was inclined to believe his ſincerity; therefore, when he received a letter from his friend, ſir Geo Middleton, then in the court of k. Cha. II. telling him, that the anarchy with which the kingdom was over-run, would end in the reſtoration of monarchy in the perſon of k Charles, and aſſured him, that he might make his own terms, by inviting his majeſty to Dunkirk, he replied, ' I am truſted by the commonwealth, ' and cannot betray it.' His majeſty having been adviſed by Monk to go from Flanders, and wiſh-ing to avoid Holland, by going to Dunkirk, ſent to Lockhart, by a perſon of honor, offer-ing him his own terms, if he would declare for him, but he was ſo deceived by the artifice and duplicity of Monk, that he declined doing it, and was ſoon after ſurpriſed by the three nations uniting in their recall of their exiled ſovereign. Sir William now ſaw his error; he had procured ſo many perſonal affronts to be put upon Charles, that he might juſtly dread feeling the effects of his reſentment, to ſoften which, may 11, 1660, he made his ſubmiſſion, by diſpatching col. Lilling-

ſton

ſton to general Monk, with an addreſs, ſigned by
himſelf and his garriſon, declaring his and their
ſubmiſſion to, and acquieſcence in the reſolutions
of the convention parlement, relating both to his
majeſty, and all other things that might in any
manner fall under their conſideration . this was too
late to afford him any real ſervice; but had he
made a timely ſubmiſſion, he might have aſked
honors and wealth, both for himſelf and his friends.
He was ſuperſeded by ſir Edw. Harley in his
government; a moſt ſenſible mortification it muſt
have been, to quit the command of what he had
conquered with ſo much bravery, and governed
with ſuch conſummate prudence; and to be obliged to quit the brave garriſon, who almoſt ido-
lized him; however, he retired to Britain a private man, ſtripped of his honors and great employments; nobly refuſing a marſhal's ſtaff of
France, with other great offers which cardinal
Mazarine made him, if he would betray his truſt,
and deliver up the places under his government
to the crown of France. The loſs of rank and
office were the leaſt of the mortifications he dreaded, however, he found a reception better than
he could have imagined; the earl of Middleton,
the miniſter of Scotland, was his particular friend,
and the earl of Clarendon was far from being an enemy to him; his lordſhip extremely admiring the fine-
neſs of his underſtanding and his addreſs in buſineſs;
the earl of Lauderdale alſo profeſſed a regard for
him, but he was a perſon whoſe actions were almoſt ſolely ſwayed by pecuniary motives; and the
ſteady loyalty of ſir James, his father, was of much
ſervice to him at this criſis · king Charles, himſelf, is ſaid to have ſpoken of him with tenderneſs,
and expreſſed his regard for him as a man of honor; nor had his majeſty been long at Whitehall,
before he was introduced to him, and permitted

to

NUM. XXIII.

Lockharts
Sir Will Lock-
hart, knt am-
baſſador to the
court of France,
from his uncle
the prot Oliver.

to kiſs the king's hand; at which time he made
his apologies for his conduct, endeavouring to
ſoften the tranſactions he had been engaged in as
much as poſſible: his majeſty accepted the ex-
cuſes ſir William made, bidding him go home
and live quietly, and not engage in any deſign
againſt his perſon or government, and he might
rely upon his protection. Sir William knew how
little dependence was to be placed in mere words,
he therefore ſeized the preſent opportunity of obtaining an indemnification for all the tranſactions
he had been employed in, either in England,
France, or Spain, excepting any thing relating to
the violent death of k. Cha. I. or the iriſh rebellion: theſe exceptions gave ſir William no alarm,
for he was not any ways acceſſory to depriving
that ſovereign of life; but, on the contrary, much
attached to his cauſe, and deſirous of his ſafety;
and it was well known, that he was not in Britain,
but reſided in France when the Iriſh rebellion commenced.

Having now in ſome meaſure ſecured himſelf,
he retired into Scotland, courting privacy and retirement, amuſing himſelf in firſt teaching his
countrymen the engliſh method of agriculture,
which was at that time entirely unknown to them;
and he had the ſatisfaction to ſee his good intentions and care crowned with ſucceſs, but as his
father was ſtill living, and he could not upon that
account reſide at Lee, he made it an excuſe for
retiring into England, for Scotland was then ruled
with a rod of iron, and thoſe who had been entruſted with any power during the king's exile,
were treated with a ſeverity that nothing could excuſe, what then was the nephew of Oliver, and the
ambaſſador, that under his ſanction had driven out
the royal family from France, and occaſioned ſuch
great ſlights to be put upon his majeſty himſelf,

to expect? his situation was torturing to excess; he therefore left his native kingdom, and, with his family, seated himself in Huntingdonshire, where he took a lease of an estate, situated amongst his lady's relations; here he lived in much splendour, but without courting popularity; yet he so won the affections of his neighbours, that it was with difficulty he prevailed upon them not to elect him a knight to represent the county at a general election, it being his aim to remain in privacy, unless called forth by his sovereign. Whilst he remained in this desirable situation, he was surprised one morning by having the house surrounded by a detachment of horse, the commander of whom acquainted him, that he had orders to conduct him to London, upon a charge of high treason, sir William knowing his own innocency, immediately surrendered himself a prisoner, and was conveyed to London, and accused as an accessory in a plot of the republicans Sir William's accuser pretended that he had been one of his officers, and that he had consented to the design, promising them to command the army they were to raise. Sir William was examined before the council, where he manifested his innocence in the clearest manner, requesting that the person might be confronted to him, declaring that no person of that name had ever been an officer under him, which he could prove by producing lists of all the officers that he had ever commanded, professing that if this man's name could be found in any one of them, he would confess himself guilty; but there was little occasion for this, as upon their asking the accuser what kind of man sir William was in size and complexion, he replied low and swarthy; whereas he was quite the reverse in both respects: and when he was admitted to the council at the time sir William was present, he did not know

NUM XXIII.

Lockharts. Sir Will Lockhart, knt ambassador to the court of France, from his uncle the prot. Oliver.

NUM. XXIII

Lockhart.
Sir Will. Lock-
hart, knt. am-
baffador to the
court of France,
from his uncle
the prot Oliver.

him, therefore finding himfelf detected, he fell at
fir William's feet, confeffing, that his party had
agreed to declare fir William would be at their
head, to give themfelves confequence, imagining,
that by its being fuppofed that a perfon of his importance would fupport the undertaking, government would be impreffed with a greater idea of
their ftrength and power, and confequently
would be more cautious of inquiring and punifhing thofe of their party, for fear of alarming fo
confiderable a body of men, and occafion them to
put themfelves upon their own defence. It is much
to the judgment of Charles, that he never believed
fir William capable of fo wild and extravagant a
project, faying he had too much fenfe and experience to be engaged in fo defperate and ill-con-
certed a fcheme with fuch low and mean men.

As fir William was exculpated even by his ac-
cufer, he was foon fet at liberty, and inftead of
leffening, it heightened him in his majefty's
good graces, but yet there was a political cloud
hung over him, which he could not difperfe, for
when a foreign minifter requefted his majefty that
he might impart his bufinefs to him, the king replied, ' that he believed Lockhart would be true to
' any body but himfelf.' But fortunately in
1671, the duke of Lauderdale, then fecretary of
ftate, who thought from his difagreeable fituation,
he fhould be able to make him the creature of his
ambition, introduced him again to the court at
London, whither he went, not from any defire to
be employed, but for his own fafety. In a fhort
time afterwards, upon a levee day, his grace of
Lauderdale acquainted the fovereign, that the regiment of foot which his majefty had ordered to be
raifed in Scotland, was come to Newcaftle, but the
officers above the rank of captain, were not yet
named, and requefted that he would be pleafed to appoint

point them; his majesty, after some short silence, looking round him, perceived sir William, and told him he had a regiment to dispose of, which he would bestow upon him, if he chose to accept of it, which he instantly did, and kissed the king's hand upon his promotion, with proper expressions of his gratitude and fidelity, and upon his asking whom his majesty would be pleased to name as lieut.-colonel and major, the king replied, ' I ' leave it to your own choice;' when he mentioning sir Will. Banatyne and capt. Windram, both experienced officers in Dumbarton's regiment, their commissions were immediately expedited: probably all this was previously agreed upon between Charles and his minister, however that was, sir William made rapid advances in court favor, for a few days after, asking permission to have another battalion added to his regiment, his request was granted, and the officers being named, they were raised in eight or ten days, in the environs of Edinburgh. His majesty was so sensible of his great knowledge in continental affairs, that he was frequently closetted respecting them; and soon after he had been restored to the royal favor, he was sent envoy extraordinary to the protestant princes of Germany, to justify his majesty's declaring war against Holland, this commission he executed with so much satisfaction, that he was appointed, in 1672, again ambassador to France, this was one of the most acceptable things the court did, for the people's just apprehensions respecting the secret friendship between Lewis and Charles, had caused great animosities, which in a great measure subsided when they found sir William, who had acted with so much spirit at that court, was sent again thither. His public entrance into Paris was extremely magnificent, and though he had not, as before, an unlimited allowance, yet

NUM. XXIII.

Lockharts,
Sir Will Lockhart, knt ambassador to the court of France, from his uncle the prot Oliver.

his

NUM XXIII

Lockharts
Sir Will. Lock-
hart, knt. am-
baffador to the
court cf France,
from h.s urcle
the prot. Oliver

his falary was double to what had been ufually given
to his predeceffors in that high office ; and though
k. Charles II. was a fovereign of a very different
character to the protector Oliver, yet fir Will
procured, by his own merit, great deference and
attention to be paid him as an eminent character,
though but little as the reprefentative of a fupine
monarch ; for, fir William told bifhop Burnet, that
when he was fent ambaffador to France by that
prince, he found he had nothing o˜ that regard that
was paid him in the time of Cromwell, however,
he ftill bore fo great an afcendancy, that
Genoa, when they had incurred the difplea-
fure of Lewis, applied to him to moderate that
haughty monarch's vengeance : the republic was
fo much pleafed with his excellency, and grateful
for the fervices he rendered them, that they
prefented him with a very rich and curious fet of
hangings of arras, and recorded his fervices in a
moft honorable manner in their archives. Cofmo,
the eldeft grand prince of Tufcany (afterwards
Cofmo III.) in his tour through feveral kingdoms
in Europe, became perfonally acquainted with fir
William, and had fo high an efteem for his prodigious abilities, that he committed all his affairs
at the french court to his management, and his
highnefs ever after retained fo high an idea of his
merit, and of the obligations he had laid upon
him, that when a relation of the fame name paid
his refpects to this prince at Florence, the grand
duke expreffed himfelf in the nobleft manner, ex-
preffing in the warmeft terms, the efteem and gratitude he had for fir William, out of compliment
to whom, he paid his relation all the honors of
his court   Lewis XIV. was fo fenfible of the merit of his excellency, that he diftinguifhed him
above all the ambaffadors at his court : fir William was unfuccefsful only in his negociations with
the

the elector of Brandenburgh, and the duke of Lu-
nenburgh, whom he endeavoured, but in vain,
either to enter into an alliance with the crown of
Britain, or at leaft to free them from thofe ap-
prehenfions they juftly dreaded from the policy of
k. Charles II.

NUM XXIII.
Lockharts.
Sir Will Lock-
hart, knt am-
baffador to the
court of France,
from his uncle
the prot Oliver.

In 1673, the duke of Monmouth, one of the
natural fons of k. Cha. II. was fent over to command a body of britifh troops in the fervice of
France, and his majefty knowing fir William's
military merit, directed him to attend the army,
and give the duke, who was then very young, his
advice and direction, at the fiege of Maeftricht,
where his grace was repulfed at the head of his
troops , but the ambaffador advancing to him, faid,
the king of Great Britain's fon, and the foldiers
under him, muft not be foiled, when rallying the
men, he led the duke and thofe his grace commanded, on to the attack, and they carried the
breach: fir William fhewed his cool and collected
courage during this fiege, by fettling his worldly
concerns , it is written with fo much devotion, that
it is a convincing proof, that even amidft the buftle of camps and courts, ' he kept up an high in-
' tercourfe with heaven.' Sir James Lockhart, his
father, dying in 1674, his majefty would not permit any one to fucceed to his place as juftice-clerk,
but fir William, though great intereft was made
for feveral others , and this his excellency continued to enjoy with his embaffage to his death,
which happened March 20, 1675-6 *, when a patent was making out to create him a peer, his
death was owing, it is fuppofed, either to a pair
of poifoned gloves, or elfe to chagrin and difap-
pointment, in difcovering the fecret negociations

* A MS. I have, fays, fir Will. Lockhart died at the
Hague.

carried

N U M. XXIII

Lockharts.

Sir Will. Lock-
hart, knt. am-
baffador to the
court of France,
from his uncle
the prot Oliver

carried on between k. Cha. II. and Lewis the
french king, to which he was moſt averſe, and his
ſovereign was ſo well aware of it, that nothing of
the kind was diſcoverable in his inſtructions,
when he went to France, as biſhop Burnet witneſſes, who ſaw the original, but theſe ſhameful
tranſactions could not long eſcape the penetration
of a perſon of ſir William's wonderful ſagacity:
however, though he was appriſed of the undue
influence of the french court over that of London, yet he always acted in ſuch a manner as ſecured the honor · of the britiſh crown, during the
whole of his ſtay in France; regardleſs of the
diſpleaſure of either the ſovereign whoſe perſon
he repreſented, or him to whom he was ſent: two
inſtances will evince the truth of this: the french
taking advantage of our neutrality during the
dutch war, took many engliſh ſhips, ſome of them
extremely valuable, pretending they were dutch
under engliſh colors, the merchants complained
loudly, as the ſhips and cargoes were valued at a
million ſterling, and at laſt claimed one, proving
in the council that it was engliſh property, this
was told to ſir Will. and he preſſed it ſo cloſe to
the french miniſter, that he procured an order to
ſurrender it up, but, in the interim, the king of
Great-Britain was prevailed upon by ſecretary
Pepys, to acquaint the french ambaſſador, that
he did not concern himſelf about the ſhip, and
that ' he believed the merchants were ſuch rogues
' that they could bring witneſſes to prove any
' thing, and therefore the french court might
' do as they pleaſed reſpecting the veſſel.'　This
was communicated to the Court of Verſailles, the
conſequence was an order to ſtop the ſhip then
in the port of Dunkirk, ſir William hearing of it,
complained in the moſt pointed manner, and to
his great ſurpriſe was told the meſſage they had
received

received from the king his master; but instead of
being discouraged, he acted up to the dignity of
his elevated employment, by answering them re-
solutely, that the king only spoke by him. This
usage of the british court he so much resented,
that he requested to be recalled, as he could
serve no longer with honor, after he had been so
disowned; Charles seemed to have as little regard
for the national honor, as sir William was determined it should not be sullied by his means,
and if his conduct had not such an effect upon his
supine sovereign as it ought, yet his majesty found
it necessary to his affairs to excuse the matter,
which he did in a letter written by himself, justi-
fying sir William's conduct, and a secret order
was issued for the vessel's immediate discharge.
The other instance which I shall mention of sir
William's firmness whilst ambassador in France
was this: one of his french servants, when at the
point of death, sent to have the sacrament admi-
nistered to him according to the rites of the ro-
mish church, which they were going to do, not
privately, but with all the idle ceremonies of pro-
cession used by them, which so offended sir William as the ambassador of a *(supposed)* protestant
monarch, that he ordered his gates to be shut;
and when the enraged populace were going to
force them open, he ordered all his family to
stand to their arms, and repel force by force, see-
ing his determined resolution, they desisted, but
perhaps nothing made a greater noise, and,
considering the bigotry of the french king, a
bolder action could not be done. Conscious of
the resentment he should receive from Lewis, he
determined to complain first, so going to court,
he expostulated upon the affront he had received,
observing, that his house was the king his master's, and that a public triumph was attempted

NUM XXIII.

Lockharts.

Sir Will Lock-
hart, knt, am-
bassador to the
court of France,
from his uncle
the prot Oliver.

over

NUM. XXIII

Lockharts
Sir Will. Lock-
hart, knt. am-
baſſador to tne
court of France,
from his uncle
the prot. Oliver

over his ſovereign's religion, declaring, that if
the prieſt had brought the ſacrament privately he
would have connived at it, but as they had acted
ſo contrary, he demanded reparation for the inſult: This ſo ſenſibly touched Lewis, who had a
blind attachment to the religion of Rome, that
he was offended in the higheſt manner, declaring
it was the moſt public indignity that his God had
ever received in his reign, and diſpatched a
meſſenger after his excellency to acquaint him,
that he would uſe force to prevent any of the
ſubjects of France to ſerve him. ſir William replied to this menace, that he would order his
coachman to drive the quicker to Paris to prevent
it, leaving Pompone to gueſs the meaning, but
which was ſoon diſcovered, for immediately upon
his arriving at his own houſe, he ordered all his
french ſervants to be paid off and diſmiſſed, and
his britiſh majeſty, whatever real ſentiments he
might entertain, was obliged, in decency, to juſtify
the matter, and even wrote him a public letter of
thanks for his conduct. the haughty monarch of
France was neceſſitated to digeſt this affair as he
would, though he never forgave what he judged
ſo direct an inſult to his religion, but ever after
behaved to ſir William with evident coolneſs.

It is ſuperfluous to ſay much in praiſe of this great
character, his penetration, aſſiduity, and fidelity,
are as univerſally acknowledged, as his conſummate prudence and valor, and he certainly would
have rendered the nation the higheſt ſervices in his
laſt, as he had done in his former embaſſy, had he
been the ſervant of a patriotic ſovereign. The
whole nation bore teſtimony of his uncommon
worth, for when the news of his death reached
London, the parlement, that was then ſitting, ordered a committee of the houſe to wait upon the
king, to condole the loſs his majeſty had received
by

by being deprived of so able and faithful a minifter, declaring that they were senfibly touched
for the misfortune the whole kingdom had experienced by his death. Bifhop Burnet calls him,
and I think with the utmoft juftnefs, the greateft
man Scotland ever gave birth to in the age in
which he lived, with a fingle exception in favor
of fir Rob. Murray, perhaps many of my readers
would have thought his lordfhip might have even
omitted fir Robert. The particulars of his em-
baffies would fill a confiderable volume of themfelves; they were as honorable to his employers
as to himfelf; his firft embaffage is fully related
in his numerous letters given in Thurloe's ftate papers: and his conduct at the treaty of the Pyrenees
has been done by a foreign hand* ; nor is it neceffary to fay more of his great worth the beft
proof of his abilities and his virtues, is Oliver's
felecting him for the hufband of his near relation;
no one formed a truer judgment of the merit of
others, and it may be obferved, that by his ju-
dicioufly marrying his female kinfwomen, he
greatly advanced them in rank, or elfe fixed upon fuch perfons, who, by their own peculiar merit,
or from the caft of the times, muft (with his
patronage) advance themfelves, as well as materially ferve both himfelf and the public. Sir
William's remains were brought over from Paris
with all poffible folemnity to Leith, where they
lay in the church for fome time, from whence, with

---

* Monficur de Wicquefort, privy-counfellor to the duke of
Brunfwick and Lunenburg-Zell, in his 'Ambaffador and his
'functions,' has given a relation of the embafly of mr. Lockhart, minifter of England, at the Pyrenean treaty, with many
others of the moft celebrated of the englifh nation, about the
year 1715, mr Digby tranflated the work into englifh. I never met with it,

NUM. XXIII.

Lockharts.

Sir Will. Lock-
hart, knt am-
baſſader to the
court of France,
from his uncle
the prot. Oliver
great funeral pomp and ceremony, they were carried to Lanerk, and interred in the church amongſt
his anceſtors. There is a portrait of ſir Will at
lord Aberdeen's, and the family poſſeſs a miniature of him painted by Cooper, it is extraordinary that we have no engraving of this truly
great man.

Sir William had two ladies; the firſt he married
after his return into Scotland from Poland; ſhe
was a miſs Hamilton, daughter of —— Hamilton, eſq. of Orbiſtown, one of the ſenators of the
college of juſtice, and lord-juſtice-clerk in the
reign of k. Cha. I. by her he had one ſon, James,
who died unmarried at the age of 20 years · ſir
William's ſecond lady, was Robina, the daughter of
John Sewſter, eſq. by Anna, ſiſter of the protector
Oliver, for whom he had the higheſt eſteem and
regard, and which her amiable behaviour and
prudence entirely deſerved. ſhe ſurviving him,
was left guardian, and had the care of the education of his children, he alſo gave her the ſole
adminiſtration of all his affairs ſhe executed her
truſt with the greateſt care and fidelity; her memory is ſo precious to the family, that her name
has been conſtantly retained by her deſcendants
ſhe retired into England, where ſhe died, but at
what time or place is not known, ſhe was living
ſo late as 1684. It appears by Thurloe's ſtate
papers, that ſhe was near dying of a lying-in,
when in France during her huſband's firſt embaſſy. ſhe was, it is evident, much beloved by
her uncle the elder protector, over whom ſhe
had much influence, ſhe requeſted, and probably
obtained of his highneſs, a company in her huſband's regiment, for her brother-in-law Lockhart.
‘ She was a lady of great wit and ſpirit.' By lady
Robina, ſir Will. had 3 daughters and 7 ſons; 1.
Robina,

Robina, married to Archibald Douglas, earl
of Forfar, whofe only fon, a moſt lively youth,
was appointed envoy in 1715 to the court of Sir Will Lock-
Pruſſia, but the rebellion unhappily breaking out, hart, knt. am-
he came poſt from London to Scotland : moſt baſſador to the court of France,
unfortunately he received a dangerous wound in from his uncle
the battle of Sherry-muir, fought nov. 13th in the prot. Oliver.
that year, of which he languiſhed until dec. 15th
following, when he died univerfally lamented.
2. Martha, ſhe had fome employment in the
bed-chamber to q. Mary II. and had a penſion for
life granted her after thē death of her majeſty ; ſhe
and mrs. Cutts, ſiſter of lord Cutts, had apartments in the palace of Somerſet-houfe : ſhe was
living at her brother James's death, and appointed
by him executrix of his will. 3. Elizabeth, who
died young and unmarried. 4. Cromwell, who,
as his half brother James died a bachelor before his
father, fucceeded to the family eſtates, he married twice, firſt Ann, daughter of Sir Daniel Harvey, who had been ambaſſador to Conſtantinople,
ſhe was niece to the duke of Montagu, and fecondly, to Martha, only daughter of his uncle ſir John
Lockhart, by neither of whom he had any child :
it is fingular, that he had fo great a diſlike to have
any hereditary honor in his family, that he limited his eſtates in fuch a manner, that if any of his
heirs ſhould accept of any dignity of that kind,
it ſhould prevent their enjoying the family eſtates.
5. Rich. who fucceeded his brother as laird of
Lee, he had no iſſue by Jean, daughter of ſir
Patrick Houfton, of that Ilk, bart. 6 Julius, who
was killed at Tangiers ; he was a bachelor. 7.
William, who alfo never married. 8. Geo. he
likewife died fingle. 9. John was a captain
in a company of dragoons, he died fept. 6.
1707,

NUM XXIII.

Lockharts.
Sir Will Lock-
hart, knt. am-
baſſador to the
court of France,
from his uncle
the prot. Olver.

1707, having married Eliz. daughter of ſir Tho. Scot, of Scotſhall in Kent, by whom he had an only child, Robina, who married Edw. Alſton, profeſſor of botany in the college of Edinburgh, whoſe only child is alſo named Robina, and is now living; ſhe is married to ——— Birnie, of Broomhill, in Lanerkſhire, eſq. 10. James, who ſucceeded to the family eſtate of Lee, he was a commiſſioner of the equivalent, and member in the firſt parlement of k George I. for the county of Lanerk, in which ſtation he continued until his death, which happened ſuddenly in 1718, leaving the character of being a ' perſon of great ability and integrity.' by his wife Dorothy, daughter and co-heireſs of ſir Will. Lockyn, of Waltham-abbey, in Eſſex, bart. he had four ſons and three daughters, all of whom died young, except John, and Ann, his eldeſt daughter, who married to captain John Pollock, ſon of ſir Rob. Pollock, of that Ilk, ſhe had an only child named Robina, married to ſir Hugh Crawford, of Jordan-hill, bart. now living, and the mother of many children. and John Lockhart, eſq. the third but only ſurviving ſon of Ja Lockhart, eſq. ſucceeded to the family eſtate, which had been enjoyed by the Lockharts, his anceſtors, for 600 years, and what is ſtill more extraordinary, he was the eighteenth perſon in lineal deſcent, if my authority is good; an inſtance, perhaps, unparallelled. Mr. Lockhart married twice, firſt, Jean, daughter and ſole heireſs of Rob. Alexander, of Blackhouſe, in Airſhire, eſq and ſecondly, Mary, eldeſt daughter of John Porterfield, of Falwood, in Renfrewſhire, eſq but he leaving no child by either of them, at his death, which happened in 1775, the intailed eſtate of Lee, with others, deſcended

descended to the heir of a younger brother of sir
Will. Lockhart the ambassador.

As I have been so highly favored by the Lockhart family, as not only to have had a memoir of the ambassador's life, with an account of his descendants, but also of his two younger brothers, I will request leave to mention them, and their children, and I am the more inclined to this, as I am enabled to give some new materials to those sent me.

Sir Geo. Lockhart, of Carnwath, a younger brother of sir William's, was bred to the bar, and became advocate to his highness Oliver; he was returned for the sheriffdom of Lanerk, in 1658-9; after the restoration he was knighted, and became lord-president of the court of Session; by his profession (of which he was at the head) he amassed a great fortune: he was shot dead as he came from a church in Edinburgh, on Easter-day, in 1689. Sir Geo. married the lady Philadelphia, daughter of Phil. lord Wharton, and sister to the duke of that title; she surviving him, re-married to captain John Ramsey, son to the bishop of Ross: she died July 3, 1722 Sir Geo. by this lady had two sons, and one daughter; 1. Geo. of whom below. 2. —— who died unmarried. 3. —— whose name is unknown.

Sir Geo Lockhart of Carnwath, knt son of sir Ja. Lockhart, and younger brother to sir Will Lockhart, knt ambassador.

Geo. Lockhart, esq. a commissioner for settling the articles of union between the kingdoms of England and Scotland; he was a true patriot, as his memoirs witness: he died about 1732, having married lady Euphemia Montgomery, daughter to the earl of Eglintoun, by whom he had 5 sons and 3 daughters; 1. Geo. of whom presently. 2. Alexander, born in 1701, and died in 1782: he was the greatest barrister Scotland ever produced: by Margaret Pringle, of Edgefield, whom he married

Geo Lockhart, of Carnwath, esq

married in 1725, he had 5 sons and four daughters, the eldeſt died young. Tho. the 2nd, repreſented the boroughs of Kintore, Bamff, Cullen, Elgin, and Inverurie, from the year 1768, until his death. he left no iſſue by his wife, the daughter of ——— Danby, of Swinton, in Yorkſhire, eſq. Alex. the 3rd ſon, was killed at the battle of Minden. Will. the 4th ſon, lately married ——— daughter of ſir Rob. Henderſon, of Fordell, in Fife. Rob. the 5th ſon is at Bencoolen, in the Eaſt-Indies. Rebecca, the 6th, married to lord Boyd, ſon of the amiable, but unfortunate lord Kilmarnock, and became ſince earl of Errol, by the death of his aunt: they have a daughter married to general Scot. Flaminia, the 7th, is unmarried; as is Suſan, the 8th. Ann, the 9th, married to the hon. Cha. Boyd, eſq. 2nd ſon of the laſt earl of Kilmarnock, ſhe is ſince dead, leaving no child. 3. William, who is ſtill living and unmarried. 4. James. 5 Philip, both of whom died bachelors 6. Grace, married to the earl of Aboyne, by whom ſhe had three ſons, the preſent earl of Aboyne, married firſt to Margaret, daughter of the earl of Galloway, the iſſue of which marriage is a ſon and a daughter, lord Strathaven, and Margaret, married to William Beckford, of Fonthill, eſq. lord Aboyne's 2nd counteſs was Mary, daughter of the earl of Morton, by whom he has one ſon, the lord ——— Douglas *, John, 2nd ſon of the firſt mentioned earl of Aboyne, died a colonel in the army, leaving 3 ſons and 2 daughters, by miſs Clementina Lockhart, his couſin-german, by his mother. John, in the Eaſt-

---

* The earl of Aboyne leaving his 2nd lady a widow, ſhe remarried Fra. lord Down, eldeſt ſon of the earl of Moray, by whom ſhe had the preſent earl of Moray, and Euphemia, who died unmarried. The preſent earl of Moray, by Jean, daughter of lord Gray, has three ſons and four daughters.

India company's fervice at Calcutta. Geo. a mid-
fhipman in the navy. James, who died young.
Clementina and Grace, both unmarried. Lockhart, third fon of the earl of Aboyne, married
mifs Wallop, fifter to lord Portfmouth. 7.
Euphemia, married to the earl of Wigtown, who
died without any iffue; and Mary, married to
John Rattray, efq. brother to ———— Rattray, in
Angusfhire, fhe had only Mary, who is unmarried.

    Geo. Lockhart, efq. died in 1761 : by Fergufia, Geo Lockhart
daughter and heirefs of fir George Wifhart, of of Carnwath,
Clifton-hall, he had fix fons and two daughters; efq
1. Geo. who engaging in the rebellion in 1745,
was attainted : he died in Paris in 1761, leaving
no child; 2. James, of whom hereafter, as continuator of the eldeft branch of the Lockhart family, 3. John; 4. Alexander; 5. William, all
of whom died young; 6. Charles, born feb. 28,
1740-1, he married, aug. 17, 1762, Eliz. daughter and heirefs of John Macdonald, of Largie, in
Argylefhire, a family of much refpect and fufficient
fortune; and in confequence of this lady's being
an heirefs, he has added her family name to his
own the iffue of their marriage has been Geo.
who died young : John, whofe death was occafioned from fatigue at the fiege of Mungalore, upon
the Malabar coaft; James, Alexander, Norman,
Eliz. Helen, who died young; Clementina, Matilda, Mary, Charles-Sarah, and Euphemia; 7.
Clementina, who married the hon. John Gordon,
fecond fon of the earl of Aboyne, her coufin-ger-
man, and 8 Euphemia, who died unmarried; 9.
Ann-Matilda, born in november, 1774.

    James Lockhart, efq. born nov. 16, 1727, Gen. James
who, from his brother's imprudence, fucceeded Lockhart, of both
to the Lee and Carnwath eftates, and is now the Lee and Carn-
reprefentative of this very ancient family; when wath
                          young,

young, he entered into the fervice of the dutch, but about 1752, he went into the auftrian army, and became lieutenant-general, was alfo created count of the holy roman empire, chevalier de l'ordre de Marie Therefe, and is the only proteftant that has been fo honored. it was conferred upon him in confideration of his fignal military fervices: his income muft be very large, as befides the great emoluments of his high pofts abroad, he poffeffes the largeft eftate in his own county, except the duke of Hamilton: he married, firft, Matilda, fecond daughter of John Lockhart, of Caftle-hill. fhe died at Pifa in 1768, and, fecondly, Mary-Ann, daughter of —— Murray, efq. allied to the family of Stormont, this unfortunate lady died lately: the iffue by the former of thefe wives, is a fon and a daughter, and by the latter, two fons and a daughter, 1. Geo. who died young, 2. Therefa, born jan. 19, 1764; 3 Jofeph, who died young; 4. Cha. born may 6, 1778, and 5. Mary. Having taken all the defcendants of fir George Lockhart, of Carnwath, I fhall fpeak of John, the youngeft brother of him, and alfo of fir Will. Lockhart, the ambaffador to France.

Sir John Lockhart, of Caftlehill, knt. youngeft brother of fir Will Lockhart, knt the ambaffador to France.

Sir John Lockhart, knt. youngeft fon of fir James Lockhart, was feated at Caftle-hill, he ferved for the fheriffdoms of Dumbarton, Argyle, and Bute, in the parlement called by the protector Oliver, in 1656, and for the city of Glafgow, and the boroughs of Lanerk, Rutherglen, Rothfay, Renfrew, Ayre, Trevyn, and Dumbarton, in 1658-9. King Charles II knighted him, and appointed him one of the fenators of the college of juftice, and lord-jufticiary: he left an only child, Martha, who married twice, 1ft, her coufin Cromwell Lockhart, efq. eldeft fon of fir Will. Lockhart, the lord ambaffador, by his fecond lady Robina.

bina, niece to the protector Oliver; but he dying
young, she re-married to ———— Sinclair, of Stevenson, esq. by the latter husband she had three
sons, 1. ————; 2. John, and 3. Rob. Sinclair,
sheriff of Lanerkshire, and unmarried; John, the
second son, succeeded to the estate of Castle-hill;
he had only three daughters, Ann, married to
Tho, Millar, of Barskimming, the present lord
justice clerk of Scotland, by whom she has no
issue. Matilda was the first wife of general Lockhart, of Lee. Isabella, married to Will. More-
head of Hertfordshire. As the estates were devised to heirs male, they went upon the death of
John Sinclair, the father of these daughters, to
his brother's eldest son, who is sir John Sinclair,
of Stevenson, the second son of whom has changed
his name from Sinclair to Lockhart, to enjoy the
estate of Castle-hill; he has one son and three
daughters *.

* The hist. of sir Will. Lockhart is chiefly taken from a
memoir written at the desire of his grandson, and most obligingly communicated to me, with other information, by mrs.
Lockhart, and Cha Lockhart Macdonald, esq. various histories of England, Thurloe's state papers, several lives of Oliver
lord protector, &c.

No. XXIV.

The history of the Disbrowe family, allied to the Cromwells by the marriage of John Disbrowe, esq. one of Oliver the protector's lords, with Jane, sister to that sovereign.

Disbrowes Arms.

THE family of Disbrowe are of a genteel, rather than an ancient or honorable descent, it is probable that though they had assumed arms, they were not intitled to that distinction, for in the last visitation of Cambridgeshire, though there is an entry that they had taken, or, on a bend gules, three bears heads couped and muzzled argent, yet there is this memorandum opposite to it: ' Mr. Disbrowe vouched his arms to be or, a fesse ' gules, charged with three bears heads erased ' argent, muzzled of the second; but, on his gold ' ring he gives it with a fesse between three bears ' heads erased. Qu. Ergo for no right appears to ' either bearing *.'

—— D.f-owe, gent.

The Disbrowes seated themselves at Eltisley, in Cambridgeshire, which manor and advowson they possessed. ——Disbrowe, gent. was the common ancestor of all of those who have risen to eminence, he had at least two sons; from John the eldest, came the major-general, and the lord chancellor

* Gwillim's 4th edition says, ' Argent a fesse between ' three bears heads couped sable, muzzled or; which is the ' seal of the hon. John lord Disbrowe, one of his highness's ' privy council, and major general of the west.' So here are three bearings used, which looks as if they had no right to any.

of

of Scotland, and from the youngeſt, a numerous
family.

John Diſbrowe, gent. the eldeſt ſon, was buried
at Eltiſley, may 24, 1610, he had ſeven ſons
and two daughters; 1. William, who died an infant, 2. John, who died at the age of twenty years,
and unmarried; 3. James the father of the two
celebrated perſons mentioned above, 4. Laurence,
who died an infant; 5. Joſeph, who, by Ann his
wife, had a daughter named Dinah; 6. Iſaac, who,
by Mary his wife, had ſix ſons and three daughters;
7. Sarah; and 8. Joan.

James Diſbrowe, gent. the third, but the eldeſt
ſurviving ſon of John Diſbrowe, was alſo lord of
the manor of Eltiſley, where he was buried oct. 23,
1638, aged 56: by Eliz his wife, who alſo was
buried at Eltiſley, jan. 26, 1628-9, he had iſſue
eight ſons and five daughters; 1. James, baptized jan. 4, 1606-7, and who ſucceeded his father
in his eſtates at Eltiſley; 2. John, the major-general, of whom below; 3. Bruno, bapt. aug. 18,
1613, and buried aug. 27, following, 4. Bruno,
baptized oct. 26, 1616, and buried july 17, 1618;
5. Samuel, who became lord chancellor cf Scotland, whoſe life will be given after that of his
brother John's, the major-general, 6. Matthew,
baptized feb. 23, 1622-3, and buried march 1,
following; 7. Iſaac, baptized march 20, 1624, he
was one of the protector Oliver's aſſeſſors of
Cambridgeſhire, he had a family, 8 Tho. bapt.
oct. 25, 1625, 9. Rebecca, baptized may 9,
1615, ſhe married, nov. 15, 1631, to mi. Geo.
Green, 10. Ann, 11. Sarah, 12. Ann, all of
whom died children, and 13. Elizabeth, baptized
jan 7, 1628-9.

Before I proceed to the life of John Diſbrowe,
eſq. the major-general, who was the ſecond ſon,
I ſhall ſay ſomewhat of James, the eldeſt. He

was

was remarkably difaffected to the monarchical, as well as epifcopal government, and he rendered El-tifley, the place of his refidence, memorable for being an afylum for the moft extravagant fa-naticifm, having placed over that parifh mr. H Denne, an ambitious time-ferving clergyman, whom he had (through the intereft of the all-powerful mr. Cromwell) releafed from prifon, this man, to pleafe his patron, and the loweft of the rabble, fell in with all the ridiculous folly that fo much difgraced the æra of liberty. Pfalm-finging was as heinous a fin at Eltifley, as bend-ing the knee to Baal, and it was then as much noted for the *devout exercifes* practifed there, as any other canting place in the kingdom, fo great a patron of the godly was fure of gaining the friendfhip of the party, he was appointed a fe-queftrator, an office he was peculiarly well qua-lified for, and Oliver nominated him one of the affeffors of his monthly payments. Mr. Dif-browe, july 13, 1630, married Ann Proby, by whom he had iffue; his defcendants remained lords of the manor and patrons of the church of Eltifley, until the beginning of this century, when the rev. Ja. Difbrowe, of that place, dying in 1703, leaving two daughters his co-heirefses (Eliz. one of them, married the fucceeding year to mr. Rob. Shipfea), they difpofed of the manor of Eltifley to ——— Barron, of Everfden, in Cam-bridgefhire, efq.

John Difbrowe, efq the fecond fon of James Difbrowe, gent. and the brother of the above Ja. Difbrowe, efq. was baptized at Eltifley, nov 13, 1608; he was bred an attorney, with which pro-feffion he cultivated an eftate of 70l. per. ann bequeathed him by his father, until the civil wars broke out, when he quitted the pen and the fpade for the buftle of the camp. At the age of 28, he he married Jane the daughter of Rob Cromwell, efq. and fifter to mr. Oliver Cromwell, afterwards Difbrowes fo celebrated, he joined the parlement in their John Difbrowe, difpute with k. Cha. I. and firft became a captain efq the major-general, brother in his brother-in-law Cromwell's troop of horfe, in law to Oliver but he foon difcovered that as an officer he deferved lord protector a fuperior poft; the parlement was fo well pleafed with his gallantry at Woodftock, that they gave him 100l. and the thanks of the houfe, he continuing to merit their favors, obtained a colonel's commiffion of horfe, he rendered the army moft important fervice, by being greatly inftrumental in quelling the levellers, and in 1648, he rofe to be a major-general; he was one who took up the petition againft the eleven members of the houfe of commons, and was named one of the commiffioners of the high court of juftice to try the king, but refufed to fit.

The commonwealth appointed him governor of Yarmouth, and in 1650, he had the care of the Weft entirely given to him : Whitlock fays he gave great contentment in this poft, that he vifited in that year, Taunton, and all the garrifons from Weymouth to Pendennis-caftle, and put them in a pofture of defence; the fame author alfo commends him for a charge he delivered at the feffions at Exeter, which in fome meafure contradicts the affertion, that he made no proficiency in the law line, and that this had occafioned his going into the army. King Charles II was near falling into his hands after the battle of Worcefter, when his majefty was not far from Salifbury, and at that time difguifed as a fervant, riding before a female relation of col. Windham's, conducted by col. Philips, but though they were obliged to pafs through a regiment of horfe, and met Difbrowe and four others, and the road was

T 3 full

full of soldiers, yet Charles escaped even suspi-
cion, either because his person was not known by
the colonel, or because the king was so disguised
in the servant, that majesty could not be recon-
noitred.   In the same year he was declared one of
the council of state, and a commissioner of the
treasury, in jan. 1652-3, he was appointed and
acted as one of the commissioners who tried and
condemned Theobald viscount Mayo, to be shot
to death, upon a charge exhibited against him of
several murders committed during the rebellion
in Ireland: in this year he was, during the dutch
war, declared one of the four generals of the fleet,
a member of the council, and he was one of those
who were voted to sit in that parlement which
gave Oliver the government of these nations;
but he was so entirely a republican, that though
nearly allied to, and greatly courted by Cromwell, yet he was always an enemy to the office
of protector, as to regal dignity, he could not
bear the idea of it, and it was chiefly through
him that Oliver did not take the crown, as he
procured a petition from the army against his
assumption of the title of king; which, unknown
to the latter, was presented to the parlement
his conscience, however tender it might be, was
not so delicate, but that he accepted of many
places of trust, as well as of great power and emolument, under Oliver's government: for he was
declared one of his privy council in 1653, he
was returned a member of parlement for the counties of Cambridge and Somerset, and for Totnefs,
in the year 1654, one of the scotch council in
1655; a commissioner with admirals Blake and
Montagu, to superintend naval affairs; a commissioner of the treasury, a lord of the Cinque
Ports, a visitor of the university of Cambridge,

major-

major-general of the counties of Wilts, Dorset, Somerset, Devon, and Cornwall; in 1656, he represented the county of Somerset, the city of Gloucester, and the town of Lynn; and in 1657, he was removed to the other house, where he took his seat without making any objections. The protector Richard endeavoured to win him to his interest, by appointing him one of his privy-council, and chancellor of Ireland, but without effect. He submitted with unwillingness to Oliver, and as he was conscious his son did not possess his abilities, and that he was courted by Richard only from fear, he joined with the Wallingford junto to dethrone him; add to this perhaps an haughtiness that could not brook to see any other his superior.

Lord Broghill says, that as a means to effect the ruin of the protector Richard, he proposed, in the great council of officers, that as *the Lord* had been so gracious to them, to secure his favor, they should admit none but the saints; wherefore he would recommend them to purge the army, by proposing a test, 'that every one should swear ' that he did believe in his conscience, that the ' putting to death the late king Charles Stuart, ' was lawful and just:' the lords Howard and Fauconberg deserted the assembly, as fearing no good could be effected, however lord Broghill remained, and defended the government of Richard, which was intended to be destroyed by this proposition and his lordship, to effectually counteract the other's intentions, proposed an oath to defend the established government under the protector and the parlement, which his lordship said was reasonable, since their political existence depended upon it; and lawful, because it would defend and preserve the present government;

NUM. XXIV.

Disbrowes.
John Disbrowe, esq the major-general,-brother in-law to Oliver lord protector.

T 4   declaring,

NUM. XXIV

Disbrowes
John Disbrowe,
esq the major-
general, brother-
in-law to Oliver
lord protector.

declaring, that should the proposition be rejected
there, he would move it in parlement, where he
knew it would be well received, this was so acceptable to colonels Whalley and Gough, persons
easily moved, that they in the most forcible
manner declared for the last test, which obliged
both the major-general and Fleetwood to com-
promise the matter, and they thought themselves
happy in having neither of the engagements insisted upon.

. Upon the resignation of his nephew, the restored parlement gave him a colonel's commission,
but, as he leaned more to the interest of the army than the parlement, and only meant to make
them the dupes of the former, they so far resented his accepting the rank of commissary-general
at the time when the army tumultuously declared
Fleetwood their general, and were so much alarmed at his conduct, that they deprived him of his
regiment: his conduct was so preposterous and
so violent, that both he and Fleetwood were ri-
diculed by all parties, and his own regiment had
such a dislike to his person, that it revolted. The
parlement, however, fearful of exasperating him
too much, elected him one of the council of state,
and one of the ten who were to consider of fit
ways to carry on the affairs of government, and
likewise appointed him governor of the island and
fort of Plymouth, all in the year 1659, but he
continuing to cabal with the army, the parlement
confined him to his seat, farthest removed from
the capital, but released him upon his submission
and promise to live peaceably, his rudeness,
perhaps, as much provoked them as his restless-
ness, for the former he is thus lampooned in one
of the loyal songs.

                                        And

And Defborough's gotten into his Farm,
    With a Hey-day, &c.
Until they do him need.
Meant the houfe no harm,
But took it for a Barn,
His Lord and he's not agreed *.

NUM XXIV.

Difbrowes.

John Difbrowe, efq the major-general, brother-in-law to Oliver lord protector.

Upon the profpect of the reftoration he endeavoured to leave the kingdom, but was arrefted by the fheriff of Effex, near the coaft, and confined again by the parlement, which excepted him out of the act of indemnity, but not to extend to the forfeiture of life. He was fcarce fet at liberty, but he was again feized in London, and fent to prifon, under a fufpicion of being engaged in an affaffination plot againft the royal family; but as the plot itfelf never, in all probability, exifted, he foon obtained his freedom. Finding himfelf fufpected of difaffection, he wifhed to fpend the remainder of his life upon the Continent in quietnefs; but in this he was difappointed, the court was ftill jealous of him, upon an idea that he and others of the old party would affift in reviving the republican fpirit, and as the exceffes of majefty never were greater than during the reigns of the two royal brothers, Charles and James, we

---

* It has been before obferved, that Difbrowe had employed himfelf, before the civil wars, in agriculture, which the preceding ftanza alludes to, as well as the two following verfes of different fongs

> Who can gain-fay that it was a ftrong F-rt
> Which blew the Lord Defborough back to his Cart,
> And taught filly Fleetwood of crying the art,
>   Which nobody can deny.
> Jantzuy Defborough then look'd pale,
> For, faid he, if the Rump prevail,
> 'Twill blow me back to my plow tail,
>   Which nobody can deny.

cannot

NUM. XXIV.

Difbrowes.

John Difbrowe, efq. the major-general, brother-in-law to Oliver lord protector.

cannot wonder at their apprehenfion, that thofe fevere judges would take advantage of their conduct to revive their beloved commonwealth, and efpecially, as they were encouraged in it by the dutch ; the court, to prevent any fuch defigns, determined to fecure his perfon, with the other heads of the party *, to effect which, they fet forth a proclamation, in 1665, to require him, with feveral of his friends, to be in England before july 23, in the following year, and furrender himfelf into the hands of fome juftice of peace in that county where he fhould land in, on pain of being declared a traitor, in confequence of this, he came over from Oftend, yet, although he fo readily obeyed the proclamation, he was committed a prifoner to Dover caftle, july 18, 1666, until the king's pleafure fhould be further known, how long he continued there does not appear, but he regained his liberty, and was again fummoned by a proclamation publifhed by k. James II. april 21, 1686, requiring him to return again into this kingdom by july 22 following, or he would be fubject to the fame penalties as were expreffed in the former one.

What became of him after this is uncertain, but, probably, he furvived the revolution, and fpent the latter part of his old age in his native land : that event muft have given him the greateft pleafure ; it would not, indeed, come up to his idea of liberty, but to fee driven from the throne an unfortunate family, who were particularly odious to him, from the injuries he had done to, and the hardfhips he had experienced

* The other gentlemen who were commanded to return into England with major-general Difbrowe, in 1665, were colonels Kelfay and White, major Grove, fir Rob. Honeywood, jun and capt. Nichols.

under

undei them, muſt have been ſuch as can only be known to a perſon of his diſpoſition. Diſbrowe poſſeſſed a great deal of turbulence, pride, avarice, and ambition, but had not a capacity ſufficient to raiſe himſelf to the head of a party *; his perſon and addreſs were little likely to inſpire reſpect, or gain affection, Granger ſays, ' he was clowniſh in ' his manners, and boiſterous in his behaviour;' this alſo is pointedly expreſſed in two ſtanzas of the loyal ſongs, entitled, ' the committee of ſafety,' and the ſecond part of ' the Gang, or the Nine ' Worthies :'

NUM XXIV.
Diſbrowes.
John Diſbrowe,
eſq the major-
general, brother-
in-law to Oliver
lord protector.

Deſborough's a Clown, of whom it is ſed,
That to be a ſtates-man he never was bred,
For his ſhoulders are far better proof than his head,
 Oh bleſſed reformation !

Deſborough was ſuch a country ſwain,
 With a hey down, down, a down, down.
An Eaſter ſun ne'er ſee ;
 He drove on amain
 Without any brain
Such a jolt-head knave was he,
 With a hey down, &c.

There is a portrait of him on horſeback, ſold by Stent, 4to ſize, and a wooden cut of giant Diſbrowe, a great club in his right hand, jointly with Lambeit, leading the meek knight, i. e. Rich. the protector, giving in the comical hiſtory of Don Juan Lamberto, and which, perhaps,

* Under the protectors the major-general enjoyed places, whoſe annual amount was many thouſand pounds, and he acquiied a prodigious property, conſideiing his ſlender beginning.

did

NUM XXIV

Difbrowes
John Difbrowe,
efq the major-
general, brother-
in-law to Oliver
lord protector

did not a little help to fell the book *. The major-general had, I apprehend, a fecond wife, as a MS. in the Britifh Mufeum, fays he married Bolton's wife's fifter, and with her had 2000l. but probably there was no iffue of this marriage : by his firft wife, Jane, fifter to the eldeft protector, he had a daughter, who died unmarried, and feven fons, 1. John, the eldeft, was baptized at the church of St. John the Baptift, in Huntingdon, april 27, 1637, it muft be he who is thus hand-fomely fpoken of by Lockhart, in a letter to Thur-loe, dated from Paris, may 2, 1657 : ' Mr. Dif- ' browe is really a very ingenious gentleman, and ' I am confident will anfwer the height of all ' your expectations concerning him.' It appears he was fent to France, to qualify him for foreign embaffages, the protector greatly wanting fit per-fons for that office, as few of his own relations were in all refpects equal to that employment. the other fons are not named, except Rich. and the two youngeft, Valentine and Benjamin : I will firft fpeak of the former of thefe two fons, and his defcendants.

Valentine Difbrowe, efq. the fixth fon of the major-general, was feated at Bocking, in Effex, he was the father of two fons and four daughters· 1. John, who probably died unmarried, 2. Va-lentine, who died a youth, the names of the two eldeft daughters only are known.

Mary, daughter
of Val Dif-
browe, efq and
the families de-
fcended from
her

The Davys.

Mary, married in dec. 1694, to mr. Rob. Davy, by whom fhe had a fon and two daughters, Rob. who died young; Eliz. married to mr. Ely, of Dedham, in Effex, mr. Tho. Ely, their eldeft fon, by mifs Peacock, has left many defcendants.

---

* In the 2nd impreffion of the above book was a 2nd part added, before which was a portrait of col Hewfon, who had been a cobler

Elizabeth,

Elizabeth, the daughter of mr. Ely, by miſs Davy,
married to mr. Will. Parker, a clothier, of Dedham, Will. their only ſon, left alſo an only child,
Will. Parker, now a minor. Saiah, the younger
daughter of mr. Davy, married mr. Bright : from
this marriage there were at leaſt two ſons and
a daughter: one of whom was mr. Edward Bright,
a grocer, at Malden, in Eſſex, ſo well known
by the name of the *Great Bright*, as the fatteſt
man that has been known; of this very remarkable man, the beſt account extant is in this letter,
written by dr. T. Coe, phyſician at Chelmsford,
in Eſſex, to dr. Cromwell Mortimer, ſecretary
to the Royal Society, dated from Chelmsford,
april 16, 1751, and read to the ſociety, may 9
following.

'SIR,

' I now ſend you a plain, but true and authentic
account of an extraordinary man, whom you your-
ſelf have ſeen, and whom I have known ever ſince
he was a boy, viz. mr. Edward Bright, grocer,
late of Malden, in Eſſex, who died there the 10th
of november laſt, in the thirtieth year of his age.
He was a man ſo extremely fat, and of ſuch an
uncommon bulk and weight, that I believe there
are very few, if any ſuch inſtances to be found in
any other country, or upon record in any books;
at leaſt I have never read or heard any genuine account of a man, who was equal, or even came
near to him in weight. I know that dr. Allen, in
his Synopſis univerſæ medicinæ practicæ, quotes
Sennertus for a woman of 450 pounds, and for a
man, who weighed 600 pounds, and Chambers,
in his dictionary, mentions the ſame preciſely
the ſame way, which, therefore, I ſuppoſe he
took from Allen. But the numbers are falſely
printed in Allen, for, as they ſtand in Sennertus,

cap.

cap. de corpulentia nimia, the weight of the woman is 480 pounds, and that of the man ſeveral
pounds more than 400.

'If the following ſtory of mr. Bright ſhould exceed the faith of any in the preſent age, there are
a great many witneſſes, who can atteſt it ; and if
poſterity ſhould find themſelves at a loſs to believe
it, upon his bare relation, they may have further
evidence, if they will be at the pains to conſult a
public record of the corporation, made by the or
der of the preſent magiſtrates, and alſo the regiſter
of the pariſh of All Saints, in Malden, where he
was buried ; in both which they will find the main
facts properly vouched.

'Mr. Bright was deſcended from families greatly
inclined to corpulency, both on his father's and his
mother's ſide. Many of his anceſtors and relations
have been remarkably fat, though very far inferior to him in bulk. He was always fat from a
child, and yet very ſtrong and active, and uſed
a great deal of exerciſe, both when a boy, and after
he became a man, which he continued to do till
within the laſt two or three years of his life, when
he became too unwieldy. He could walk very
well, and nimbly too, having great ſtrength of
muſcles, and could not only ride on horſeback,
but would ſometimes gallop, after he was grown
to between thirty and forty ſtones weight. He
uſed to go to London about his buſineſs, till the
journey of forty miles, and going about there, became too great a fatigue for him, and he left it
off for ſome years before he died. But he was
grown to ſuch a ſize before he left it off, that he
was the gazing-ſtock and admiration of all people,
as he walked along the ſtreets. In the laſt year or
two he could walk but a little way, being ſoon
tired and out of breath, and travelled abroad but
little, and that in a chaiſe. He was ſo large and

fat

fat a boy, that at the age of twelve years and a half, he weighed ten ſtone and four pounds, horſe-man's weight, i. e. 144 pounds *, and he in-creaſed in bulk as he grew up, ſo that in ſeven years more, that is, before he was twenty, he weighed twenty-four ſtones, or three hundred and thirty-ſix pounds. He went on increaſing, and probably in pretty near the ſame proportion; for, the laſt time he was weighed, which was about thirteen months before he died, his weight was forty-two ſtones and twelve pounds, with only his waiſtcoat, ſhirt, breeches and ſtockings on; and theſe cloaths, being afterwards weighed, were found to be ſixteen pounds, ſo that his neat weight at that time was forty-one ſtones and ten pounds, or five hundred and eighty-four pounds. What his exact weight was at the time of his death, cannot be told, but as he was manifeſtly grown bigger ſince the laſt weighing, which he himſelf and every body about him were ſenſible of, if we take the ſame proportion, by which he had increaſed for many years upon an average, viz. of about two ſtones a year, and only allow four pounds addition for laſt year, on account of his moving about but very little, while he continued to eat and drink as before (which allowance is, perhaps, leſs than might be granted); this will bring him to forty-four ſtones, or ſix hundred and ſixteen pounds neat weight : and that I find by the judgment of the moſt rational people, who knew him well, and ſaw him often, is reckoned a very fair and modeſt computation, and the loweſt that can be made.

* ' There is at this time (1751) at Malden, a boy not fourteen years old (no relation to mr Bright), who weighs as much. Tulpius, Obſ. medic. lib. 3, cap. 55, tells us of a boy of vaſt bulk and ſtrength, who at five years of age weighed 150 pounds, but does not ſay what became of him afterwards.'

" As

'As to his meafure, he was five feet, nine inches and a half high. His body round the cheft, juft under the arms, meafured five feet fix inches, and round the belly fix feet eleven inches. His arm in the middle of it was two feet two inches about, and his leg two feet eight inches.

'He had always a good appetite, and when a youth, ufed to eat fomewhat remarkably; but, of late years, though he continued to eat heartily, and with a good relifh, yet he did not eat more in quantity than many other men, who, we fay have good ftomachs.

'As to his drink, though he did not take any liquor to an intoxicating degree, yet, perhaps, upon the whole, he drank more than might have been advifable to a man 'c his very corpulent difpofition. When he was a very young man, he was fond of ale and old ftrong beer; but for fome years paft his chief liquor was fmall beer, of which he commonly drank about a gallon in a day. In other liquors he was extremely moderate, when by himfelf, fometimes drinking half a pint of wine after dinner, or a little punch, and feldom exceeding his quantity; but when he was in company, he did not confine himfelf to fo fmall an allowance.

'He enjoyed, for the moft part of his life, as good health as any man, except that in the laft three years he was two or three times feized with an inflammation in his leg, attended with a little fever, and every time with fuch a tendency to mortification, as to make it neceffary to fcarify the part. But, by the help of fcarification and fomentations, bleeding largely once or twice in the arm, and purging, he was always foon relieved. I fay bleeding largely, for it was always the cuftom with him to have not lefs than two pounds of blood taken away at a time, and he

was

was no more fenfible of the lofs of fuch a quantity, than another man is of 12 or 14 ounces.

'He married when he was between twenty-two and twenty-three years old, and lived a little more than feven years in that ftate; in which time he had five children born, and left his wife with child of the fixth, near her time.

'There was an amiable mind in this extraordinary over-grown body. He was of a cheeiful temper, and a good-natured man, a kind hufband, a tender father, a good mafter, a friendly neighbour, and a very fair, honeft man. So that he was beloved and refpected by all who knew him, and would have been as much lamented by his acquaintance, as any man in any ftation of life ever was, had it not been, that they looked upon him for feveral years as a man who could not live long, and out of regard and compaffion to him, confidered his life as a burthen, and death as a happy releafe to him, and fo much the more as he thought fo himfelf, and wifhed to be releafed.

'His laft illnefs, which continued about fourteen days, was a miliary fever, as I am well informed by the apothecary who attended him. It began with pretty ftrong inflammatory fymptoms, a very troublefome cough, difficulty of breathing, &c. and the eruption was extremely violent. For fome days he was thought to be relieved in the other fymptoms by the eruption; but it feems to be no wonder at all, that his conftitution was not able to ftruggle through fuch a difeafe, which proves fo fatal to many, who appear to be much more fit to grapple with it.

'His body began to putrify very foon after he was dead; fo that notwithftanding the weather was cool, it became very offenfive the next day, before they could get a coffin made. As the corpfe was of a furprifing bulk, the coffin muft be fo too.　It was three feet fix inches broad at the fhoulders, two feet three inches and a half at the head, twenty-two inches at the feet, and three feet one inch and a half deep.

‘ Great numbers of people came to fee the coffin while it was making, and at the funeral there was a vaft concourfe, not only of the town, but from the country for feveral miles round about, out of curiofity to fee how fuch a corpfe could be got to the ground.　It was drawn to the church on a low-wheel’d carriage by ten or twelve men, and was let down into the grave by an engine fixed up in the church for that purpofe.

I am, fir,

Your moft humble fervant,

T. COE.’

There have been engravings of mr. Bright.

Jane, the daughter of mr. Val. Difbrowe, is anceftrefs of many families, I fhall, therefore, be as particular as poffible, fearing the reader may not otherwife well comprehend me . fhe was married to mr. John Walford, a wealthy clothier in Effex, as were moft of his defcendants ; by whom fhe had two fons and a daughter, William, Richard, and Jane ; mr. Will. Walford, the eldeft fon, was alfo a clothier ; he married mifs Mary Bacon, and died in 1766, leaving 3 fons and 4 daughters : 1. William, who married mifs Ann Ruggles, by whom he had only the rev. Will. Walford, of Terling, in Effex, who married mifs Sarah Tweed, and has by her two infant fons. 2. Tho. who died in 1766, by Mary his wife, he had Tho.-Will. and Mary, who is unmarried. 3. John, who married twice, firft, mifs Maria Sworder, and, fecondly, mifs Mary Cook ; the iffue of thefe marriages were, John, Maria-Ann, Ifabell-Jane, and Frances (the only child of the fecond marriage).

riage). 4. Mary, married to mr. Arthur Tabrum, by whom she had mr Arthur Tabrum, who is married, and has an infant daughter, Will. Tabrum died young, Rob. Tabrum and Jane Tabrum, now unmarried. 5. Jane, married Joſ. Green, a merchant in London, by whom she has Joſ. Green (who by miſs Cowell, has an infant ſon), Will. John, Jane married to Iſaac Le Fevre, eſq. but has no iſſue; Mary, married to mr Luke-William Walford, Douglas, Fra. Ann and Charlotte are unmarried. 6. Eliz. died young. 7. Fra married mr. Rich. Daniel, but died without iſſue in 1780. I now return to John, ſecond ſon of mr. John Walford, and Jane Diſbrowe · John was bred to the church, and became vicar of Great Bardfield; he died about the year 1770: by miſs Goldſtone his wife, he had 2 ſons and 4 daughters, 1. Luke-Will. Walford, who by his relation, miſs Mary Green, has Will. Joſ. John and Jane. 2. John, unmarried. 3. Mary, alſo unmarried. 4. Jane, married to mr. Dick, by whom she has Geo. John, Tho Jane, Mary, Ann, Eliz. and Fra 5. Elizabeth, died unmarried. 6. Ann, unmarried. Jane, the only daughter of mr. John Walford by Jane Diſbrowe, married Rob. Tweed, of Halſted, in Eſſex, eſq. she died in 1781; the iſſue of this marriage was John Tweed, who died young whilſt at the univerſity; and Jane, who married J. B. Whalley, of Colcheſter, eſq. by whom she has John, unmarried. Jane the wife of the rev. —— Pooley, of Boxtead-Hall, in Suffolk, who has one ſon, an infant; and Ann Whalley, unmarried. Another of the daughters of Valentine Diſbrowe, married mr. Bowtle, by whom she had two daughters, Eliz. and Jane, Eliz. the eldeſt, married mr. Martin Lane, their iſſue is 2 ſons and a daughter, 1. Lionel Lane, who has had no child by either of his wives, miſs Ann May, or by the widow of

Side notes: NUM XXIV. Diſbrowes. The Tabrums. Greens. Le Fevres. Walfords. Dicks. Tweeds. Whalleys. Pooleys. Bowtles. Lanes.

mr.

mr. Parker.   2. Martin Lane, who by Eliz. daughter of mr. Walford, of Witham, has two daughters, Eliz. and Jane, both unmarried; and 3. Eliz. married to mr. Hen. Ray; they have had four children, Hen. Eliz. Jane, and Mary; Eliz. died young, the others are unmarried.   Jane Bowtle, the youngest daughter of mr. Bowtle by the daughter of Val. Disbrowe, married mr. Rous, by whom she had Simon, Ja. Jane, Eliz. and Fra. several, if not all, of whom have married.

Of the youngest daughter of Val. Disbrowe, I have not been able to obtain any information.

Benj. Disbrowe, the seventh son of the major-general, received from his father, half of West-Thurrock, in Essex, of which county he was sheriff in 1689, he died feb. 21, 1707-8, and was buried in Downham church, in Essex.   He married thrice : 1st. Eliz. daughter of ——Arm-sted, of Thorelby, in Lincolnshire.   2nd. Sarah, daughter of Rob. Norden, and widow of Andrew Sanc, a merchant of Dort, in Holland (by whom she had an only child named Rob.) and also widow of Cornelius Vanden Anker, of London, merchant ; she died apr. 9, 1692, and is also buried in Downham church.   3rd. Mary Norden, sister of his second wife ; she was buried at Downham, april 22, 1728 : by the first wife he had one son, and by the last, five daughters.   Before I proceed to speak of them, and their descendants, I shall observe, how fortunate this mr. Disbrowe was in his alliances, for Sarah, his 2nd wife, had, by the will of mr. Vanden Anker, the whole of his personal estate, and the manor of Trimnalls, or Hern-nels, in the parish of Downham, which he had purchased for 3100l. and three parts of the manor of West-Thurrock, also in Essex, which he had purchased of sir Rob Clayton, knt. (part of the money had been paid at the time of mr. Vanden Anker's death, but the deeds had not been sealed

how

however the purchafe was afterwards completed) :
all thefe premifes were left free of all incum-
brances, except the payment of his debts, and
1500l. to the child that fhe was then bearing, when
of age, but it was to be educated at her expence :
the pofthumous child was Cornelia, who afterwards married Cromwell Difbrowe, Benjamin's
heir. Mr. B. Difbrowe, jointly with his wife,
levied a fine of the manor of Trimnalls, to the
ufe of Sarah for life, remainder to Cornelia, and
the heirs of his body, remainder to Rob. Norden,
brother to Sarah, and his heirs and affigns for
ever ; but he fold the eftate of Weft-Thurrock to
Caleb Grantham, a gentleman of Yorkfhire. It
will appear that he muft have obtained a very
confiderable fortune from only one of his three
wives, but there is the greateft reafon to fuppofe
he had much with the others. I fhall now mention his children. they were Mary, Sarah, Eliz.
who died a child, Eliz. Jane, and Cromwell, of
whom below.

Cromwell Difbrowe, efq. this, his only fon, by
the marriage of Cornelia Vanden-Anker, enjoyed
the eftate of Trimnalls, he joined with his wife to
fuffer a recovery, and bar the intail to their iffue,
as they by will fhould appoint, and, in default, to
Platt their eldeft fon; he died march 4, 1717-18,
in the 44th year of his age, and was buried in the
abbey-church of Bath. His widow furvived him
many years, and was buried at Downham, april
14, 1750; their iffue was feven ,fons and two
daughters, 1. Platt Difbrowe, efq. born in 1699
or 1700, fucceeded to the eftate of Trimnalls for
want of any appointment to the contrary by his
father and mother, he died there a bachelor nov.
22, 1751, and was buried in Downham church-
yard. 2. Cha. died young before his father. 3.
Benj. died a bachelor, and was buried aug. 13,

Disbrowes.

Defmadrylls

Lunns.

1714, at Downham.   4. John, buried at the fame
place, oct. 28, 1722; he alfo never married.   5.
Nehemiah, died young before his father.   6.
Cromwell, furvived his father, but died before
he was of age in the Eaft-Indies, whither he
went as a writer in the fervice of the company.
7. Samuel, died of the fmall-pox in London,
but was brought down and buried at Downham,
fept. 7, 1729.   8. Mary, baptized may 12, 1717,
at Downham, fhe was married to John Cha.
Defmadryll, of All-Saints, Barking, in London,
jan. 25, 1741-2; he died at Trimnalls, and was
buried at Downham, oct. 8, 1763, aged 63 years;
fhe died nov. 12, 1770, and was buried at Camberwell, in Surry, the iffue of this marriage was
three fons and one daughter.   Cha. Defmadryll, a
merchant, he died a bachelor at the age of 40, at
Coggefhall, where he was buried may 29, 1782.
Rich. Defmadryll, went to fea, he died a bachelor at the age of 23, at Chelmsford, and was buried at Downham, nov. 23, 1767.   John Defmadryll, of London, merchant, born in 1748, he
married in 1776, Ann Deman, of Helfton, in
Cornwall, by whom he has John Defmadryll, an
infant; and Louifa Defmadryll, married april 4,
1778, to the rev Hen du Cane, of Coggefhall,
in Effex, by whom fhe has two daughters, Louifa,
and Anna-Maria.   9 Cornelia Difbrowe, the
youngeft daughter of Cromwell Difbrowe, was a
pofthumous twin with her fifter Mary, I apprehend, as they were both baptized at the fame
time, fhe married Will Lunn, of Cambridge,
furgeon, fon of Will. Lunn, D. D. archdeacon of
Huntingdon, and rector of Elfworth; they had
no iffue: he died feb. 2, 1769, aged 69 years,
' whofe integrity and fkill in his profeffion joined
' to a chearful, amiable, and pious difpofition,
' juftly rendered him refpected whilft living, and

' no

'no lefs lamented at his death.' Cornelia, his widow, 'after a few years bewailing this feparation,
'was again united to him in feb. 11, 1775,' when
in the 65th year of her age; they are buried in
the church of Elfworth, part of the infcription
upon their grave-ftone I have here copied, their
arms are alfo cut upon it. The eftate at Trimnalls, valued at 200l. per ann was fold about 20
years ago for 6000l. for the co-heireffes, mrs.
Mary Defmadryll, and mrs. Cornelia Lunn, after
a long, tedious and expenfive law-fuit *.—Having
taken the life of the major-gen. John Difbrowe, and
what defcendants I could obtain, I fhall now fpeak of
his brother Samuel, the lord chancellor of Scotland.

Sam. Difbrowe, efq. was the fifth, but third fur- Sam Difbrowe,
viving fon of James Difbrowe, of Eltifley, where efq keeper of
he was born nov. 30, 1619; but little of his life the great feal of
is known until the civil war had fubfided, only Scotland
that he refided fome years in New-England, whither he went probably to enjoy his religious opinions, and from whence he returned in 1650-1,
in which year he was fent to Scotland, in fome employment under the ftate, through the intereft of
his brother, and Oliver Cromwell, the general;
when he arrived in Scotland, he fent a preffing
letter to know whether he might expect a permanent fettlement there, that he might be certain of
procuring a fuitable provifion for himfelf, his
wife, and children; he was chofen to reprefent the
city of Edinburgh in parlement; and at a council
held at Whitehall, may 4, 1655, he was appointed by the protector Oliver, one of the nine counfel-

---

*A friend of mine fays, the manfion at Trimnalls was large,
furrounding a court and where he has feen the major-general's buff-coat, and hat of the fame materials, lined with an iron
plate, with the furniture he left behind him, and alfo two good
three-quarter portraits of mr. and mrs. Vanden Anker.

lors for the kingdom of Scotland, in the following
year, he was returned a member of the britifh parlement, for the fheriffdom of Mid-Lothian : he fo
well pleafed the protector, that, fep. 16, 1657, he
gave a patent for the office of keeper of the
great-feal of Scotland to him, or his deputy, during his natural life, with all fees due from may 1,
preceding, fubject only to fuch regulations, in
refpect of fees, or otherwife, as fhould be made
by his highnefs, or his fucceffors, with the advice of the privy-council of England : he was
continued in all his employments by the protector
Richard, he prudently embraced the royal proclamation fent from Breda, in the prefence of
general Monk, he figned his fubmiffion to his
majefty, may 21, 1660, and he alfo obtained the
king's warrant, october 24, following, to the attorney or folicitor-general, to prepare a bill for
the royal fignature, of a pardon of all fuch of-
fences, but with fuch reftitution of lands and goods,
and fuch exceptions and claufes in all things, as
were expreffed in the form of a pardon prepared
for that purpofe, and remaining with them under
the fignet and fign manual, and he obtained his
pardon, in confequence of this, dec. 12, in the
fame year. After this, he retired to his feat at
Elfworth, in Cambridgefhire, which, with the
manor and advowfon of the church, he had purchafed of Tho Wendy, efq. (whofe anceftor, Tho.
Wendy, phyfician to k. Edw. VI. had received a
grant of them from that fovereign, to be held in
capite). he remained here in privacy until his
death, which happened dec. 10, 1 0, and was
buried upon the fouth fide of the communion rails
in the chancel of Elfworth church, over whofe remains is a black marble flab. The rev mr. Lunn
thinks he had either three or four wives, he married his laft wife in 1655, fhe was Rofe, widow of
Samuel

Samuel Pennyer, of London, merchant; prior to
which, march 26, in the fame year, there was a
deed executed, by which it was agreed, that both
he and fhe fhould give 1000l each, within fix
months, to the truftees, who were the right hon.
John Difbrowe, Will. Hobfon, of London, efq.
and Will. Pennyer, of London, merchant, to be
laid out in purchafes to the ufe of them for life,
then to their children, remainder to him in fee,
and a bond was given by him in the penalty of
3000l. to perform the agreement. ' This virtuous
' and pious lady's foul returned to God who gave
' it,' march 4, 1698, in the 83d year of her age;
fhe is buried on the north fide of the communion
rails, in Elfworth chancel, oppofite to her laft hufband, mr. Difbrowe, as appears by her grave-
ftone: the arms upon both hers and his are very
erroneoufly cut. The iffue that mr. Difbrowe had
by his former wives, I apprehend, all died unmarried. by his laft, he had,

Dr. James Difbrowe, a phyfician, who refided
at Chefhunt, in Hertfordfhire, where he is buried;
he married Abigail, the daughter of John Marfh,
of Garfon, Herts, efq. immediately after whofe
marriage, march 9, 1678, his father, in confideration of her fortune, which was 1500l. fettled the
manor and advowfon of Elfworth, with a walk for
500 fheep, to Samuel for life, without impeach-
ment of wafte, with remainder to James, in fee;
and a meffuage, with fifty acres of arable, four of
pafture, and five of meadow, to Rofe, his wife,
for her life, with the remainder to James, in fee;
and, by a deed of fettlement, dated oct. 14, 1681,
the manor, &c. of Elfworth, was fettled upon
James and Abigail, for their joint lives, and the
furvivor of them, with remainder to the heirs of
their body, in fee, by which limitation the eftates
at Elfworth, and, I think, at Fenny-Draiton, came

to Elizabeth, their only daughter, who married to Matthew Holworthy, eſq. the dates of their deaths, and thoſe of their deſcendants, will be ſeen by the following inſcription, which I copied from an elegant mural monument, with the arms of the Holworthys impaling thoſe of the Diſbrowes over it, placed above the door of the dormitory, on the north ſide of Elſworth chancel.

To the Memory
of *Eliz^{th.}* and *Matthew Holworthy*, late Lord and Lady of this Manor,
whoſe exemplary Piety, liberal & extenſive Charity,
Probity, Humanity, & Candour, were
equalled by few.
To them and their Deſcendants, whoſe Remains are
depoſited within this Dormitory,
this Monument is erected by *Saml Holworthy*, Eſq.
ye 17th of Mar. 1756.
Matthew Holworthy, Eſquire,
only Son of Sr *Matthew Holworthy*, of *Great Palgrave*, in Norfolk, Knt.
died the 18th of May, 1728, aged 54 years:
Elizabeth Holworthy, Relict of *Matthew Holworthy*,
Eſq. & Daughter of *James Diſbrowe*, Eſq^r
Doctor of Phyſick,
died the 19th of Aug^{ſt} 1749, aged 67 years.
Matthew, ſon of *Matthew & Elizabeth Holworthy*,
died the 4th of June, aged 1 month.
Diſbrowe, Son of *Matthew & Elizabeth Holworthy*,
died the 22d of May, 1721, aged 21 years
Suſanna, daught^r of *Matthew & Eliz^{th} Holworthy*,
died the 2^d of June, 1721, aged 16 years
Elizabeth Heathcote, daught^r. of *Matthew & Eliz^{th.} Holworthy*,
died ye 6th of May, 1726, aged 27 years.

Mrs. Heathcote, to whom the eſtates at Elſworth came, having no iſſue by mr. Heathcote
(who

(who was a merchant of London), devifed them to
Matth Heathcote, efq. fon of her fifter Sufanna,
with an injunction, that he would take the name
of Holworthy, which he did, his fon, —— Holworthy, efq. is the prefent poffeffor. he married
a daughter of mr. Difbrowe, furgeon, of Huntingdon, defcended from the family at Eltifley. Mr.
Holworthy poffeffes three portraits of the Difbrowes, who lived in the laft century, they are
faid to be the reprefentations of three brothers, one
is certainly the lord-chancellor of Scotland, as it
agrees in the likenefs to an invaluable miniature
of that perfon by Cooper, by both the portrait
and miniature, he appears to have been, when in
the middle age of life, of an oval face, with fmall
whifkers, and a lock of hair beneath the lower lip;
he has an engaging countenance, and fuch as be-
fpeaks great fenfe. There is at Elfworth, the travelling cheft of the major-general, as it is called,
and there lately was a cloak, alfo faid to have been
his, but I fuppofe they belonged to his brother,
the lord-keeper, but what are moft obfervable,
are two large chefts, that evidently belonged to
k Cha I. when prince of Wales, and which he
brought out of Spain, where they were made; they
are moft curioufly carved, many parts of which
are allufive to his reception there, and the intended
marriage between him and the infanta. I have
dwelt perhaps too long upon the lord chancellor
of Scotland's hiftory, efpecially as he did not ally
himfelf to the blood of the Cromwells; but I
thought every particular of fo memorable a perfon
worthy recording *.

* The hiftory of the Difbrowe family is taken from the regifters and funeral monuments of the churches of Eltifley, Elfworth, and Downham, laft vifitation of Cambridgefhire, felect
papers communicated by L. Brown, efq.——Holworthy, efq.
the

No. XXV.

Some account of dr. Peter French, brother-in-law to the prot. Oliver, and the descendants of his marriage with Robina, the youngest sister of that sovereign.

NUM XXV.

The li.e of dr. French, b, otner-in-law to the protector Oliver

OUR histories are silent respecting the life of dr. Peter French, more than that he was educated at Emanuel-college, in Cambridge, he was of puritanic principles, and was incorporated a bachelor of divinity, dec. 16, 1650, and, upon his brother in-law's raising himself to the sovereignty of these kingdoms, he was presented by

the rev. Will Walford, the rev Hen. du Cane, the rev Rob Masters, mr. Longmate, and other friends, Thurloe's state papers, secret hist. of Europe, mr Morant's hist. of Essex, Clarendon's hist of the rebellion, Whitlock's memorials, and other contemporary historians The major-general, and the chancellor, no doubt, assisted to improve the fortunes of many of their relations Nathaniel Disbrowe, esq. married Letitia, eldest daughter of Adam Lottus, visc. Ely, lord-chancellor of Ireland, and widow of lieut -col Phi. Feinly, another Nathaniel Disbrowe, esq. married Ann, daughter of sir John Corbet, of Stoke, created a baronet by k Cha. I. These gentlemen were, probably, the sons of Isaac Disbrowe, gent uncle to the major-general, and of —— Disbrowe, the youngest son of the mr Disbrowe, with whom the genealogy commences John Disbrowe, esq. by act of parlement changed his name to Spencer; he died may 31, 1730 and —— Disbrowe, of Staffordshire, esq who changed his name for Smith Cha Disbrowe, esq. an old sea officer, and some time capt. of the Fubbs yacht, died in march, 1723 From the registers of Wicken, it appears that Alice Disbrowe, widow, was buried nov 8, 1680, and Benj Disbrowe, oct. 19, 1603, as was Ann his wife, may 20, in the same year, they had James, born 1684, who died a child; Benj born in 1688, Mary in 1679, probably they were drawn there by Hen. Cromwell, lord-lieutenant.

him

him to the canonry of Chrift-church, in the uni- NUM XXV.
verfity of Oxford, upon the fhameful ejection of
dr. Edward Pocock * . he was one of the com- The life of dr.
miffioners, or delegates, during the abfence of dr. French, &c
Owen, the vice-chancellor of the univerfity of Oxford. In december 1653, he was diplomated doctor
of divinity at Oxford, and appointed one of the
protector's chaplains, and frequently preached at
Whitehall, having arrived at the height of his
honors and preferments, he died june 17, 1655;
from our knowing fo little of him, we may conclude, that it was his marriage, more than his
literary merit, that occafioned his rifing in the
church †.

There was no other iffue of this marriage, than Some particulars
an only daughter, Eliz who was married, in 1664, of dr John Til-
to mr. afterwards dr. John Tillotfon, who became bifhop of Can-
lord archbifhop of Canterbury; one of the greatest terbury, nephew
ornaments that the church of England ever had, by marriage, to
and of whom it may be obferved, that he was bred Ol lord prot.
a puritan, was confecrated primate when only a
dean, and that he was the third in that exalted
dignity that was married.

---

* Dr. Pocock was ejected for not taking the engagement;
he was one of the greatest ornaments to literature that this
country has produced, he would have been expelled from his
living at Childrey, for *ignorance and infufficiency*, had he not
been faved by dr Owen—fuch was the profound *wifdom* of
the parlement vifitors'

† There was a John French, of Broughton, near Banbury,
in the county of Oxford, who practifed phyfic in the parlement
army, he died in 1657, near Boulogne, in France. He had a
brother named Will. French, of Caius-college, in Cambridge,
who was alfo fuppofed to be a doctor of phyfic, and acted in
that capacity, in the fcotch army, and died in the beginning
of 1650. Alderman French was a committee-man for the univerfity of Cambridge: probably thefe were allied to the
brother-in-law of the prot. Oliver.—Wood's Athen. Oxonienfes, and ordinances of parlement.

                                        This

NUM. XXV.

Archbifhop
Tillotfon

Antiquity of the
Tilftons or Til-
lotfon..

This great, and truly good man, was defcended from the Tilftons, feated at a place of that name in Chefhire; the anceftor of whom was Nicholas de Tilfton, efq. lord of the manor of Tilfton, from whom defcended another Nich. de Tilfton, who was living in the 9th year of the reign of k. Edw. III. his grandfon and heir was Roger Tilfton, efq. who was alive in the reign of k. Hen. V. he married Catharine, fecond daughter of fir John Leigh, of Baguly, in Chefhire, knt. Tho Tilfton, his fon and heir, by Eliz. daughter and heirefs of Hugh Heath, of Huxley, in that county, had iffue two fons, Richard, the fecond fon, married Maud, daughter of Rich. Boftock, by whom he had feveral children, Ralph, the third fon, fettled at Newport, in Shropfhire, and married Eliz. the fecond daughter of Will. Leighton (2nd fon of fir Tho. Leighton, of Wattlefborough, in Chefhire, knt.) Thomas, their third fon, was feated at Wook-liff, in the parifh of Craven, in Yorkfhire, and altered the orthography of the family name to Tillotfon, he left a fon named George, who, by Eleanor, daughter of Ellis Nutter, of Pendle-Foreft, in Lancafhire, had Robert, his fon and heir, father of the archbifhop

Mr. Rob. Tillotfon was a confiderable clothier of Sowerby, in the parifh of Halifax, in Yorkfhire, and was extremely attached to the tenets Calvin taught, which he ftrenuoufly perfifted in, and it was with difficulty his fon, who became archbifhop of Canterbury, could wean him from thefe fentiments *; he had the fatisfaction to live to fee the doctor, dean of Canterbury, dying fome time after, may 1679, : mi. Tillotfon was remarkable

* Archbifhop Tillotfon's family feem much inclined to diffent from the eftablifhed church; mr Nath Tillotfon, an eminent quaker-fpeaker, was nearly allied to his grace.

for an uncommon knowledge in the fcriptures, NUM XXV.
and for an excellent underftanding ; he married
Mary, daughter of Tho. Dobfon, alfo of Somer-
by, gent. She was a moft amiable perfon, but, to
the grief of all her friends, loft her fenfes many
years before fhe died, the iffue of their marriage
was three fons· 1. John, afterwards archbifhop
of Canterbury. 2. Jofhua, who was a wet and
dry-falter, or oilman, in London, he died fuddenly,
fept. 16, 1678, by a vomiting of blood, which
very greatly affected his eldeft brother, who immediately wrote to mr. Timothy Bentley, their relation, to break the matter to his father, and to in-
treat him ' to bear it with patience and fubmiffion
' to the will of God, and to comfort himfelf, as,'
fays he, ' I defire to do, with the hope of meeting
' and enjoying him in a better life.' He left a
fon named Robert, whom the archbifhop's widow
generoufly, out of her fmall income, brought up
for fome time, at Clare-hall, in Cambridge, but
being unable longer to fupport the expence, he was
fupplied with every thing neceffary to continue
there, chiefly by lord chancellor Somers, who, out
of regard to his uncle's memory, honored him
with his particular notice, which he acknowledged
in a latin letter to his lordfhip, he received the
finecure of Elme, of confiderable value, in the ifle
of Ely, upon his entering into holy orders: this
preferment was given him by the archbifhop's executors, to whofe difpofal that option was left.
3. Ifrael, whofe grandfon, the rev. Jofhua Tillotfon, M. A. ' the worthy and learned furmafter of
' St. Paul's fchool, in London,' communicated to
dr. Birch the pedigree of the Tilfton, or Tillotfon
family, drawn out in 1682, and compared with
one in the herald office ; from which, with other
information contained in dr. Birch's hiftory of the
life

life of the archbishop, thefe pages are chiefly borrowed.

Dr. John Tillotſon, archbiſhop of Canterbury,
was born in the end of ſeptember, or the beginning of october 1630, in the pariſh of Sowerby,
and baptized oct. 3, in that year, one of his god-
fathers was the rev. Joſhua Witton, a native of that
village, and afterwards rector of Thornhill, in
Yorkſhire; but he loſt that preferment by the Bartholomew act in 1662. Mr. Tillotſon, his father,
though he poſſeſſed but a ſmall eſtate, gave this ſon
the beſt of educations; of which he was always ſo
ſenſible, as it was the ſole cauſe of his attaining the
high rank that he afterwards held, that he ever
ſhewed his gratitude by kindneſſes to the whole
of his family; deſirous to make it appear how much
he wiſhed to compenſate them for the ſums expended upon him in the beginning of his life, looking upon it as taken, in ſome meaſure, from the
ſhares of his brothers, and as having deprived his
father of more money than he could ſpare without
inconveniencing himſelf, probably his father was
induced to this liberality from the vaſt facility
with which he attained a knowledge of the latin
and greek languages, for, april 23, 1647, when
only ſeventeen years of age, he was admitted a
penſioner of Clare-hall, in Cambridge, matricu-
lated july 1 following; commenced bachelor of
arts at midſummer, 1650; and was elected fellow
of Clare-hall, in 1651, in the room of his tutor,
the rev. David Clarkſon, B D author of ' No evi-
' dence of dioceſan epiſcopacy in the primitive
' times,' and other books in behalf of preſbyteri-
aniſm; and who, by retaining theſe ſentiments, loſt
his preferment of Mortlack, in Surry, in 1662, but
whoſe piety and learning made him always highly
valued by his pupil. Mr. Tillotſon, in 1654, took a
master

mafter of arts degree; and, in 1656, became tutor
to the fon of Edm. Prideaux, of Ford-abbey, in
Devon, efq. attorney-general to the protector
Oliver, but, at the death of his highnefs, mr. Tillotfon was in London, and probably out of employment.

Though born of a father who was a rigid prefbyterian, and educated by and amongft perfons of
thofe fentiments, yet it is well known he early imbibed a diflike to their opinions, and an utter
averfion to their writings, as exceffively heavy and
tirefome, however, he was too great a friend to
human nature not to value the good of every perfuafion, and no one ever acted with more caution
and tendernefs to thofe whofe confciences would
not fuffer them to comply with the practice of the
national church. It is fingular, that the time of
his ordination, and by what bifhop he was ordained,
are unknown; conforming to the church of England at the reftoration, he became curate to dr.
Hacket, vicar of Chefhunt, in Herts, but after
promoted to the bifhopric of Litchfield and Coventry: here, by his mildnefs and eloquence, he
won many of the fectaries to the church. In 1662,
he declined accepting the church of St. Mary,
Aldermanbury, upon the deprivation of mr. Ca-
lamy, but accepted of the rectory of Keddington,
in Suffolk, in 1663, to which he was prefented by
fir Tho. Barnardifton, knt. that living having become vacant by the refufal of mr. Sam. Fairclough
to conform: nov. 26 following, he was elected
preacher of Lincoln's-Inn, in 1664, he was appointed Tuefday-lecturer of St. Lawrence-Jewry;
and, in 1666, he took a doctor of divinity's degree.

At this time, perhaps, few perfons were more
popular than dr. Tillotfon, not only as the reformer
of the dull and pedantic declamation that difgraced
the pulpit, but as the moft modeft and candid of

any of his brethren; fetting himfelf againft the two reigning evils of the day, atheifm and popery, and recommending moderation and chriftian charity amongft all men, efpecially the proteftants, as the only means to defeat the defigns of the court of Rome, whofe aim was vifible to every eye. His popularity increafing, he continued to rife equally rapid; for, in 1669, he was preferred to a canonry of Chrift's-church, in Canterbury, and to a prebend of St. Paul's in 1675, from thence he was removed to the deanery of Norwich, which he exchanged for that of Canterbury.

At the revolution he was looked upon with particular favor, on account of his moderation, and he was appointed, fucceffively, refidentiary of St. Paul's, clerk of the clofet to their majefties, and dean of St. Paul's, all in the year 1689; and upon the deprivation of dr. Sancroft, in 1691, he was (much againft his own inclination) raifed to the archiepifcopal throne, which he filled with the greateft honor to himfelf, and advantage to the church. His grace died at his palace of Lambeth, nov. 22, 1694, in the arms of his beloved friend, the pious Rob. Nelfon, efq. having lived 65 years: his remains were buried upon the left fide of the altar of the church of St. Lawrence-Jewry; to whofe memory an handfome monument is erected. King William fo feverely lamented his death, that he never mentioned him, but with fome teftimony of fingular efteem for his memory, and he ufed often to tell his fon-in-law, mr. Chadwick, 'I loved your father, I never knew an honefter man, and I never had a better friend.'

The lady of the archbifhop furvived him, whom he left in a very indifferent fituation, as he himfelf had forefeen, for, when he was preffed by k. William to accept of the primacy, amongft other objections, he urged, that he knew he fhould

not

not be able to fave any thing; and, as his private fortune was fmall, he fhould leave a poor widow of Canterbury; his majefty promifed then, that if fhe furvived him, he would obviate that inconvenience, which he faithfully performed: his grace having, from the expences of coming to the archiepifcopal fee, and the repairs and improvements he had made in the palace, died worth fo little, that even his debts would not have been all paid, had not the firft fruits been forgiven him; and his family had nothing but what the copy of his manufcript fermons fold for (which was 2500 guineas): his majefty therefore compaffionating mrs. Tillotfon, granted her, may 2, 1695, an annuity of 400l. during her natural life; and, as her grandchildren were left deftitute by the death of her fon-in-law, mr Chadwick, who died infolvent; the king gave mrs Tillotfon a further annuity of 200l. both of which were continued until her death, which happened jan 20, 1701-2; and becaufe no diminution or delay fhould be made, his majefty always, from his own hands, punctually fent the quarter's allowance as foon as it became due.

The archbifhop, by Oliver the protector's niece, (his only wife) had three children: 1. A fon, who died when juft arrived at the age of manhood; whofe lofs the archbifhop deplores in a letter to mr. Hunt, a friend of his grace's. 2. Elizabeth, who died, unmarried, in the fummer of 1681, of whofe lofs he fays, in anfwer to mr. Nelfon's condolence, ' I thank you for your compaffionate fenfe ' of my lofs, which went very near me, but God's ' will is always beft, and I have no doubt but fhe ' is infinitely moie happy and fafe than fhe could ' have been in any condition in this world.' 3. Mary, who married to Ja. Chadwick, efq. fhe died in nov. 1687, this lofs, as he acquainted mr. Nelfon, deeply pierced his heart; ' but I endeavour,'

he

he fubjoins, ' to do as becomes me, and as I know
' I ought.'　However, it made fo great an impreffion upon him, that he retired to Canterbury.
Probably the death of one or both thefe children
is alluded to by his grace in his letter to lady
Ruffel, dated april 19, 1689, in which, after ex-
preffing his fears that the king fhould appoint
him fucceffor to archbifhop Sancroft, he fubjoins,
' and now I will tell your ladyfhip the very bot-
' tom of my heart, of late God has been pleafed
' by very fevere ways, but in great goodnefs to
' me, to wean me perfectly from the love of this
' world.'　It is much to the honor both of the
archbifhop and of his fon-in-law, that the one never
afked, and the other never requefted him, to petition for any place at court, nor did the latter ever
interfere in ecclefiaftical affairs, or receive any
place under the primate: it would be doing them
injuftice not to give the archbifhop's own words
upon this fubject, in a letter to mr. Nelfon,
fpeaking of mr Chadwick, he fays, ' my fon
' hath no place at court, nor did I ever mention
' him to the king, but only to beg leave of his
' majefty for him to attend upon him into Hol-
' land, where he met with my lord and lady
' Durfley *.　I never afk any thing of the king,
' unlefs upon the account of charity for perfons
' in diftrefs, and whom he had reafons to confider,
' as the poor french and irifh proteftants, or for
' fome poor widows, whofe hufbands have died
' in his fervice, and for whom nobody elfe will
' fpeak, or elfe to do fome good office for a friend,
' which cofts the king nothing, and this but very
' rarely　And indeed I have no occafion to afk
' any thing of him, who hath done for me what

---

* Cha. lord Durfley was, in 1689, created baron Berkley
of Berkley, and fent envoy extraordinary into Holland.

' I wi

'I was fo far from defiring, that I did for paft a
'year and an half decline it with all my might.
'And yet I have no reafon to doubt, but that
'upon the leaft intimation of my defire he would
'give my fon any place that is fit for him: but
'as well as I love my fon, I can hardly afk any
'thing. I had much rather the king would pre-
'vent me, or, if he do not, I believe the queen
'will. And I fhould not be a little pleafed to
'have him one of the commiffioners of the cuf-
'toms, for which he is much fitter, than for any
'other place that I know. And I am the more
'defirous to have fomething done for him, not
'only for the fake of my grandchildren, but be-
'caufe he is fo very kind to us, and confiders fo
'well what becomes him and me, that though he
'is ftill willing to live with me, he will not only
'take no place from me, but has not fo much as
'fpoken to me for any perfon whatfoever, nor
'will he ever intermeddle either in ordering my
'family, or in any of my affairs as archbifhop.'
I apprehend mr. Chadwick was afterwards appointed one of the commiffioners of the cuftoms.
However praife-woithy this moderation might be
in not foliciting fomething proper to fupport the
family according to their fituation in the world,
yet it was nearly involving the defcendants of the
primate in abfolute want and beggary, for mr.
Chadwick dying in 1697, when in the middle
age of life, and but indifferently provided for, his
affairs were exceedingly involved, the whole of
his eftate being fpent, except what had been fettled upon his wife, fo that his younger fon, and
his daughter, had not any fortune whatfoever, but
depended wholly upon mrs. Tillotfon, their grandmother, whofe fituation was rendered the worfe by
mr. Chadwick's having given no declaration of
truft for 1000 l. of hers, which he had put into

the

the Bank in his own name, though fhe had often
defired him to give her a proper acknowledg-
ment. but what added ftill to mrs. Tillotfon's
perplexity, was, that the eftate mr. Chadwick
poffeffed in the foreft, called Valentines, near
Wanfted, in Effex, being copyhold, and only
purchafed for his life at 300 l. was obliged to be
paid for again, and the houfe which fhe had at
his importunity built at a great expence, was by
his death rendered too large for her. The lord-
chancellor Somers, compaffionating the misfortunes of the archbifhop's family, out of reverence
for his memory, interceded with his majefty k.
William, who, as I have before mentioned, augmented mrs. Tillotfon's penfion, by adding 200 l.
to the 400 l. before given, but it is probable, that
had not mrs. Tillotfon been obliged to folicit dr.
Sherlock to get a provifion for the archbifhop's
nephew, whom he had, before thefe misfortunes,
fupplied with fufficient fums to defray the expences of an univerfity education, it had never
been known what misfortunes fhe and her grandchildren were involved in, but her two friends,
dr. Sherlock and mr. Nelfon, faithfully, and without folicitation, or perhaps her knowledge, acquainted the chancellor with their pitiable fituation. It is greatly to her honor, that fhe conftantly,
from a grateful refpect and veneration for the
memory of her hufband, fhewed the utmoft attention and kindnefs to all his relations. The
iffue of mr. Chadwick, by the archbifhop's daughter, were three children: 1. Geo. Chadwick,
efq. who received his education at Catherine-hall,
in Cambridge, and was under the tuition of mr.
Benjamin Hoadley, then fellow of that hall, and
who afterwards became bifhop of Winchefter. mr.
Chadwick retired from college to his paternal
eftate in Nottinghamfhire, which was of no higher

value

value than 300l. per annum. he died young,
leaving a fon, Evelyn Chadwick, efq. 2. John
Chadwick, the other grandfon of the archbifhop,
became a turkey merchant; he died about 1735.
3. Mary, the grand-daughter of archbifhop Tillotfon, became the wife of mr. Edw. Fowler, fon
of dr. Fowler, bifhop of Gloucefter · mr. Fowler
was a confiderable linen-draper in Cheapfide,
London: he died june 29, 1710, and his wife
may 9, 1728, when nearly 42 years of age ·· they
are buried in a vault on the north corner of the
church at Hendon, in Middlefex. Bifhop Fowler's monument is within the church, and theirs
on the outfide; the latter is an altar-tomb and
farcophagus with two weeping boys, it was erected
by John Chadwick, and Tho. Mansfield, efqrs.
the executors of her will. By this monument it
appears, that fhe left by mr. Fowler two daughters, Anna-Maria, and Elizabeth *.

* The hift. of dr. French, and archb. Tillotfon, and his family, is taken from Wood's Athen. Oxon. various hift of Engl.
lives of the prot Oliver, information communicated by mr.
Longmate, dr Birch's life of archb. Tillotfon and another by
F H. M. A who compiled it from the minutes of the rev. mr.
Young, dean of Salifbury, to whom dr. Burnet promifed to
give fome further account of his grace's family, but unfortunately he died immediately after, Nonconformifts memorial;
lives of illuftrious perfons who died in 1712, and Gent. magazine.

No. XXVI.

The life of dr. Wilkins, bishop of Chester, brother-in-law to the protector Oliver.

DR. John Wilkins was the son of mr. Walter Wilkins, a goldsmith and citizen of Oxford. This son was born at Fausley, near Daventry, in 1614, in the house of his maternal grandfather, the rev. John Dod, the celebrated decalogist *. The arms of the Wilkins are, arg. on a bend engrailed between two plain cottices, sable 3 martlets, or. Dr. Wilkins received the first rudiments of learning from mr. Edw. Sylvester, who kept a private school in Oxford, and where he made so great a progress, that at easter term 1627, when he was no more than thirteen years old, he was admitted a student at New-Inn, in that university: after a short stay there, he was removed to Magdalen-Hall, and placed under the care of mr. John Tombes, the celebrated anabaptist disputant, that gentleman leaving the university in 1630, occasioned his pupil's not taking his first degree at the regular time, for he did not receive that of bachelor of arts till michaelmas term, oct. 20, 1631: in act term 1634, he became master of arts: at this time he was 21 years of age, and taking holy orders, was immediately appointed chaplain to Will. lord visc. Say and

---

* John Dod was born at Shortledge, in the county of Chester, where his father had a competent estate. He was educated at Jesus's college, Cambridge, and was, says Fuller, ' by nature, ' a witty, by industry, a learned, by grace, a godly divine ' He ended his ministry at Fausley, in Northamptonshire, of which he was vicar, and was buried there, aug. 19, 1645

Sele,

Sele; and afterwards fucceffively ferved lord Berkley, and pr. Cha. count-palatine of the Rhine, whilft he refided in this kingdom in the fame capacity, a mutual love for the ftudy of the mathematics was the caufe why he obtained this laft honor; whilft he attended upon the prince, he omitted no opportunity of improving himfelf in this his favorite ftudy. The dr. (then mr. Wilkins) was early biaffed in favor of the puritans, and therefore complied, without any reluctance, with the order of the parlement, in taking the folemn league and covenant, to qualify himfelf to retain his chaplainfhip. As the univerfities were clouded with the bigotry of the times, and little improvement could be obtained there, by the affociation of men of equal liberality with himfelf, he propofed a philofophical meeting in London, which gave the firft hint to the royal fociety.

The parlement committee for the reformation of the univerfity of Oxford, wifely viewing him as one of the greateft and moft refpectable of their party, chofe him, in 1648, to be warden of Wadham-college, to qualify himfelf for which, april 12, he took his degree of bachelor of divinity, and the day following, was put in poffeffion, upon the ejection of the rev. John Pitt, B. D. dec. 18, in the fame year, he obtained the degree of doctor of divinity, and foon after took the engagement, ' to be true to the commonwealth of ' England, as it was then eftablifhed without a ' king or houfe of lords.' Being obliged to quit London to refide in his college, he endeavoured to eftablifh a meeting of the learned there, upon a fimilar plan of that in the capital, which met at dr Petty's lodgings, until that gentleman left this kingdom to refide in Ireland: after which time the members conftantly came to Wadham-college as long as he remained warden, so that it might be justly said, that wherever he came he was the patron of the sciences. In the year 1656, he became the brother-in-law to the sovereign of these kingdoms, by marrying Robina, the widow of dr. French, and sister to the protector Oliver *, who granted him a dispensation to retain his wardenship, though it was contrary to the founder's statute to be held by a married man; this favor was all that he received of that protector: Richard, his nephew, also gave him a like dispensation, and knowing his universal benevolence, promoted him, in 1659, to the mastership of Trinity-college, in Cambridge, upon the death of dr. Arrowsmith, as thinking he would be as serviceable in that, as he had been in the other university. Richard not only loved, but trusted him, for he appointed him one of his cabinet council, and, with lord Broghill and col. Philips, took his advice upon most affairs. The use he made of his alliance with the Cromwell family was the most noble, instead of aggrandizing himself and his friends, he made it only subservient to the great wish of his heart, the promotion of learning, then threatened to be overcome by bigotry and fanaticism, for this reason it was that he opportunely interposed to shelter Oxford from the moroseness of Owen and Goodwin.

The restoration threatened him with ruin, he was equally odious to the minister and the archbishop, his conformity to the legal establishment was less thought of, than his complying with the parlement ordinances; but even this was trifling

---

* It is most probable that dr. Wilkins well knew his lady in her first husband's life-time for we must suppose them to have been very intimate acquaintance, as they two of the commissioners, or delegates, during the absence of dr. Owen, the vice-chancellor of Oxford.

in comparifon of his having allied himfelf to the

intruding family. So great a divine and philofopher, however, could not long languifh in difgrace: the honorable fociety of Gray's-Inn, fo well calculated to judge of merit, chofe him their preacher, fo early as 1660. It was a fenfible pleafure for him to be called to the capital, where he had an opportunity of promoting the philofophical meetings, which he took every means of advancing, and, by his care, it foon came to have fome appearance of a permanent fociety; as in the latter end of this year, it was refolved, that himfelf, and as many as were profeffors of Grefham college, as were of the fociety, fhould be joined to them, and that any three, or more, fhould be a committee to receive experiments. Upon the promotion of dr. Seth Ward to the bifhopric of Exeter, in 1662, the living of St. Lawrence-Jewry becoming void, his majefty prefented him with it, the following year he was elected one of the council of the royal fociety, then finally eftablifhed, and became a noble contributor to it Government now began to view him with greater confidence and regard, he was promoted to the deanery of Rippon. and the bifhopric of Chefter falling vacant, by the death of dr Geo. Hill, in 1668, he was, through the intereft of the duke of Buckingham, fixed upon to fucceed him, and, nov. 15, he was confecrated at Ely-houfe, by drs. Cofin, Laney, and Ward, lords bifhops of Durham, Ely, and Sarum; and a fermon was preached upon the occafion by his fonin-law, dr. Tillotfon. In this year bifhop Wilkins was appointed, by the lord-keeper, in conjunction with mr. Burton, chaplain to the keeper, to hold a conference with dr. Manton, dr. Bates, and mr. Baxter, about a comprehenfion, and a toleration of the prefbyterians, independents, and others,

others; the latter certainly might be done, and it might be a humane and politic thing to do it, but the former was an impoffibility: his lordfhip drew up the lord-keeper's propofals. In his epifcopal character he obtained the love and efteem of all, by continuing invariably his accuftomed moderation to every defcription of men, however widely differing from him, romanifts and fanatics, with which his diocefe was crowded, were treated with equal humanity and benevolence. He held this fee to his death, which happened in London, nov. 19, 1672, occafioned by a ftoppage of urine when he was acquainted with his approaching end, he replied, ' I am prepared for the great ' experiment.' His remains were depofited in the church of St. Lawrence-Jewry, and his funeral fermon was preached by dr. Lloyd, afterwards bifhop of Worcefter: the great number of coaches that attended his funeral fufficiently befpoke the eftimation he was held in, for, though it was a rainy day, yet more than 400 coaches and fix followed the hearfe, befides a great number of other carriages. As a token of his regard to Wadham college and the royal fociety, he bequeathed to the former 200l. and to the latter 400l. though, it muft be confeffed, it was a liberality ill-timed, as he did not leave his widow fufficient to fupport herfelf as fuch: his lady, during her widowhood, refided with dr. Tillotfon, and died at his houfe, whilft he was dean of Canterbury.

His lordfhip obliged the world with many publications, all excellent, feveral of them are peculiarly whimfical, the moft fo, is his ' difco- ' very of a new world,' in which he endeavours to prove, that the moon may be habitable, but what is moft extraordinary, he pretends, that it is poffible for a man to go there, it was printed in 1638: when the duchefs of Newcaftle faid to him,

him, ' Where am I to find a place for baiting
' at in the way up to that planet?' he replied,
' Madam, of all the people in the world, I never
' expected that question from you, who have
' built so many castles in the air, that you may
' lie every night at one of your own*.'   Had dr.
Wilkins been fortunate enough to have lived to the
æra of the air balloons, he would certainly have
himself attempted to find a passage to his favorite
planet, the moon.   We have three engravings
of him, the first is by Blooteling, large half sheet,
from a picture painted by M. Beale, the second
is by White, in the frontispiece to his ' principles
' and duties of natural religion.' 1675, 8vo. and
the third by Sturt, of the same size.

The avowed moderation of this great and good
man to the protestant dissenters, and his principle
—that it is the duty of all to submit to whatso-
ever power gains the government, procured him
the greatest abuse, which, both from his virtue
and learning, he ill deserved, even the captious
Anth.-à-Wood allows, that ' there was nothing

---

* The other literary works of the very learned and romantic
dr Wilkins, are, ' a discourse concerning a new planet, printed in 1640.—Mercury, or the secret and swift messenger, 1641,
a book of great merit —Ecclesiastes, or a discourse of the gift
of preaching, 1646 —Mathematical magic, or the wonders that
may be performed by mechanical geometry, 1648.—A discourse
concerning the beauty of Providence, in all the rugged passages
of it, 1649.—A discourse concerning prayer, 1653.—An essay
towards a real character and philosophical language, 1668.—A
sermon preached before k. Cha. II on Proverbs iii. 16 printed
in 1669.—Another sermon preached before that king, upon
Ecclef xii. 13. printed in 1670 —Also another sermon, preached before that monarch, from Ecclef. xii 14. printed in 1671
Dr Tillotson, his trustee, published in 1675, his principles and
duties of natural religion, and, in 1682, a volume of sermons,
preached upon various occasions

                                                ' de-

Bp Wilkins

'deficient in him, but a conſtant and ſettled
' mind.' the biſhop of Sarum had a proper ſenſe
of his worth, for he ſums up his character, by
ſaying, ' he was naturally ambitious, but he was
' the wiſeſt clergyman I ever knew. He was a
' lover of mankind, and had a delight in doing
' good' Granger ſpeaking of him, ſays, ' he
' was a very able naturaliſt and mathematician,
' and an excellent divine,' and that this ' excel-
' lent perſon's character was truly exemplary, as
' well as extraordinary *.'

* For a more minute life of dr. Wilkins, ſee the Biographia Britannica, under that article.—Biſhop Wilkins had a
brother named Timothy, who was ' bedel of divinity, formerly a
' capt. in the parl army, afterwards one of the ſtout defendants
' of Pontefract-caſtle againſt Cromwell's army. He died at his
' houſe in Holy-well, oct 4, 1671, aged 54, and was buried,
' according to his will, in the remoteſt part of Holy-well
' church-yard, i e. near the ſouth door that leadeth there-
' unto.' M. S. of Anth. à-Wood's remarks de com. Oxon.
p 122, and Guillim's diſplay of Heraldry, 6th edition.

No.

No. XXVII.

The life of Henry Ireton, esq. son-in-law to the protector Oliver, one of k. Cha. I.'s judges, and lord deputy of Ireland.

HENRY Ireton, so well known for his republican principles, and the great sway he bore in the distractions of his country, was the eldest son of German Ireton, of Attenton, in the county of Nottingham, esq. and was born in the year 1610. He was entered a gentleman commoner of Trinity college, Oxford, in 1626, and so early as june 10, 1629, took the degree of bachelor of arts. From college he removed to the Middle-Temple, where he studied the common-law, but the civil war breaking out, put a stop to his pursuits in that line, and led him to serve in the parlement army; where he made so great a proficiency in the military art, that some have not scrupled to say that Cromwell himself learned the rudiments of it from him. In the year 1646, he married Bridget, eldest daughter of mr. O. Cromwell (afterwards protector), which, with his own merit, soon gained him a captain's commission of horse, and almost immediately after, that of colonel: and upon the new-modelling the army in 1645, he was raised to the rank of commissary-general. He greatly distinguished himself at the battle of Naseby, in which his ardor having led him too far from his men, he was taken prisoner by the royalists: but in the confusion that soon after ensued in the

king's

king's army, he made his escape. In 1647[*], he
joined his father-in-law, and the independents,
in professing an inviolable attachment to his majesty, in opposition to the presbyterians, whom they
greatly hated, fearing that Charles should close
with their propositions. He at this time either
was, or pretended to be, exceedingly strenuous
for his sovereign's interest, expressing an entire affection for his person, and a keen sense of his sufferings, declaring, that rather than ' the king
' should continue thus enslaved by the presbyte-
' rian party, if but five men would join with him,
' he would venture his life in order to his re-
' demption;' adding, that he would ' purge and
' purge again, till they had brought the house of
' commons to such a temper as would do his ma-
' jesty's business, and rather than fall short of these
' promises, he would join with french, spaniard,
' cavalier, or any other who would concur with
' him to force them.' Notwithstanding these pro-
fessions, he was, perhaps, more than any other,
the cause of the king's death, which is said
to be owing to his intercepting a letter sent from
his majesty to the queen, in which both his de-
struction was fixed, as also that of his father in-
law[†], he therefore ceased to listen to any terms

---

[*] Perhaps in 1647, Ireton was in the long-parlement, as
he was returned for Appleby, but not until some time after
the parlement met in 1640, however, he was a committee man
for Nottinghamshire so early as 1643, and continued so during
the civil war.

[†] Cromwell and Ireton, finding, by their spies, that his
majesty had written to his queen, and that it was sent in the
skirts of a saddle, they dressed themselves as troopers, and met
the man carrying the saddle into an inn, in Holborn, when,
after telling him that they were sent there to search all that
came, added, that as he seemed a very honest fellow, they would
not give him that trouble, and would only take the saddle for
form's sake, which he readily permitted, not knowing its value:
having searched it, they discovered the fatal letter.

of accommodation with his fovereign, and refolved, be the confequence what it would, to deftroy the perfon of the king, and with him the
monarchy. Bifhop Burnet fays, Cromwell was
wavering, whether to put the king to death, or not,
but that ' Ireton, who had the principles and tem-
' per of a Caffius, ftuck at nothing that might
' have turned England into a commonwealth,'
hoping, ' by the king's death, that all men con-
' cerned in it would become irreconcileable to
' monarchy, and would, as defperate men, deftroy
' all that might revenge that blood.' We cannot
wonder, then, at finding his name as attending
moft of the fittings, both public and private, in the
high-court of juftice, that he fentenced his fovereign to die, and that his name is in the warrant
for his execution.

NUM XXVII.

Lord-deputy
Ireton.

Upon the eftablifhment of the commonwealth,
he was, june 1649, appointed to go into Ireland,
next in command to Cromwell, and embarked
for that kingdom in the auguft following. In jan.
1649-50, he was made prefident at Munfter, and,
laftly, upon the departure of his father-in-law, in
the following june, was declared lord-deputy.
and, what is obfervable, he almoft finifhed the reduction of that ifland without fighting a battle,
which was more owing to fear of his cruelty,
than his valor Amongft many inftances of the
former, this will be fufficient the inhabitants of
an irifh barony having revolted a fecond time,
he determined to deftroy man, woman, and child,
but lord Broghill would not leave him until he
had perfuaded him to lay afide fo horrid a refolution. Whilft in his laft appointment, in the
height of his moft profperous fucceffes, he was
feized, nov. 15, 1651, before Limerick, with the
plague, which carried him off on the 26th of the
fame month, and, if we believe fir Philip War-

wick (who had it from a perſon that was preſent) that he died raving, crying out ' I will have more ' blood, blood, blood!' His remains were brought to England for interment : they were landed at Briſtol, dec. 17 ; and as ſoon as the mayor of that city knew, that the ſhip in which the corpſe was, had ſailed into the river, he ſent a boat, with a tilt covered with black, and brought the body into the city, where a hearſe was provided, and it was accompanied to the caſtle by him, the aldermen, and council, in their formalities; the governor, officers, and great number of the people alſo attending · during the ceremony, the great guns were fired from both the caſtle and the fort ; afterwards, it was conducted to London, and laid in ſtate in Somerſet-Houſe. The room in which Ireton's body lay at Somerſet-Houſe, was hung with black, and an atchievement over the gate of that palace, with this motto, ' Dulce eſt pro pa-
' tria mori ,' which a wag thus engliſhed · ' It is
' good for his country that he is dead.' Dr. Goodwin preached his funeral ſermon : a ſtately tomb, with the effigies of himſelf and wife, was placed over his grave, which was mutilated ſoon after, and, at the reſtoration, entirely deſtroyed, upon it was an epitaph to his praiſe, written in a ſtile much above the common cant of the times, it is too long for inſertion. The body was, on feb. 6, depoſited with great funeral pomp, in k. Hen. VII.'s chapel, in Weſtminſter-abbey, O. Cromwell, afterwards protector, walked as chief-mourner, attended with the members of parlement, in black, who firſt ſhewed his ambition and ſtate over others, in this pompous funeral of his ſon-in-law. At the reſtoration, the lord-deputy's body was taken up, and indecently expoſed upon a gibbet at Tyburn, the trunk was there buried, and the head ſet upon a pole.

Ireton

Ireton was the moſt artful, dark, deliberate man
of all the republicans, by whom he was in the
higheſt degree beloved; they revered him as a
ſoldier, a ſtateſman, and ſaint; there is no one
but will allow him to be an able, though not a
virtuous ſtateſman; few will now regard him as a
ſaint: if we believe the following anecdote, his
perſonal courage may be queſtioned, or elſe his ad-
herence to his religious principles was very great;
for, when he had groſsly affronted mr. Hollis in
parlement, the latter challenged him, but he refuſed it, ſaying, it was againſt his conſcience;
and when mr. Hollis pulled him by the noſe, and
told him, that if his conſcience would not keep
him from giving men ſatisfaction, it ſhould keep
him from provoking them, yet he ſilently put up
the affront.   It muſt, however, be obſerved, that
the independents greatly ſet themſelves againſt
duelling.   It muſt be ſaid in his praiſe, that
though he had no objection to the delicacies of
high life *, yet he abſolutely perſiſted in refuſing
grants of the public money, nor had his family
the 2000l a year offered him out of the confiſcated
eſtate of the duke of Buckingham, until his death,
when the parlement, out of gratitude for the ſervices he had done them, and to oblige Cromwell,
ſettled it upon his widow and children. He has
been called the ' ſcribe,' from his ſkill in drawing
up declarations, petitions, &c. the remonſtrance
in behalf of the army for juſtice againſt the king,
the agreement of the people, the ordinance for
the trial of the unfortunate monarch, and the
precept for proclaiming the high court of juſtice,

---

* Ireton, though he hated the kingly office, from its ſtate
and expences, yet indulged himſelf in a coach and four which
coſt him 200l this was rather too luxurious for a ſaint, particularly when we reflect on the difference between the middle
of the laſt century, and the latter end of the preſent.

are all fuppofed to be his. We have the following
engravings of Ireton, mentioned by mr. Granger,
general Ireton, Cooper p. Houbraken, fc. 1741,
Illuft. Head, in the poffeffion of David Polhill,
efq. The lord-deputy Ireton, fold by Walton,
whole length, large 8vo. Henry Ireton, &c. Van-
dergucht, &c. 8vo. There is a medal, fuppofed
to be defigned for him, from its great refemblance,
by Simon, it is of filver, and reprefents his buft
in a circle, and the neck without any drapery, the
infcription is, *Quid tibi retribuam*, the reverfe
fhews a foldier climbing up a rock near the fea,
and reaching with a torch to an eagle's neft, which
he endeavours to fet on fire, the motto is, *Juftitia
neceffitafq. jubet.*

*The children of the protector's daughter Bridget,
by Ireton.*

1. Hen. Ireton, efq. who married Cath. daughter of the right hon. Hen. Powle, efq. fpeaker of
the houfe of commons, and mafter of the Rolls
there was no iffue of this marriage.

2. Eliz. eldeft daughter of the lord-deputy Ireton, was married to Tho Polhill, efq. or, as the
family anciently wrote it, Polley, of Deeley, in the
parifh of Hollingborne, in Kent, but more latterly
of Otford, in the fame county, where this gentleman refided · ; the iffue of this marriage was
3 fons, 1 David Polhill, of Cheapfted, in Kent,
efq. he was a member of parlement for the city
of Rochefter, and keeper of the records of the
Tower, at the time of his death, which happened

---

* The family of Polhill were friends to k. Cha. I David
Polhill, efq and mr Swan, were fent prifoners, in 1643, from
Kent, for inciting others againft the parlement, he, however,
procured his liberty, but at the expence of a fine, to be levied
by the deputy-lieutenant of Kent, as the fequeftrators fhould
order.

jan 15, 1754, in the 80th year of his age; he
was buried with his anceftors, in Otford church,
where there is an elegant mural monument, with
his bufto before a pyramid of grey marble, and
at the top, the arms of the deceafed and his three
wives . as part of the infcription is fo expreffive
of his worth, I here give it: ' He was very active,
' and fteady in promoting the true interefts of his
' fovereign, and defending the juft liberties of the
' fubject, both civil and religious, with which
' laudable view, he generoufly hazarded his own
' fafety, by being one of the Kentifh petitioners
' in the reign of k. Will. III. His humanity to
' his dependants, generofity to his relations, ten-
' dernefs and affection to his family, fteadinefs and
' fincerity to his friends, added to a moft bene-
' volent temper, merited, and gained him a very
' general approbation and efteem.' He married
three wives; 1 'Eliz. daughter of Tho. Trevor,
of Glynd, in Suffex, efq. 2nd. Gertrude, fifter of
the moft noble Tho Holles, duke of Newcaftle,
by neither of whom he had any iffue, and laftly,
Eliz daughter of John Borret, of Shoreham, in
Kent, efq by her he had 4 fons and 1 daughter,
viz. Cha. Tho. John, ———— and Eliz. Cha.
Polhill, of Cheapfted, efq. the eldeft, married
twice, firft, Penelope, daughter of fir John Shelly,
bart by whom he has a daughter, and by his fecond wife he has one or more fons. 2 Henry,
who died before his father. 3 Charles, who was
born oct. 3, 1679: ' The early part of his life he
' fpent at Smyrna, in a fteady application to bufi-
' nefs, as a merchant; on his return to England,
' he was appointed one of the commiffioners of
' Excife, which office he executed many years with
' diligence and integrity.' He married Martha,
daughter of Tho. Streatfield, of Sevenoaks, in

NUM XXVII.

Defcendants of
lord-deputy
Ireton

Y 3   Kent,

Kent, efq. by whom he left no iffue : fhe died in
may 1741, aged 55; he fept 30, 1755, their lives
were in a ftate of friendfhip and mutual affection;
his body was buried in Otford church, near his
wife's remains, and where, by his will, he ordered
that a monument fhould be erected to their memories; and, accordingly, a magnificent one was
placed there, inclofed in an iron railing; it gives
the ftatue of mr Polhill, ftanding, as large as life,
leaning againft an urn of Sicilian marble; above
him is a medallion of his wife; upon the fides of
the farcophagus fit the figures of Faith and Hope,
beautifully executed; and, upon a tablet of black
marble at the bafe, is an infcription in gilt letters,
which I have before in part copied.

3. Jane, the eldeft daughter of the lord-deputy
Ireton, married Rich. Lloyd, efq. The iffue of this
marriage was Jane, an only child, who married
Nich. or Hen Moore, efq. by whom fhe had, 1.
David. 2. Hen. 3. Nich. 4. Daniel. 5. Eliz.
married to —— Oyle, M D and mother of
Eliz. the wife of mr. Samuel Codrington. 6. Jane,
married to mr. Burroughs; and, 7. Ann, married
to mr. Roberts.

4. Bridget, the 2nd daughter of the lord-deputy
Ireton, who was one of the moft extraordinary
beings that ever lived. if the reader wifhes to
know what kind of a figure Oliver the protector,
her grandfather, would have made in petti-
coats, I would recommend him to read this lady's
character, drawn by various hands, and given
in future pages, which I have put feparately, to
prevent too great a break into this genealogy.
fhe was married to Tho. Bendyfh, of Gray's-Inn,
Middlefex, and of Southtown, in Suffolk, efq.
defcended of a very ancient and refpectable family: one of whom was fir Tho. Bendyfh, bart.
ambaffador

ambaſſador from both k. Cha. I. and the prot.
Olivei : the Bendyſh's were attached to the parlement; for Tho. Bendyſh, eſq. was a committee-
man for the county of Cambridge, they bore for
their arms, arg. a chevron ſable, between 3 rams'
heads, erazed azure. he died april 27, 1707,
aged 61, and was buried in the church of Yarmouth * Mrs Bendyſh died in 1727, or 1728;
they had three children, who lived to the age of
manhood, 1. Tho who married twice; his ſecond
wife was miſs Cath. Smith, of Colſkirk, near
Fakenham, in Norfolk, with whom he had an
eſtate at that place, he died in the Weſt-Indies,
where he had a conſiderable property, and to
which he was obliged, from his extravagance, to
retire †, he left one ſon, by the firſt marriage,
named Ireton Bendyſh, who enjoyed a place under
government; he died in 1730, unmarried, and

* The inſcription upon the monument of mr Bendyſh, ſays
he was deſcended from Sir Tho. Bendyſh, bart the ambaſſador, that Bridget, his wife, was the daughter of Henry Ireton,
of Ireton, in Derbyſhire, eſq. ſometime lord-lieut. in Ireland :
but I do not think he was deſcended from, though nearly allied
to, the ambaſſador probably the Iretons took their name from
a village of that name in Derbyſhire but it had not been poſſeſſed by them ſo late as the 17th century. Hen Ireton, eſq.
was never lord-lieut but lord-deputy of Ireland.---At Bower-
hall, in Binneſtead, in Eſſex, is the original appointment of
ſir Tho. Bendyſh, ambaſſador to the Porte, with many other
writings and pictures of that family, in the church of Binneſtead, is a very fine monument of ſir Hen Bendyſh, the laſt
heir male, and another of his ſiſter, mrs. Pike, who limited
the eſtate with many remainders, ſeveral have dropped. it is
now poſſeſſed by a gentleman whoſe name was Biſhop, but
who has changed it to Bendyſh, in compliance to the will of
mrs Pike

† There was a Tho. Bendyſh, a clerk of the Inner-Room,
in the treaſury, in the reign of q. Ann. Query, Was it the
above gentleman ?

Y 4   greatly

great'y lamented, as ' he was in his perfon, tem-
' per, and breeding, a very amiable young gen-
' tleman.' 2. Bridget, who refided in the feat
at Southtown; fhe died unmarried, long after her
mother. 3. Henry, who refided at Bedford-row,
he married Martha Shute, fifter to the amiable
lord vifc. Barrington, whom fhe refembled ' in her
' perfon, in her voice, in the grace and politenefs
' of her addrefs, and in the extent of her under-
' ftanding.' Henry died in the year 1740, leaving
three fons and two daughters; 1. Henry Bendyfh, of Chingford, on Epping-foreft, Effex, but
chiefly at the Salt-pans, or Southtown, in Suffolk,
in the latter part of his life, where he had a patent place under the lord chancellor, he died, unmarried, at Tempsford, in Bedfordfhire, in june,
1753. 2. Tho. 3. Geo. 4. Mary, married to
Will. Berners, alfo of Hanover-fquare, and Wolverton-park, Suffolk, efq. he died fept. 1783, and
fhe juft before him; they had iffue Cha. Berners,
alfo of Hanover-fquare, and Wolverton-park, efq.
who married Cath daughter of ———— Laroche,
efq by whom he had feveral children, and the
rev. Hen. Berners, rector of Hambleton, in Bucks,
unmarried in 1775. 5. Eliz. who married march
27, 1756, to John Hagar, of Warefley-park, in
Huntingdonfhire, efq. fon of the admiral of that
name.

5. Mary, the fourth and youngeft daughter of
the lord deputy, married to a mr. Nathaniel Carter, a wealthy merchant of Yarmouth, feb. 21,
1677-8, in the licence fhe is called Fleetwood,
and not Ireton, as thinking it better to pafs for
the daughter of her mother's fecond, than firft
hufband, the reafon is obvious. Ireton was a
chief in k. Cha. I.'s death, Fleetwood had no
concern whatfoever in it: fhe had no iffue by
mr.

mr. Carter, who furvived her: her death is fup-
poſed to have happened about 1722 *.

————

No. XXVIII.

*Various Anecdotes of the extraordinary Mrs. Bendyſh,
by different hands.*

THE character of mrs. Bridget Bendyſh,
grand-daughter of Oliver Cromwell, written in 1719, on account of the cloſing words of
lord Clarendon's character of her grandfather,
' he, Cromwell, will be looked upon as a brave
' wicked man,' by mr. Say, a diſſenting miniſter,
dr Brookes, and mr. Hewling Luſon. ' The character of Oliver ſeems to be made up of ſo many
inconſiſtencies, that I do not think any one who
was not perſonally and thoroughly acquainted
with him, or, at leaſt, with his grand-daughter,
mrs. Bridget Bendyſh, capable of drawing it
juſtly. She was the daughter of his ſon-in-law,
Ireton a lady, who, as ſhe exactly reſembled the
beſt picture of Oliver, which I have ever ſeen,
and which is now at Roſe-hall, in the poſſeſſion

NU XXVIII.
Anecdotes of
mrs Bendyſh,
grand-daughter
of Oliver lord-
prot by mr.
Say.

* The hiſt of the deputy-lord Ireton is taken from his life
in the Biograph Britan with other books of the ſame kind, as
alſo from the writers of the engliſh hiſtory during the reigns
of k Cha I and the plot. Oliver; his deſcendants are taken
from Hughes's letters, and various papers, given in the London magazine, relating to the Cromwell family, and its alliances, in 1774 and 1775, Swinfen's hiſt of Yarmouth, and
materials communicated by miſs Cromwell, and mr. Longmate.

of ſir Rob. Rich *, ſo ſhe ſeems alſo exactly to reſemble him in the caſt of her mind. A perſon of great preſence and majeſty, heroic courage, and indefatigable induſtry, and with ſomething in her countenance and manner, that at once attracts and commands reſpect the moment ſhe appears in company, accuſtomed to turn her hands to the meaneſt offices, and even drudgeries of life †, among her workmen from the earlieſt morning to the decline of day; inſenſible to all the calls and neceſſities of nature, and in a habit and appearance beneath the meaneſt of them, and neither ſuiting her character nor ſex. and then immediately, after having eaten and drank almoſt to exceſs, of whatever is before her, without choice or diſtinction, to throw herſelf down upon the next couch or bed that offers, in the profoundeſt ſleep, to riſe from it with new life and vigour, to dreſs herſelf in all the riches and grandeur of appearance, that her preſent circumſtances or the remains of better times, will allow her, and about the cloſe of evening, to ride in her chaiſe, or on her pad, to a neighbouring port ‡, and there ſhine in converſation, and to receive the place and precedence in all company, as a lady who once expected, at this time, to have been one of the firſt perſons in Europe, to make innumerable viſits of ceremony, buſineſs, or charity, and diſpatch the greateſt affairs with the utmoſt eaſe and addreſs, appearing every where as the common friend, advocate, and patroneſs of all the poor, and the miſerable in any kind, in whoſe cauſe ſhe will receive no denial from the great and rich, rather demanding than requeſting them to perform their duty, and who is generally received

---

* The reader, by referring to the life of the late mr. Hollis, may ſee an engraving of her.
† 'Salt-works.'   ‡ 'Yarmouth.'

and

and regarded by thofe who knew her beft, as
a perfon of great fincerity, piety, generofity, and
even profufion of charity . and yet poffeffed of all
thefe virtues, and poffeffed of them in a degree
above the ordinary rate, a perfon of no truth,
juftice, or common honefty (I am tempted to fay),
who never broke her promife in her life, and yet,
on whofe word no man can prudently depend, nor
fafely report the leaft circumftance after her: of
great and moft fervent devotion towards God, and
love to her fellow-creatures and fellow-chriftians;
and yet there is fcarcely an inftance of impiety, or
cruelty, of which fhe is not capable · fawning,
fufpicious, miftruftful, and jealous without end,
of all her fervants, and even of her friends, at the
fame time that fhe is ready to do them all the fervice that lies in her power, affecting all mankind
equally, and not according to the fervices they
are able to do her, but according to the fervice
their neceffities and miferies demand from her; to
the relieving of which neither the wickednefs of
their characters, nor the injuries they may have
done herfelf in particular, are the leaft exception,
but rather a peculiar recommendation.

NU XXVIII.

Anecdotes of
Mrs Bendyſh.

‘ Such are the extravagancies which have long
appeared to me in the character of this lady,
whofe friendfhip and refentment I have felt by
turns for a courfe of many years acquaintance
and intimacy; and yet, after all thefe blemifhes
and vices, which I muft freely own in her, he
would do her, in my opinion, the greateft injury,
who fhould fay, fhe was a great wicked woman;
for all that is good and great in her feems to be
owing to a true magnanimity of fpirit, and a
fincere defire to ferve the intereft of God and all
mankind, and all that is otherwife, to wrong
principles, early and ftrongly imbibed by a tem-
perament of body (fhall I call it?) or a turn of
mind

mind to the laſt degree enthuſiaſtic and viſionary.
It is owing to this, that ſhe never hears of any
action of any perſon, but ſhe immediately mingles
with it her own ſentiments, and judgment of the
perſon and the action, in ſo lively a manner, that
it is almoſt impoſſible for her to ſeparate them
afterwards, which ſentiments, therefore, and judgment, ſhe will relate thenceforwards, with the
ſame aſſurance that ſhe relates the action itſelf.
If ſhe queſtions the lawfulneſs or expediency of
any great, hazardous, and doubtful undertaking,
ſhe purſues the method, which, as ſhe ſays, her
grandfather always employed with ſucceſs, that
is, ſhe ſhut herſelf up in her cloſet, till, by faſting
and praying, the vapours are raiſed, and the
animal ſpirits wrought up to an unuſual ferment,
by an over-intenſeneſs and ſtrain of thinking,
and whatever portion of ſcripture comes into
her head at ſuch a ſeaſon, which ſhe apprehends
to be ſuitable to the preſent occaſion (and whatever comes in ſuch circumſtances, is ſure to come
with a power and evidence, which, to ſuch a heat-
ed imagination, appear to be divine and ſuper-
natural); thenceforward no intreaties nor perſuaſion, no force of reaſon, nor plaineſt evidence
of the ſame ſcripture alledged againſt it, no con-
viction of the impropriety, injuſtice, impiety, or
almoſt impoſſibility of the thing, can turn her
from it, which creates in her a confidence and induſtry, that generally attains its end, and hardens
her into the ſame practice for ever, " ſhe will
" truſt a friend that never deceived her." This
was the very anſwer ſhe made me, when, upon
her receiving a conſiderable legacy at the death
of a noble relation *, I urged her to ſuſpend
her uſual acts of piety, generoſity, and charity

* Moſt probably lady Fauconberg, aunt to mrs. Bendyſh

upon

upon such occasions, till she had been just to
the demands of a poor woman, and had heard the
cries of a family too long kept out of their money,
for "how," said I, "if you should die and leave
such a debt undischarged, will it be paid, as no
one will think himself obliged to pay, after the
decease of a person from whom they have no
expectations?" She assured me she would never
die in any one's debt. "But how is it possible
you should be assured of that, who are for ever in
debt to so many persons, and have so many other
occasions for your money than discharging of
your debts, and are resolved to have so many as
long as you live?" Her answer was as before-
mentioned *(added after her death)*, and the event
justified her conduct, if any thing could justify a
conduct, which reason and revelation must condemn.
Such was this grand-daughter of Oliver, who
inherited more of his constitution of body and
complexion of mind, than any of his descendants
and relations with whom I have happened to be
acquainted, and I have had some acquaintance
with many others of his grandchildren, and have
seen his son Richard, and Richard's son Oliver,
who had something indeed of the spirit of his
grandfather, but all his other distinguishing
qualifications seemed vastly inferior to the lady,
whose character I have sincerely represented as it
has long appeared to S S '

' The old lady (mrs. Bendysh) was a very singular character, and there was something in her
person when she was dressed, and in company,
that could not fail of attracting at once the
notice and respect of any strangers that entered
the room wherever she was, though the company were ever so numerous, and though many
of them might be more splendid in their appearance. Splendid, indeed, she never was, her

highest

NU. XXVIII.

Anecdotes of
mrs Bendysh.

Anecdotes of
mrs Bendysh,
grand-daughter
of Oliver lord
prot by mr.
Brooke

Nᵒ XXVIII

Anecdotes of
mrs. Bendyſh.

higheſt dreſs being a plain ſilk, but it was uſually of the richeſt ſort, though, as far as I can remember, of what is called a quaker's colour, and ſhe wore beſides a kind of black ſilk hood, or ſcarf, that I rarely, if ever, obſerved to be worn by ladies of her time, and though hoops were in faſhion long before her death, nothing, I ſuppoſe, could have induced her to wear one. I can ſo far recollect her countenance, as to confirm what is obſerved by mr Say, of her likeneſs to the beſt pictures of Oliver, and ſhe no leſs reſembled him in the qualities of enterprize, reſolution, courage, and enthuſiaſm. She looked upon him as the firſt and greateſt of mankind, and alſo as the beſt; in talking of herſelf, on the mention of any good quality, ſhe would ſay ſhe learned it of her grandfather, and would add, if ſhe had any thing valuable, ſhe learned it all from him. She muſt certainly have had an engaging and entertaining turn of converſation, or ſhe could not have fixed the attention of myſelf, when a boy of twelve or fourteen, and of another ſtill younger, and as volatile, and have made us often happy in liſtening to her diſcourſe, whether it concerned the hiſtory of herſelf and her own times, or whether it conſiſted of advice and inſtruction to us, or was a mixture of both It is impoſſible to ſay what figure ſhe might not have made in the world, had ſhe been placed in an elevated ſtation, and been honoured with the confidence of a prince or miniſter, and I believe there is no ſtation to which her ſpirit would have been unequal. In the circumſtances, therefore, in which ſhe was left, with an income, I think of 2, or 300l. a year, it was natural that ſometimes as far, or rather farther than her fortune would admit, ſhe engaged in projects of buſineſs of different kinds, by which, I have been

told

told, she was much oftener a loser than a gainer. Nᵁ XXVIII.

One into which she entered, was the grazing of
cattle; her going to fairs to buy them, in the
only equipage she had, a one-horse chaise, afforded
exercise at once for her courage and enthusiasm;
travelling in the night was to her the same as in
the day; and in the worst roads and dangers,
in which it would be too little to say she was perfectly fearless, it comes nearer to her character
to say, which she would most enjoy. I have
heard her say, that when in the darkest night, on
a wild open heath, with the roads of which she
was quite unacquainted, she has had to encounter
the most dreadful thunder storm, she has then been
happy, has sung this or that psalm, and doubted
not that angels surrounded her chaise, and protected her. She was as little fearful of encountering other dangers, in particular, she delivered
a relation from imprisonment for high-treason, on
account of the Rye-house plot, by a bold and well-
concerted stratagem, though perfectly sensible of
the vindictive spirit of the king and duke, and
that her own life must have paid the price of his
escape, had she been detected. I have heard that
she was privy to this plot when it was hatching,
and you know it never came to more. I have
also heard from herself, and it was confirmed by
my father, and others, from good authority, that
she was in the secret of the revolution, that she
would go into shops in different parts of the town,
under a pretence of cheapening silks and other
goods, and in going out to her coach, would take
the opportunity to drop bundles of papers, to
prepare the minds of the people for that happy
event, for she might safely be trusted with any
secret, were it ever so important. This art of
secret-keeping, I have heard her say, she learned
from

from her grandfather, for that when ſhe was only
ſix years of age, ſhe has ſat between his knees
when he has held a cabinet-council, and on very
important affairs, and on ſome of them objecting
to her being there, he has ſaid ' there was no ſe-
' cret he would truſt with any of them, that he
' would not truſt with that infant.' And to prove
that he was not miſtaken, he has told her ſomething as in confidence, and under the charge of
ſecrecy, and then urged her mother and grandmother to extort it from her by promiſes, careſſes,
and bribes, and theſe failing, by threatenings and
ſevere whippings; but ſhe held ſteady againſt all
with amazing diſpaſſionate firmneſs, expreſſing
her duty to her mother, but her greater duty to
keep her promiſe of ſecrecy to her grandfather,
and the confidence he had repoſed in her. I have
heard both my father and mr. Say, and others,
mention this; and I know they had no doubt of
the truth of it: I recollect too, that archbiſhop
Tillotſon introduced her to q. Mary, in order
that a penſion might be ſettled upon her, to ſup
port her in ſome degree of dignity to what ſhe
had known in the beginning of her days; but the
death of that excellent prelate following ſoon after,
and the queen's the month ſucceeding to it, all hope
was defeated. Happening to travel in a London
ſtage, in company with two gentlemen who had
ſwords on, ſhe informed them of her deſcent from
Oliver, and as uſual was extolling him with all that
rapture to which her idolizing him to enthuſiaſm
led her; when one of her fellow-travellers deſcended ſo much below the man, though his appearance was that of a gentleman, as to treat his
memory with groſs indignity and abuſe, ſhe an-
ſwered it with all the ſpirit that was inherent in
her, till the coach ſtopped and they got out, on
which ſhe inſtantly drew the other gentleman's
                                        ſword

ſword, called this a poltroon and a coward, for

behaving as he had done to a woman, and now
challenged him to ſhew himſelf a man, told him
ſhe was prepared to treat him as he might expect
from his inſolence, were ſhe a man, and inſiſted,
if he would act like ſuch, on his not taking ſhel-
ter under pretence of her ſex In a violent fever,
being thought paſt recovery, and inſenſible to any
thing that might be ſaid, her aunt, lady Fauconberg, and other company being in the room, and
her ladyſhip, though Oliver's daughter, giving too
much way to things ſaid in diſhonor of his memory by ſome preſent, to the aſtoniſhment of all, ſhe
raiſed herſelf up, and with great ſpirit ſaid, " if
ſhe did not believe her grandmother to have been
one of the moſt virtuous women in the world, ſhe
ſhould conclude her ladyſhip to be a baſtard, won-
dering how it could be poſſible that the daughter
of the greateſt and beſt man that ever lived could
be ſo degenerate, as not only to ſit with patience
to hear his memory ſo ill-treated, but to ſeem herſelf to aſſent to it." I have often heard her ſay,
that " next to the twelve apoſtles, he was the firſt
ſaint in heaven, and was placed next to them "
On evenings that ſhe has ſpent at my father's, ſhe
has ſeemed to be in enthuſiaſtic raptures, when religion made part of the ſubject of converſation;
and ſeldom would leave the room, though it were
twelve at night, or later, without ſinging a pſalm;
ſhe then would go into her chaiſe in high joy, to
return to her houſe, which was a conſiderable way
from the town where my father lived. My account of mrs. Bendyſh's poſterity is not ſo exact
as I could wiſh, but a letter which I expect in a
few days from my friend mr. Luſon, who is one
of the beſt and moſt amiable men I know, will, I
hope, enable you to place in your collection, and
tranſmit to poſterity, a complete character of this

very extraordinary woman, who wanted only to have acted in a superior sphere to be ranked by historians amongst the most admirable heroines. Had she been in the situation of a Zenobia, she would have supported her empire, and defended her capital with equal skill and resolution, but she would never have lived to decorate the triumph of an Aurelian, or have given up a secretary of the fidelity and abilities of a Longinus to save herself. If she had been in the situation of Elizabeth, she would, without scruple, have cut off the heads of twenty Marys, who, by surviving her, might have overturned the happy establishment she had formed, and would as gloriously have defended her kingdom against a spanish armada, or any hostile force whatever, and have rather inwardly triumphed, than been intimidated at the most formidable preparations against her   On re-perusing mr. Say, I find I have said something similar of this lady, to what is said by him, but it was from my own original ideas of her and not from having read his account.   J. BROOKE."

Says mr. Hewling Lufon, in a letter to dr Brooke, ' I find, sir, that mr. Say's character of mrs Bendyfh, has much engaged the public notice, the first sight I had of this character was about twelve years ago, when it was put into my hands at London, by a lady who asked me my opinion of it, because she knew I was well acquainted with Yarmouth and its neighbourhood.   The copy which was shewn to me, was taken, as I was informed, from a manuscript in the library of sir Rich. Ellys. Cromwell was so great in his courage, in his parts, in his hypocrisy, in his politics, and in his fortune, and these conjoined, produced effects in his own days, so astonishing, and even down to

* This letter is dated Norwich, april 28, 1773

oui

our times fo interefting, that the public curiofity
is naturally excited to trace the fate of his own family from his time to our own. He fucceeded
in giving the mortal wound to *monarchical tyranny*;
it was wounded, but did not expire, it languifhed
indeed, yet lived through the two fucceeding
reigns, till at length, exhaufted by the wafting
wound of the republican hero, it finally gave up
its horrid ghoft, with the abdication of James.
This, and no more, was the merit of Cromwell.
Nothing could be more remote from national freedom, than the politics and government of the
ufurper, unlefs it were the principles and manners
of the times, thefe were too warlike, too vindictive, and too illiberal, to receive a conftitutional
eftablifhment of public liberty. Cromwell conquered tyranny, but he did not eftablifh freedom.

‘ Mr. Say’s character of mrs. Bendyfh is perfectly juft, in my opinion, it is well drawn, and
exhibits a ftriking likenefs. Mr. Say, with whom
I was perfectly well acquainted, was a moft ingenious, modeft, worthy man, he fought his happinefs, and found it in domeftic peace and contem-
plative retirement. his wife was one of the beft of
women, he married her out of the family of mr.
Carter, a wealthy merchant at Yarmouth, to whom
mr Say was nearly related*· this mr. Carter married the daughter of general Ireton, and the fifter
of mrs. Bendyfh, fo that mr. Say, being thus
connected with the family, had every poffible advantage for an accurate examination of mrs. Bendyfh’s character. This fon-in law of Ireton died
at a very advanced age, about the year 1723, I
well remember his perfon, but his wife died long
before my time. There was no iffue from this

* She died in 1744-5, within a year after her hufband.

Z 2   marriage.

marriage*. I was young, not more than sixteen,
when mrs. Bendysh died, in 1727, or 1728, yet
she came so often to my father's house, that I remember her person, her dress, her manner, and
her conversation (which were all strikingly peculiar) with great precision, and I have heard much
more of her than I have seen, she was certainly,
both without and within, in her person and in her
spirits, exactly like her grandfather the protector,
her features, the turn of her face, and the expref-
sion of her countenance, all agreed very exactly
to the excellent pictures I have seen of the protector, in the Cromwell family, and whoever looks
upon the print, prefixed to the octavo " life of
Cromwell,' said to be published by the late bishop
Gibson, about the year 1725, which exactly agree
with these pictures, will have a clear idea of mrs
Bendysh's person, if their imaginations can add a
female dress, a few years in age, and a very little
softening of the features. I refer to that print, be-

---

* ' When I was a boy says mr. Luson, they used to shew
a large chamber in the house of mr Carter, which had also
been the house of his ther, in which, as the tradition went
the infamous murder of Cha I on the scaffold was finally
determined. A meeting of the principal officers in the army was held in this chamber, they chose to be above stairs
for the privacy of their conscience they strictly commanded
no person should come near the room, except a man appointed
to attend, their orders whoever was ordered to tout, was pre-
of, from time to time, till past eleven at night, they then
came down, took a very short supper, and immediately after on post, many for London, and some for the quarters of
the army. Thus fiore, sir, I give you from the very doubtful
authority of tradition, or that has no better foundation' Th
though it relates materially concerns mrs Bendysh, is
too curious to be omitted, particularly as it was so short I
is generally fixed, that the violent death of k Cha I was
finally determined at or near Windsor, but there can be little
doubt, that so momentous a circumstance would require no
than one. probably many meetings.

CAU

cause the fine engraving of Cromwell in the Houbraken collection bears very little resemblance to the pictures in the Cromwell family, and no resemblance at all to mrs Bendyʃh.

'Mrs Bendyʃh had as much of Cromwell's courage as a female conʃtitution could receive, which was often expreʃʃed with more ardor than the rules of female decorum could excuʃe. That enthuʃiaʃm, in which Cromwell was generally but an actor, in her was ʃincere and original, ʃhe had not merely the courage to face danger, but ʃhe had alʃo that perfect undiʃturbed poʃʃeʃʃion of her faculties, which left her free to contrive the beʃt means to repel or to avoid it. Mrs. Bendyʃh lived through, what the diʃʃenters but too juʃtly called " the troubleʃome times," by which they meant the times when the penal laws againʃt conventicles were ʃtrained to their utmoʃt rigor the preaching of this ʃect was then held in the cloʃeʃt concealment, whilʃt the preachers went in momentary danger of being dragged out by ʃpies and informers to heavy fines and ʃevere impriʃonments. With theʃe ʃpies and informers ʃhe maintained a perpetual war. This kind of buʃtle was, in all reʃpects, in the true taʃte of her ʃpirit, I have heard many ʃtories of her dealings with theʃe ungracious people, ʃometimes ʃhe circumvented and outwitted them, and ʃometimes ʃhe bullied them, and the event generally was, that ʃhe got the poor parʃon out of their clutches Upon theʃe occaʃions, and upon all others, when they could expreʃs their attachment to her, mrs Bendyʃh was ʃure of the common people, ʃhe was, as ʃhe deʃerved to be, very dear to them, when ʃhe had money, ʃhe gave it freely to ʃuch as wanted, and when ʃhe had none, which was pretty often the caʃe, they were ʃure of receiving civility and commiʃeration ʃhe was not barely charitable; ʃhe practiʃed an exalted

humanity,

humanity,—if in the meaneſt ſick room, ſhe found
the ſufferer inſufficiently or improperly attended,
ſhe turned attendant herſelf, and would ſit hours
in the pooreſt chamber to adminiſter ſupport or
conſolation to the afflicted : in this noble employment ſhe paſſed much of her time.   As mis. Bendyſh was thus beloved by the poor, to whom ſhe
was beneficent, ſhe was reſpected by the richer
ſort of all parties, to whom, when ſhe kept clear
of her enthuſiaſtic freaks, ſhe was highly entertaining   She had ſtrong and maſculine ſenſe, a
free and ſpirited elocution, much knowledge of
the world, great dignity in her manner, and a moſt
engaging addreſs.   The place of her reſidence was
called the Salt-Pans, whilſt the ſalt-works were
carried on there, but the proper name is South-
Town, i. e. ſouth of Yarmouth. in this place,
which is quite open to the road, I have very often
ſeen her in the morning, ſtumping about with an
old ſtraw hat on her head, her hair about her ears,
without ſtays, and when it was cold, an old blan-
ket about her ſhoulders, and a ſtaff in her hand,
in a word, exactly accoutred to mount the ſtage
as a witch in Macbeth, yet if, at ſuch a time, ſhe
was accoſted by any perſon of rank or breeding,
that dignity of her manner, and politeneſs of her
ſtile, which nothing could efface, would inſtantly
break through the veil of debaſement, which concealed her native grandeur, and a ſtranger to her
cuſtoms might become aſtoniſhed to find himſelf
addreſſed by a princeſs, while he was looking at
a mumper.

    ' Mrs. Bendyſh reſembled the protector in no-
thing more than in that reſtleſs, unabated activity
of ſpirit, which, by the coincidence of a thouſand
favorable circumſtances, conducted him to the
ſummit of power and of fame, and entangled her
generally, unfavored by ſucceſs, in a thouſand
                embariaſſments

embarraffments and difgraces, yet fhe never faint-
ed or was wearied, " One profpect loft, another
ftill fhe gain'd," and the enthufiafm of her faith
kept place with, or to fpeak more truly, far out-ran
the activity of her mind. Perhaps warm enthufiafm of all kinds, and in all tempers, by attach-
ing the temper folely to the attainment and fruition
of its object, either entirely overlooks, or lightly efti-
mates every objection, however invincible, and
every obftacle, however infurmountable, which
may arife in the neceffary path of its progrefs.
Thus it was with her, and the habit of her mind
and her temper concurred to render her inflexibly
obftinate, and incurably deaf to every fuggeftion
in oppofition to her refolves. Mrs Bendyfh had,
however, one conftant, never-failing refource
againft the vexation of difappointments, for, as
fhe determined, at all events, to " ferve the Lord
with gladnefs," her way was to rejoice at every
thing as it arrived· if fhe fucceeded, fhe was
thankful for that, and if fhe fuffered adverfity,
which was generally her lot, fhe was vaftly more
thankful for that, and fhe fo managed, that her
fpiritual joy always increafed with her outward
fufferings. Happy delirium of pious enthufiafm!

' Mrs. Bendyfh's religion was in the higheft
ftrain of calviniftic enthufiafm, and dr. Owen, in
his writings, was her fpiritual guide. She never
doubted the validity of her election to the kingdom of heaven. But mrs Bendyfh's enthufiafm
never carried her to greater lengths of extravagance than in the juftification of her grandfather,
of whofe memory fhe was paffionately fond. It,
however, unfortunately happened, that her fancy
led her to defend him exactly in that part of his
character which was leaft defenfible. She valued
him, no doubt, very highly, as a general and
politician, but fhe had got it fixed in her head,

Z 4   that

that this kind of fame was vain and worthless,
when compared with the gracious glory of Oliver's
saintship. " A chosen veffel," he was, " a re-
generated child of God, divinely infpired," and
much more jargon of this fort, fhe was perpetu-
ally attempting to tranflate from her own imagination into her auditors, now, it could not
but happen, that, for five hundred who might
be prevailed with to receive Oliver as a great
general, not five could be found who would admit him as a great faint; and this conftant kick-
ing againft Oliver's faintfhip, wrought the lady
fore travail. On fuch occafions her friends gave
way to her whims, or laughed them off, but,
when her faith in Oliver was gravely contefted by
ftrangers, great and fearful was her wrath. Mrs.
Bendifh gravely infifted in converfation with her
friends, that Oliver was one day feeking the Lord,
with fuch fervor of devotion, and ftriving for a
gracious anfwer with fuch vehemence of fpirit,
that the tears were forced from him in fuch
abundance, as to run under the clofet-door into the
next room. This, to be fure, was fnivelling to
fome purpofe. A gentleman, to whom this information was particularly addreffed, obferved, in
reply, " that it was difficult to fay precifely, what
abundant fountains of tears might fill up and run
over the Lord's chofen veffels, yet he could not
help fufpecting, that the flood under the clofet-
door, occafioned by the protector's ftruggles, was
derived from fome other fource than his eyes."
This fhe bore pretty well. But it happened in a
ftage coach, where fhe was not known, mrs. Bendyfh fell into a violent difpute in behalf of the
protector. the opponent was as hot and as violent
as the lady, and if, towards the end of the ftage,
their anger fubfided, it was not for want of wrath,
or of words to keep it up, but for want of breath

to give it utterance. After they went out of the
coach and had taken some refreshment, the old
lady very calmly and respectfully desired to speak
apart with the gentleman who had been the opponent in the dispute. When she had him alone,
she told him with great composure, " he had, in
the grossest manner, belied and abused the most
pious man that ever lived, that Cromwell's blood,
that flowed in her veins, would not allow her to
pass over the indignities cast on his memory in
her presence, that she could not handle a sword,
but could fire a pistol as well as he, and that she
demanded immediate satisfaction to the injured
honor of her family." The gentleman was exceedingly amazed at the oddness of this address;
but, as he happened to carry about him good
sense enough to teach him how to act upon the
spot, he immediately told her, ' there were many
great qualities in Oliver, which he honored as
much as she could, that, if he had known, or
suspected, her relation to him, he would not have
said a word on the subject to give her offence;
and that he sincerely asked her pardon." This
submission completely satisfied her, and they finished their journey with much pleasure and good-
humour, but saint Oliver was not again brought
upon the tapis. The truth of this story I never
heard questioned

As the whole of mrs Bendysh's personal œco-
nomy was not of the common form, her hours
of visiting went generally out of the common
season. She would very frequently come and visit at my father's at nine or ten at night, and
sometimes later, if the doors were not shut up.
On such visits she generally stayed till about one
in the morning. Such late visits, in those sober
times, were considered by her friends as highly
inconvenient, yet nobody complained of them to
her.

her. The respect she universally commanded gave her a licence in this, and many other irregularities. She would, on her visits, drink wine in great plenty, and the wine used to put her tongue into very brisk motion. but I do not remember that she was ever disgracefully exposed by it There was an old mare, which had been the faithful companion of mrs. Bendysh's adventures during many years. The old mare and her manoeuvres, were as well known at Yarmouth as the old lady. On this mare she was generally mounted, but towards the end of her life, the mare was prevailed with to draw a chaise, in which mrs. Bendysh often seated herself. Mrs. Bendysh would never suffer a servant to attend her in these night visits : " God," she said, " was her guard, and she would have no other." Her dress on these visits, though it was in a taste of her own, was always grave and handsome At about one in the morning, for she never finished her round of visits sooner, she used to put herself on the top of the mare, or into the chaise, and set off on her return. When the mare began to move, mrs Bendysh began to sing a psalm, or one of Watts's hymns , in a very loud, but not a very harmonious key. This I have often heard and thus the two old souls, the mare and her mistress, one gently trotting, and the other loudly singing, jogged on the length of a short mile from Yarmouth, which brought them home.'—I could not shorten these curious and well-written anecdotes of mrs. Bendysh, without doing an injustice to these memoirs

─ Dr Watts was well known to mrs Bendysh, and her family, for in the Horæ Lyricæ of the doctor's, is a copy of verses, dated 1699, to mrs B Bendysh against tears another, dated sept ., 1701, intitled, the Indian Philosopher, addressed to mr Hen Bendysh, her second son, upon his marriage, and a third called, the rise of souls, dated 1704, to dr Tho. Gibson, the protecto'

No. XXIX.

The life of Cha. Fleetwood, esq. lord-lieut. of Ireland, and one of his father-in-law, the protector Oliver's lords.

THE Fleetwoods are sprung from an ancient family, formerly seated in Lancashire, and from the offices many of them held, and the honors so liberally bestowed upon them, especially by k. Ja. I. and k Cha. I. it might have been expected that all of the name would have been eminently loyal, but the particular subject of these pages, with others of his relations, were much attached to republican principles. It will not, I presume, be unacceptable to my readers, to have the history of this family precede the life of the lord-lieutenant Fleetwood, as it will be curious to mark the difference of sentiment, as well as employments of the Fleetwoods.

John Fleetwood of Little-Plumpton, in Lancashire, gent. lived in the reign of k. Edw. III. his eldest son and heir was Hen. Fleetwood, of the same place, gent. who was living the 3d k. Hen. VI. he left Edm. his son and heir, of Hesketh, in the same county, gent. living 13th k Edw. IV he married Eliz. daughter of Rob. or Roger Holland, esq their eldest son was Will. Fleetwood, also of Hesketh, esq. who married Helen, daughter of Rob. Standish, esq. by her he had 4 sons and 2 daughters; 1. John Fleet-

NUM XXIX.
Fleetwoods.

Antiquity.
Genealogy.

protector Richard's son-in-law. A paper, signed I. D. in the London magazine for 1775

wood,

　　　　MEMOIRS OF

wood, of Penwortham, in Lancashire, esq who
obtained a confirmation of the following arms
from Will. Harvey, esq. clarencieux, party per
pale, nebule, azure and argent, 6 martlets coun-
terchanged, and they have since added for a crest,
a wolf trippant, regardant, or, wounded in the
shoulder proper. Rich. the grandson of this John,
was seated at Calwicke, in Staffordshire, and was
created by k Ja I. a baronet, he was a roman-
catholic, and one of those whom the house of Commons, in 1641, petitioned k. Cha. I. to secure as a
recusant; this, however, did not discourage him
from following the royal banner, under which he was
taken prisoner at the relief of Namptwich, in 1643
the title is still enjoyed by his descendant, who is also
of the church of Rome: if I am rightly informed,
this branch is much impoverished by supplying the
unfortunate part of the royal family upon the continent with very large sums of money. the estate
of Calwicke is disposed of, and the seat of these
baronets is now in Cheshire.　2. Tho. of whom
below.　3. Rob of Penworthm, esq. whose descendants were also loyalists · John Fleetwood,
of that place, esq was fined for his attachment
to k. Cha. I. 641 l. 3 s 4 d. his son Edward
was set down a knight of the royal oak, his
estate was then valued at 1000 l per ann. The
Fleetwoods, of Wisham, in Lancashire, were
also descended, I suppose, from Rob. of Pen
wortham, but the most memorable of this family was sir Will. his natural son, who was called
to the degree of serjeant-at-law, in 1580, and in
1592, appointed queen's-serjeant, he was also
knighted, and made recorder of London. Sir
Will. was a great wit, as well as a good antiquary and historian, which several valuable literary works evince, but he was a sycophant to the
court, the worst actions of which he justified,

4　　　　　　　　　　　　　　　　　sir

fir Will. purchafed an eftate at Great-Miffenden,
in Bucks, where he was buried, his death hap- Fleetwoods of
pened feb 28, 1594-5: by Mariana, daughter of Great-Miffen-
John Barley, of Kingfley, in Bucks, efq. and den, Bucks.
widow of Rich. Serjeant, of Kimble, in that
county, efq. he had 2 fons and 2 daughters, fir
Will. was knighted at the Charter-houfe, by k.
Ja I. may 11, 1603, he reprefented the county
of Bucks, in the 1ft, 18th, and 21ft of k Ja. I.
and the 3rd of k. Cha. I.'s reign. This fir Will.
married Ann, daughter of fir Ranulph Barton,
of Smethels, in Lancafhire, efq. Sir Tho. Fleetwood, knt. fon of fir Will. the elder, was of the
Middle-Temple, and attorney-general to Hen.
prince of Wales Sir Will. the elder's daughters
were, Cordelia, married to fir David Foulis, bart.
and Eliz married to fir Tho Chaloner, knt. tutor to prince Henry, by whom fhe had feveral
children, three of the fons were, fir Will. Chaloner,
created a baronet by k. Cha. II. Tho. and James,
two of k Cha. I's judges. 4 Edm. Fleetwood,
4th child of Will. of Hefketh, was a Monk at
Sion, in Middlefex 5 Agnes, married to John
Jellibrand, of Choiley, in Lancafhire, efq and 6.
Janet, who became the wife of John Blackledge,
of Leyland, alfo in Lancafhire, efq.

Tho Fleetwood, efq. 2nd fon of Will was Tho Fleetwood,
born at his father's feat of Hefketh, but purchafing of the Vache,
the manor of the Vache, in Bucks, he fettled there, Bucks, efq
he was treafurer of the royal mint, in Southwark,
and furveyor of the poffeffions of k. Edw VI in
Chefhire, a member of parlement for Bucks, 5th q
Eliz and alfo fheriff for that county and Bedford,
he died nov 1, 1570, aged 52, having married twice;
1ft Barbara, who was an heirefs, and 2dly, Bridget,
daughter of fir John Spring, of Lavingham, in fuf-
folk, knt (fhe furviving him, re-married to fir Rob.
Wingfield, of Letheringham, in Suffolk, knt) the
                                                    iffue

Fleetwoods

issue by these marriages were 18 children by the former wife, and 14 by the latter, the names of such as survived him, that I have met with, were, 1. Everard Fleetwood, esq. member for Chipping-Wycomb, 43d q Eliz. (who, by Joan Cheney, had a son named John, and other children) 2. Rob. 3. Fra. (both of them minors at their father's death). 4. Mary, married to Peter Dormer, esq these were by Barbara his first lady: from the second marriage came, 5. sir Geo. Fleetwood, knt. 6. Sir Will. Fleetwood, knt. 7. James, lord bishop of Worcester. 8. Edw. 9. Mich. 10 Hen. seated at Longby, in Bucks, a member for Chipping-Wycomb in that county, 43d of q. Eliz.'s reign, he married Eliz daughter of Edward Fust, of London, esq. 11. Edm.

Fleetwoods of Roshall, in Lancashire.

ancestor of the Fleetwoods, of Roshall, in Lancashire. 12. Bridget, married to sir Will. Smith, of Hill-Hall, in Suffex, knt ancestors of the baronets of that place 13. Joyce, married first to sir Hewit Osborne, knt. ancestor of the dukes of Leeds; and 2dly, sir Peter Frechville, of Stavely, in Derbyshire, knt The three sons of this marriage, sir Geo sir Will. and dr Ja Fleetwood, require to be particularly mentioned, I shall defer noticing sir Will. until I have given the history of the others, as he was the ancestor of Cha. lord-lieut. of Ireland, and I will notice

Dr Fleetwood, bishop of Worcester.

the bishop before his brother sir Geo. —— Dr. Ja. Fleetwood, son of Tho. Fleetwood, by his 2d lady, was celebrated for his loyalty, which occasioned his being ejected from all his ecclesiastical preferments, then very considerable, after this he became chaplain to the earl of Rivers's regiment, and had the care of the two eldest princes at the battle of Edgehill, for his services there, he was, by special command of k. Cha. I. honored with a doctor of divinity's degree, appointed

ed chaplain to Cha pr. of Wales, and was prefented to the rectory of Sutton-Coldfield, in
Warwickfhire, being deprived of which, he became tutor to the earls of Litchfield, Kildare,
and Sterling, and afterwards to Efme, duke of
Richmond and Lenox, and to Cha. who fucceeded
to thofe ducal honors, with the former of thefe
dukes he retired into France, and returned at
the reftoration, when k. Cha. II. in reward for
his fufferings, gave him many preferments, and
ultimately, the bifhopric of Worcefter · his lordfhip died july 17, 1683, aged 81 years, leaving
a family —— Sir Geo. Fleetwood, knt. another
fon of Tho. Fleetwood, efq. * was feated at the
Vache, in Bucks, he was member of parlement
for Chipping-Wycomb, 28th q. Eliz. and was
knighted by k. Ja. I at the Charter-houfe, may
11, 1603, he died dec 21, 1620, and was buried at the church of Chalfont St. Giles, near his
feat· fir Geo married Cath. daughter of Hen.
Denny, of Chefhunt, Herts, efq (by Honora,
daughter of Will. lord Grey, of Wilton, and
fifter of fir Edw. Denny, earl of Norwich), fhe
died march 9, 1634 5, and was buried near her
hufband: they had 8 fons and 5 daughters, 1.
Arthur. 2 Sir Edw. Fleetwood, knt a commander, in 1624, of a regiment of foot, in the
expedition under count Mansfeld, for the recovery of the Palatinate, he was alfo an adventurer
for cultivating Virginia 3. Cha. of the Vache
(who by Ann his wife, had a daughter, Honoria,
married to Sam Cradock, efq.). 4. Geo. who
alfo became poffeffed of the manor of the Vache .
he died may 28, 1628, having married Ann,

---

* Probably fir Geo Fleetwood, knt was the eldeft fon of
the 2d marriage. as he had the family feat of the Vache, and
it is not unlikely that the male defcendants of the firft marriage
became extinct in his time.

fifter

Fleetwoods.

fifter of fir David Watkins, knt. fhe was buried at Chalfont St. Giles, june 3, 1673, by her he had Geo. Fleetwood, of the Vache, efq. (who by Hefter his wife, had Cha. Geo. Rob. and Eliz. the two former died infants) and David Fleetwood, alfo of the Vache, efq. buried at Chalfont, jan. 26, 1692-3. 5. Tho. 6. Henry. 7. James 8. Will. 9. Sibel. 10. Bridget, married to Lawrence Afhburnham, of Bromham, efq. father of fir Denny Afhburnham, created a bart. 11. Ann. 12 Honoria, and 13 Joyce.

Sir Will Fleetwood, of Cranford, Northamptonfhire, knt.

Sir Will Fleetwood, a fon of the 2d marriage of Tho. Fleetwood, of the Vache, efq. fettled at Cranford, in Northamptonfhire. he was knighted, and appointed receiver of the court of Wards. Sir Will. by Joan, daughter of Will. Clifton, efq. and fifter of Gervace, lord Clifton, the relict of —— Copleftone, efq had 6 fons and 5 daughters. 1. Sir Miles Fleetwood, of Aldwinckle, in Northamptonfhire, knt alfo receiver of the court of Wards, he reprefented Hyndon, in Wilts, in the long-parlement By Ann, daughter of —— Luke, efq he had fir Geo. Fleetwood, knighted by k. Cha I june 3, 1632, who was in the royal army before the civil war, but fubmitted to the protector Oliver, and was appointed by his highnefs, in 1657, one of the committee of Bucks; Will. Roger, Cha. Dorothy, Ann, Martha, and Eliz.

Fleetwoods, of Crowley, in Northamptonfhire.

2 Sir Gervace Fleetwood, of Crowley, in Northamptonfhire, knighted by k. Ja I. at the feat of his brother fir Will he was returned a member of parlement for Chipping-Wycomb, 4th of that reign, and adhering to k. Cha. I he was fined by the parlement 5661. 13s. 4d. He married Eliz. daughter of —— Lambert, efq. 3 Tho 4. Sir John Fleetwood, knt alfo member for Chipping-Wycomb, 4th k. Ja. I. 5. Sir Will. of whom fee below. 6. Geo lord Fleetwood, in Sweden,

Sweden, whither he went, and diftinguifhed himfelf fo much in the army under the illuftrious k.
Guftavus-Adolphus, that he was declared a ge- Fleetwoods.
neral, and created a baron of that kingdom: his
lordfhip was well known, and much efteemed by
the protector Oliver, to whom he applied in
1655-6, requefting men and money to affift his
fovereign, k. Cha. IX. to which his highnefs
confented, if the treaty then carried on with the
fwedifh ambaffador came to a good conclufion;
in that cafe, it being ftipulated, that he fhould
have commiffions to raife 2000 men, in addition
to the 4000 already granted, whom he defigned to
form into two regiments, and to command both
of them himfelf: by a fwedifh lady, named Gylen-
ftierna, he had Guftavus-Miles, 2nd lord Fleetwood, Geo.-Will. Fleetwood, and Adolphus-
Jacobus Fleetwood, naturalized in England, in
1656. 7. Hefter. 8. Bridget. 9. Cath. 10. Joan;
and 11. Eliz.

Sir Will. Fleetwood, of Aldwincle and Wood- Sir Will. Fleet-
ftock, knt. 5th fon of fir Will. Fleetwood, of wood, jun knt.
Cranfield, was knighted by k. Ja. I. when that feated at Ald-
monarch honored him with a vifit in 1603; to winckle and
which fovereign and his fucceffor, k. Cha. I. he Woodftock.
was cup-bearer, and comptroller to both of them,
of Woodftock-park. Sir Will. was a member of
the long-parlement for the borough of Woodftock, and retained his loyalty to k. Cha. I. but
when his majefty retired from Oxford, he was
obliged to furrender himfelf a prifoner to col.
Rainfborough, and threw himfelf upon the mercy
of the parlement, who fent him a prifoner to War-
wick-caftle, and fined him 510l. He furvived the
reftoration, and again reprefented the fame place,
as he had done in the long-parlement, and was
reftored to his place of cup-bearer. Sir Will. had
two wives; his firft lady's name is unknown; his

2nd was of the family of Harvey; by the former, he had three fons; by the latter, feveral. 1. Sir Miles Fleetwood, of Aldwinckle, knighted by k. Cha. II. who left defcendants. 2. Colonel Will. Fleetwood. 3. Geo a col. in the parlement-army, one of k. Cha. I.'s judges, and a lord of the protector Oliver's other-houfe: his life has been already given in vol I. 4. Charles, fon-in-law of the elder protector, whofe hiftory will be given in the fucceeding pages, and feveral other children.

From this hiftory it appears, that the Fleetwoods, from a very private family in Lancafhire, made a rapid progrefs in honors, acquiring in a fhort time, the hereditary titles of baron of Sweden, and baronets in England, gave a bifhop to Worcefter (as they have fince to Ely *) with many knights: exclufive of thefe, were Oliver the protector's lords, Cha. and Geo. the former of whom was fon-in-law to that fovereign, who appointed him to the government of Ireland, and, after his death, he was declared commander in chief of the britifh army.

Charles Fleetwood, efq fon-in-law of the protector Oliver, in contradiction to the fentiments of moft of his family, early efpoufed the caufe of the fubjects againft k. Cha. I. which fo pleafed the parlement, that, upon their depriving fir Will. Fleetwood, his uncle, of the receiverfhip of the court of Wards, they gave it to him, an ordinance for that purpofe was paffed by both houfes at Weftminfter, in the beginning of 1644. He was one of thofe gentlemen of the Inns of court, who learnt the military duties, and formed themfelves into a guard, to protect the perfon of the earl of Effex, the parlement general. In march,

---

* Dr. Will. Fleetwood was elected bifhop of St. Afaph's, and was tranflated from thence to Ely, where he fat until his death, in 1723.

1644-5, he was a trooper under that nobleman ;
soon after, he obtained the rank of colonel of foot, had the government of Briftol given him upon its reduction by the parlement , and, in october, in that fame year, he was conducted to the houfe of commons in triumph, as one of the returned knights for the county of Bucks. The parlement appointed him, in june, 1647, one of their commiffioners to treat with the king; but, from the temper of both parties, it was attended with no good effect : though he was fo partially difpofed to the intereft of the army, he was no ways concerned in the violent death of the fovereign ; after that unhappy cataftrophe, he was inferior to few in the power he had in the army, fo that he poffeffed fome of the firft places under the commonwealth, he wa raifed to the rank of lieutenant-general, and made one of the council of ftate. He particularly diftinguifhed himfelf at the battle near Worcefter, in which k. Cha. II fuffered a total defeat; and he and Lambert fo won the regard of Cromwell that day, that it was with difficulty that he was prevented from knighting them.

Upon Ireton's death, Cromwell fixed upon him to marry his widow, not only on account of his own intereft, but alfo for that of his numerous relations; feveral of whom were perfons of no fmall weight in the army, particularly Lambert *. As he was now the fon-in-law of the lord-general Cromwell, he procured him, in june, 1652, the poft of commander in chief of all the forces in Ireland , and, at the fame time, got him invefted with a commiffionerfhip for the civil department ; and this, that he might pave the way

* Befides the relations of mr. Fleetwood, mentioned in the pedigree, Lambert, Col. Scudamore, mr Fairclough, and many others, then confpicuous perfons, were allied to him.

for his intended grandeur: he embarked for that kingdom in september following *, and so entirely secured the island to the interest of his father-in-law, that the council was prevailed upon to proclaim him protector of Ireland, as well as England; which so pleased Oliver, that he declared him lord-lieutenant. But, notwithstanding his compliances to the protector, he joined with Disbrowe and Lambert, in violently opposing his taking the title of king, though the parlement, in 1657, offered it him: he was certainly greatly attached to a republican form of government; and which, some say, he imbibed from the prejudices his wife entertained against the kingly office: his affection to a commonwealth, and to the sectaries, how wild soever their tenets were, particularly the anabaptists, was well known to the Cromwell family; and it is curious to see how artfully they endeavour to deceive each other, particularly the father and the son-in-law. Oliver, not thinking it safe to trust him in Ireland, where there were so many disaffected persons to his government, and the presbyterian worship, wrote him a most canting letter, to excuse sending his son Henry over; who, indeed, only went with a military commission; but, in fact, was to watch and guard his conduct, till an opportunity should offer to supersede him in that government, which some time after offered. To sweeten this disgrace, he was, in december following, made one of the new created lords,

---

* Whilst mr. Fleetwood was in Ireland, he was elected, in 1654, member for Woodstock and Marlborough, it was customary, during the protectoral governments, as may have been observed by the reader, to return the same member for various places · the same happened to Fleetwood in 1656, when he sat as member for the counties of Oxford and Norfolk, and the borough of Marlborough.

and

and placed in the other houfe : he had before been
appointed principal of the major-generals, which
were fet over England and Wales, and to whom
the government of the nation was arbitrarily
committed. The counties he prefided over were
numerous ; they were Norfolk, Suffolk, Effex,
Cambridge, Huntingdon, Oxford, Bucks, and
Hertford ; the three latter he governed in perfon,
the others were left to the care of his deputy,
major Haynes*.

He wifhed to be declared commander in chief
in Scotland ; but the fame reafons forbad that as
occafioned his recall from Ireland. He was a dif-
content during the latter part of Oliver's protectorfhip, but much more fo in Richard's ; however,
there is no truth in what either Heath or Bates
fay, that he refufed to go to Whitehall, which was
the more obferved, one of them pretends to remark, becaufe he lived fo near, and his fifter
Claypoole was then dying, and all the family were
bewailing fo great a calamity —But fo far is this
from being the cafe, that he conftantly attended
both during her's and the protector's illnefs, and
gave Henry Cromwell, lord-deputy, conftant,
and even tender relations refpecting the fituation
of their diforders. He had (to keep him from
abfolute revolting) been cajoled by Oliver, with
the hopes of fucceeding to the fovereignty, and,
probably, he had been once appointed his fucceffor, for Thurloe, in a letter to Henry Cromwell, lord-deputy, dated auguft 30, 1658, fays,
that he did not think his father had declared a

---

* A perfon of the name of Farr wiote a letter to Haynes,
and directed it ' To the right rev. Father in God, right hon.
' in his highnefs the lord piotector's council, right worfhipful
' in his country, and right worthy in himfelf, majoi-geneial
' Haynes.' Fleetwood fhewed this letter to Oliver, who replied, ' They will jeei us! Has he any fleece upon his back ?'
' No.' ' Then we had better take his jefts, and let him alone.'

fucceffor ;

succeſſor; though, before he was the ſecond time inſtalled, it is certain that he had, and ſealed it up in form of a letter, and directed it to Thurloe, but kept both the name of the perſon and the paper himſelf, and that after he fell ſick at Hampton-court, he ſent mr John Barrington for it, telling him it lay upon the ſtudy table at Whitehall, but it was not found there, nor elſewhere, though it had been narrowly looked for.—Some think, that one of the protector's daughters, knowing its contents were in his favor, deſtroyed it.

Richard knowing his chagrin, and the extenſive power he had in the army, durſt not take upon him the government till he had aſked and obtained his conſent to be declared protector, and he ſigned the proclamation for that purpoſe, only becauſe he thought he ſhould rule him, as Richard was entirely unacquainted with public buſineſs. He was continued in all thoſe places the protector Oliver left him poſſeſſed of, and honoured alſo with being named one of his highneſs Richard's privy counſellors, and appointed (with Diſbrowe) one of the lords of the Cinque-ports, and conſtable of Dover; but, as the protector knew his ſentiments, with regard to himſelf, and diſliked him alſo for that over-righteouſneſs, which was by no means his own diſpoſition; he never favoured him with any of his confidence, but treated him with caution, if not diſlike: perceiving this, he was determined to dethrone Richard, in hopes of attaining to what he pretended he could never be ſatisfied in his conſcience in permitting another to enjoy, however near to him, but the ſectaries, perhaps, led him into this idea, by flattering him, 'that 'a truly godly man, that had commanded them 'in the wars, was to be preferred to ſuch a one 'as Richard, whom they conceived to have no 'true godlineſs.' To effect his purpoſe, he obliged

the

the protector to diffolve his parlement; and in the end to fign his own quietus. Upon the reftoration of the rump-parlement, and with it the republic, he was appointed one of the council of ftate, and next month lieutenant-general; but the parlement perceiving that his aim was to again fubject the nations to the rule of the army, recalled their commiffion, which they gave to fir Anth. Afhley Cooper, fearful, however, of exafperating him, they made him one of the commiffioners to govern all the forces; they alfo gave him a company of horfe, and another of foot, and complimented him with the rangerfhip of St. James's park; all this however was not fufficient to fatisfy his ambition, or to atone for the affront he thought they had put upon him he, therefore, forcibly withheld the members from going to the houfe, by which he fufpended their authority, fo that the government became again vefted in the army · to oblige him, or rather Lambert (whofe abject tool he was), they made him a member of their general council of ftate, commander in chief, and one of the feven who were to confult about a new form of government. Weak man! he now thought he had near brought his fchemes to bear; when the nation, effectually tired of the almoft weekly revolutions, thought that the only way to give the nation quietnefs and peace, was to recall the exiled king.

Alarmed at the danger, and finding his intereft rapidly decline, he wifhed much to reftore the government to the long parlement, but, perceiving that in vain, he turned his thoughts upon making his peace with his fovereign; and it is certain, that had he acted with boldnefs and refolution, in favor of the reftoration, he might have not only fecured his pardon, but have acquired honor and riches, as his fituation made him, at this time, of no small importance ; he did, indeed, profefs great duty and refpect to his majefty, and promifed that, upon the landing of either the king, or the duke of York, in any part of England, he would openly declare for monarchy ; but this was fcarcely faying any thing, when fo many were forward to offer their fervices; he fhould have thrown afide all parleying and embraced the moment, that, when loft, was never to be regained. Whitlock, who had great penetration, and the beft intelligence, urged his declaring openly for the king, and even undertook to be the meffenger ; and had, at one time, obtained his promife to fend him, but the next moment came in Vane, Difbrowe, and Berry, who gave him contrary advice ; timid and irrefolute, he declared he could not do it without Lambert's confent; and though Whitlock told him that there was neither time nor reafon for waiting Lambert's anfwer, yet he could not prevail. The folly of not following Whitlock's advice was near cofting him his life : the well-known hatred he had for monarchy, and the intereft he had in the army, made the court anxious to have him taken off, but through the interpofition of lord Litchfield, he was with difficulty faved, but not without being fubject to fuch pains, imprifonment, and confifcation, as a fubfequent act of parlement fhould adjudge. Happily for him he experienced fo much mercy as to be fet at liberty, and permitted to fpend the remainder of his life, in the moft contemptible obfcurity, amongft his friends at Stoke-Newington, near London, where he died foon after the revolution ; the taking place of which muft be highly acceptable to one who ftood in fo much fear of that dreadful monfter prerogative. He had the courage to continue a non-conformift (I think of the prefbyterian perfuafion), for which he underwent many hardfhips,

4

particularly

particularly in the year 1686, when the informers against those who frequented meeting-houses, broke in upon him at Stoke-Newington, and levied a very heavy fine *.

Fleetwood was indebted neither to his skill in the military line, nor to the depth of his capacity, for his grandeur: his influence in the camp was owing entirely to his gift of praying, which, in an army composed of religious fanatics, must make the possessor of such a powerful accomplishment, however else ridiculous, of no small consequence: it is almost incredible to what excesses his devotion carried him; praying he thought the best means of opposing an enemy: it was better, he said, than trusting to ' carnal weapons,' or ' exerting the arm of the flesh.' If his pious rhapsodies were not heard, he reconciled it, by saying, that ' God had spit in his face, and would not hear him †;' and when the dissentions in the army were so high as even to render his person in danger, he would be upon his knees, and it was with difficulty that he was rouzed from his devout reveries, by the most earnest entreaties of his dearest friends. The cavaliers thought it proceeded from another motive, fear ‡. He was overbearing and

* The fines at Stoke-Newington, from Fleetwood, sir John Hartopp, and others, amounted to 6000l. or 7000l.

† Alluding to this expression of his, the poet, in the song of the rump, thus speaks.

Then suddenly Fleetwood fell from grace,
And now cries, *Heaven has spit in his face,*
Tho' he smelt it came from another place.

‡ It is certain, that Fleetwood, though he displayed on several occasions personal courage, has been taxed with cowardice—the songs of the ' committee of safety,' and of the ' cobler's last will and testament, or the lord Hewson's translation,' thus records his valour;

Charles

adventurous in profperity, ruining that intereft which alone could have kept him from contempt; but, in the hour of diftrefs, he loft all firmnefs, making at one time mean fubmiffions to that very parlement, which juft before he had treated with the greateft fcorn ; and, at another, furrendering himfelf tamely, upon their proclamation, before his party was ruined. He was religious, and had the greateft veneration for civil liberty ; but his ideas of both were fo romantic, fantaftical and erroneous, that they were blemifhes, inftead of ornaments to his character: he had formed better notions of the vanity of accumulating money ; he thought 'God's bleffing with a little, great riches *.' The kindnefs which he fhewed to the Cromwell family, after their fall, proceeded more from po-licy than real goodnefs : he only held them forth to affright the republican parlement ; he had both too much feared and injured them to have a real value or regard for them.

The lord-lieutenant Fleetwood married two wives, his firft was Frances, fole daughter, and, in the end, fole heirefs of Tho. Smith, of Winfton, in

Charles Fleetwood is firft, and leads up the van,
Whofe counterfeit zeal turns cat in the pan,
And dame *Sarkey* will fwear he's a valiant man
    Oh bleffed reformation.

Firft to the new lords I would give *all*,
But that (like me) they're like to fall,
Though heartlefs Fleetwood has no *gall*.

* Letter to Henry Cromwell, lord-deputy, dated jan. 18, 1658-9, given in Thurloe's ftate-papers, and in which he alfo fays—' You know my ftate and condition ; I cannot make an ' advantage of my public employments, as many have, or ' others fuppofe I doe.'

Norfolk,

Norfolk, efq. * by whom he had two fons and one daughter (of whom in a future page); the former were Smith, and Charles, who was buried at Stoke-Newington, oct. 12, 1675, the eldeft fon, Smith Fleetwood of Winfton, and Feltwell-St.-Mary, both in the fame county, efq. was born in 1644, as appears by the regifter of Feltwell-St.-Mary, in which is this item: ' Anno dom. 1647, ' Smyth Fleetwood (Smyth) the fon of Charles ' Fleetwood and Frances his wife, was baptized ' july 29, nomine dedito per Simonem Smyth ' armig. Idem Smyth Fleetwood, filius ejufdem ' Caroli Fleetwood Armig. natus erat apud Felt-' well, feb. 9°, 1644.' He was buried at Stoke-Newington, feb. 4, 1708-9, by Mary, daughter of fir Edw. Hartopp, bart. whom he married oct. 15, 1666, at Feltwell, and who was buried at Stoke-Newington, jan. 21, 1680-1, he had two fons and fix daughters †. 1. Cha. Fleetwood, of Armingland-Hall, and Winfton, efq. who died unmarried. 2. Smith Fleetwood, of the fame places, and alfo of Wood-Dalling, efq. where he was buried oct. 28, 1726, aged 52, by mifs Eliz. Athill (who re-married to John Gibfon, efq.) he had only Eliz. his fole heirefs, who was alfo buried at Dalling, dec. 2, 1732, aged 22: fhe was married to Fountain Elwin, of Thurning,

* Tho. Smith, efq. was the fon of Simon Smyth, of Beccles, in Suffolk, efq. by the daughter of ——— Roberd. Tho. married ——— Crampton, and by her he had mrs. Fleetwood, and two fons, Simon and Nicholas, the former of them was feated at Winfton, and Feltwell, in the right of his wife Eliz. daughter and heirefs of fir Edw Mundeford, of that place, knt. It is reafonable to fuppofe, that neither of the brothers had iffue, as the eftates came to their fifter, or her children.

† It is fuppofed, mr. Smyth Fleetwood re-married, and by the laft wife had a ftill-born child, buried at Stoke-Newington, jan 31, 1683-4, and that Ann, the mother, was alfo buried there feb. 29, 1683-4.

in

in Norfolk, gent. (where he was buried in 1735), by whom she had Fleetwood Elwin, who died young, and was buried at Thurning. 3. Mary, married to the rev. Abraham Coveney, of Oulton, in Norfolk; by whom she had no child: she was buried at Dalling, in 1720. 4. Frances, died unmarried, and was buried at Stoke-Newington, april 14, 1749. 5. Eliz. who also died single, and was buried at the same place, june 30, 1728. 6. Caroline, who likewise never married; she was also buried at Stoke Newington, april 18, 1744. 7. Ann, married to Will. Gogney; she died at Boston, leaving no child. 8. Jane, died single, and was buried nov. 7, 1764, at Stoke-Newington. These sisters, by the death of their great nephew, Fleetwood Elwin, became co-heiresses; Jane, the youngest, devised the whole of the estates of the Fleetwoods held in Norfolk, to her distant cousin, miss Hurlock.

Elizabeth, the only daughter of the lord-lieutenant Fleetwood, by miss Smyth, has been supposed by her descendants, to have been by the second marriage; but, upon a careful examination, it is certain she was not; for she was married nov. 8, 1666, as appears by the register of Feltwell-St.-Mary, and, supposing her the eldest child, of the second marriage, she could not, at the very most, be more than thirteen years of age at that time; which I think is scarce credible. The lord-deputy Ireton died in 1651, we cannot, therefore, allow less time than two years for his widow's marriage, and the birth of her first child by her second husband, which will place her birth in 1653, supposing her to be the first child of this second marriage, and to have been born within the first year. Another, though no direct, yet a strong presumptive proof, that Eliz. was the daughter of Fleetwood, by miss Smyth, is, that no notice

notice is taken of any descendants of the second marriage, in the many additions made by miss Cromwell, to their pedigree, however, as it may be curious, I will add the descendants of this daughter of the lord-lieutenant Fleetwood; she married sir John Hartopp, bart. the third of that title*, he thrice represented the county of Leicester in parlement, during the reign of k. Cha. II. sir John's only sister was the wife of Smyth Fleetwood, esq. This baronet died april 1, 1722, in the 85th year of his age, his lady, nov. 9, 1711; they were both buried in a vault in Stoke-Newington church: their issue was four sons and eight daughters. 1. Cha. born june 5, 1672. 2. Edw. buried jan. 25, 1675-6 †. 3. John, buried may 28, 1679; these three sons died infants. 4. Sir John Hartopp, bart. of whom below. 5. Ann, buried may 8, 1674. 6. Helen, buried dec. 8, 1691; they both died in their infancy ‡. 7. Martha, buried feb. 15, 1738-9.

* The Hartopps are an ancient family, seated in Leicestershire so early as the reign of k. Rich II. Sir Edw. Hartopp was created a baronet by k. Ja. I. in 1619, by Mary, daughter of sir Erasmus Dryden, bart. he had sir Edw. Hartopp, his successor, who, by Mary, daughter of sir John Cook, of Melburn, in Derbyshire, knt. principal secretary of state to k. Cha. I. had the above sir John Hartopp, bart. and mrs. Fleetwood. Sir Edw. Hartopp, the second baronet, was a strenuous parlementarian, leaned much to a republican form of government, and was a bigotted dissenter, these sentiments were always cherished by his descendants.

† All the children of sir John Hartopp, except the eldest, were buried at Stoke-Newington.

‡ No. IX. of the Bibliotheca Topographica Britannica, has given Mary, as another daughter to sir John Hartopp, and says, she was buried at Stoke-Newington, jan. 2, 1648-9, observing, that there are few instances where there is a space of 90 years distance between the deaths of two sisters; but Mary could not possibly be the daughter of sir John Hartopp, by Miss Fleetwood, as she was buried several years before they were married.

8. Eliz.

8. Eliz. buried march 15, 1754. 9. Ann, buried april 6, 1764. 10. Bridget, buried jan. 15, 1741-2. 11. Dorothy, buried april 23, 1755; all of whom died unmarried. 12. Frances, died nov. 15, 1711, surviving her mother only six days, she married to Nathaniel Gould, of Stoke-Newington, esq. a Turkey merchant, and governor of the Bank in that and the following year, and was after her death knighted; he had a considerable estate at Stoke-Newington by inheritance and purchase, and greatly enlarged his seat there, or rather built another adjoining to it, in which he died july 20, 1728, and was buried near his wife, by whom he had two daughters; Mary, married to sir Fra. St. John, of Longthorpe, in Northampton-shire, bart. their descendants are given in a former page of this volume; and Eliz. who died jan 15, 1763, aged 63, and is buried at Stoke-Newington, she married Tho. Cooke, of Stoke-Newington, esq. also a governor of the Bank, and a Turkey merchant, he was for some years in the commission of the peace for Middlesex. Mr. Cook died at Stoke-Newington, aug. 12, 1752, whilst a governor of the Bank, he gave 1000l. amongst the clerks; he directed that his body should be conveyed to Morden College, upon Blackheath, of which he was a trustee, and that he should there be taken out of his coffin (which was to be laid by for the use of the first pensioner that might want it), and that his corpse should be set upright in the ground, close to a stile very near the college, which whimsical request was complied with: his two children by miss Gould, were Frances, who was buried in the church of Stoke-Newington, nov. 3, 1728, aged six years; and Margaret, also buried there, nov. 20. 1749, aged 23 years, and unmarried.

Sir

Sir John Hartopp, the fourth baronet, inherited
his father's title, as eldeſt, and indeed only ſurviving ſon; he died jan. 15, 1762, aged 82, and
is buried in Stoke-Newington church.   He married twice; his firſt lady was Sarah, daughter of
ſir Joſeph Woolfe, of Hackney, knt. an alderman
of London: ſhe died ſept. 12, 1720, aged 35 years,
and was buried at Stoke-Newington. Many years
after her death, he re-married mrs. March, by
whom he had no child, and who did not long ſur-
vive him, and, from want of heirs male by theſe
ladies, the title is become extinct. The daughters,
his co-heireſſes, were Sarah and Eliz. the latter
married about december 1759, to Timothy Dal-
lowe, M. D. who is dead, leaving her a widow,
and without iſſue, ſhe reſides at Epſom in Surrey.
Sarah, the eldeſt ſiſter, died march 27, 1766,
aged 47, and was buried at Stoke-Newington;
ſhe married to Joſ. Hurlock, eſq. governor of
Bencoolen.   They had only one child an heireſs,
Ann, born at Stoke-Newington, april 1, 1756 * ;
ſhe married aug. 8, 1777, to Edmund Bunny, of
Leiceſter, eſq. who obtained an act of parlement
to take the ſirname of Cradock for the eſtates his
mother poſſeſſed, and alſo Hartopp for thoſe of
his wife. He is ſeated at Newbold, and Aſton-
Flamville in Leiceſterſhire, and at Merivale-
priory, in Warwickſhire. Their iſſue has been,
1. Edm.-Joſeph, born at Florence, july 8, 1778 ;
he died at Bath, march 29, 1779, and is buried
at Aſton-Flamville. 2. Anna-Maria, born at Pynes-
houſe, Devon, feb. 8, 1780.   3. Caroline, born

* She became heireſs and the repreſentative of the very reſpectable families of Hartopp and Fleetwood, and by the will
of mrs Jane Fleetwood, her relation, ſhe came into the poſſeſſion of the eſtates of that family in Norfolk.

ſept.

fept. 14, 1781. 4. Emilia, both of whom were also born at the fame place, may 26, 1783, 5. Frances, born at Merivale, july 27, 1784.*

Having now taken all the defcendants of the lord-lieutenant Fleetwood by his firft wife, though not defcended from the Cromwells, I muft obferve, that it is moft probable that he had alfo iffue by his fecond wife, Bridget, eldeft daughter of the protector Oliver, and widow of the lord-deputy Ireton; efpecially as he mentions that fhe was in an increafing way, in feveral of his letters, written in 1654 and 1655. I think it highly probable, ' mr. Charles Fleetwood, the fon of efq'. ' Fleetwood,' who was buried at Stoke-Newington, ' 14 may, 1676,' was his fon by the protector's daughter, as perhaps was Ellen Fleetwood buried in the fame place in a velvet coffin, 23 july, 1731, if fo, fhe muft have been, at the time of her death, upwards of 70 years of age.

* The following extracts from the regifter of Stoke-Newington are too curious to be omitted. 1711, dame Elizabeth Hartopp was buried in woollen, the 26th day of november, according to an act of parlement made, *one*, that behalf attefted before mr Goftling, minor Canon of St Paul's, London; fir John Hartopp, bart. was buried in the church, april 11, 1722, and paid information money My lady Hartopp was buried in a velvet coffin, fept. 22, 1730, in the church, fir John Hartopp, bart 28 jan 1762 Over the laft fir John and his lady is a grave-ftone, infcribed. ' Dame Sarah Hartopp, ' daughter of fir Jofeph Woolfe, knt. ob. fept. 12, 1730, æt 35 ' Sir John Hartopp, bart. ob. jan. 15, 1762, æt. 82 ' Mr. Gafkins obligingly obferves to me, that he finds no infcription in the church relative to the former fir John and dame Eliz. nor does he believe they were buried in the fame grave with the latter, efpecially as the fexton told him, that when the vault, where the manorial family has ufually been buried, was opened for the interment of mrs Abney, a coffin or coffins were vifible, with an infcription denoting that they were Hartopps, and probably one of thefe coffins contained the body of the former baronet.

It

It appears by the life of Tho. Hollis, efq. that NUM XXIX the Simons modelled or engraved a portrait of Fleetwood, fon-in-law of the protector Oliver, as Fleetwoods. alfo his fecond wife, daughter of that fovereign, and her firft hufband, there have been thefe engravings of him, Walker, p. Houbraken, fç. 1740, as lieutenant-general. this belongs to the fet of illuftrious heads, from a painting in the collection of Tho. Cook, efq. and two of him as lord-deputy, one a whole length, in armour, the other on horfeback.

I cannot difcover what relations to the lord-lieutenant Fleetwood thefe three gentlemen were. Captain Fleetwood, who was in Jamaica in 1657; lieutenant-colonel Fleetwood, whom Lockhart recommended to the protector Oliver, in june 1658, and Will. Fleetwood, efq clerk of the privy-feal *.

---

* The hiftory of the Fleetwoods is taken from materials communicated to the author by the earl of Sandwich, the bifhop of Peterborough, fir Hugh Pallifer, bart Edm. B C Hartopp, efq the rev. C T Smith, rector of Eaton, mr Geo. Gafkin of Iflington, and mr Longmate, vifitations of feveral counties, Cole's efcheats, various authors who have written hiftories of England during the reigns of k Cha I. the interregnum, or the reign of k. Cha II lord Clarendon's, Thurloe's, Rufhworth s, and Nelfon's ftate-papers, with feveral biographical writers, efpecially the lord-lieutenant Fleetwood's he, by dr Birch, No ix of the Bibliotheca Topographica Britannica, Baronetage, Whitlock's memorial, lifts of the loyalifts who compounded for their eftates, Magna Britannia, Wood's Athenæ Oxonienfes, Mf. hiftory of Dinton by B. Willis, MS catalogue of k. Ja I's knights, Walkely's knights of k Cha. I. Willis's not parliamentaria, Val. Green's hift of Worcefter, admiral Smith's hiftory of Virginia, the protector Oliver's acts publifhed by Field, journals of the houfe of commons, and trials of the regicides.

No. XXX.

The history of the Claypooles, especially the life of John Claypoole, esq. son-in-law to the protector Oliver, one of his lords, and also master of the horse to both Oliver and Richard, with his descendants by Mary, the favorite daughter of the elder protector.

I SHALL commence the history of the Claypoole family in the person of James, who was a yeoman of considerable property, and making great additions to his paternal inheritance, thought his fortune sufficient to support him as a gentleman. He therefore applied to, and had a grant of arms from Robert Cooke, clarencieux, dated june 17, 1588, viz. topaz, a chevron, sapphire between 3 hurts, and for a crest they have taken on a wreath a fleur-de-lis, enfiled with a ducal coronet or. He purchased in 1571, for 440 l. of Edm. Elves of Walton, in Northamptonshire, gent Walhamparks, containing about 75 acres of fenny land, lying in the parish of East-Deeping, alias Deeping St. James's, in that county, and in the following year he bought for 500 l. of John Brown of London, draper, the manor of Norborough, or Northborough, in Northamptonshire, with certain premises belonging to and lying in that lordship, which he had occupied long before, it is singular, that in the title deeds to these estates he is called only yeoman, when in 1588, in the grant of arms he was stiled gentleman. Besides these estates he added some inconsiderable purchases within the manor of Norborough

borough. In the latter part of his life he was appointed receiver of the taxes of a great part of the
county of Northampton, in the commiſſion for which
he was complimented with the title of eſq. but
he loſt this place ſome little time before his death,
he was buried at Norborough, oct. 16, 1599, to
whoſe memory is erected a very magnificent monument in the chancel of that church, this coat of
arms appears thrice upon it· I apprehend that he
himſelf cauſed it to be ſet up, my reaſons are,
becauſe it has no other inſcription than, 'All
'good bleſſings unto man, cometh of the free gift
'of God. Ja. Cle. 1594,' which is 5 years before his death. The ſentence ſeems to allude to
his gratitude to Providence for his ſingular good
fortune *. By Joan his wife, who was buried at
Norborough, nov. 14, 1598, he had two ſons and
four daughters, ſir James Claypoole, who was
ſworn in 1594, ſurveyor of the royal ſtables, under the earl of Eſſex, and was knighted by k. Ja.
I. at Greenwich, june 18, 1604 in the following
year he conveyed the eſtates which his father had
poſſeſſed, and left to him, to his brother Adam, it
is therefore reaſonable to ſuppoſe that he either never married, or at leaſt had no children, probably
he died at London attending the court. 2. Adam,
of whom hereafter. 3. Ann, married Oct. 19,
1573, to John Norton of Northamptonſhire, eſq.
4. Dorothy, married ſept. 30, 1577, to Maurice
Blount. 5. Bonye, died unmarried in 1567, and
6 Hella, who alſo died ſingle in 1575.

Adam Claypoole, eſq. the ſecond ſon of James, Adam Claypoole,
and heir to his brother ſir James, was of eſq
Gray's-Inn, where he ſometimes reſided during

---

* Mr Tho. Simpkins of Peterborough moſt obligingly ſent
me a drawing of this monument, together with others of the
ſeat, and church of Norborough, which are proofs of his ſkill
and taſte in that pleaſing art.

the

the former part of his first marriage, at others, at Norborough or Maxey. Upon an inquisition taken upon his death in 1634, it appears he possessed not only the manor of Norborough and estate of Waldram-parks, but also the manor of Lolham. His first wife was Dorothy, daughter of Rob. Wingfield of Upton, in Rutlandshire, esq (by Eliz. daughter of Rich. Cecil, esq. and sister to William, lord Burleigh) a connection that led the Claypooles to have interest at court. She was buried at Norborough, nov. 7, 1619. His second wife was Jane Bird, whom he married at Norborough, sept. 25, 1620 *. by the former he had 10 children, and by the latter three. 1. James, born in 1588, who died in his father's lifetime, leaving no child. 2. Edward, the eldest surviving son, was, at the time of his father's death, more than thirty-six years of age: it is reasonable to suppose that he had displeased his father, as Norborough was left from him, but it is supposed he had Lolham, but perhaps only that for life. as, upon his death, without issue, the whole of the estates devolved to his next brother. 3. John, of whom below. 5. Wingfield, born in 1593-4. 6. Rich. born in 1594, who died in 1673   7. Rob born in 1599. he died an infant. 8. Henry, born in 1608-9. 9. Rob. born in 1613. 10. Joanna, born in 1602   11. Dorothy, born in 1605. 12. James, born in 1621. 13. Adam Claypoole, of West-deeping, in Lincolnshire, esq was born in 1622. He was a loyalist, and was fined for his delinquency 600l. He died in 1600. And 14. Jane, born 1623 †.

---

* Mrs. Claypoole, the second wife of Adam, is supposed to have been of a West-deeping family, as Tho. Bird, of that place, struck a token in the last century.

† Edw and John, sons of Adam Claypoole, esq. were probably baptized in London whilst their father resided at Gray's

Inn,

John Claypoole, of Gray's-Inn, efq. where he chiefly refided, which accounts for the baptifms of his children not appearing in the regifters of Nor- borough or Maxey, it plainly appears that he was the favored fon, as his father in 1622, upon his marriage with Mary, the daughter of Will. Angell of London, efq. conveyed to him in fee, with power to fettle upon his wife, the manor and lands of Norborough, and thirty-two acres, part of Wal-dram-parks; the whole of which was worth about 200l. per ann. the lady's fortune was 1500l. Her brother John is mentioned in the fettlements. The fentiments he entertained refpecting the then ftate of the nation, were probably the fame as thofe which mr. O. Cromwell (afterwards protector) poffeffed, when he firft gained a feat in the long-parlement; and as he had fuffered hardfhips from k. Cha. I's defpotifm, it might occafion an intimacy that end-ed in an alliance between the families, it is not un-likely that he and Oliver might be ftudents of the law together, which might alfo promote this union. He was fummoned in 1637 before the ftar-chamber, and the attorney-general was ordered to commence a profecution againft him for refufing to concur in the payment of fhip-money, which the court demanded, it cannot therefore be won-dered at, that he declared for the parlement when the civil war broke out. In 1643, 1644, and 1647, he was appointed one of the affeffors for the county of Northampton, he was a juftice of the peace, and, probably fheriff for his own county in 1655, as major-general Boteler recommends him to Thurloe, in a letter to him, dated nov. 16. He was a member of parlement in 1654, for the

Inn; the births of Wingfield, Henry, and Dorothy, with the deaths of Rich. and Adam, are taken from the regifter of Nor-borough, the births of the others from that of Maxey.

county

county of Northampton, and for Carmarthenshire in 1656: in the following year he was made a commissioner with his son, for levying the taxes upon the county of Northampton. The protector appointed him clerk of the Hanaper in the court of Chancery, created him a knight, and soon afterwards gave him a patent for a baronet, dated july 16, 1657, and march 13, 1659-60, he had a new grant, jointly with dr. Tho. Clarges, M. D. of the place of clerk of the Hanaper during their lives, and the survivor of them. The whole of his estates were worth about 450 l. per ann. and the same premises do not now bring in more. He survived his wife, who died april 10, 1661, and was buried the day following at Norborough: his name appears in the court rolls of that place until the year 1664, three or four years before which he had granted his manor of Norborough to his eldest son, John. Mr. Claypoole is supposed to have died and been buried at London; he left 8 sons and 4 daughters. 1. John, of whom presently. 2. Rob who died an infant. 3. Wingfield, who became an officer in Ireland in the army of the protectors Oliver and Richard: he and another of his brothers had done something wrong, as the lord Claypoole, their eldest brother says, in a letter to Henry Cromwell, lord-deputy of Ireland, dated april 16, 1658, ' I wish he (Wingfield) had not presumed upon your goodness in so long an absence, and requested the lord-deputy's pardon on his behalf, yet he desired he might be reprehended, and that his other brother might be reproved, as he feared he would stand in too much need of it. 4. Christopher, who was also in the army, and was sent by the protector to the Hague in 1658. 5. Henry, seated at Peakirk and Glinton, in Northamptonshire; he writes himself gentleman deman in his will, which is dated april 21, 1670, and was proved oct. 22 following; he appoints his brother Rob. sole executor, and gives small legacies to his sister Patrick and her children, Jane, Fra. Edw. Eliz. and Joanna, he also mentions his nephew Shield, his niece Holled, and nephews, Ja. Benj. Norton, and Cromwell Claypooles; and he gives to mr. Stoughton, the rector, any book out of his library that he shall choose. 6 Rob. 7. Gravely. 8. Norton, all of them living in 1678. 9. Mary, married dec. 26, 1655, to Will. Shield, esq. *. 10. —— married to major Staples. 11. —— married to mr. Patrick, and 12. —— to mr. Holled.

John Claypoole, the eldest son and heir of the above gentleman, of both his names, was also bred to the law. in 1645-6, he was married to Mary, the second, and most favored daughter of Oliver Cromwell, then of Ely, in Cambridgeshire, esq. but afterwards lord protector of these kingdoms, with this lady he had a fortune of 1250 l. his father, at the same time, gave him the manor of Lolham, with the lands and tenements appertaining thereto, and seven acres and three roods of meadow adjoining, called Nunton-Holm, which then was, and now is worth about 200 l. per ann. this was settled upon miss Cromwell, in case she survived him, and as a provision for the eldest son of the marriage. He was certainly very young when he married (but more than fifteen, as the Annual Register for 1738 mentions), however, probably, he was not twenty.

margin note: John Claypoole, esq son-in-law to the protector Oliver, and one of his lords

---

* Mr Shield is supposed to have been the son of mr Mark Shield of Preston, in Rutlandshire, of an ancient family, still seated there. Mr. Shield, by miss Claypoole, had many children, their grand-daughter married to mr. Balgrave, whose son now resides there.

The

376

Claypooles

The firſt mention I have found of him in a public capacity, is, his having permiſſion, aug. 20, 1651, to raiſe a troop of horſe, of ſuch as ſhould voluntarily come to him in the counties of Northampton and Lincoln, or elſewhere, and they were to be paid by the parlement, according to the eſtabliſhment of the army, and, in 1647, he was one of the parlement committee for the former county. When his father-in-law was inveſted with the title of protector, he received from him the office of maſter of the horſe, and as ſuch led the horſe of ſtate at the inauguration, going bare-headed on one ſide of the protector's body-coach, with Strictland, captain of the guard to his highneſs. he acted in the ſame capacity at the ſecond, or more magnificent inveſtment, when he ſtood immediately behind the protector during that ceremony. He was a member of Oliver's parlement, in 1654, for the county of Northampton, and alſo in 1656 * : in the latter he oppoſed the power of the major-generals, the particulars of which I will give in Ludlow's words ' Mr. ' Claypoole ſtood up in the houſe, which was ' unuſual for him to do, and told the houſe, he ' could but ſtart the game, and muſt leave it to ' them that had more experience to follow the ' chace, and, therefore, ſhould only ſay, that he ' had formerly thought it neceſſary, in reſpect of ' the condition in which the nation had been, that ' the major-generals ſhould be entruſted with the ' authority which they had exerciſed, but in the ' preſent ſtate of affairs, he conceived it incon- ' ſiſtent with the laws of England, and liberties ' of the people, to continue their power any

---

* Major-gen. Whalley ſays, in a letter, dated aug 9 1656, that if his couſin Claypoole would offer himſelf for Lincoln, and acquaint him with it in time, he thought he could procure his return Thurloe's ſtate papers

' longer.

‘ longer. This ſpeech (adds Ludlow) was a

‘ clear direction to the ſycophants of the court,
‘ who being clear that Claypoole had delivered
‘ the ſenſe, if not the very words of Cromwell, in
‘ this matter, joined as one man in oppoſing the
‘ major-generals, and ſo their authority was
‘ abrogated.’ His mild and gentle diſpoſition
rendered him unfit for any ſervices of Cromwell’s,
but ſuch as were of the peaceable kind, and which
he was laviſh in giving him, both as the huſband
of his favorite child, and as a moſt amiable
perſon. Oliver nicely adapted the places to the
perſons he employed; inſtead therefore of appointing mr. Claypoole to be a major-general,
where ſeverity and rigor were neceſſary, he gave
him places of great honor and emolument, but
of ſuch a nature as the moſt ſcrupulous might
accept, even during an uſurpation, perhaps he
had a further deſign in this, that he might not
feel the effects of any future revolution, which
might endanger his fortunes, and conſequently
thoſe of his deareſt daughter, her delicacy too in
theſe matters might alſo have its weight, from
ſome, or all theſe cauſes, we do not ſee him employed in any office of magiſtracy.

He was appointed by his father-in-law one of
the lords of his bed-chamber, ranger of Wittle-
wood, or Wittlebury foreſt, in Northamptonſhire,
where he built a lodge, which now belongs to his
grace of Grafton, the firſt duke having had a
grant of the foreſt in 1685, with the title of
hereditary ranger, to raiſe him ſtill further above
the rank of a private gentleman, he was made
one of the lords, and placed in his father-in-law’s
other-houſe. The grand-daughter of mr. Claypoole’s cook, ſays, that Oliver, his father-in-law,
uſed to come and ſpend his chriſtmas at Norborough it is not at all improbable that he ſhould

paſs

NUM. XXX.

Claypooles.

pass that time at the seat of the husband of his favorite daughter; but this must have been before his exaltation to the protectorship· the same person also remembers to have heard, that the plate of k. Cha. I. used to grace the side-board at Norborough. I have seen no other transaction of his, during Oliver's life-time, except that he was sent by him to receive the Dutch ambassadors upon their return to London, in march 1654; and that he entrusted him to go to Lilly, the astrologer, to ask for advice, which that conceited coxcomb says, Oliver frequently sent for, and which he honestly gave him, without any gratuity whatever; but the most wonderful is, that the protector should act as Lilly directed, I rather think that he was an instrument to further Cromwell's artful schemes, and it is pretty certain, that by his conjuration he got rid of Whitlock, by sending him into an honorable banishment to Sweden. During the short reign of his brother-in law Richard, he retained all his places at court, and carried the sword of state when his highness went to open his parlement.

As he had never during the whole of his relations holding the helm, done any action that could even inconvenience an individual, at the restoration he found not an enemy, but in every one a friend, and he had the humanity, as well as courage, to give an asylum to his mother-in-law, the relict of the protector Oliver, until the time of her death.

He by some means had fallen into debt, for he was obliged to dispose of Lolham manor, with the estates he had belonging to it, which he was in treaty to sell to lord Fitzwilliam, but that nobleman objecting to the price, he sold it to mr. Clitherow. About this time he had a dispute with the rev. John Stoughton, rector of Norbo-

rough,

rough, for in the regifter of that parifh remains the following item, after the laft entry of baptifms in 1670: ' The reafon of this defect in the regif-' ter was, becaufe one mr. John Claypoole, a ' factious gentleman, then living in the parifh ' of Northborough, caufed the regifter to be ' taken away from me Jo Stoughton, their rec-' tor, for which I was by the ecclefiaftical court, ' then holden at St. Martin's, adjudged for fatif-' faction, the fum of two pounds ten fhillings; ' the money was pd. at the charge of the parifh ' by Robt. Cooke, then churchwarden—Sic tefta-' tur Joannes Stoughton—Rectr. ibm.*' Per-haps his being involved in debt might make him fix upon a rich widow for his fecond wife, who was Blanch, the widow and executrix of Lancelot Staveley, of London, merchant, whom he mar-ried march 21, 1670, this did not retrieve his affairs, for in 1677, he refigned up the manor of Norborough, to his eldeft fon and heir apparent, together with the premifes he held in that lord-fhip, with Waldram-Parks, for 1500l. which then was incumbered with a heavy mortgage, and when thefe eftates came again to him by the will of his fon, he was obliged, in 1682, to difpofe of them for 5600l. to William lord Fitzwilliam, 4765l. of which was to be paid to the mortgagee, fir Rob. Dacres, and 400l. to remain in his lord-fhip's hands, as a fatisfaction for the claim of dower which Blanch his prefent wife might have in thofe eftates, if fhe refufed to join in levying a fine to bar dower, or fhould furvive him, the fmall remainder too was charged with the payment of the debts and legacies of his deceafed fon,

* The rev. John Stoughton was prefented in aug. 1660, to the rectory of Norborough, by the dean and chapter of Peter-borough. Bifhop Kennet's chronicle.

the

the teſtator, ſo that he could have little, or nothing, remaining of the purchaſe money.

When the court and the country vied with each other, which could invent the moſt improbable and ridiculous plots, he, the moſt unlikely man in the three kingdoms, was fixed upon to be the head and contriver of one againſt the royal family, in concert with the old republican party. Upon this pretence he was apprehended in june, 1678, and ſent to the Tower: obtaining an habeas corpus to the King's-Bench, he thought to procure bail, but though many perſons, to whom no objections could be made, offered themſelves for that purpoſe, yet chief-juſtice Scroggs, who was the tool of the court, ſet the penalty ſo high, that his friends thought proper to decline it, he was, therefore, removed back to the Tower, but the next term, as no evidence appeared againſt him, and what was, perhaps, much more fortunate for him, a counter-plot began to work, he was diſcharged. ' His only (political) crime,' ſays an hiſtorian, ' ſeems to be his having married one ' of Cromwell's daughters,' which k Cha II. would gladly have done, if he could by it have recovered his crown.

It might have been ſuppoſed, that he would have returned to his eſtate in Northamptonſhire, where he reſided when he was taken into cuſtody, and there have ſpent the remainder of his life in a happy tranquillity, which his former virtues deſerved, and which, from his taſte for ſtudy, he certainly might do, without ever looking back to thoſe gay ſcenes his youth had been ſpent in, eſpecially as he had a taſte for mathematics, and, probably, for architecture, as he was the intimate friend of mr. (afterwards ſir Chriſtopher) Wren ,

* Mr. (afterwards ſir) C Wren, when dining with mr. Clay poole, was ſurpriſed by the protector Oliver's coming into the room,

but this was by no means the cafe, for, inftead of living in the country, he made London his refidence, and an unhappy difunion between him and his fecond wife taking place, he feparated from her, and lived entirely with a woman of the name of Ann Ottee, who had obtained the moft abfolute dominion over him; this connection, fo injurious to his character and fortune, continued for fome years, and until his death, which happened june 26, 1688, at which time he was of the Middle-Temple, London, and was buried no doubt in that city, probably near his father and other relatives. In religious fentiments he was a prefbyterian, and in that communion died, in mr. Vertue's engravings of Simon's works, is a medal of him, which has no reverfe; there is no ftriking feature in his face. Mr. Snelling has copied it in his Englifh Series.

By the protector's daughter he had, at leaft, three fons and a daughter, 1. Cromwell, to whom his father refigned the manor of Norborough, with Waldram-Parks, which, however, was greatly mortgaged, and, as the fum of 1,00l. was to be paid as a confideration, it feems to have been but a very moderate favor, he was buried may 28, 1678, in the chancel of Norborough chuich, as near to the body of his grandmother Cromwell as convenience would admit, according to his own exprefs direction, there

---

room, and (without the leaft notice being taken) fitting down and eating with then, during the repaft turning to mr Wren, he faid, 'you have a relation who has long been in the Tower, 'he may have his liberty if he choofes it.' 'Will your high-'nefs give me leave to acquaint him with what you fay?'— 'Yes' Mr Wren went with great joy to the old bifhop of Ely, but his anfwei was, 'this is not the firft intimation of 'the fame kind, but I fcorn to receive my liberty from a tyrant 'and ufurper' And he remained a prifoner until the reftoration fet him free.

is a grave-ftone with fome little remains of a rude infcription upon it in his will, as he died a bachelor, he left his eftates, after bequeathing fome legacies, to his father, and, as he had no brother or fifter that would regard the valuables once belonging to his mother, he bequeathed them all to her relations. As I have been indulged with a copy of this will, I cannot omit giving it entire, it being every way worthy attention *. 2. Henry, it is fuppofed went into

---

* In the name of God, amen, I Cromwell Claypoole, of Norborough, in the county of Northampton, Gentn doe make and ordaine this my laft will and Teftament in manner and form following. Imprimis, I give and devife unto Sr. Will. Ellis, knt. and mi. Tho. Percival, of Newmarkett, Attorney, their heirs and affigns, all my Mannors, Meffuages, Lands, Tenem⁵ and Hereditam⁵. whatfoever, in Norborow aforefaid, or elfewhere in the countyes of Northampton and Lincolne, and all my right, title, equity of redemption, claime, and demand, of, in and to, the fame, upon fpecial truft and confidence that by fale of the fame or any part thereof, or otherwife, they, or the furvivour of them, and the heirs of the furvivour, fhall, with all convenient fpeed, raife moneys for the payment and difcharge of the debts charged upon the fame, and all other debts of mee the sd Cromwell Claypoole. And after the s⁴ debts fhall be payd and fatisfyed, I give the refidue of the s⁴. mannors and premifes unto my honoured father John Claypoole, Efq. and his heirs, and will that the fame be conveyed unto him and his heirs by any perfon or perfons ftanding feized thereof, upon truft and confidence that the s⁴. premifes fhall be charged with and liable to the Legacies herein after mentioned. Item, I give to my loving unkle Gravely Claypoole, the fum of 100l Item to my uncle Norton Claypoole the fum of 50l Item to mr Percivall the fum of 50l Item to Rich. Kipwell the fum of 20l. Item to John Peacocke the fum of 5l. Item to my fervant Rich. Deane the fum of forty fhillings with my wearing apparell. Item to my Cozen Elizabeth Ruffell I bequeath my pearl neck lace with the picture of my Grandmother and mother † Item to my Cozen S Will Ruffell I bequeath my Grandfather's medall of gold, being a three pound piece, in a black cafe ‡

† It is much to be wifhed that thefe felect miniatures were engraved query?
In whofe poffeffion they now are

‡ Probably the larger medall ftruck upon the death of Oliver lord protector

Item

the army, where he died; but it muſt have been before his brother Cromwell's death, as no mention of him is made in his will, the ſame reaſon ſhews that he had no children, and, probably, never married. 3 Oliver, who died juſt before his mother, the grief for whoſe loſs haſtened, we may ſuppoſe, her death 4. Martha, of whom we have the following remarkable circumſtance: it having been repreſented to the protector, that the Oceana,* which was then in the preſs, was a reflection upon his government, it was ſeized by his order; Sir Ja. Harrington, the author of it, alarmed for the ſafety of his manuſcript, determined to apply to lady Claypoole, becauſe, ' ſhe

Item to my couſin Oliver Cromwell of Hurſley, I bequeath my young bald horſe (bought of mr Underwood) with my piſtols and holſters. Item to my cozen Henry Ireton my young horſe called Crickett Item to my good friend mr. Tho Jorden I bequeath my black gelding that was lately put to graſs by Richardſon, with my beaver hatt which I lately bought of mr. Grne, haberdaſher All which Legacyes and ſums of money aforeſayd I will ſhall be pyd out of the ſⁱ. premiſes within ſix months after my deceaſe. And finally I do nominate, conſtitute and appoint my ſᵈ. father executor of this my will Willing alſo that my body be carried in a hearle to Norborow and interr'd as near my Grandmother Cromwell as convenience will admitt, and that at my interrmᵗ tenne pounds be given amongſt the poor people of Norborow. In witneſs whereof I have hereunto put my hand and ſeale the tenth day of may, in the year of our Lord 1678—Cromwell Claypoole.
—Signed, ſealed and publiſhed as the laſt will and teſtament of the ſᵈ. Cromwell Claypoole, and atteſted in his preſence by us
—Henry Panton, George Shaw, John Kenton

* The Oceana was a political romance, recommending a republican form of government It is the chimera of a man intoxicated with liberty, and the plan of a government which never can be put in practice The protector ſaid that he had gained his power by his valor, and he would not be beaten out of it by a little paper ſhot.

' acted

' acted the part of a princefs, very naturally ob-
' liging all perfons with her civility, and fre-
' quently interceding for the miferable,' flattering himfelf that by her affiftance he fhould
regain the work.   As lady Claypoole was entirely a ftranger to him, he was led into her anti-
chamber; whilft he waited the return of one of
the fervants of the palace, with an anfwer to his
humble requeft, that fhe would admit him into
her prefence, fome of her women came into the
room followed by her little daughter, about three
years old, who regarding the ftranger, permitted
the women to leave the room without following
them; fir James entertained the child fo divert-
ingly, that fhe fuffered him to take her up in
his arms, till her mother came, when ftepping
towards her, and fetting the child down at her
feet, faid, ' Madam, 'tis well you are come at
' this nick of time, or I had certainly ftole this
' pretty little lady.'   ' Stolen her?' replied the
mother, ' pray what to do with her? for fhe is
' yet too young to become your miftrefs.'
' Madam,' faid he, ' though her charms affure her
' of a more confiderable conqueft, yet I muft
' confefs, it is not love, but revenge that prompted
' me to commit this theft.'   ' Lord,' anfwered
the lady again, ' what injury have I done you,
' that you fhould fteal my child?'   ' None at all,'
replied he, ' but that you might be induced to
' prevail with your father to do me juftice, by
' reftoring my child that he has ftolen.'   But fhe
urging it was impoffible, becaufe her father had
children enough of his own, he told her at laft,
it was the iffue of his brain, which was mifre-
prefented to the protector, and taken out of the
prefs by his order.   She immediately promifed
to procure it him, if it contained nothing pre-
judicial to her father's government. and he af-

furing her, that it was fo far from containing any treafon againft her father, or even any. paffage that could difpleafe him, that he hoped fhe would acquaint his highnefs he defigned to dedicate it to him, and promifed that fhe herfelf fhould be prefented with one of the firft copies; the lady was entirely fatisfied, and fo well pleafed with the manner of introducing himfelf, that the whole that was feized was foon after reftored to him. But to return to Martha—fhe died young and unmarried, and was buried in the chancel of the church of Norborough, jan. 14, 1663-4. Mr. Claypoole, her father, by his laft wife Blanch, whom he again left a widow, had John, who died a child, and Bridget, who probably was fo named from mrs. Fleetwood, who might be her god-mother, fhe was fourteen years of age at her father's death, who moft unnaturally left neither this his daughter, nor her mother, any thing by his will, but made Ann Ottee, then of St. Clement's Danes, Middlefex, his fole executrix, leav-ing her all he had to difpofe of; her mother there-fore filed a bill in Chancery, in which fhe was made a party, as fole heirefs of her father, to com-pel lord Fitzwilliam to give the particulars of the eftate his lordfhip had purchafed of the truftee of her late hufband, in which fhe fet forth that he had by the fubtleties, wiles, and intrigues of Ann Ottee, prevailed upon, and feduced him to for-fake her, and cohabit with the faid Ann, which he had done for feveral years before his deceafe; that fhe was worth, upon her marriage with mr. Claypoole, 10,000l. and more, and that he had promifed, in cafe fhe furvived him, he would leave her that fum, and a great deal more, yet fhe and her daughter were both of them likely to be ftripped, and defeated of all the real and per-fonal eftates of her faid late hufband, by the contrivance of this Ann Ottee, and her confederates, who had prevailed upon him to sign a will, made by him in favor of his mistress, and had even so contrived that his said widow knew nothing of his death, until a fortnight after it had happened; and having compelled lord Fitzwilliam to give the particulars of those estates he had purchased of mr Claypoole, she brought a writ of dower against his lordship, and recovered her thirds of them, which, indeed, had not been refused to be allowed her, but only an objection had been made to her estimate. At this period it will be impossible to determine what were the reasons that induced mr Claypoole to desert his wife: his attachment to another woman would have exculpated her, if she had not betrayed some immodesty of behaviour, as was probably the case, for no other reason can be assigned for his abandoning the daughter, which she bore after his marriage with her, and unless something of that kind had been presumed, sure her brother Cromwell Claypoole, and her uncle, Henry Claypoole, would have mentioned her in their wills. Bridget became the wife of Cha. Price, a col in the guards, and surviving him, died in oct. 1738, of a cancer in her breast, in the 64th or 65th year of her age. I believe there are descendants of this marriage, but as they have none of the Cromwell blood, I have not thought it necessary to trace them.

The seat of the Claypooles at Norborough, is in part standing, and used as a farm-house, but the wings are pulled down, the gateway, which is the entrance to the house, conveys the idea of great antiquity, the north view shews that the mansion is as ancient as the gateway, and was built, probably, long before the Claypooles owned it; two of the windows are very large, and have

stone

ſtone diviſions, and are in the manner of our
gothic churches, the ſtables have been very elegant, and ſpacious enough to contain more than
twelve horſes with convenience. Ja. Claypoole
was an admired friend of the famous Will. Penn,
the quaker· there are many Claypooles now in
Lincolnſhire of this family, but they are rather
below than above the middle rank of life. Thoſe
of Tallington, in that county, now ſpell their
name Claypon*.

* The hiſtory of the Claypooles is taken from very valuable
information, communicated to me through the lord biſhop of
Peterborough (to whom I cannot too warmly expreſs my very
many and great obligations) from mr. Smith, the rev. mr.
Laying, rector of Maxey Wm. Strong, eſq rev Hen. Free-
man, mr Landen, of Milton, near Peterborough, F R S a
gentleman well known to the literary world, as a mathematician, and another gentleman of taſte, whoſe name I am ſorry
to be forbidden to mention Vertue's engravings of Simon's
works, Ruſhworth's collections, ordinances and journals of
the houſe of commons, lives of the prot Oliver, Ludlow's
memoirs, Wood's faſti· Mr Pennant's tour from Cheſter to
London, perfect politician, or life of O. Cromwell, Thurloe's
ſtate papers, Lilly's life of himſelf, hiſt. of the civil wars of
Great-Britain, containing an exact hiſtory of the occaſion,
original, progreſs, and happy end of the civil war, by an impartial pen, London, 1661, ſecret hiſt of Europe hiſt of
Engl during the reigns of the Stuarts, Toland's life of Harrington, prefixed to his Oceana, Biographia Britannica, under
the article of dr. Wren, biſhop of Ely, hiſtorical regiſter for
1738, and the hiſtory of Rutlandſhire.

No. XXXI.

The life of Thomas, viscount, afterwards earl Fau-
conberg, who married Mary, thi d daughter of the
protector Oliver.

THOMAS, viscount Fauconberg, was descended from an ancient family in the north
of England, of the name of Bellasyse : sir Tho.
Bellasyse, baronet, his grandfather, was created
by k. Cha. I. baron, and afterwards viscount
Fauconberg, of Henknowle, in the county palatine of Durham *, and son of Henry, who died
in the life-time of his father, the first viscount, by
Grace, daughter and co-heiress of sir Tho. Barton, of Smithalls, in the county of Lancaster,
knight. This nobleman's youth alone prevented
his embarking in the royal cause, as all his relations had done (lord Fairfax excepted), they having shewed themselves much attached to k. Cha.
I in opposition to his parlement, but, perceiving that the monarchy was dissolved, and no
prospect of its restoration, he cast his eyes upon
that quarter where power only could be obtained ; this was the effect of his ruling passion,
ambition : the death of his first lady † paved the

* Thomas, the first viscount Fauconberg, very eminently
distinguished himself in the army of k Cha. I. but leaving that
monarch's service in 1644, he returned to Hamborough, and
died so late as 1652, he had a younger son, John, who, for
his exemplary loyalty, was created by k Cha. I. lord Bellasyse,
of Worlaby, in the county of Lincoln he died in 1689
† The first lady of Thomas, the second lord Fauconberg,
was Mildred, daughter and co-heir of Nicholas Sanderton,
viscount Castleton.

way

was for his attaining the height of his wishes, in NUM XXXI
becoming son-in-law to the chief magistrate of
the kingdom.

Whilst he was abroad in the beginning of 1656-7,
he endeavoured to ingratiate himself into the favour of Oliver, and strove to convince him how
much he was attached both to his person and
government *, which was the more wondered at,
because, not only his lordship's relations, but
most of his own order, wished to express their dislike (if not a studied contempt) for both. He
came to court with every advantage from his
rank, the antiquity and interest of his family,
their connections and alliances, his education, improved by travel, fine person, and address, a behaviour winning and conciliating affection ; and,
besides all these, a solid and strong understanding,
as we may well judge from the character both
Lockhart and Thurloe gave of him: the former
says, ' in his humble opinion, he is a person of
' extraordinary parts, and hath, appearingly, all
' these qualities, in a high measure, that can fit
' one for his highness and country's service.'
The secretary remarks of him, that ' he is a
' person of very great parts and sobriety.' These

---

* Upon lord Fauconberg's return from Italy to Paris, in
1656-7, Lockhart, the protector's ambassador at that court, in
two letters, dated in march, acquaints Thurloe of his lordship's
being there in the letter, he says, that nobleman ' owns a par-
' ticular zeal for both his highness and his country's service,'
and that he seemed much troubled for a report he heard, that
' the enemy,' (the loyalists) ' gave him out to be a catholic, and
' did purge himself from having any inclinations that way. He
' desires his highness may cause strict inquiries to be made after
' his carriage in England, and hoped, by that means, his in-
' nocency would be vindicated, and the malice of his enemies
' discovered. He is of opinion, that the intended settlement'
(the establishment of Oliver's government) ' will be acceptable
' to all the nobility and gentry of his country, save a few, who may
' be biassed by the interest of their relations.'

C c 3   valuable

valuable qualifications were not loſt in the ſight of the protector, or his daughter, lady Mary · his highneſs reflected, that ſuch a nobleman would be a very deſirable match for his daughter, for, beſides ſecuring ſo powerful, deſerving, and accompliſhed a gentleman in his intereſt, the marriage would tend to conciliate the affections of the nobility, whoſe good wiſhes he was anxious to engage, and was what he ſeduloufly courted, and, likewiſe, he was ſecuring to his child an huſband, who had a fortune of five thouſand per annum, and would raiſe her to the rank of a viſcountefs.

Such conſiderations were too weighty to be rejected by ſo wiſe a man as Oliver : his lordſnip, therefore, did not long ſue in vain, but obtained the lady, from the hands of her father, in the ſame year, and, to honor the wedding, even the gravity of the times were ſuſpended for near a week ; and, to do his lordſhip ſtill further honor, his rank of viſcount was allowed him*. It is impoſſible to ſeriouſly read what lord Clarendon has written of this marriage. his lordſhip avers, that he was ‘ the owner of a very fair eſtate ‘ in Yorkſhire, and deſcended of a family emi- ‘ nently loyal. There were many reaſons to be- ‘ lieve, that this young gentleman, being then ‘ of about three or four and twenty years of age, ‘ of great vigor and ambition, had many good ‘ purpoſes, which he thought that alliance might ‘ qualify and enable him to perform †.’ It may

---

* As the title of viſcount had been given to the family of Bellaſyſe, ſo late as jan 31, 1642-3, and, conſequently, after the civil war broke out, neither the pariement, nor the commonwealth would allow its legality

† Sir Philip Warwick, ſpeaking of the earl of Fauconberg's marriage with the protector's daughter, ſays much more to the purpoſe. ‘ he was a nobleman of great parts, and, by
‘ his

readily be believed his lordſhip had ambition, but
Jerry White would probably have ſtrongly diſ-ſented from the noble author, reſpecting his vi-gor, the good purpoſes the viſcount thought this marriage would enable him to perform, were to riſe at court, by being the ſon-in-law of the pro-tector, to ſuppoſe any thing elſe, is to ſuppoſe the greateſt nonſenſe, for he accepted every place and employment his father-in-law choſe to honor him with, as is evinced in the ſubſequent part of his life.

In the year 1657, he was placed in the new houſe of peers; and when the french king and cardinal Mazarine came oppoſite Britain, Oliver ſent his lordſhip ambaſſador, to congratulate his majeſty upon the occaſion, fixing upon him to honor that prince the more, as his lordſhip was ſo near a relation, and the beſt qualified of any of the protectoral family for ſuch an embaſſy, from the ſuperior advantages of his education and knowledge of the world -; and, as the honors he received will ſhew how far the haughty Lewis ſtooped to court one whom he thought an uſurper, I will give a particular relation of his reception. The protector, to pay the greater compliment both to his moſt chriſtian majeſty and to his ſon-in-law, gave him more than an hundred per-ſons to attend in his train, and, that grandeur and utility might be united, the ambaſſador pre-ſented his majeſty with a letter, written by the protector himſelf to the king, and another to the cardinal, earneſtly deſiring the conqueſt of Dun-

' his friends ſuppoſed not to have wanted therein an ambition
' to ſerve the king, at leaſt he ſaid ſo ' both lord Clarendon
and ſir Philip call him lord Falconbridge

+ Some writer remarks, that Cromwell had no other rela-tion, who was capable of viſiting France as ambaſſador, ex-cept lord Fauconberg, but this is certainly a miſtake.

kirk,

kirk, as it was an harbour for pirates *. Lord
Fauconberg was received with all the honors due
to a sovereign prince : all rules in the ceremo-
nials were paſt over . the cardinal received him
as he alighted from his coach, and conducted
him back to the very gate , honors, my lord ſays,
' particular and unuſual.' His majeſty not only
kept bare at his public audience, but, when he
made a private viſit, the king remained uncovered
for an hour or two ; and the proud Mazarine,
not to be leſs aſſiduous than his maſter, paid him
an homage that had never before been given to
any ambaſſador , for, diſpenſing with the ſtate of
a public audience, he came out of his own apartments to meet his lordſhip, and conducted him
into his own cabinet , and, after an hour's private
conference, his eminence, the cardinal, conducted
him down to the very door where his coach
ſtood , a ceremony which was never paid by him
to any other ambaſſador, nor even to his own
ſovereign himſelf ; he alſo gave him the right
hand in his apartment, which the emperor's ambaſſador, or the pope's nuncio, had never received. This gave great diſpleaſure, not only
to the repreſentatives of the firſt civil and eccle-
ſiaſtical powers in Europe, but to all the other
foreign miniſters at that court. During the time
his lordſhip remained at the french court, which
was five days, he was royally treated, both by
the ſovereign and his prime miniſter, and two
handſome tables were provided at the public expence, for the ambaſſador and all his retinue. At
the audience of leave, his majeſty preſented him
with a gold box, inlaid with diamonds : upon the

* The original inſtructions that lord Fauconberg received
from his highneſs the protector, are in the hands of mr Railic,
who alſo poſſeſſes the original inſtrument of Oliver, for diſ-
ſolving his firſt parlement.

lid

lid on the outſide was the arms of France, com-
poſed of three large jewels, in the inſide was that
monarch's picture, alſo ſet round with diamonds;
the whole valued at five thouſand crowns. Gold
medals were given to ſeveral gentlemen of his
train, and one thouſand louis d'ors diſtributed
amongſt the ſervants From the cardinal his
lordſhip received a preſent of a dozen pieces of
the richeſt genoeſe velvet; and in return for two
ſets of engliſh horſes of eight each, which the
ambaſſador, in the protector's name, had preſented his majeſty with, he received for his father-
in law, a magnificent ſword, as characteriſtic of
the prince to whom it was deſigned, valued at ten
thouſand crowns, and the cardinal who had alſo
received one ſet of horſes, preſented his highneſs,
by the hands of his ambaſſador, a ſet of tapeſtry
hangings, made in the Gobelins, in Paris, in the
perſian ſtyle: his lordſhip (in the letter written
by him to his brother in law, and given in
Thurloe's ſtate papers) ſays, 'in ſumme, through
' all their actions, not the leaſt circumſtance was
' omitted that might witneſſe the truth of theſe
' reſpects they beare his highnes and the engliſh
' nation,' and to exceed all, the french king ſent
an embaſſy to return the compliment, that, if
poſſible, exceeded that of lord Fauconberg's in
ſtate and grandeur, at which time the ambaſſador, the duke de Crequi, firſt lord of the bedchamber, preſented the keys of Dunkirk to the
protector, with this handſome compliment, ' My
' maſter takes pleaſure in parting with them to
' the greateſt captain upon earth.'

Lord Clarendon prepoſterouſly pretends, that
this nobleman was by no means attached to his
father-in-law. The noble hiſtorian's words are,
' Cromwell plainly diſcovered that his ſon Faul-
' conbridge's heart was ſet upon an intereſt de-
' ſtructive

' ſtructive to his, and grew to hate him perfectly.'
It is eaſy to aver any thing; but there is not
the leaſt reaſon to believe what my lord chancellor has affirmed, much leſs any proof for
it: the death of ſir Henry Slingſby, uncle to lord
Fauconberg, was, no doubt very diſtreſſing to
him, whoſe life, both by the intereſt of his lady,
the protector's daughter, and other friends, he
endeavoured to ſave, but this made no breach
between the father and ſon-in-law; ſo far from it,
that his lordſhip accepted this embaſſy after the
decapitation of ſir Henry *; and upon the death
of the protector, he ſtyles him, ' the greateſt per-
' ſonage, not only our own, but any other age
' ever produced,' and places him, for his virtues,
in the ' firmament of happineſs.' Lord Clarendon, by ' another intereſt,' evidently means king
Charles II s, but the viſcount had then no pre-
dilection for his majeſty, we may be aſſured, for,
upon the protector Oliver's death (which was ſoon
after his return from France), he was ſworn of the
privy-council of his highneſs, Richard, his brother-
in-law, whom he ſupported to the utmoſt of his
power. I have before obſerved, that his lordſhip's
grand feature was ambition, and would he not
then conclude it more for his honor to be ſo near
a relation to the ſovereign, than to ſink into only
a ſimple nobleman ?

These certainly were his ſentiments, for he was
the trueſt friend to the protectoral family † they

---

* Sir Henry Slingſby was a loyal roman-catholic, univerſally
beloved, and his death as greatly lamented. He ſuffered with
the unfortunate dr. Hewitt their deaths were determined upon by Oliver, that it might prevent every attempt againſt his
government, by ſhewing that none, however befriended, muſt
expect mercy, who roſe againſt him

† Lord Fauconberg's regiment was one of the eight that the
protector Richard could depend upon. It is obſervable, that
the republicans were ſo jealous of him on account of his attachment

had, and particularly to Henry Cromwell, lord-
deputy of Ireland, between whom there was the
moft cordial and brotherly amity, and from their
epiftolary correfpondence, given in Thurloe's ftate
papers, it appears, he remained with Richard * till
that prince's imprudencies, want of policy, and
the turbulency of his republican relations, were
preparing the way by hafty ftrides, for that revolution that foon enfued. Unable to ftem the
torrent that was, he perceived, coming, he prudently retired to his own domain in the north,
where he was received in a manner the moft flattering, and fuch as befpoke the regard the people
in that part of the kingdom had for the protector,
and a nobleman of lord Fauconberg's merit; for
he was received in Yorkfhire by above one thoufand gentlemen on horfeback, befides many others
who met him near the city of York, and to do
him ftill greater honor, the lord-mayor and aldermen, in their robes, attended to congratulate his
lordfhip upon his coming there. This was july
20, 1658, a very different fcene was tranfacted
in a very little time after; for, as he forefaw, fo
it happened, that the feeble Richard was depofed,
and the republicans, who were jealous of his lordfhip upon every account, fent him to the Tower,
where he remained from feptember 26, to november 2 following, when he regained his liberty only
by promifing not to moleft their government. As
he found all hopes of reftoring the Cromwell family at an end, he determined to affift in the

tachment to the Cromwells, fo early as march 1657, that Difbrowe, with others, prevented his then gaining a place in the
army

* The peerage hints that lord Fauconberg was one of the
relations of the protector Richard that betrayed him, but
much to his lordfhip's honor, the preceding pages exculpate
him from that bafe charge

4 re-eftablifh-

re-eſtabliſhment of monarchy, where he ſuppoſed
he ſhould be better received than by the four republicans, who looked upon him with jealouſy,
and from whom he had experienced hardſhips.
his ſentiments were not unknown to general Monk*,
who for that reaſon gave him Haſilrigge's regiment,
and entruſted him with the ſecret of reſtoring his
majeſty, which he promoted to the utmoſt. His
zeal towards the reſtoration made his marriage
with the uſurper's daughter forgotten ; his majeſty
received him with pleaſure ; and july 27, 1660,
gave him the lieutenancy of the biſhopric of Durham, and the ſame year conſtituted him lord-
lieutenant and cuſtos-rotulorum of the north-riding
of Yorkſhire, and ſent him ambaſſador extraordinary to Venice, to the duke of Savoy and grand-
duke of Tuſcany : upon the ſurrender of his
lordſhip's uncle, John lord Bellaſyſe, of Worlaby,
in 1672, he ſucceeded him in the poſt of captain
of the band of penſioners ; and when his majeſty
declared he was determined to no longer govern
by a ſingle miniſter, at the expence of the ſubjects
freedom, he was ſworn, april 21, 1679, a privy
counſellor. In the following reign, when none
that were not pliant enough to profeſs the royal
faith were truſted, he loſt his influence at court,
and in 1687, his place of cuſtos-rotulorum · this

---

* The hiſtory of England, during the reign of the Stuarts,
acquaints us, that lord Fauconberg went to Monk into Scotland, under pretence of advancing Richard the protector's
intereſt, but in fact to conſult with Monk about the reſtoration. I do not find by any other author that his lordſhip did
go into Scotland at all Ludlow ſays, that lord Fauconberg
and colonel Howard were the two chief inſtruments againſt
the parlement, though before they went into the north (which
they did, becauſe it was in the neighbourhood of Scotland,
where Monk was), they attended upon Fleetwood to aſſure him
of their reſolution to acquieſce in the late change.

did

did not, however, prevent his conftantly declaring his attachment to that unfortunate mifguided
monarch; even after the prince of Orange had
landed, he protefted that he would oppofe all that
were enemies to his majefty; yet, no fooner were
k William and q. Mary feated upon the throne
than he ingratiated himfelf fo far into their favor,
that he was immediately fworn of their moft honorable privy-council, and march 29, 1689, reftored to the place the abdicated king had deprived
him of, and as a ftill further mark of their royal
regard, he was created an earl, by patent. This
nobleman died dec. 31, 1700, and was buried at
Cockfwould, in the county of York. The epitaph
upon his monument, erected over the vault in which
the body was depofited, is given in Le Neve's Monumenta Anglicana, it is very long. I have elfewhere
obferved that his lordfhip had no child, at leaft that
lived, by the protector's daughter, who left all fhe
had from the Bellafyfe family, even the houfe fhe
refided in, ftanding in Soho-fquare, called Faucon-
berg-houfe, and adjoining to what is now called
Fauconberg-court. The prefent earl of Fauconberg poffeffes fome valuables, which were the firft
nobleman's of that title, and prefented to him by
his highnefs, his lordfhip's father-in-law, amongft
thefe are a fabre worn by the protector Oliver, at
Nafeby, his head is engraved upon the blade, with
this infcription, 'Oliver Cromwell, general, for the
englifh parlement, 1652;' above it 'Soli Deo
Glorior,' below it, 'Fide fed cui vide,' on the
other fide of the blade is the fame head and infcription as above, and a man on horfeback, with
the infcriptions, 'Spes mea eft Deo,' below it,
'Vincere aut mori' A broad fword alfo of Oliver's,
with the fame head and infcription, except the
'Spes mea eft Deo' is omitted, and in its ftead
is 'Pro aris et focis.' Alfo a gold watch, which
was

was worn by the same protector; it is in a shagreen
case, richly studded, with a viscount's coronet
upon the back, and a heart transfixed with two
arrows; appendant to it is a seal of a lion rampant,
double tailed, also given by Oliver, but it is improperly represented, the crest of the Cromwells
is a demy lion, double tailed, holding a gem ring
in his fore-gamb.　I shall also observe here, that
mr. Tho. Beckwith, of York, painter, and F. A. S.
has a knife, fork, and spoon, in a shagreen case,
the latter is silver gilt, as are the hafts of the others,
they are very small and neat, they were lady Fauconberg's, who said they were the elder protector's,
her ladyship gave them to miss Eliz. Plaxton, afterwards the wife of mr. Rob. Edwards, their
grand-daughter marrying to mr Beckwith, brought
them to him.　Drawings of these were presented
to me by my very good friend Samuel Pegge, esq.
Lord Fauconberg has in his town-house a fine
portrait of Tho earl of Fauconberg, and another
of his second lady, the protector's daughter, painted both by Walker, and one of them by the same
hand at his lordship's seat in the country.　There
are two engraved portraits of this earl Fauconberg,
mentioned by Granger, they are, Thomas Bellasyse,
lord viscount Fauconberg, &c Maria Beale, p. A.
Blooteling, sc. 1676, large h. sh scarce and fine.
Thomas Bellasyse (or Bellasis) viscount Fauconberg; White, h. sh given in Guillim's heraldry.
His lordship was succeeded as viscount by his nephew Thomas, eldest son and heir of sir Roland
Bellasyse, created a knight of the Bath preceding
the coronation of king Charles II. ancestor of the
present noble viscount and earl Fauconberg [*].

[*] The life of lord Fauconberg is taken from Jacobs's and
Collins's peerages, Thurloe's state papers, Whitloc's memorial lord Clarendon's history of the civil wars, sir Philip
Warwick's memoirs, and other contemporary writers, the
author

No. XXXII.

The life of the hon. Robert Rich, esq (grandson of the earl of Warwick) the first husband of the lady Frances, youngest daughter of the protector Oliver.

THE honorable Robert Rich, esq. was the eldest son of lord Rich, and grandson of Robert, earl of Warwick *, the parlement-admiral, who by praying with, and laughing at the puritan preachers, gained the esteem of them and the failors. the celebrated Cromwell and he continued friends during all the different fortunes that the latter experienced, this earl did not think it beneath his nobility, both for himself and his sons, to assist at the inauguration of investing him with the protectoral power, he himself carrying the sword of state at that ceremony, in 1657; and was one of the few nobles called to sit in Oliver's house of lords †. The mutual regard between the protector and the earl, produced a

NUM XXXII.

The hon R Rich, esq grandson of the earl of Warwick, and son in law to Ol. ld prot.

author of the history of England during the reigns of the Stuarts, and several other historical books, together with some information that lord Fauconberg was pleased to honor me with.

* Rob earl of Warwick, was the son of Rob. the first earl of the name of Rich, who was grandson of Richard created lord Rich, of Leeze, in Effex, feb. 17, in the first year of k. Edw VI in which reign he was lord chancellor of England; these Riches derived their origin from Richard Rich, who was sheriff of London, in 1441, and from the mr. Rich, who, to please a tyrant, swore away the life of the very venerable sir Tho Moore.

† Echard says that all the other branches of the Rich family 'treated Cromwell's alliance with a perfect hatred; ' and that though the earl and Oliver had little resemblance ' either in their humours, or natures, yet they were fast friends, ' and Oliver lamented the death of his son-in-law on all
' accounts.'

marriage, though it was, some say, very much
reprobated by all the relations of the latter . many
difficulties arose, but the regard of the young
people overcame them; and if we believe Ludlow, it was, at last, performed without the consent
of their parents, and sir Edward Sydenham, who
passed for the contriver of the match, was, to
save appearances, for some time forbid the court,
but this, though spoke confidently, is certainly in
part erroneous, as the reader may see by referring
to the life of the lady Frances.

Mr. Rich losing his mother when very young,
was, at her dying request, put under the tuition
of dr. Gauden, afterwards bishop of Worcester,
after remaining some time under his care, he was,
by his desire, sent to Trinity-college, in Cambridge, where mr. Mole, the university orator,
was appointed his tutor, here he continued for
two years, and then went a second tour into France,
under the care of his old tutor, dr. Gauden, during
which time the reverend pedagogue wrote a large
volume for his use, but fortunately for his lordship's literary reputation (if that could be injured)
it was never published, though he had intended it.
Upon his return into England he married the protector's daughter, though at that time he was in a
very bad state of health; his disorder soon encreas-
ing, carried him off two months after his nup-
tials, and five from the commencement of his ill-
ness; during his sickness, as he was unable to bear
long discourses from the violence of his cough, he
directed dr. Gauden, who now attended him as his
ghostly comforter, to send him his advice in writing, that he might, when able, either read or have
it read to him, which was done by him with all the

' accounts.' The above must be taken with some latitude,
for the lord Sherard, the earl's nephew, assisted with lord
Rich, in bearing Oliver's train at his second investment.

attention

attention and regard that could be expected from
his weak ftate of body; he alfo would frequently
have particular parts of the fcriptures read to him,
and when ' that perfon whom he moft loved
(whofe tears in reading beft interpreted, not the
text, but her own heart and fympathies to him)
he would pray her to repeat fome *verfes* once and
again, to give *him leave to paufe* upon them; and
fometimes he ended his meditations and conference with fuch an humble ejaculation, as, ' O how
infinite is the mercy of our heavenly Father, that
hath given us poor finners fuch gracious promifes
to lay hold on !' His diforder was the king's-evil,
as we learn by dr. Gauden; and he was rather
fuffocated by it, than worn down, for it being
internal, and not having a fufficient difcharge,
he was fuddenly fuffocated, immediately after he
had fpoken, and removed himfelf, with much
feeming ftrength and earneftnefs : this cataftrophe
happened in his apartments in Whitehall, at four
o'clock, upon feb. 16, 1657-8, at the early age
of twenty-three years, having furvived his mother
feven, and whofe age, he had ufed frequently
to fay, he fhould not exceed ; but which he did
not arrive to by four years. His remains were
conveyed from Warwick-houfe, in Holborn, with
great funeral pomp, through the city, followed
by a very great number of coaches, and in that
manner conducted to the family vault at Felfted,
in Effex, where they were depofited : the funeral
fermon was preached by dr. Gauden.

Mr. Rich's tutor fays, that he never was guilty
of profanenefs in any refpect, and that he wifhed
to have proper books recommended to him by
which he might be inftructed, both in piety and
prudence . he feems to have been well-difpofed,
and good-natured without any brilliancy of parts:
his untimely death was feverely felt both by his

own, and his lady's family : his grandfather, the
earl of Warwick, said, when he heard of it, that
if they would keep the body a little, they might
convey his with it, and indeed, he survived only
until the eighteenth of april following, when he
died suddenly; and mr. Rich's father, who succeeded to the title of earl of Warwick, died may
29, 1659, surviving his father and his son only
about a year. It would be unjust to the memory
of mr. Rich not to remark, that his brother-in-
law, Henry Cromwell, in a letter of condolence,
that he wrote to lady Devonshire, dated, feb. 24,
1657-8, speaks highly of him : ' I am sure,' says
he, ' the loss of the only son of an only daugh-
' ter, and the hopes which, madam, you had of
' that blessed person, cannot but grieve your lady-
' ship *.'

---

* The life of mr Rich is taken chiefly from Echard's and
other histories of England, Thurloe's state papers, Tindal's
history of Essex. but more especially from ' Funerals made
cordials, in a sermon prepared and (in part) preached at the
solemn interment of the corpse of the right honorable Robert
Rich. heir apparent to the earldom of Warwick, &c. by John
Gauden, D D of Bocking, in Essex.' This is, perhaps,
the most complete piece of pedantic bombast, that disgraces
the english language, it consists of 124 small quarto pages,
exclusive of a dedication to the widow, he has also added a
prayer, in order to prepare for death, the return of the phy-
sicians who inspected the body of the deceased, a long latin
epitaph upon mr. Rich's mother, by himself, and a much
happier one in english, by Sidney Godolphin as a frontispiece to this curious sermon, is a good engraving of the arms
of Rich impaling Cromwell, hung upon a tree, whose top and
branches are cut off, at the first and fourth corners are the
coats of Rich, and at the second and third the Cromwells,
the demy lion holds the broken javelin in his fore-gamb instead of the gem ring.

No. XXXIII.

The history of the baronet family of Ruffell, of Chippenham, who were allied to the protectoral-houfe of Cromwell by frequent inter-marriages.

THIS family commences in Thomas Ruf-fell, of Yaverland, in the ifle of Wight, where he held the manors and advowfons of Yaverland and Wathe, with the manor of Rou-burg, and the caftle of Carifbroke, all in capite; he died in the eighteenth year of the reign of k. Henry VI. leaving his fon, Mau-rice Ruffell, efq. feated at the fame place, who was father of William Ruffell, of Surry, efq. who had a fon, William, created a ba-ronet, and of whom and his defcendants I fhall be the more particular, as they were fo often allied by inter-marriages to the Cromwells.

Sir William Ruffell was firft knighted, and afterwards created a baronet, by the name and ftile of fir Will. Ruffell, of Chippenham, in the county of Cambridge, knt. the patent bears date jan. 19, 1629-30: this dignity was conferred upon him for his many years fervices as treafurer of the Navy. He was buried at Chippenham, feb. 3, 1653-4. Sir William was thrice married; his firft lady was Elizabeth, daughter of fir Fran-cis Cherry, knt. by whom he had no child, fhe was buried at Chippenham, oct. 14, 1626. 2. Elizabeth, daughter of Tho. Gerard, of Burwell, in Cambridgefhire, efq (a younger fon of the

side notes: Nu XXXIII. Ruffells Their antiquity.

Sir William Ruffell, the firft bart.

family

family of that name, ſeated at Flamberds, on Harrow-on-the-Hill, in the county of Middleſex): by this lady ſir William had ſeven ſons and three daughters: the third and laſt marriage of this baronet was with Elizabeth, daughter and co-heir of Michael Smallpage, of Chicheſter, gent. *, and relict of John Wheatley, of Catesfield, in the county of Suſſex, eſq. and a barriſter of the Middle-Temple: the iſſue of this marriage was two ſons. 1. Sir Francis Ruſſell, bart. of whom preſently. 2. Sir William Ruſſell, knt. ſirnamed the black ſir William, to whom k. Charles I gave the treaſurerſhip of the navy with ſir Henry Vane. he was not ungrateful, he never deſerted his royal maſter, for which he was ſtiled the cream of the Ruſſells; his attachment to his ſovereign occaſioned his impriſonment by the parlement in 1646. He married Ann, daughter of —— Bendyſh, by whom he had an only child, a daughter, who died an infant, near whom he is buried, at Burwell, in Cambridgeſhire †. 3. Gerard Ruſſell of Fordham, in the county of Cambridge, eſq. was member for the county of Cambridge in

---

* Catherine, the wife of Michael Smallpage, eſq. and mother of ſir William Ruſſell's laſt lady, was the daughter and co-heir of William Devenish, of Hellingleigh, in Suſſex, eſq. deſcended from lord Hoo.

† In the chancel of the church of Burwell is a neat monument of marble, to the memory, I ſhould ſuppoſe, of the lady of ſir William Ruſſell, knt called the black ſir William, and, if ſo, ſhe muſt have lived to a great age. The inſcription is.

> Neare this Place
> Lyeth the Body
> of the Lady Ruſſell,
> who departed
> this life
> Auguſt the 10 h
> 1717.

the

the parlement called in the 31ſt year of the reign of k. Cha. II. He married twice; firſt, Mary, daughter of ———— Cherry, of Surry, his ſecond, was mrs. Mabel Floyd, to whom he was married at Fordham, aug. 21, 1671, ſhe was buried there ſept. 1, 1674; and he, dec 7, 1683: by the firſt wife, he had four ſons, Will. Ruſſell, of Fordham, eſq. who was buried there, june 26, 1701: he was one of the parlement-committee for Cambridgeſhire. he married Eliz. daughter of Henry Cromwell, lord-lieutenant of Ireland, ſecond ſon of the protector Oliver, the deſcendants of which marriage will be given in ſubſequent pages of this volume, Gerard *, John, Killephet, who was one of the parlement aſſeſſors for Cambridgeſhire, in the years 1644 and 1645, he was buried at Fordham, aug. 1, 1677. By the laſt wife mr. Gerard Ruſſell had Mabel, who was baptized at Fordham, aug. 15, 1673, and married at the ſame place, april 5, 1693, to Rich. Ruſſell, of St. Mary's Woolnoth, London, eſq. ſecond ſon of ſir John Ruſſell, bart. 4. Edward Ruſſell, buried at Chippenham, july 10, 1647. 5. Robert Ruſſell, alſo buried at Chippenham, feb. 17, 1640-1. 6. John Ruſſell, baptized in the pariſh of All-Hallows, Barking, London, jan 31, 1623-4: who died an infant. 7. John Ruſſell, eſq. baptized in the ſame pariſh, nov. 29, 1624, was a colonel in the parlement army, and diſtinguiſhed himſelf both in the battle of Marſton-Moor, and in Oliver's army employed againſt Spain he died unmarried. 8. Elizabeth, the eldeſt daughter of ſir Will. Ruſſell, bart who was married firſt to Edward Lewknor, of Denham, in Suffolk, eſq. the iſſue of this marriage was Mary, married to

---

* There was a Gerard Ruſſell, eſq appointed governor of the ports and forces of Yarmouth, ſept. 26, 1718, who, probably, was the Gerard mentioned above, or his ſon.

Horatio the firft lord vifcount Townfhend: after the death of mr. Lewknor, fhe became the lady of John Gauden, D. D. afterwards bifhop of Exeter, and laftly of Worcefter: his lordfhip died at his palace, in his own city, fept. 20, 1662, aged 57 years, after governing the latter diocefe only four months. Bifhop Gauden was buried in his cathedral of Worcefter, as was his relict alfo, and near to his remains: fhe died march 21, 1671, in the 56th year of her age. K. Cha. I. gave this divine the care of examining his Eikon Bafilicon, to which it is fuppofed he made fome alterations or additions: at the reftoration, he pretended, that he wrote the whole, for which he was promoted to a bifhopric: perhaps there is no one thing that has made more difputes, than this book, for as it has great merit, the enemies of the unfortunate, mifguided monarch, not contented with taking his head, wifh to rob him of his credit as an author; it was the moft confummate prefumption in dr. Gauden to father it upon himfelf, it being fo very far fuperior to any thing he ever wrote, the parts he altered, or added are more eafily known by their inferiority, than by the different manner of fpelling. upon his monument this book is confpicuous. It was the fate of k. Cha. I. always to truft to others, though his own judgment was much fuperior to thofe upon whom he placed a reliance; his giving d. Gauden the perufal of this book is a moft convincing proof of this obfervation. 9. Ann, the 2d daughter of fir Will. Ruffell, bart married to John Bodville, of Bodville-caftle, in Carnarvonfhire, efq. Sarah, their daughter, was married to John, lord vifcount Bodmyn, and, as he died in the life-time of his father, the earl of Radnor, his majefty granted this lady a warrant to entitle her to the rank and precedency of

a coun.

a countefs. 10. Sarah, the 31d daughter of fir
Will. Ruffell, bart. became the lady of fir Tho.
Chichley, of Wimpole, in Cambridgefhiie; a
gentleman who was one of thofe whom Cha. I. in
1645, agreed to commit the militia to· he was
member of parlement for the boiough of Huntingdon, 43rd of q. Elizabeth, for the town of
Cambridge 12th of k. Ja. I. and for the county
of Cambridge in the long-parlement: he was,
I think, favored by the protector Oliver. 11.
William Ruffell, the eldeft fon of fir William
Ruffell, bart. by his laft lady, was baptized in
the paiifh of All-Hallows, Barking, London,
dec. 7, 1621; he died young. And 12. Sir
Will. Ruffell, of Langherne, in Carmarthenfhiie,
knt. youngeft child of fir Will Ruffell, bart.
was firnamed white fir William, his majefty k.
Cha. II. for his loyalty, created him a baronet,
nov. 8, 1660, as he left only a daughter, the
title of baronet in this line became extinct. Sir
Will. married Hefter, daughtei of fir Tho. Roufe,
of Roufe-Lench, in Worcefteifhire, bart. their
only child, Mary, fiift married to Hugh-Calver-
ley Cotton, efq. fecond fon of fir Robert Cotton,
of Cumbermere, in Chefhire, bart and after his
death to the lord Arthur, fecond furviving fon of
Henry duke of Beaufort

Sir Francis Ruffell, bart. fon and heir of fir
William, the firft baronet, was retuined a mem-
bei for the county of Cambridge in the long-
parlement, and was as warm a friend to their
inteieft, as he was a fteady enemy to k. Cha. I.
for his activity in the feivices of the former, he
was by them appointed, aug. 20, 1642, deputy-
lieutenant of Cambridgefhire, at which time an
indemnity was ordered to be caiiied fiom the
commons to the lords foi him (jointly with mr.
Oliver Cromwell, afterwards piotector, and mr.

Valentine

Valentine Walton) for preventing the removal of the plate from Cambridge to York, and to which the lords aſſented. He was alſo one of the committee of his county for ſequeſtering the eſtates of the delinquent loyaliſts, from the commencement to the end of the civil war. The parlement gave him a colonel's commiſſion upon the breaking out of the wars, they appointed him governor of the iſle of Ely (if not of Crowland alſo); to the former he was ordered in 1646 by his employers, he was likewiſe named governor of the city of Litchfield, which, in 1643, he was obliged to ſurrender to prince Rupert, and afterwards he had the government of the iſles of Jerſey and Guernſey given him. During the protectorſhip of his relation Oliver, he was entruſted with many employments, and was returned a member of parlement for the county of Cambridge in 1654 and 1656, but ſtill to raiſe him to a more elevated ſtation, the protector placed him in his houſe of lords. Sir Francis ſurvived the reſtoration, and was buried at Chippenham, april 30, 1664 His lady was Catherine, daughter and ſole heir of John Wheatley, eſq. (mentioned above) by Eliz. Smallpage, his wife, to whom he was married at Chippenham, dec. 19, 1631, by her he had 14 children. 1. Sir John Ruſſell, bart. of whom hereafter. 2. William, baptized at Chippenham, march 9, 1635-6; probably he died young. 3. Robert Ruſſell, of Feckenham and Mildenhall, in Suffolk, eſq. was born at Chippenham, oct. 21, 1644, he married a widow, who was daughter and co-heir of Tho Soame, of Thurlow, in Suffolk, a captain of foot in the ſervice of k. Cha. I*. 4. Gerard Ruſſell, eſq. at Hamburgh

---

* There was a ſir Tho Soame, an alderman of London, who upon the decapitation of k. Cha I. refuſed to proclaim
the

merchant, born at Chippenham, jan. 2, 1645-6;
he married the daughter of —— Yonker, a
merchant of that city. 5. Killephet, born at
Chippenham, april 21, 1647, and buried at the
fame place, april 16, 1650. 6. Killephet Ruffell, of
Mildenhall, in Suffolk, efq. was born at Chippenham, march 11, 1652: he married; his fon Francis
died an infant, and was buried oct. 1, 1680, at
Ifelham, in Cambridgefhire. 7. Edward, baptized
at Chippenham, oct. 12, 1653. 8. Elizabeth,
married to Henry Cromwell, lord-lieutenant of
Ireland, fecond fon of the protector Oliver; their
male defcendants are given in the firft volume,
and their female in this. 9. Sarah, baptized at
Chippenham, may 14, 1636; fhe died an infant.
10. Sarah, baptized at the fame place, may 3,
1637; fhe alfo died an infant. 11. Sarah, baptized at Chippenham, aug. 24, 1638. This lady
firft married John Reynolds of Cambridgefhire,
efq. a famous officer in the fervice of the parlement,
the commonwealth, and the protector Oliver;
in the year 1657, in his paffage to England from
France, he was caft away*; immediately as it
was known, his highnefs moft humanely difpatched
a meffenger to this lady, to defire fhe would not
come up to London, as fhe intended, with the
hopes of meeting her gallant hufband crowned
with victory, that the melancholy cataftrophe
might be properly divulged to her. She had
no child by him, and though his real eftates

the act againft kingfhip, for which he was called to the bar
of the houfe of commons, and upon his declaring that the
reafon why he did not do it, was becaufe ' it was againft feveral oaths which he had taken, as an alderman of London,
' and againft his judgment and confcience.' he was difabled
from being a member of parlement, deprived of the office of
alderman, and rendered incapable of any public employments.
* The life of general Reynolds is given in No. 34, in this
volume,

defcended

deſcended to his ſiſter's children, he left her a
very rich widow; her brother-in-law, Henry
Cromwell, then lord-deputy of Ireland, adviſed
her, that as the will was perplexed, and as his
perſonal eſtate lay chiefly in debenture lands, to
compromiſe the affairs with his heirs, by having
5000l. per ann. ſecured to her, and what was due
from arrears in Ireland, which, though ſmall,
' by the help of friends might be made conſider-
' able,' and they doing this, ſhe ſhould give up
her right in the debentures, by which his other
legatees would have his freehold eſtate of Carrick,
and 16000 acres of land, after his debts and her
jointure were paid ſo ample a proviſion procured her the hand of Henry earl of Thomond;
ſhe left a family by that nobleman *. Fleetwood,
the protector's ſon-in-law, in one of his letters
to Henry, lord-lieutenant of Ireland, gives her
a great character; and ſhe certainly merited it.
12. Frances, baptized at Chippenham, nov 18,
1648, ſhe became the wife of John Hagar, of
Bourn, in Cambridgeſhire, eſq 13. Ann, baptized at Chippenham, july 14, 1650, was married
to Hugh Underwood, of Whittleſey, in the iſle
of Ely, eſq. who was one of the deputy-lieu-
tenants of that iſle, ſhe was his ſecond wife†.

* The deſcendants of the counteſs of Thomond are given
in No 25, in this volume.
† The Underwoods are a very ancient and reſpectable family;
for it appears by the monk Odericus Vitalis, in his hiſtory of
Normandy, that Herbrean de Underwood was living in the
time of William the Conqueror, and that he was the father of
three noble knights, Jordan, William, and Robert, all of
whom had the ſurname of Underwood, and a virtuous lady
named Avice, married to Walter, lord of Alfage and Hu-
gierville, by whom ſhe had iſſue, Jordan, lord of Altage, who
married Julin the daughter of Godſcal, who came into
England, with Adeliza of Lovain, the queen of k. Henry I.
it is remarked by mr Edw. Gwin, the antiquary, that the
the father of theſe children ſtands ſeventh in the roll
of

14. Catherine, baptized at Chippenham, december 23, 1651, it is supposed she became the wife of ———— Sheers, of Hertfordshire, esq

Sir John Ruſſell, bart. was baptized at Chippenham, oct. 6, 1632, he was firſt a royaliſt,

of the names of thoſe chieftains, who accompanied the duke of Normandy when he came to ſeize the engliſh crown, and it is farther ſaid, that having found the diadem, that the unfortunate Harold had worn in the field of battle, he had a grant of theſe arms, ' argent, an oak tree proper, growing ' out of a mountain's baſe, vert, ſurmounted of a lion paſſant ' gules, crowned with the imperial crown, and gorged with an ' open crown, for a creſt, the head of one of the roman Cæſar's; ' with this motto, " Be ever mindful ," and for ſupporters, on ' the dexter ſide, a woman attired azure, holding a book in ' her hand or, and upon the ſiniſter, a chevalier armed at all ' points, holding in pale or.' Theſe bearings are no doubt more modern than the norman invaſion by k. William I. nor are they properly expreſſed. A deſcendant of this family was Fra Underwood, of Whittleſey, eſq whom I ſuppoſe to be the father of the above Hugh, Francis was a great favourite of Oliver the protector, to whom he was probably known before the civil war broke out, Oliver was ſo pleaſed with his adroitneſs, in the ſurpriſe of, and maſſacre at Woodcroft-caſtle, that he gave him a commiſſion of a captain of foot of a company conſiſting of 150 men, it is dated dec 12, 1643, and is given to him by Cromwell in right of his power as governor of the iſle of Ely, to which he had been appointed by his excellency the earl of Eſſex it is worthy of remark, that the ſeal of arms of the Cromwells to this commiſſion is cut in the vileſt manner, all the quarterings are wrong given, and the proper arms of Williams, alias Cromwell, is put in the third, inſtead of the firſt quarter, probably it was cut by a very bad engraver, and done in great haſte. But to return to mr Underwood, he roſe to the rank of major, colonel, and laſtly lieutenant colonel, ſo early as june 8, 1648, he was appointed governor of Whittleſey and Crowland, for he is ſo ſtiled in the thanks of the parlement, ſigned by the ſpeaker Lenthall, for ſuppreſſing the forces under Hudſon and Stiles, which were raiſed to favour the royal cauſe, it appears by the papers now in the hands of mr Maydwell, that he was greatly intruſted by the commonwealth, the protectors, and the reſtored republic, theſe original papers are chiefly letters ſigned by the protector but afterwards a colonel of foot under the earl of Manchester, the parlement-general*, and diftinguifhed himfelf at the battle of Marfton-Moor, and in the protector's wars in Ireland and Flanders†. He enjoyed the office of chamberlain of Chefter during thefe times, and probably many others of confequence; he died in 1669, and was buried at Chippenham, march 24, in that year. He married Frances, youngeft daughter of the protector Oliver, and relict of the hon. Robert Rich, efq. eldeft fon of lord Rich, and grandfon of Robert earl of Warwick. The life of this lady has been given before; fhe long furvived fir John, fpending the latter part of her life with her fifter lady Fauconberg: though fhe had fo great a jointure from her firft hufband, fhe was a great misfortune to the Ruffell family,

protector Oliver, Thurloe fecretary of ftate, Lawrence prefident of the council to his highnefs, Bulftrode Whitlock, Johnfton, and Rich. Salwey, prefidents of the council of ftate, alfo one from Rufhworth, and another from col. V. Wauton, figned Walton   He was certainly a ufeful perfon to his party, but his government was odious from his feverity, and by having the cuftody of many loyalifts, and others that were fufpected to be fo; his name is yet remembered and reprobated in that part of the kingdom, he was undoubtedly vindictive, and having taken fome umbrage, quarrelled with fecretary Thurloe; but the matter was fettled by the latter's declaring his having no intention to offend him.   The family of Underwood poffeffed very confiderable property at Whittlefey, before the commencement of the feventeenth century; no doubt it was much augmented by colonel Underwood his defcendants continued there for many years.

   * Wood, in his Fafti, fays this of the baronet Ruffell, who married the protector's daughter, but calls him fir Francis, inftead of fir John, fo query, Whether this belongs to the father or the fon

   † I apprehend that fir John Ruffell was the mi. Ruffell, appointed with others, to be arbitrators about the differences between the commonwealths of England and Holland, and the fhips each nation claimed.

h ving

having diſſipated the greateſt part of the very fine eſtate at Chippenham: the iſſue of ſir John by her, was five children. 1. Sir William Ruſſell, bart. of whom hereafter. 2. Rich Ruſſell, the former name he received from lord Rich: he married his couſin Mabell, daughter of Gerard Ruſ-ſell, of Fordham, eſq. and, after her death, miſs Catherine Barton; mr Rich Ruſſell was buried at Chippenham, june 13, 1672. 3. John Ruſſell, poſthumous, whoſe life, as he was the continuator of the family, I will reſerve till the eldeſt branch became extinct. 4. Chriſtian, bu-ried at Chippenham, auguſt 28, 1669. 5. Elizabeth, born at Chippenham, november 4, 1664; ſhe married ſir Tho. Frankland, bart.*. the deſcendants of which marriage are given in the following pages.

Sir William Ruſſell, bart. who with more pa-triotiſm than prudence, finiſhed the ruin of his family's fortune, in promoting the revolution, and was obliged to part with the fine eſtate and ſeat of Chippenham, one of the moſt elegant in the kingdom†, was a member of the convention parlement, and voted the throne vacant. As the name of his lady is not given in the baronetage, nor in any of the genealogies ſent me, it is

* Vide the deſcendants of ſir Thomas Frankland, bart. by miſs Ruſſell, No. 34, in this volume.

† Chippenham is near Newmarket, the earl of Orford pur-chaſed it. Le Neve ſays, he was informed that Spinney-Abbey, the ſeat of the ſon of Henry Cromwell, lord-deputy, was by the artifice of one Perceval, a lawyer, confounded with it; but it ſeems impoſſible.—Chippenham is now, or late was, the ſeat of George Montgomery, eſq and Spinney-Abbey is poſ-ſeſſed by the earl of Aylesford, who, in 1779, repaired both the church and manor-houſe. I am informed that there are various portraits of the Cromwell family at Chippenham, but I ſhould ſuppoſe it was not ſo.

reaſonable

NO XXXIII reaſonable to ſuppoſe, he married much beneath
himſelf; lady Ruſſell died feb. 19, 1724-5, ſir
William died diſpoſſeſſed of every acre of land,
in 1707, leaving two ſons.

Sir Will Ruſ-
fell, the 5th bart. 1. Sir William Ruſſell, bart. he died unmarried
at Paſſage, near Waterford, in Ireland, in may 1738,
and was ſucceeded in his title by his only
brother.

Sir Fra Ruſſell,
the 6th bart. 2. Sir Francis Ruſſell, bart. who was one of the
council, and afterwards governor of Fort-William,
in Bengal, in the Eaſt-Indies; in 1725, he married
Ann, daughter of ———— Gee, a merchant, by
whom he left only one ſon, his ſucceſſor in the title.

Sir Will Ruſ-
fell, the 7th bart. Sir William Ruſſell, bart. who was a lieutenant
in the firſt regiment of guards, and dying a
bachelor in 1757, the title of baronet deſcended
to the late ſir John Ruſſell, bart. his ſecond couſin,
whoſe deſcent is thus:

John Ruſſell, third and poſthumous ſon of ſir
John Ruſſell, the third bart, was born in London,
oct. 4, 1670, and became firſt a factor for the
Eaſt-India company, at Bengal, and afterwards was
governor of Fort-William there, he died at Bath,
dec. 5, 1735; having married twice, firſt in Bengal,
dec. 17, 1697, Rebecca, ſiſter of ſir Cha. Eyre,
of Kew, in the county of Surry, knt. by whom
he had one ſon and three daughters, he re-married ſept. 7, 1715, Joanna, ſole daughter and
heireſs of ———— Thurban, ſerjeant-at-law, of
Checkers, in Bucks, niece to lord Cutts, and
widow of colonel Rivett, of the guards, who
ſo gallantly diſtinguiſhed himſelf at the battle
of Malplaquet, where he fell *, by this laſt
marriage mr. Ruſſell had only one daughter.

* See the particulars of the honorable death of colonel
Rivett, in Tindall's continuation of Rapin, and the Tatler,
No 65.

6   1. Charles

1. Charles Ruffell, efq. of whom below. 2. Frances, born jan. 6, 1699-1700, bedchamber woman to the princefs Amelia, fhe married to John Rivett, efq. formerly of the guards, only fon of colonel Rivett, who was killed in the battle of Malplaquet. he died in 1763, fhe in 1775. There is a moft excellent anecdote of this lady the late prince of Wales came into the room upon the 30th of January, when fhe was adjufting fome part of the drefs of the princefs Amelia. Ah! mifs Ruffell, are you not at church to endeavour to avert the judgments of Heaven from falling upon the nation for the fins of your anceftor Oliver? to which fhe inftantly replied, Is it not humiliation fufficient for a defcendant of the great Cromwell to be pinning up the tail of your fifter?—As there was no iffue of this marriage, the Checkers eftate fell to Mary, his fifter, the wife of Charles Ruffell, efq. as will be mentioned below. 3 Mary, born aug. 6, 1701, who married to ——— Holmes, efq. who refided in the Eaft-Indies. There was no iffue of this marriage. 4. Elizabeth, born july 20, 1704; fhe married to Samuel Greenhill, of the Eaft-Indies, efq. he purchafed Swincome, in Oxfordfhire, but difpofed of it again, their iffue was two fons, the rev. dr. John-Ruffell Greenhill, rector of Cotisford, in the fame county, guardian to the prefent baronet, fir John Ruffell, who, by mifs Eliz. Noble, of Sunderland, has Robert, now a ftudent at Chrift-church-college, in Oxford, Charles, the other fon of mr. Sam. Greenhill, died young. 5. Ann, the only child of the fecond marriage: fhe died an infant.

Charles Ruffell, efq. born jan. 8, 1700-1, was appointed a major in the fecond regiment of guards, dec. 17, 1751, he was in the battles of Dettingen and Fontenoy, and greatly diftinguifhed himfelf in the latter, where he commanded the battalion, and was afterwards colonel of the thirty-fourth regiment;

NU XXXIII.

Ruffells.

NU XXXIII
Ruffells.

giment; he caught a diforder, when in Minorca with his regiment, that occafioned his leaving that ifland; he returned to his native clime, but his diftemper had made too confiderable a progrefs for it to reftore him; he died in London, nov. 20, 1754, and his remains were depofited at Kew. He married, june 18, 1737, Mary-Joanna-Cutts Rivett, daughter of colonel Rivett, who, as has been mentioned before, was flain at Malplaquet; fhe by the death of her three brothers, John, James, and William, became heirefs of Checkers. She died in may 1764: the iffue of this marriage was two children.   1. Mary Ruffell, born dec. 13, 1739, was bedchamber-woman to the princefs Amelia, and

Sir John Ruffell,
the 8th bart.

2. Sir John Ruffell, who fucceeded to the title of baronet, upon his fecond coufin fir William's dying unmarried, fir John was born oct. 31, 1741; was a ftudent of Chrift-church Oxford, and afterwards a barrifter-at-law, in Lincoln's-Inn: he died of an inflammation in his bowels, aug 7, 1783 (occafioned by eating melon), at the feat of fir Henry Oxenden, in Kent, univerfally lamented by all who had the honor of his acquaintance, he was a truly amiable character, and had a fine tafte, his library was felect, he had alfo a fmall but choice collection of medals, gems, and other rarities; he married Catherine, daughter of the hon. general Geo. Cary, brother to lord Falkland, by mifs Ifabella Ingram, a rich heirefs of Yorkfhire, whofe only children were the prefent lady Amherft (who has no child) and the late Lady Ruffell, who died dec. 26, 1782, both her ladyfhip and fir John Ruffell, bart. are buried at Checkers; their iffue is only two children.   1.

Sir John Ruffell,
the 9 h bart

Sir John Ruffell, the prefent baronet, born in may 1779.   2. George Ruffell, born in april 1781.

Checkers, the feat of this family, is very ancient, but not elegant, there are many valuables in it, efpecially

eſpecially pictures; in the drawing-room are ſeveral of the Cromwell family, painted by the beſt
artiſls*. There are ſome good prints of the protector Oliver, and a fine impreſſion in ſulphur of
the commonwealth, taken from Simon's dye, when
it was cracked. I was much hurt that I could not
ſee the miniature of the protector Oliver, and a
painting upon glaſs of lord Cutts, as they, with
other valuables, were locked up. Amongſt the
arms painted upon the glaſs in the windows, I
obſerved the Hampdens, with the creſcent.

It is with ſingular pleaſure that I acquaint the
reader that the preſent baronet will, beſides the
eſtate at Checkers, inherit a very ample fortune
from the family of the late lady his mother †.

* In the gallery at Checkers, are ſome very fine family
pieces, eſpecially one over the chimney-piece, there is alſo a
valuable piece, as large as the life, of the emperor Charles V.
on horſeback, and a fine one in the drawing room of the lady
of that lord Cutts, who was the uncle to the maternal grandmother of the late ſir John Ruſſel, ſhe is exquiſitely handſome.

† The hiſtory of the baronet family of Ruſſell I have given
very fully, as they more than once intermarried with the
Cromwells, and to improve and correct the many errors and
omiſſions in the baronetage, which I have been the better able
to do, from examining regiſters and other authentic memorials,
and from pedigrees moſt obligingly ſent me of this family, by
the late lord Grantham, the late ſir Tho Frankland, bart.
miſs Cromwell, dr. Greenhill, the rev. Sam Pegge, and Sam.
Pegge, eſq I have alſo had recourſe to many hiſtorical
books, eſpecially thoſe relating to the engliſh affairs during
the reign of k Cha. I. the government of the republic, and
during thoſe of the protectors Oliver and Richard.

No. XXXIV.

The life of general John Reynolds, allied to the Cromwells by marriage.

THE Reynolds's were of a family that could not boaft either of its antiquity or fplendor, for it had never been noticed by any of the heralds in their vifitations, the firft of that name that is known was of Chefterford, in Cambridgefhire; he grew rich by agriculture, and by diffembling with the world, (to which he always pleaded poverty) he obtained the furname of the beggar, his fon and heir was fir Ja. Reynolds, of Camps, alfo in Cambridgefhire; his eftate was fuppofed to have been 300l. per ann. by his fecond wife, whofe maiden name was Mordaunt, he had three fons, the eldeft was an officer in the army, the fecond was Robert, who procured an eftate of 2000l. per ann. he married thrice, his firft wife was the daughter of ——— Deards, efq. the fecond was the widow of fir ——— Calthorp, and the third the relict of ——— Wyndham, efq. This Robert early diftinguifhed himfelf as an advocate for the parlement, who appointed him one of the commiffioners named to try k. Cha. I. but he prudently declined attending any of the fittings, he was in fuch high favor in 1659, that he was appointed attorney general, and one of the 21 commiffioners for managing the affairs of the admiralty and navy, alfo one of the 14 perfons who were members of parlement, who met to accommodate matters with the fuperior officers in the army, he had Abbington-Hall, and lands

tt

to the value of 400l. per ann. granted him by the long-parlement, and 2000l. in money *. The third brother was general John Reynolds, whose life is given here.

NU XXXIV.
Reynolds.

General fir John Reynolds, allied by marriage to the prot Oliver.

John Reynolds, of Cambridgeshire, esq. took up arms to support, as he supposed, the liberty of the parlement; he was a captain under lieutenant-general Oliver Cromwell, afterwards so celebrated, he first distinguished himself in 1645, in the storming of Bridgewater, where entering with a forlorn hope of horse, he scoured the streets, and beat the royalists out of the first town into the other; for which service the parlement ordered him 100l. and after the king's death, in reward for his important exploits, they settled upon him 500l. per annum, at the recommendation of the general. In 1647, he was sent prisoner to Windsor, for attempting to have the king tried as a criminal; but when the army were of the same mind, the parlement set him at liberty. In may 1649, he defeated and took prisoners the levellers at Banbury, and had it in his power to have put them all to the sword, but mercifully spared them; for this the parlement raised him to the rank of a colonel. The same year he was ordered, with his troop of horse, to Ireland, where he gained great honor by his conduct and bravery, in one of his first actions in that kingdom, he defeated the marquis of Ormond, took his rich camp, and in it his lordship's cabinet, with all his letters, commissions, &c. with a prodigious number of prisoners, amongst whom were many officers and persons of distinction, particularly the marquis's brother, whom he threatened to pistol, until he

---

* Sir Ja. Reynolds, knt. and Ja. Reynolds, esq. were committee-men for Cambridgeshire, as was Rob. Reynolds, esq. for that county and Suffolk.

shewed

NU XXXIV shewed him Ormond himself, which he was obliged to do

Reynolds
General fir John
Reynolds, allied
b marriage to
the prot. Oliver.

After he had defeated the marquis, he was left at Carrick with his regiment of horse, a troop of dragoons, and two companies; but soon after he had the command of sixteen troops of horse, and two thousand foot; being ordered to march to the capital of that province, in his way thither he beat the enemy, and took lord Offory's captain lieutenant, and another lieutenant of horse, prisoners; and in his march to Rofs, he reduced Eniftegoe, a fmall walled town, about five miles from that place, and removed the garrifon of the irifh, and then joined the main army under Cromwell. After this, in 1650, he fell into the earl of Caftlehaven's quarters, and obliged his lordfhip's army to retire into a bog for protection, whilft he continued watching the earl's motions, he was called to affift dr. Theophilus Jones, in relieving the governor of Dublin; and marching for that purpofe back to his own garrifon of Carr.ck, he repulfed the enemy, who had endeavoured to ftorm that place, his ammunition being foon fpent, he beat them off chiefly with fwords and pikes, with the lofs of fome hundreds of their men. Towards the clofe of this year, he again fell upon the earl of Caftlehaven, and defeated him a fecond time, killing 1200 of his men, and taking as many prifoners, which was the caufe of that nobleman's making fcarce any further refiftance this ftruck fuch a panic into the earl of Clanricarde, that though his army increafed, he durft not engage with him.

He alfo took Bellebeg-caftle, and difperfed Dungan's forces, and marching into Caterlough, he took their garrifons, the foldiers deferting two of them, and the third opening their gates the day after fummoning them to furrender, it was
the

the more obfervable, as the whole country was
in the irifh intereft—a plain proof of the eftimation his valor and military knowledge was
held in · this fervice was the more important, as
one of the forts was the only place in that part of
the kingdom which commanded the Shannon.
In 1652, he took and garrifoned a fort in the
Callowe, and two others bordering upon Ulfter;
he alfo, jointly with colonel fir Charles Coote, be-
fieged Galway, and obliged general Prefton, the
governor, to quit the place, and retire from Ireland, and difperfed the enemy's army at Letrim;
in fine, having taken all the provifions of the irifh,
and driven them into their bogs, he obliged all
the rebel commanders to lay down their arms, and
by his permiffion to leave the kingdom, excepting
fuch as had been engaged in the horrid maffacre,
or thofe who were otherwife great offenders,
whom he detained to fuffer that punifhment
their enormous crimes deferved. It was really
aftonifhing with what rapidity he over-run a great
part of Ireland, and the reduction of that kingdom
was more owing to his fervices, than to thofe of
any other perfon, the general's excepted. In 1652,
he diftinguifhed himfelf when Anthony Young,
vice admiral, attacked and punifhed a dutch naval
officer for not ftriking his fail to the englifh flag
upon the italian coaft

His merit was fo well known to Oliver, that
he employed him as foon as he was declared
protector · feb. 8, 1653-4, when his highnefs
went to dine in great ftate at Grocer's-hall, he,
with Whalley, led a troop of three hundred horfe.
He reprefented the counties of Galway and Mayo,
in Ireland, in the britifh parlement called in 1654.
In reward for his merit in the reduction of that
kingdom, he had grants of debentures there to
a very confiderable amount He had alfo 1000l.

N⁰ XXXIV.

~~~~

Reynolds
Gen-ral fir John
Reynolds, allied
by marriage to
the prot Oliver

E e 3   per

NU XXXIV

Reynolds
General Sir John
Reynolds, raised
by marriage o
the prot. Oliver

per ann out of the duke of Ormond's eftates, and a grant of dean and chapter lands in Cambridgefhire, to the annual value of 500l. his highnefs alfo honored him with knighthood in 1655, and difpatched him to Ireland to accompany his youngeft fon, Henry, as one who could give him the beft information of that country, and its particular intereft, and what caft of characters the leading men bore. In 1657, he was fent over to affift the french in the war againft Spain, he landed in Picardy, in the latter end of may, with 6000 foot under his command, with which he was very inftrumental in taking Mardyke from the fpaniards; that important place was delivered into his hands december 12, in the fame year. In his return home, in a dutch pink of one hundred tons, he was, with colonel White, his fecretary, D'Evaux, and others, caft away in a ftorm, as is fuppofed, near Goodwin's fands, for his cheft, fword, and belt, were found there. His death was greatly lamented by the protector, and the nation in general: Heath, in his chronicle fays, that his highnefs commanded him home to anfwer to a complaint in having paid too great a refpect to the duke of York (afterwards k. Ja. II.) at a conference held between Dunkirk and Mardyke; Clarendon, on the contrary, fays, that fir John intended to come into England only for the purpofe of paying a vifit to his friends.

It is far from improbable but fome perfons had endeavoured to leffen him in the opinion of the protector, which he took more notice of than it deferved, and perhaps defired to come over to vindicate himfelf in perfon. This appears plainly by the following well-written letter from fir Francis Ruffell to him, when he was general of the englifh forces in Flanders.

‘ Sonne

' Sonne Reynolds,

NU. XXXIV.
Reynolds
General fir John
Reynolds, allied
by marriage to
the prot. Oliver.

' According to my promife, and your defire, I am now at Whitehall, and have folicited his highnes, my lord Fleetwood, and mr. Secretary for your returne. His highnes told me, that you fhould have leave granted you very fuddenly, and mr. Secretary likewife fayed, that himfelfe would wright unto you, to let you know fo much, but his highnes did fay, when I wrote unto him about this bufynes, that you muft not expect to make any long tarrying heie from your employment: however, I am glad that your friends have fome hopes of feeing you. Your laft letter I did receive, and I have tow for your wife, which I intend to fend downe unto hir by the poft this night. Within this tow or three days I fhall return back for Chippenham, for my chiefeft bufynefs here was to fullfill that love, which I owe unto you. As for news, this place affords me but little. all our ftate-affaires are very private, and to enquire or fearch them out, is not my bufynefs. I hope all things will goe well, yet tis poffible, all our ftate-doctors, are not of one opinion, tis poffible, the wifeeft of them cannot gueffe at the event and iffue of things, nor fay what will be biought to paffe in a fhort time. His highnes takes the prefent of your hoife very kindly   I doe believe his love and refpect towards you is very reall: let therefore no darke thoughts oveifhadow your mind; keep but all things cleaie and honeft at home in your owne hart, and that fun wil fcattei all thofe mifts, that others can caft over your eyes. Expect bad report as well as good to be your portion here below, a wife good man is not much concerned at either. Above all things remember to make a wife ftout warr with all your own enemys within you, for that warfare concernes you moft;

E e 4   and

NU XXXIV
~~~~
Reynolds
General fir John
Reynolds, allied
by marriage to
the prot. Oliver

and the end of it will be a good happy peace. The Lord bleffe and keepe you fafe inwardly and outwardly. I have in this fent you a letter from your wife. fhe will be glad to fee you, and ready to goe along with you to any place you fhall defire her.

I am,

deare fir,

WHITEHALL,
Nov 24, 1657.

Yours in all faithfullnes,

FRANCIS RUSSELL.'

---

* The life of geneial Reynolds is taken from various hifto-ries of England and Ireland, Thurloe's ftate papers, and MSS. in the Britifh mufeum. I have been more particular in fpeak-ing of this commander, as our hiftorians and biographers have not done his valor juftice. It is fingular that dr Leland has not fo much as mentioned him in his hiftory of Ireland — Whitlock knew his merit, and fpeaks of him with honor. Charles Longland, the proteftoi's agent at Leghorne, fays to fecretary Thurloe, in a letter, ''tis very fad news the lofs of that worthy great man, fir John Reynolds.'

No. XXXV.

The history of Henry, earl of Thomond, allied to the protectoral house of Cromwell, by the marriage of Sarah, daughter of sir Francis Russel, bart. and widow of general Reynolds.

HEnry O'Brian, seventh earl of Thomond, was descended from the ancient kings of Ireland · upon the breaking-out of the civil war, he declined giving any assistance to the parlement, from his fear of offending the irish, and injuring his relations, he therefore left Ireland, and came into this kingdom, under pretence of business: when the parlementarians solicited money of him, he excused himself from advancing any, under pretence of inability; but the soldiers, in searching his seat, discovered 2000l. buried in the walls, which they appropriated to the public use *.

In the year 1660, he married the widow of general Reynolds, whose large dower made her no inconsiderable fortune to him, and though he had submitted to bear offices under the Cromwells, yet

NUM XXXV.

Hen earl of Thomond, allied by marriage to Hen Cromwell, lord-lieut of Ireland

---

* The lady Honora O'Brian, the eldest sister, having assisted the royal party after she had sought the protection of Ireton, the parlement lord-deputy of Ireland, he sent for her, and said, he expected a more ingenuous carriage from her, to which she replied with tears, that if he would pass over this fault, she would faithfully promise not to transgress again, and when he retired, she recommended her cause to mr. Ludlow, beseeching him to intercede for a continuance of the lord-deputy's favor; Ireton replied to him, that ' As much a cynic as I am, the tears ' of this woman moved me,' and he condescended to give the protection she asked, which was next to a miracle.

he

he profeſſed all loyalty towards the royal brothers, Charles II. and James II to both of whom he was one of the lords of their moſt honorable privy-council in Ireland. I have mentioned that, to the former of theſe ſovereigns he introduced, or intended to introduce, Henry Cromwell, who had been lord-lieutenant in Ireland His lordſhip died at his ſeat of Billington, in Northamptonſhire, the ſecond of the ides of May, 1691, in the 73d year of his age, having married twice, the lady O'Brien, his firſt couſin, and Sarah, the daughter of ſir Francis Ruſſel, bart. and widow of general Reynolds, by each of whom he had children, the male line failing in the deſcendants of both theſe marriages, the title of earl of Thomond (together with that of Tadcaſter) became extinct *.

It is obſervable, that not a word is mentioned in the peerage, or upon the monument of the earl of Tnomond (erected by Sarah his counteſs, who long ſurvived him) that his lordſhip's laſt lady was the widow of general Reynolds,—was it omitted in the peerage from delicacy to the royal family, or upon the monument of the gallant officer, becauſe his knighthood could not be mentioned? Miſs Cromwell has portraits of the earl and his laſt counteſs †.

* Upon the death of the laſt earl of Thomond and Tadcaſter, Cha. O'Brien, marſhall of France, col of an iriſh regiment of foot, and governor of New Briſac, and Alſace, ſtiled himſelf earl of Thomond, he died in ſept. 1761.

† The hiſtory of the earl of Thomond is taken from the peerages, Le Neve's monumenta anglicana, the ſame author's hiſtory of illuſtrious characters, who died in 1712, Ludlow's memoirs, and a letter ſent the author by miſs Cromwell.

No. XXXVI.

The history of the baronet family of Frankland, ever since they had been allied to that of the Cromwells, by sir Tho. Frankland's marrying Eliz. daughter of sir John Russell, bart. by Fra. youngest daughter of the protector Oliver.

THE family of Frankland is of great antiquity, they originally were of Hertfordshire, but for some time have resided at Thirkesby, in York-shire. Sir Tho. Frankland, bart. eldest son and heir of sir Will. Frankland, created a baronet by k. Cha. II. and grandson of sir Hen. Frankland, knt. married the youngest daughter of sir John Russell, by Fra. the protector's youngest daughter, which was a most fortunate marriage for him, as his uncle, lord Fauconberg *, who had married Mary, the protector's third daughter, was so well pleased with it, that, at the time of the wedding, he settled upon him several considerable estates, one of them was at Chiswick, in Middlesex; and his lordship left him Sutton-court, a delightful seat, in the same county, with its fine furniture and valuable curiosities. This distinction was due to him from his great merit. he represented the borough of Thirsk in several parlements, and was ever the friend to his country, having eminently distinguished himself in promoting the revolution. His character and employments will be seen in this sketch of him, given by Mackey, in his me-

NU XXXVI.
Franklands.
Antiquity.
Sir Thomas
Frankland, 2nd
bart.

* Sir Will. Frankland, bart. married Arabella, daughter of Hen. Bellasyse, esq. eldest son of Tho vil. Fauconberg.

moirs:

moirs : ' Sir Thomas Frankland, poftmafter-ge-
' neral, is chief of a very good family in *Yorkſhire*,
' with a very good eftate , his being my lord *Fau-*
' *conberg*'s nephew, and marrying a grand-daugh-
' ter of *Oliver Cromwell*, firft recommended him
' to king *William*, who at the *revolution* made him
' commiſſioner of the *Excife*, and, in fome years
' after, governor of the Poft-office , by abundance
' of application, he underftands that office better
' than any man in *England* , and, notwithftanding
' we had no intercourfe with *Fierce* laft war, he
' improved that revenue to ten thoufand pounds a
' year more than it was in the moſt flouriſhing years.
' He was the firft that directed a correfpondence
' with *Spain* and *Portugal*, and all our foreign
' plantations, to the great advantage of our
' traffick , and is turned from greater matters, when
' the government ſhall think fit to employ him.
' The queen, by reafon of his great capacity and
' honefty, hath continued him in the office of pay-
' mafter-general. He is a gentleman of a very
' fweet, eafy, affable difpofition ; of good fenfe,
' extremely zealous for the conftitution of his
' country, yet does not feem over forward ; keeps
' an exact unity amongft the officers under him,
' and encourages them in their duty, through a pe-
' culiar familiarity, by which he obliges them, and
' keeps up the dignity of being mafter   He is a
' handfome man, middle ftature, towards forty years
' old ' This was written in 1713   Sir Tho. died
oct 29, 1726, and his lady in july, 1733   their
iſſue was feven fons and three daughters.

1. Sir Tho Frankland, bart of whom in a following page

2. Will Frankland, efq. F R S. who was made
page to q Mary at the revolution, then comptroller
of the General-poft-office , and, nov 20, 1714,
treafurer of the Stamp-office , he was alfo, dec 9,
following,

following, appointed conful in Bifcay. he died NUM XYXVI.
nov. 28, 1714. his firft wife was Marg. daughter
and heirefs of ——— Afcough, efq. and his fecond, Franklands.
Eliz. daughter of mi. Bawdowin, by the former
he had a fon and daughter, who both died infants ;
by the laft, a daughter, named Eliz. who died unmarried.

3 John Frankland, efq. who died a youth at John Frankland, efq
Hamburg, in Germany.

4. Henry Frankland, of Matterfea, in Not- Hen Frankland, efq
tinghamfhire, efq. He obtained a very confiderable property in the Eaft Indies, in which
country he died, aug. 23, 1728. By Mary,
daughter of Alex. Crofs, merchant, he had fix
fons and a daughter, 1. Cha.-Hen. 2. Tho. both
of whom became baronets, and will be fpoken of
hereafter, 3. Will. a merchant, and who continued in the fervice of the Faft-India company
for twenty years, at Bengal, but refides now at
Montham, in Suffex, was fheriff for that county
in the year 1738, and was alfo a member of parlement for the borough of Thirfk. he has never
married. 4. Rich. who died young, 5. Rob.
who died a captain of the Yarmouth man of war,
at Bombay, in dec. 1757, 6. Frederick, who died
in july 1752, at Lifbon. he was major in the
Blues, in the britifh army, he married Meliffa,
the daughter of the rev. ——— Laying, who furviving him, re-married to Edm -Cha. Blenberg,
efq By Meliffa, mr. Frankland had an only child,
alfo named Meliffa, who married to Penifton
Powney, efq fhe died in 1774, leaving alfo one
daughter, named Mel ffi and, 7. Harriot, who
died upon her return to England from India, when
an infant.

5 Richard Frankland, efq. was educated at Rich Frank-land, efq
Jclus-college, Cambridge, and was created a doctor
of civil law, he was a commiffioner of the Salt-
office,

office, and also comptroller of the penny-post office many years . he died a bachelor, sept. 21, 1761.

Fred Frank-
land, esq

6 Frederic Frankland, esq. was a barrister at law, a commissioner of the revenues in Ireland, then a commissioner of the Excise in that kingdom, afterwards a commissioner of the Excise in England, and lastly a comptroller of the accounts in that office   He was returned a member for the borough of Thirsk, in several parlements, and died march 8, 1768.   His wives were, Ann, relict of Adam Cardonnel, esq. secretary to John, the celebrated duke of Marlborough, who dying jan. 27, 1736-7, he re-married jan. 19, 1739-40, lady Ann Lumley, sister to the late earl of Scarborough, who died march 28, 1739-40, by the former he had two sons and three daughters; 1. Fred. 2. Arthur. 3 Ann, and 4. Fran. who all died young; and 5. another Ann, who was married in 1754, to the present Tho. lord Pelham, of Stanmer, in Sussex, by whom she has had four sons and four daughters, Tho. Hen. Geo. Fred. who died an infant, Henrietta-Ann, married in 1778, to Geo. visc. Middleton, of the kingdom of Ireland, who died june 26, 1783 (leaving one daughter, named Fra) Ann, Lucy, and Amelia. Mr. Fred. Frankland had no issue by his last marriage.

Rob. Frankland,
esq.

7. Rob. Frankland was supercargo (of the governor, his brother's ship) from Calcutta to the Persian-Gulph, and, after finishing his trading voyage, and being ready to return to Bengal, the natives rose and murdered him, and all the other europeans, at Juda. The occasion of this barbarity was, that the bodies of some lascar indians, who died in the ships, and had been buried below the high water mark, were washed up by the tide, and by the floods brought up the river,

which

which the people fuppofed, or pretended to fuppofe, had been butchered in the fhips, fo to re-
taliate the injury, they proceeded to the outrage
that involved this gentleman in ruin.

8. Eliz. who married Roger Talbot, of Wood-
end, in Yorkfhire, efq. by whom fhe had, 1. a fon
of the fame names, who married Sarah, widow of
fir Rob. Fagg, of Whifton, in Suffex, bart. and
left no iffue; and, 2. Arabella, married to col.
Gee, who was killed at the head of his regiment,
at the battle of Fontenoy: their only fon, Roger
Gee, married Cath. Wharton, by whom he left two
daughters, Sarah, and Caroline.

9. Frances, married to Tho. Worfley, of Ho-
vingham, in Yorkfhire, efq by whom fhe had 2
fons and 4 daughters: 1. Tho. the eldeft, married Eliz. Lifter, and left 2 fons, Edw. and
Geo. and two daughters, Fran. and Amelia. 2.
the rev. Ja. Worfley, married Dorothy Penny-
man, and left 4 children, Ja. Ralph, Rich. and
Dorothy. 3. Mary Worfley, married to Marmaduke Conftable, of Waffand, by whom fhe
had 2 fons and 2 daughters, Marmaduke, and the
rev. Tho. Conftable (who, by mifs Sarah Goulton,
has 2 fons and 3 daughters, Cha. Marm. Fra.
Marian, and Sarah). Mary, married to Jonathan
Aclom, of Wiftom, in Nottinghamfhire, efq. by
whom fhe has one fon and four daughters, Rich.
Ann, Mary, Lucy, and Rofe. 4. Eliz. Worfley,
married and became the widow of Will. Slaen-
forth, efq. 5. Cath. Worfley, now unmarried.
6. Fra. Worfley, married to fir Tho. Robinfon,
knt. of the Bath, created april 7, 1761, lord Grantham, by whom fhe had 2 fons and 6 daughters,
all born at Vienna, whilft his lordfhip (then fir
Tho) was envoy-extraordinary and plenipotentiary at that court. 1. Tho. the late lord Grantham. 2. Frederic. 3. Frances, both of whom died

unmarried

NUM XXXVI

Franklands.

unmarried in 1768. 4. Ann, died an infant 5.
Ann, now unmarried. 6. Mary, died very young
7. Terefa, became fecond wife to John Parker, efq.
who, may 18, 1784, was created lord Boringdon;
fhe was married may 18, 1769, by whom fhe had
John, born may 3, 1772, and a daughter, named
Terefa. Mrs. Parker died fept. 21, 1775, and
was buried at Plympton St. Mary, in Devonfhire,
leaving a moft exalted character, both as an amiable and accomplifhed lady, and, 8. Eliz. died an
infant. Tho. the late lord Grantham, amongft
others, his moft honorable employment was ambaffador to Spain, firft lord of the board of trade
and plantations, and fecretary of ftate for the foreign department, his lordfhip married, aug. 17,
1780, lady Mary-Jemina Yorke, 2nd daughter and
coheirefs of Phil earl of Hardwicke, by Jemina,
marchionefs de Grey, and baronefs Lucas of
Crudwell, in her own right, by this lady, lord
Grantham had 3 children, Tho. the prefent lord
Grantham, Fred. and Philip.

Arabella Frank-
land

Sir T Frank-
land, bart.

10 Arabella, who died unmarried.

Sir Tho. Frankland, bart. eldeft fon and heir to
the baronet of both his names, was in many places
of great importance, being appointed a clerk of
the deliveries in the Tower, dec. 28, 1714, and of
the ordnance ftores, apr 7, 1715, comptroller of the
penny-poft-office; a commiffioner of the revenue
of Ireland, apr. 8, 1724, one of the commiffioners
for trade and plantations, may 8, 1728, likewife fecretary to the mufter-mafter general, and was many
years one of the lords commiffioners of the admiralty, the borough of Thirfk returned him one of its
members in five fucceffive parlements Sir Tho died
in march 1727, his ladies were Dinah, daughter and
heirefs of Fra Topham, of Agelthorpe, near Richmond, in Yorkfhire, efq with whom he had a very
confiderable fortune, fhe died feb. 2, 1740-1, and

2   Sarah,

Sarah, daughter of mr. Mosely, of Worcestershire :
she died in oct. 1783, by her he had one son, born
in aug. 1743, who died nov. 27 following   by
his first lady he had two daughters   1 Betty, married to John-Morley Trevor, of Glynn-Bourne, in
Suffex, esq. a member of parlement for Lewes, in
that county.   There is no issue of this marriage.
2. Dinah, she became countess to Geo.-Hen. Lee,
earl of Lichfield : she died without issue in 1772.
This was a most memorable alliance, as the countess was descended in the fourth degree from O. Cromwell, and the earl in the same degree from k. Cha. I.

The title of baronet failing in the elder branch,
for want of male issue, it descended to sir Cha.-
Hen. Frankland, nephew of sir Tho. and son of
Hen. Frankland, of Mattersea, esq.   Sir Cha.-
Hen. was for many years collector of his majesty's
customs for the port of Boston, in North-America : he was afterwards consul-general to Portugal,
and was buried for an hour under the ruins in
the great earthquake at Lisbon, nov. 1, 1755, but
fortunately he escaped death : sir Henry returning
to his own country, died at Bath after a long ill-
ness, jan. 11, 1768.   He married miss Agnes
Brown, of New-England, in America, who re-
married, after his death, to John Drew, of Chi-
chester, esq. a banker in that city. she died at
that place, april 23, 1783, of an inflammation in
her lungs, aged about 55 years : she accompanied
her first husband to Lisbon, and was there with him
when the earthquake happened, and what is singular, observed from her elegant seat at Boston,
the battle of Bunker's-hill, after which she returned to Britain.   As sir Cha.-Hen. died without issue *, he was succeeded in the title of baronet by his next brother.

* Sir Cha.-Hen. Frankland had a natural son, to whom he
gave the names of Henry Cromwell, who was with admiral

Sir Thomas Frankland, the late baronet, was born in july, 1718, and brought up to the naval department, he became a captain in july, 1740, and in dec. 1744, he was so fortunate as to take a french ship of great value, off the Havannah, with a spanish register, homeward bound, after an engagement of several hours: upon the death of his brother, he succeeded to the title of baronet; he rose afterwards to be vice-admiral of the red squadron of his majesty's fleet, and, as such, was one of the supporters of the canopy at his royal highness the duke of York's funeral, and was afterwards an admiral of the white: he represented the borough of Thirsk in five successive parlements. His lady was miss Sarah Rhett, grand-daughter of the chief-justice of South-Carolina, in North-America, whom he married in that province, in may, 1743: sir Tho. died at Bath, nov. 21, 1784; he had five sons and eight daughters. 1. Henry Frankland, who died an infant. 2. Sir Tho. Frankland, the present baronet, of whom below. 3. Hugh Frankland, who died an infant. 4. Will. Frankland, Fellow of All-Souls, in Oxford, and a member of the Society of Gray's-Inn. 5. Roger Frankland, B. A. a student at Christchurch-college, Oxford, and designed for the church. 6. Mary, married to sir Boyle Roche, bart. there is no issue of this marriage. 7. Sarah, died young. 8. Harriet, unmarried. 9. Ann, married, march 24, 1778, to John Lewis, of Harpton-court, in Radnorshire, esq. by whom she has Tho.-Frankland Lewis, born, may 14, 1779, and Louisa, born, july 8, 1783. 10. Dinah married to Will. Bowles, of Heale, Wilts, esq

Kempenfelt in the gallant action off the French coast, in the navy, nov. 14, 1781, and is very much esteemed, as I have been told, by gentlemen high in the naval service.

by whom she has one son, William, and three
daughters, Ann, Lucy, and Charlotte. 11. Catherine, married to Tho. Whinyates, esq. an
officer in India, their issue is two sons, Thomas,
and Manners, and also several daughters. 12.
Charlotte, married to Rob. Nicholas, of Ashton-
Keams, Wilts, esq. they have two sons and one
daughter, Edw. Rob. and Charlotte. And 13.
Grace, who is unmarried.

Sir Tho. Frankland, the present and sixth
baronet, was born in sept. 1750, and was educated at Eton, and Mereton-college, in Oxford:
he married Dorothy, daughter of sir Will. Smelt,
and niece to Leonard Smelt, esq sub-governor to
George prince of Wales: their issue is four
children, 1. Henry. 2. Rob. 3. Amelia, and
4. Marian *.

NU XXXVI.
Franklands.

*Sir Tho Frank-
land, the 6th
bart.*

---

* The history of the family of Frankland is taken from the
baronetages, various other writers, and corrected and enlarged
by information, which I had the honor to receive from the
late lord Grantham, the late sir Tho. Frankland, bart. and the
present baronet of that name, the rev. dr. Greenhill, the rev.
Sam. Pegge, and Sam. Pegge, esq It may be necessary to
correct a passage in the history of the life of the first sir Tho.
Frankland in the baronetages; they say, that the earl of
Fauconberg was descended from Mary, daughter of the protector Oliver, but his lordship married that lady instead of
being descended from her, as is sufficiently proved in these
memoirs.

No. XXXVII.

*The history of Richard Major, esq. father-in-law
to the protector Richard, with some particulars
of the Dunchs, of Pusey, in Berks.*

No. XXXVII.
Majors
A—r
An ꜱ—r

THE Majors are of a respectable family;
they bore gules, an anchor argent, on a
chief or; three roses of the first. The patriarch
of the Majors was sir Mark Major, who served
in the wars of k. Henry VII. his son was John
Major, of Handway, in the isle of Jersey, esq.
who was the father of Bonaventura Major, esq.
whose son John, was the father of John Major,
esq. who was mayor and alderman of Southampton; his son was Richard Major, esq. whose
daughter married to his highness Richard lord
protector. Mr. Major is supposed to have first
been seated at Sylton, in Dorsetshire, a manor
he owned, but whether from descent or purchase
is uncertain, however, it appears from a variety
of articles, entered in six pages of the account
book of mr. Major, which is still extant, and in
the possession of sir Tho. Heathcote, that he was
lord of that manor, from lady-day 1637, until the
end of the next year, how much longer he had
it, or whether he was possessed of it before 1637, is
uncertain, a memorandum of his, shews that a ter-
rier of the parsonage there was put in Blandford
court, in the summer of 1637. During his residence at Sylton, 1637, he had a law-suit concerning the common of that place, and, in that, and
the following year, he employed himself in re-
pairing his house, and adding to his stock and
sheep.

sheep. Probably the dislike he had to that place occasioned his purchasing of sir Gerard Napier, the seat of Hursley, about four or five miles from the city of Winchester, together with the manor of Meidon, or Marden, in which Hursley lies: Hursley house, or lodge, was an ancient mansion situated in a park of the same name this purchase was made about 1639, for the first entry in mr. Maijor's memorandum-book, concerning this place is dated in that year, and it is still further proved, by his mentioning that he had received some information respecting the coppices in that manor, by two persons concerned in the falling of them, in the years 1632, 1633, 1634, 1635, and 1637, a person of his apparent attention to his own concerns, would not have wanted information during those years, had he either resided upon, or even owned the manor, for he was most exact in collecting every information relating to Merdon.

He was high-sheriff of Hants in 1640, or 1641: in the following year he resided much with his mother, in the town of Southampton, but he informs us, that april 19, 1644, he began house-keeping, in a house rented of John Barton, in that town. may 2, in this year, he had the misfortune to break his leg, for the setting of which he gave 6 l. 13 s. 4 d. his health was not restored in the july succeeding, for he gave 2 l 10 s. to dr. Phillips for attending him in his sickness during that month. From september the nineteenth until october following, he maintained six of the parlement general's soldiers, but by his own remarks in his memorandum-book, he did not any otherwise assist in the civil wars: however, it must be observed, that in a manuscript-book, written by his reeve, it is said, he set forth horse and arms in behalf of the parlement

ment

ment cause; but as this man was his professed enemy, little reliance can be placed upon what he says, in contradiction to his master's assertion, especially when it is known, that the latter's memorandums were only for his own private satisfaction, but it is undoubted, that the parlement looked upon him as their friend, and accordingly appointed him one of their committee in the county of Southampton. It also is manifest by his own relation, that in conformity to an order of the committee, he had the care of the cures of Hursley and Otterbourne, from 1646, until the latter end of 1649; during that period he received the whole revenue of those benefices, and paid the officiating ministers; he was extremely busy in matters relating to church affairs, for it appears, that he had obtained possession of three manuscripts relating to the bishop of Winchester's court, which he was obliged to give up, june 30, 1644, to mr. Tho Baker, of Fareham, who was a sequestrator, and steward of that diocese, they being adjudged useful to the state.

He resided during the year 1645, chiefly at Southampton, in the latter end of this year he appears to have received the freedom of the city of Winchester, as he paid in november 21, ‘ fees ‘ for burgesse of Winchester 10s town-clerke, ‘ and to 4 sergeants 2s. 6d. a-piece.’ In 1650, he disposed of his farm of Horingford, in the isle of Wight, for the sum of 1220l. and nov. 18, in the following year, he purchased for 4000l. the estate of Chilbolton, which brought in at that time 280l. His daughter's alliance with the Cromwells, occasioned his having great interest in the government july 14, 1653, he was added to the council of state, and when Oliver called a convention (to which he afterwards gave the name of parlement), and it behoved him to be

careful

careful in chufing fuch whom he could depend upon, as they were to give him the fceptre, he procured mr. Maijor, his brother-in-law, to be returned a member for Southampton; and when this parlement gave him the title of protector, he was appointed by his highnefs one of his privy council. In the following year he was named by the protector, an affeffor of the taxes, for both Southampton, and the ifle of Wight; however, it is evident, by a letter written by major-general Goffe, to fecretary Thurloe, dated from Winchefter, may 5, 1656, that notwithftanding Oliver's power, and mr. Maijor's confequence in the place and neighbourhood, the magiftrates of Southampton, were againft him, and the *godly party*. In this year he made an inconfiderable purchafe of fome tenements at Southampton, called Bargow tenements above Bar, this was probably done to keep up his connections at that place: befides the eftates I have already noticed, mr. Maijor alfo poffeffed fome lands at Allington, and a fee-farm rent of 25l. a year iffuing out of the rectory of Porchefter; both of thefe places, as alfo Chilbolton, are in the county of Hants.

Mr. Maijor had obtained a commiffion in the army, and was put in the commiffion of the peace; but the protectoral power being firmly eftablifhed, he was called to the other houfe, and obtained the title of lord; and upon his fon-in-law's acceffion to the fovereignty, he was declared of his privy-council; but his lamenefs from the gout prevented his attending court, which was no little injury to the protector, as he was a man of great capacity and knowledge of men: the misfortunes of Richard, and the return of royalty, together with his bodily infirmities, terminated his life in the fifty-fixth year of his age, april 25, 1660: his remains were depofited in the chancel

F f 4 of

of the church at Hurfley : over his grave is laid a ftone upon which are the arms of Maijor, impaling thofe of the Kingfwells, and this infcription:

> Hic jacet corpus Ricardi Maijor
> Armigeri. Dominique
> Hujus Manerii de Meidon alias
> Marden, Qui obiit 25to Die
> Aprilis, Ano. Dni. 1660.
> Ætatis Suæ 56to

The protector Oliver, when lieutenant-general only, tells mr. Maijor, that it was his family's godlinefs that made him court his alliance, and not any confiderations about his confiderable property, he having, he fays, had many propofals for his fon of greater advantage than his. How true this may be, is difficult to determine. In a letter to one of their common friends, Oliver fays, he perceives that he was, ' wife and honeft, ' and, indeed, much to be valued;' but he immediately fubjoins, ' fome things of common ' fame did a little ftrike.' It is impoffible to know, at this diftance of time, what thefe ' things' the world objected againft him were, but, from the feeming attention he paid to money matters, it is not improbable, that it was either exceffive love of money *fimply*, or that he had done fome action to add to his wealth, more than what his honor ougt to have permitted, I fhould therefore fufpect, notwithftanding the elder protector's afferveration, that money was the principal inducement that occafioned him to feek the marriage of his fon to this gentleman's daughter, but, however, it muft be acknowledged, that if mr. Maijor was thrifty, he was liberal to the poor, as feveral entries are made by him of money given to different perfons, or diftributed amongft the indigent.

His

His greateſt enemy, the reeve, allows him to be
witty*.

Mr. Maijor married Ann, daughter of John Kingſwell, gent. lord of the manor of Marvel, in the iſle of Wight, with whom he had ſome lands in that and other places in the iſle of Wight, mr. Kingſwell died march 6, 1639, in the ſeventy-ſeventh year of his age, and is buried in the chancel of Hurſley church, where there is a flat ſtone with his arms, gules, a ſaltire between four lions heads, eraſed or, and underneath this inſcription

> Hic jacet corpus Johiſ. Kingſwell
> De Marvel in Inſula Vectis Gen. Qui obiit
> VIᵗᵒ Die Martii Ano. Domi. 1939 Anᵒ· que
> Ætatis Suæ 77°·

· Mrs. Maijor died june 13, 1662, aged fifty-ſix, and was buried near her huſband and father· the grave-ſtone laid to protect her remains has the arms of the Kingſwells, quartering a chevron, between three fleurs-de-lis, and this epitaph.

> Hic jacet Corpus Annæ Maijor
> Viduæ, Quæ Maritum Habuit
> Ricardum Maijor de Hurſley Ar-
> migerum, et Patrem Johannem
> Kingſwell de Marvell Generoſum
> Obiit 13ᵗ·ᵒ· Die Junii Anᵒ· Dni.
> 1662 Ætatis Suæ 56.

* There was an Edw. Maijor, eſq who was vice-conſul at Gallipoli, during Oliver's government, he was ill-uſed by the cadee, for which that magiſtrate, upon complaint, was removed, the following perſons names occur as the relations of mr. Maijor's, the protector Richard's father-in-law, in the book of his expenditures his ſiſters Waltris, Wolgar, and Lavington; whether his own, or his wife's, cannot now be determined, and his couſins, Maijor widow, Chafic, William Smith, Warner, and Harient, perhaps, alſo, ſome of theſe are likewiſe his wife's relations, but the laſt, mr. Gauntlet ſuppoſes to have been his own.

Mr.

Majors.

Mr. and mrs. Maijor and mr. Kingſwell's grave-
ſtones lie upon the ground within the rails of the
altar, parallel to, and touching each other, mr.
Kingſwell's being the middlemoſt.

The iſſue of mr. Maijor, by miſs Kingſwell,
was only two daughters; Dorothy, who married to
his highneſs Richard, lord protector, and Ann, the
wife of John Dunch, of Puſey, in Berks, eſq. as
I have given an hiſtory of the Dunchs, in a former
part of this volume, I ſhall now give all the particulars I can of this branch, which was ſettled in
Berks, eſpecially as they were by this marriage
again connected to the Cromwells.

Dunch of
North-Bad-
deſley.
Sam Dunch,
eſq.

Samuel Dunch, of North-Baddeſley, in Hants,
eſq. was a younger ſon of Samuel Dunch, of Little-Wittenham, in Bucks, eſq and brother to ſir
Will. Dunch, of that place, knt. who married
Mary, daughter of ſir Henry Cromwell, knt.
which lady was alſo aunt to the protector Oliver;
the occaſion of mr. Samuel Dunch, junior, ſet-
tling at North-Baddeſley (which is about three
miles from Winchefter) was his marrying Dulcibella, the eldeft daughter of John More, eſq. a
counſellor at law*, who reſided ſome time there,
and whoſe only ſon dying unmarried, mrs Dunch
became a coheireſs, and in the diviſion of the eſtates of mr. More, this manor fell to his ſhare.
Mr. Dunch was an active member of the long-parlement, his name frequently occurring in the journals of the houſe of commons, during the years 1643,
and 1644, and in 1650 he was appointed one of their
committee for Berks, which county he repreſented
in 1653: he was much in the confidence of the protector Oliver, who, in 1654, appointed him one

---

* Counſellor More purchaſed the manors of North-Baddeſley
of ſir Tho. Fleming, lord-chief-juftice of the Queen's-Bench,
in the reign of q Eliz. Mr. More died upon the weftern circuit,
and was brought for ſepulture to Baddeſley, his ſon died at
Oxford, of the ſmall-pox.

of

of the vifitors of the univerfity of Oxford. He died
in Berkfhire, as did his only fon and heir, and they were both buried together in one grave in the church of North Baddefley, nov. 5, 1668, they were the greateft patrons of the ejected minifters of any in their county. Mr. Dunch, by mifs More, had one fon and five daughters: 1. John, of whom below; 2. Mary, who was the firft wife of fir Rob. Pile, of Compton, Berks, bart. by whom fhe had only Frances, who died young. lady Pile is buried in Pufey church, upon a marble grave-ftone laid over her remains, is a fhield of fir Robert's and her arms, with this motto, Virginis en nobis caftæ nuptæque coronam, by the epitaph it appears fhe was born june 25, 1616, married june 9, 1634, and died jan. 1, 1638-9 3. Dulcibella or Ifabella, married to Edw. Wifeman, of Spanholts-court, Berks, efq. anceftor of the baronets of that name, by whom fhe had four fons and three daughters; fhe died november 10, 1656, aged 37 years, and is buried at Steventon church, in Berks. 4. Elizabeth married to John Pittman, of Quarley, in Hants, efq. 5. Ann. married to Gabriel Beck, of Weftminfter, efq. folicitor to the council of ftate during the commonwealth, and whom mr. Dunch, his father-in-law, wifhed to get into the houfe of commons, in 1656, as a member for fome place in Berks. And 6. Lucy, the fecond of four wives of John Twifleton, of Horfeman's place, in Kent, efq. created a baronet by his highnefs, the elder protector, fhe died without iffue, and was buried in Dartford church, where her hufband's body was afterwards depofited.

John Dunch, efq. the only fon of Sam Dunch, efq. was fortunate in his alliance, for though he received only 1000l. in money, with Ann, the youngeft daughter of mr. Major, at the time of

their

their marriage, yet, as she was a co-heiress, he afterwards divided the ample fortune of his father-in-law; and, besides this, it introduced him to the particular notice of the sovereign upon the protectoral throne, for Oliver no sooner was informed of his marriage, than he invited him to court, by the following letter.

For my loving friend, John Dunch, esq.

Sir,

I desier to speake with you, & hearinge a report from *Hursleye*, that you was goinge to yr. father's in Berkeshiere, I send this expresse to you, disiring you to come to mee at Hampton-court with my respects to yr. father, I rest

Yr. lovinge friend,

Aug. 27th. 1657.   Oliver P.

Such an invitation would not be slighted, the protector appointed him a justice of peace, and gave him a commission in the army, he was one of the county members for Berks, in the parlements called in the years 1654, 1656, and 1658-9 I have before mentioned his death. By miss Major, he had eight children, all of whom were born at Hursley, except Dorothy the youngest. they were, 1. Major Dunch, of whom hereafter. 2. Samuel, born sept 26, 1652; he was bred to the law, and resided in Red-lion street, in London, he was appointed guardian to the last male of the Dunchs, of Little Wittenham, by that gentleman's father, who called him cousin, he is buried in the church of the parish in which Red-lion street stands. By miss Sarah Lawyer he had four daughters, three of whom, Mary, Eliz. and Olivia, died unmarried. Sarah the second, married late in life, to Edw. Haylock, of Saviton, in Cambridgeshire, gent. she died feb. 14, 1773, her character was truly exemplary. Unwilling to omit what is so greatly to her honor,

I shall

I ſhall give the whole of it as drawn up by mr.

Robinſon, who preached her funeral ſermon, but as it would too much break into the genealogy of the family, I will put it in the note *. 3. Edmund, born ſept. 3, 1656, he walked as a mourner at the funeral of mrs. Dorothy Cromwell, the protector Richard's daughter, as her neareſt relation,

* The character of mrs. Sarah Haylock, given by the rev mr Robinſon in a funeral diſcourſe, preached at her death, who died the 14th of february 1773. Laſt week died in the 77th year of her age, lamented by all that knew her, mis Sarah Haylock, wife of E Haylock, gent. of Sawſtone in this county. This lady, whoſe maiden name was Dunch, was the laſt ſurviving daughter of ——— Dunch, eſq. a younger ſon of an ancient and honorable family of that name in Berkſhire, nearly allied to the dukes of Mancheſter, earls of Shafteſbury, and to ſeveral other noble families Her agreeable perſon, and great-mental abilities, refined by the moſt polite and literary acquirements, and adorned with unaffected piety, rendered her one of the moſt accompliſhed of her ſex. Superior in her early life to the futility of grandeur, ſhe declined the moſt flattering alliances, preferring an uſeful retirement in the country, though ſhe never ſeparated the affability of a well-bred lady from the life of a recluſe. She was ſtudiouſly munificent to the poor, devoting the far greater part of her income to charitable uſes, her liberalities diffuſing themſelves among people of all parties, and extending to the colonies abroad, as well as to numbers of the indigent at home Her books were few, but well read, the holy ſcriptures being her favorite ſtudy, and her life a conſtant comment on their meaning Educated a diſſenter, ſhe conſcientiouſly continued ſo to her death, but, with a modeſty equal to her ſincerity, was as far from preſuming to think for others as from reſigning the noble privilege herſelf. For ſeveral of the laſt years of her life, having loſt her hearing, ſhe avoided all company except her relations, and one diſſenting miniſter (mr Robinſon of Hauxton), to whom ſhe gave the liberty of repreſenting, and the honor of relieving a number of neceſſitous caſes. No wonder that the evening of ſuch a life ſhould be ſerene, or that her laſt ſhould be her beſt and happieſt moments. She was buried, according to her own directions, in a very plain manner, wiſely applying to the wants of the poor, what her rank might

3

and to whom she left a legacy, as she also did to his brothers Samuel and John, he left a son of his name; one of them founded and endowed some alms-houses; the father was a person of unbounded benevolence. 4. John, born oct. 5, 1657, was a Turkey-merchant, he was a gentleman of taste and enquiry, for he visited the city of Jerusalem, from whence he brought two models of the Temple, and a cross of cedar, richly inlaid with mother of pearl, he died abroad; his picture, it is supposed, is at Dean, in Kent. By Mary, his wife, he had Will. Dunch, a merchant, who married Dudley, daughter of Geo. Gent, of Moyns-park, at Bump-stead, in Essex, esq. whose father had large pos-sessions near that place, a part of which are now en-oved by her nephew, a very worthy gentleman of the same names and place, both this mr. Dunch and his father resided in Bridgewater-square, and are supposed to have been both buried in that parish; he died very young, leaving four sons, Edm. Geo. Will. and John, Edmund went abroad and died, Will. and John both died young, and unmar-ried, Geo. the 2d son, was designed for the church, and by his learning was well qualified for that profession; he married Esther, daughter of John Day, of Cambridgeshire, esq. by whom he had a son, who died unmarried, and Elizabeth, miss Dunch resides at St. Neots, and is the only de-scendant of the name from the North-Baddesley branch. 5. Dulcibella, born march 29, 1654-5. 6. Ann, born june 22, 1655, she died an infant,

might have claimed for funeral pomp and parade. What of her fortune does not go away at her death—except what she left in charitable legac es, she has divided between her disconsolate husband (whose loss nothing can repair) and her nearest rela-tion, miss Dunch, of St Neots.

and

and is probably buried at Pufey. 7. Ann, born
oct. 5, 1659, who married John Hade, of Frampton, in Gloucefterfhire, efq. fhe died july 16, 1687,
and is buried at Frampton, and 8. Dorothy, who
was the fecond wife of Will. Wright, efq. recorder
of Oxford, fhe dying may 23, 1686, aged 24
years, was buried in St. Michael's church in that
city, and upon her grave-ftone are the arms of
her hufband impaling her own.

Maijor Dunch, efq. eldeft fon of John Dunch,
efq. by mifs Maijor, was born aug. 9, 1651; he
was placed under the tuition of mr. Gunter, the
ejected fellow of Magdalen-college, in Oxford:
mr. Dunch reprefented Appleby and Richmond,
in parlement, but unfortunately died prematurely fept. 27, 1679, when only twenty-eight
years of age; and was buried in Pufey church,
where his widow fet up a monument to comme-
morate his virtue and learning, it is given in mr.
Le Neve's - monum. anglicana. He married
Margaret daughter of Philip lord Wharton, who
re-married to fir Sam. Selyard, of Boxley-Abbey,
in Kent, bart. mr. Dunch by this lady had three
children, 1. Wharton Dunch, efq. who died, leaving no child. 2. Margaret, who probably died young
and unmarried: and 3. Jane, who became heir to her
brother; fhe married to Francis Keck, of Great-
Tew, in Oxfordfhire, efq. he died fept. 29, 1728;
the iffue of this marriage was John Keck, of
Great-Tew, efq. who died without children, aug.
13, 1729; Mary, his widow, re-married to John
Nicholl, efq. 2. Anthony Keck, efq. died unmarried in november 1726. and 3. Mary, married to fir John Dutton, bart. by whom fhe had
no child.

It is fingular that this branch of the Dunch
family, which furvived the eldeft, feated at
Little-Wittenham, now has only one remaining,
a female,

a female; there is, I am informed, a family of these Dunchs in Scotland, who spell their name Dunsh, it is probable they procured some appointment in that kingdom during the government of the Cromwells, and probably marrying advantageously, settled themselves there. The manor of North-Baddesley, which the Dunchs possessed in Hants, is now the property of mr. Dance, in right of his wife, the relict of —— Dummers, esq. who purchased it of mr. Chute, who succeeded mr. Nichols; he purchased it of mr. Keck.*

* The history of the Maijors and the Dunchs, of North-Baddesley, is taken from a pedigree of the Maijors, signed J. Watson. Regr. extracted out of Brooke, C folio 101, sent me by miss Cromwell, through mr. Field; materials also communicated by a lady allied to the Dunchs, the rev. Sam. Gauntlet (chiefly taken from memorandum books written by mr. Maijor, regifters and funeral monuments), mr. Longmate, and other friends, from various writers of the civil wars, Harris's life of Cromwell, the last edition of Collins's peerage, with the supplement, baronetage, Willis's not. parliamentaria, Thurloe's state papers, and Le Neve's monumenta anglicana. Mr. Will Dunch drew out a very full pedigree of his family, which is supposed to be now in the hands of some person to whom he lent it, mis. Dunch, of St Neots, in Huntingdonshire, will esteem it a particular favor to have it returned, and I shall be happy if these volumes are the means of having it restored to the family.

No. XXXVIII.

Of the descendants of Elizabeth, daughter of Henry
Cromwell, the lord-lieutenant of Ireland.

ELIZABETH, the only surviving daughter of
Henry Cromwell, lord-lieutenant of Ireland,
was born at Chippenham, june 3, 1660, she was
married to William Ruffell, of Fordham, in Cambridgeshire, esq. who had a commiffion in the
army; he was fon of Gerard Ruffel, esq. of the
fame place, and grandfon of fir William Ruffell,
the firft baronet, a marriage concluded probably
from the several prior alliances between these two
families of Cromwell and Ruffell, it, however,
was a moft unfortunate one for the lady, as mr.
Ruffell lived at an expence far exceeding his income. He kept the firft company, and had his
coach and fix, which, with other needlefs expences,
together with a large family, brought him fo much
in debt, that his creditors became clamorous:
fortunately for himfelf, he died in 1701, and
was buried, june 26, in Fordham church His
widow, inftead of endeavouring to retrieve the
fhattered fortunes of the family, ftrove to keep
up an appearance of riches as long as it was
poffible, when, in the night-time, fhe fet off in
her coach, with as many of her children as fhe
could take, and went to London, much indebted
to all the neighbourhood, and died in that city,
in the year 1711, of the fmall-pox, which fhe
caught by keeping fome of the hair of two of
her daughters, who died a little before her of that
dreadful diftemper. She had the numerous fa-

NU XXXVIII.

Ruffells of
Fordham

William Ruffell,
of Fordham, efq.
who mar Eliz.
daughter of
Henry Crom-
well, lord-lieut.
of Ireland

mily

mily of feven fons, and fix daughters. 1. Obrian-
William Ruffell, who was baptized oct. 17, 1684,
at Fordham (as were all his brothers and fifters,
except the two youngeft); what became of him,
I could not learn, only that he was brought up
to no profeffion.   2. Henry, baptized oct. 10,
1685, he died at fea.   3. John, baptized dec.
4, 1688, he died march 23, 1694-5, and was
buried in Fordham chancel, march 25, 1695;
over whom, within the communion-rails, is a
black marble flab.   4. William, baptized dec. 6,
1689; he was alfo in the fea-fervice, in which
he died.   5. Francis, baptized jan. 19, 1691-2;
he was brought up to the hofiery bufinefs, which
he followed in London.   6. Edward, baptized
march 14, 1693-4, he died aug. 18, 1694, and
is buried near his brother John, in Fordham
church.   7. Thomas, baptized aug. 31, 1695;
he was put apprentice to his brother Francis, he
never married.   8. Elizabeth, baptized may 2,
1683; fhe married to mr. Robert D'Aye, of
Soham, of an ancient family, who, having fpent a
good fortune, was fo reduced, that he died in
the workhoufe.   The daughters of the protector
Richard leffened the weight of mrs. D'Aye's mif-
fortunes, by fending an annual prefent to her,
and by leaving her a legacy at their deaths, but
this did not prevent her experiencing very great
hardfhips from poverty; fhe died fo late as nov. 5,
1765, at Soham.   The children that lived to the
age of manhood, were, Ruffell D'Aye, whom captain Smith (pitying his condition) fent to fea,
when a boy, in which fervice he died a bachelor,
and fcarce of age; and Elizabeth D'Aye, who
was the fift wife of Tho. Addefon, of Soham,
who, from a fhoe-maker, has gradually rifen to be
a perfon of fome confideration, he was, in the
year 1781, or 1782, high conftable of Soham;
                                              his

his honefty and good fenfe have procured him the
regard of the neighbouring gentlemen, who have
on many occafions fhewed the favorable opinion
they entertain of him. Mrs. Addefon died jan. 8,
1779, aged 50; fhe was mother of three fons and
four daughters; Ruffell and Thomas, twins, born
june 10, and 11, 1767, Thomas died the fame
day in which he was born; William, born in
1770, died 1771; Mary, born in 1759, died in
1764; Elizabeth, born in 1762, Mary-Ruffell,
born in 1764, and Francis, born in 1769, died
in the fame year. 3. —— D'Aye, married one
Saunders, a butcher's fon, who was a fellow-fervant
in the family in which fhe lived; there is no iffue
of this marriage. Saunders is an idle, diffipated
man, which obliged his wife to leave him; fhe is
now a fervant in the Obfervatory in Greenwich-
park, and he an auctioneer in London. 9. Frances,
baptized dec. 15, 1686. 10. Jane, baptized jan.
15, 1687-8; thefe two daughters went with their
mother to London, where they caught the fmall-
pox, and both died of it nearly together. 11.
Mary; fhe died when only three months old, jan.
16, 1690-1, as it is noticed upon a fmall ftone, in
Fordham chancel. 12. Mary, baptized jan. 18,
1689-90; fhe became the wife of mr. Martin
Wilkins, of Soham, a perfon of good property;
fhe had two children, who both died infants.
This Mary was left a poor, deftitute, forfaken
creature, at Fordham, where fir Cha. Wager found
her, when he purchafed Fordham-abbey, the
eftate of her anceftors: fir Charles, with a humanity, which ought never to be forgotten, educated her, and, when fhe married, gave her a fortune*. 13. Margaret, who lived with her fifter,

* Sir Cha Wager was lord of the manor of Soham in 1716,
where he built a feat, but foon afterwards fold the whole to

No. XXXVIII

Russells of
Fordnam

mrs. Wilkins. Mr. Wilkins had an improper connection with her; but, to hide it from the world,
married her to one of his servants, named Peachey,
whom he put into a good farm; but the husband,
ashamed of his conduct, or having spent the hush-
money, very soon ran away, after which mr. Wilkins supported her   She had an only daughter,
named Elizabeth, whom she was supposed to be
with child of, by her brother-in-law, at the time
of her marriage. this child was brought up as a
gentlewoman, and married to mr. Peachey, no
ways allied to her nominal father, but a person of
fortune and education; by him she had Richard
Peachey, who died unmarried, when about twenty-
five years of age; William Peachey, who was, in
1780, at the university of Cambridge. he will
have an estate of about 100l. per annum, when he
comes of age: and Eliz. Peachey, married to the
rev. ——— Ellis, of Melborne, in Cambridgeshire. 14. ——— married to mr. Nelson, of
Mildenhall, by whom she had a son, a jeweller,
who went abroad, and a daughter, married to a
mr. Redderock, an attorney, at Mildenhall, who
dying in poor circumstances, mrs. Redderock now
keeps a school in that place, she is the mother of
Russell Redderock, an attorney there, and many
other children.

When we view the great Cromwell in his palace,
surrounded with his guards, and the kings of the
earth striving which should gain his friendship by
the abjectness of their submissions, we look with
astonishment at several of these, his descendants,
almost begging their daily bread. Oh Oliver!
if you could have seen, that the gratification of
your ambition could not prevent your descendants,
in the second and third generation, from falling

governor Harrison, whose daughter and heiress brought it to
lord viscount Townshend in marriage.

into

into the moſt ſevere poverty, you would ſurely have ſacrificed fewer lives to that idol. How much are they to be pitied! the elevation of their anceſtor, but humiliates them the more. In writing their ſtory, and knowing how true it is, from ocular demonſtration, I feel the greateſt ſympathy; and I have dwelt longer upon it, that the many affluent, nay, ſeveral noble and right honorable families, to whom they are allied, will remember that ſuch perſons exiſt, and that they have great claims upon them by a double tye— and even the public at large. The nation thought itſelf honored by giving birth to a Milton, and generouſly ſubſcribed towards the ſupport of his unfortunate deſcendants If the poet raiſed the fame of Britain by his lyre, ſurely Cromwell raiſed it far higher by his ſword all nations trembled at his name, and he made that of a briton greater than ever was a roman ·—it may be replied to this, that Oliver was an uſurper, to which I rejoin, Milton was his ſecretary, and openly defended thoſe actions which the protector is moſt blamed for, yet, did the royal Caroline patronize the humane diſpoſition of her ſubjects in relieving his grandchildren *.

* The deſcendants of Elizabeth, grand-daughter of Henry, lord-lieutenant of Ireland, is taken from the regiſter of Fordham, and from the teſtimony of many of the inhabitants in and near that place, particularly mr. Addeſon, who married one of them.

No.

No. XXXIX.

The history of messrs. Benjamin and William Hew-
ling, brothers of Hannah, wife of major Richard
Cromwell, and others, her relations.

NU XXXIX.
Hewlings

THESE two amiable, but unfortunate gentlemen, of the name of Hewling, were the only
sons of mr. Benjamin Hewling, a turkey-merchant
of good fortune, in London, who, happily for
himself, died before them; they were, after their
father's death, most carefully brought up by a tender mother, and their maternal grandfather, mr.
William Kiffin, who, though very much advanced in
years, as well as his wife, survived them both. the
Hewlings and Kiffins were protestant dissenters, and
the latter (if not the former) were anabaptists.

Before I proceed to speak of the young Hewlings, I will mention one or two circumstances
of their maternal grandfather, mr. Kiffin; he was
probably a native of Wales, or descended from a
family in that principality, where the name signi-
fies a borderer; he was put apprentice to John
Lilburn, of combustible memory, who was a
brewer in the city during the anarchy and confusion that the civil war produced; he warmly
attached himself to the cause of the parlement,
and distinguished himself as much by his dislike
to the religious, as the civil establishment, setting
himself up as a leader of, and a preacher amongst
the anabaptists; but, contrary to the practice of
most of that sect, he behaved with much moderation and decency: Patience and he travelled into various parts of the kingdom, to
establish their mode of faith; I think he settled
in Kent. Mr. Edwards, who was then the
presbyterian

presbyterian champion, accuses him of many
extravagancies, likening his conduct to that of a
mountebank, and charged him with not only
praying by the sick, but anointing them, as is
practised by the roman-catholic clergy; 'many
'such heathenish and atheistical passages with
'baseness,' says Edwards, 'I could relate of this
'man, and some of his members, and some others,
'but it would too much intrench upon modesty
'and your patience,' but it is probable, that this
behaviour was nothing more than what men of his
sentiments constantly practised: it is certain his
conduct was the exact reverse of his accuser, whose
bigotry and narrowness of mind were excessive *;

NU XXXIX.

~~~

Hewlings

* As a proof of mr Edwards's attachment to his own faith,
and hatred to all others, I will quote what he says of toleration—
'Toleration will make the kingdom a chaos, a Babel, another
'Amsterdam, a Sodom, an Egypt, a Babylon, yea worse than
'all these; certainly, it would be the most provoking sin against
'God, that ever parlement was guilty of in this kingdom it
'proves the cause and fountain of all kinds of damnable here-
'sies, and blasphemies—Toleration is the grand work of the
'devil, his master-piece and chief-engine he works by at this
'time, to uphold his tottering kingdom, it is the most compen-
'dious, ready, sure way to destroy all religion, lay all waste, and
'bring in all evil, it is a most transcendant, catholicque, and
'fundamental evil for this kingdom, of any that can be ima-
'gined As original sin is the fundamental sin, all sin having
'the seed and spawn of all in it, so Toleration hath all errors
'in it, and all evils; it is against the whole stream and current
'of Scripture, both in the Old and New Testament, both in
'matters of faith and manners, both general and particular
'commands; it overthrows all relations, both political, eccle-
'siastical, and œconomical, &c.' and speaking of the various
sectaries endeavouring to obtain freedom for their religious
opinions, he says, 'all the devils in hell, and their instru-
'ments, were at work to promote toleration.' The presbyterians of those times were too fond of these persecuting principles, a practice justly condemned in the roman-catholics:
probably mr. Edwards himself totally changed his opinion respecting religious liberty, if he survived the act of uniformity,
which followed the restoration

on

on the contrary, mr. Kiffin shewed a most christian patience and forbearance ; answering all these railing accusations, by a very meek and sensible letter, humbly requesting leave for himself and his followers to object to what they saw improper in mr. Edwards's preaching. The reader will find other particulars of mr. Kiffin in the succeeding pages.

Mr. Benjamin Hewling, the elder brother, made a great progress in learning, was well skilled in the mathematics, and other parts of philosophy, and was some time in Holland, to perfect himself in these and other studies. When the duke of Monmouth came into England, and laid claim to a crown, which he had not a shadow of right to, mr. Hewling, whose zeal for the protestant interest led him to depose king James, as a papist, upon any terms whatever, joined his standard, the duke gave him a troop of horse, with which he signalized himself in several skirmishes , and, as ill-chance would have it, he was dispatched with a detachment of his own troop and two more, to Minehead, in Somersetshire, to fetch cannon to the army ; he returned at the very time that the duke of Monmouth was routed at Sedgmore, which he, in vain, endeavoured to prevent , the loss of the battle is thought to be greatly owing to his absence with so considerable a part of the horse, and the most resolute of the army.

Mr. William Hewling was educated with as much care as his brother, and was also sent into Holland for improvement · he returned from thence with the duke of Monmouth, and also enlisted under his banner, and bore the rank of lieutenant of foot at the battle of Sedgmore, where he, as well as his brother, behaved with distinguished gallantry. After the army dispersed, the two unfortunate brothers continued together,

and

and took the firſt opportunity of putting to ſea, but they were driven back again, and with difficulty gained land, by climbing over the dangerous rocks. But the proſpect now before them, was as melancholy as that from which they had juſt fled; the country was filled with ſoldiers, and thoſe who had been raiſed to ſeize upon Monmouth's parti-zans, wherefore fearing to fall into the hands of the ſoldiery or the rabble, they ſurrendered themſelves to a gentleman whoſe houſe was near the place they landed at, from whence they were ſent to Exeter priſon, july 12th, and on the 27th following, were put on board the Swan frigate, and conveyed to the Thames, from whence they were taken to Newgate; from which priſon they were removed to Saliſbury, then to Dorcheſter, where mr. Will. Hewling was tried and condemned; and ſent with ſeveral others to Lyme, where he wás executed ſept. 12, 1685. Mr. Benj Hewling was tried and executed with many others, at Taun-ton, where he was put to death, ſept. 30, ſome days after his brother.

Of all the unhappy victims that died in the Weſt, none were more pitied than theſe two brothers, their youth, their beauty, their being the only ſons of their mother, and ſhe a widow, their extraordinary piety, reſignation, even excef-ſive joy at their approaching fate, made all men look up with horror at a throne, which, inſtead of being that of mercy, was not only that of ſevere juſtice, but exceſs of cruelty; for they were flat-tered with life, though not even one (which was earneſtly deſired) was ſaved. They were treated with the greateſt inhumanity, and even ſhameful barbarity, for in Newgate they were loaded with heavy irons, not permitted to be together, nor to have any of their friends ſee them, even in the preſence of the keeper of the priſon. when the

NU XXXIX.
Hewlings.

the eldeft was taken to execution, the fheriff, cal_lous to every feeling of humanity, would fcarce permit him and his fellow-unfortunates to take leave of their friends.   At the fatal tree, after two of the oldeft prifoners had prayed, he would not permit mr. Hewling * to pray apart, though it was particularly requefted, but afked him if he would pray for the king, to which he anfwered, ' I pray for all men;' and when the brutifh fheriff was afked permiffion for them to fing a pfalm, he replied, ' it muft be with ropes about their necks;' to this they chearfully complied.   The forrowing fpectators exclaimed, ' it both broke and rejoiced their hearts.'

The people, as if to reflect upon their fovereign's flintinefs of heart, ftrove who fhould moft exprefs their pity and regard for them whilft living, and when dead; the body of the youngeft was depofited in Lyme church-yard, attended by two hundred perfons, and accompanied by fome of the moft fafhionable young women in the town, though it was the day following his untimely death, and no invitation or preparation made. and moft of the inhabitants of Taunton, alfo, waited upon the remains of Benjamin, to the church in that place, where they were depofited, which was wonderful, when we recollect the horrid butchery that muft every where prefent itfelf to them under the unfeeling tyrant; and that feveral of the dreadful objects died only for affording comfort to thofe who had been in arms.   The dignity and acquiefcence in God's providence under their misfortunes, and the cruelty of their deaths, made

* It was obferved, that when mr. Benjamin Hewling was fet upon the fledge, it was half an hour before the officers could force the horfes to draw, which greatly enraged them, as there was no vifible obftruction; and at laft, the mayor and fheriffs were obliged to drag the horfes forwards themfelves.

a great

a great impreſſion upon all ſober men, and the outrages committed in the Weſt, more than any thing, contributed to overturn the throne of a tyrant, which he had diſcolored with the blood of ſo many of his ſubjects, to gratify an inſatiable cruelty.

Their characters are thus drawn in the new martyrology, from which the above is taken.—
' They were both of very ſweet and obliging tem-
' pers, as has appeared in their hiſtory, it being
' a very hard matter for their very worſt enemies
' when they once knew 'em well, not to honour
' and love 'em. Mr Benjamin, the elder, re-
' conciled the *lamb* and the *lion* exactly. In the
' field he ſeemed made only for war, and any
' where elſe, for nothing but love. He, without
' flattery, deſerved to be called a very *fine man*,
' of lovely proportion, extremely well made,
' ſo handſome a mien, and good an air, as per-
' haps few in *England* exceeded him.' His picture (a print given in the martyrology) is pretty
like him.

' The younger, mr. *William*, ſomewhat taller
' and more ſlender, his face freſh and lively as
' his ſpirit, being maſter of an extraordinary *vi-*
' *vacity* and *briſkneſs* of temper. Both of them vir-
' tuous, pious, and courageous, far above their
' years, and indeed, they ſeemed to be *men* too
' ſoon, one of them not being twenty, the eldeſt
' but two-and-twenty, when they died ; verifying
' that common obſervation, *that whatever is* PER-
' FECT *ſooner than ordinary, has generally a ſhorter*
' *period prefixed to it than what's more baſe and ig-*
' *noble.*'

It would, for many reaſons, be improper to
omit what mr. Hewling Luſon has ſaid of theſe
two young men, and others of this family, to
which he was near allied, ſpeaking of Hannah,
the

the wife of major Henry Cromwell, he fays, " this Hannah Hewling, my brother's elder fifter, is the perfon fo often mentioned in the many particular relations which were publifhed, of the bloody unrelenting perfecutions in the Weft, after the defeat of the duke of Monmouth's rebellion.

'The two unfortunate brothers of this lady, Benjamin and William Hewling, were the only males of their name, and of their family, which was in the higheft efteem and popularity among the ftaunch whigs and diffenting proteftants, at that time fo numerous and confiderable in that city. Their parts were excellent, and their education was the beft that could be given them, their morals were fpotlefs, their piety exemplary, their zeal againft popery, the ardour of their courage in the field, and the manly meeknefs and devout refignation of their deportment, to the laft, under their fufferings, concurred with their youth, the one twenty-one *, the other not quite twenty, and the uncommon beauty and gracefulnefs of their perfons, to place them the firft in the lift, which was at that time called " the Weftern Martyrology," and render the feverity of their fate moft pitied of any who fell a facrifice to the popifh vengeance of James, though there were fome other fentences much more unjuft.

'The father of this unfortunate family was dead; the mother, from her diftrefs, incapable of acting, fome of the near friends of the family were themfelves too obnoxious to act, and many more too timid, and as the other fifters were hardly out of their childhood, it fell upon this young lady alone to conduct the whole affair, in the prifon for their comfort, and with the court for their pardon.

* The Martyrology fays, mr Hewling was twenty-two.

'It

'It has been faid in moft of the accounts which ᴺᵁ. XXXIX
have been publifhed, that lord-chief-juftice Jefferies always treated Hannah Hewling according
to his ufual cuftom, with the greateft brutality ;
" but black as he is, the devil may be blackened !"
for Jefferies always treated her with the greateft
politenefs and refpect. This inftance, however,
does not much foften the horror of his general
character. Jefferies had a relation from whofe
fortune he had formed great expectations, and as
this relation was an intimate acquaintance of the
Hewlings, he exerted himfelf very warmly with
him on their behalf. He repeatedly protefted to
the chief-juftice, that " the continuance of his
" friendfhip, together with every benefit he might
" hope would refult from it, depended entirely
" upon his ufing every endeavour to fave the
" Hewlings." This Jefferies protefted he did ;
with what fincerity, God only knows, but he
always declared the king was inexorable *.

'When Jefferies was afterwards prifoner in the
Tower, he complained to dr. Scott, author of
" the chriftian life," who vifited him under his
confinement, of his hard fate. " I was hated," fays
he, " by the kingdom, for doing fo much in the
" Weft, and I was ill received by the king, for
" not having done more." He ufed almoft the fame
words when he was applied to for the Hewlings.

'When Hannah Hewling prefented a petition
to the king, in behalf of her brothers, fhe was
introduced by lord Churchill, afterwards duke of
Marlborough, while they waited in the anti-

* Sir John Dalrymple afferts, that, " when James knew
the cruelties of Jefferies, he gave orders to ftop them," but
this affertion is againft all evidence, for he knew daily of his
conduct, or campaign, as he ftyled it, was accuftomed to repeat his infamous tool's cruelties with jocularity ; and for his
glorious and pleafing fervices, he made him, after his campaign, lord-high-chancellor.

chamber, for admittance, ſtanding near the chimney-piece, lord Churchill aſſured her of his moſt hearty wiſhes of ſucceſs to her petition; "but, madam," ſaid he, "I dare not flatter you with any ſuch hopes, for that marble is as capable of feeling compaſſion as the king's heart ＊." This declaration of lord Churchill adds no ſmall degree of credibility to Jefferies' report of the king's obdurate cruelty.

'William Kyffin, the father of mrs. Hewling, was then alive; this man throughout his life had been a merchant, and was poſſeſſed of what was then thought a very large fortune; yet I think he ſometimes gave vent to his piety, by holding forth amongſt the baptiſts. He was, however, in much and general eſteem; his fortune and affluence placed him amongſt the foremoſt of the diſſenters in the city. I believe he never meddled with politics himſelf, but all his connections were amongſt the warmeſt patriots of thoſe warm times †. Hayes, the banker, who married another of Kyffin's daughters, was tried for his life, in 1684,

＊ This exactly agrees with the opinion that muſt be formed both of James's head and heart, from his own letters, in which, numerous as they are, ſir John Dalrymple obſerves, "there is ſcarcely one ſtroke of genius or ſenſibility to be found."

† Mr. Luſon was miſtaken, for mr. Kyffin was intruſted by the parlement, in 1647, to be an aſſeſſor of their taxes, to be raiſed for Middleſex, and he was at the head of thoſe that ſigned a profeſſion of the faith of anabaptiſm, in 1644, in behalf of his congregation, during Oliver's protectorate, he wrote to thoſe of that perſuaſion in Ireland, to requeſt them to live peaceably, and ſubmit to the civil magiſtrate, and alſo ſigned an apology in behalf of himſelf and his brethren, of the ſame judgment, with a proteſtation againſt Venner's fifth monarchy plot, which is called ' the late wicked and moſt ' horrible treaſon and rebellion in this city of London,' and a declaration of their loyalty to the king, promiſing that their practice ſhould be conformable—In the laſt century the anabaptiſts were powerful and turbulent, at this time they are inconſiderable and peaceable.

for remitting money to fir Thomas Armftrong, an outlaw. Hayes narrowly efcaped the halter, which the court, under Charles II. earneftly defired to be put about his neck. The trial was curious and important, as it ftruck at the root of mercantile liberty. A good account is given of it by Burnet *.

' Kyffin was perfonally known both to Charles and James; and when the latter of thefe princes, after having arbitrarily deprived the city of the old charter, determined to put many of the dif-fenters into the magiftracy; under the rofe, he fent for Kyffin to attend him at court. When he went thither in obedience to the king's com-mand, he found many lords and gentlemen. The king immediately came up to him, and addreffed him with all the little grace he was mafter of. He talked of " his favor to the diffenters," in the court ftile of this feafon, and concluded with tel-ing Kyffin, " he had put him down as an al-" derman in his new charter." " Sire," replied Kyffin, " I am a very old man, and have withdrawn " myfelf from all kind of bufinefs for fome years " paft, and am incapable of doing any fervice " in fuch an affair, to your majefty or the city— " befides, fir," the old man went on, fixing his eyes fteadfaftly upon the king, while the tears ran down his cheek, " the death of my grandfons " gave a wound to my heart which is ftill bleed-" ing, and never will clofe, but in the grave!"

' The king was deeply ftruck by the manner, the freedom, and the fpirit of this unexpected rebuke. A total filence enfued, while the galled countenance of James feemed to fhrink from the horrid remembrance. In a minute or two, how-ever, he recovered himfelf enough to fay, " Mr.

* See Burnet's "hiftory of his own times," vol. I. p. 599, and ftate trials, vol. III. p. 983.

" Kyffin,

" Kyffin, I fhall find a balfam for that fore ;" and immediately turned about to a lord in waiting.*

' When the french proteftants were driven to England for refuge, this William Kyffin received into his protection a numerous french family of confiderable rank. He fitted up and furnifhed a houfe of his own, for their reception, provided them with fervants, and entirely maintained them at his own expence, in a manner which bore fome proportion to their rank in France, and when this family afterwards recovered fome part of their ruined fortune, he would not diminifh it a fingle fhilling, by taking any retribution for the fervices he had done them. Such were the *city patriots* of thofe times !

' I give thefe feveral accounts as I have heard them in the family, I have no doubt of their authenticity, and I infert them in this letter, I hope not improperly, as they relate to public characters and events.

' It was not, I believe, above a year after the execution of her brothers, that Hannah Hewling, who died in 1731, married major Henry Cromwell, before-mentioned †.

* ' A ftroke equally unexpected, and equally deferved, this unfeeling monarch received, at an extraordinary council, which he called foon after the landing of the prince of Orange, when amidft the filent company he applied himfelf to the earl of Bedford, father to the executed lord Ruffel, faying, " My lord, you are a good man, and have great influence, you can do much for me at this time ;" to which the earl replied, "I am an old man, and can do but little," then added, with a figh, " I had once a fon, who could now have been very ferviceable to your majefty," which words, fays Echard, ftruck the king half dead with filence and confufion.'

† " May 28, 1686" fays dr Gibbons—V de the new martyrology, and dr Hughes's letters.

F I N I S.

CPSIA information can be obtained at www.ICGtesting.com
Printed in the USA
LVOW09s0751121113

360879LV00020B/904/P